Hillier
NURSERIES

THE HILLIER COLOUR DICTIONARY OF TREES & SHRUBS

THE
HILLIER COLOUR
DICTIONARY
OF
TREES &
SHRUBS

David & Charles

A David & Charles Book

First published 1981
Second impression 1982
Third impression 1984
Second edition 1993

A catalogue record for this book is available from
the British Library.

ISBN 0 7153 0091 1

Typeset by XL Publishing Services, Nairn
and printed in Hong Kong
by Regent Publishing Services Ltd
for David & Charles
Brunel House, Newton Abbot, Devon

Acknowledgements
The basic text for this book was prepared and
verified by Hillier Nurseries (Winchester) Ltd., and
especially by the following members of the Hillier
team; Sid Cox, Allen Coombes, Stan Dolding, John
Hillier, Robert Hillier, Brian Humphrey, Bill Stillwell
and Sarah Stride.

The majority of the photographs are by Michael
Warren, but additional pictures were provided by
Pat Brindley, Valerie Finnis, John Hillier, Brian
Humphrey, Roy Lancaster and Dennis Woodland.

Contents

The Sir Harold Hillier Gardens and Arboretum   6

Preface
by Christopher D. Brickell, CBE, BSc (Hort) VMH
Director General, The Royal Horticultural Society   8

Introduction   9

How to Use the Dictionary   11

Symbols and Abbreviations   13

Leaf Forms   14

Inflorescences   15

Understanding Plant Names and Classification
*International codes, generic names, specific epithets
and their meanings*   16

Choosing Trees and Shrubs
*General guidance, soil pH, hardiness
Trees and shrubs for specific purposes (tables):
    Trees; Conifers as Trees; Shrubs; Conifers as Shrubs;
    Climbers; Choosing Rhododendrons*   19

Pruning Garden Shrubs and Climbers   33

The Colour Dictionary
    Trees and Shrubs   37
    Climbers   225
    Conifers   245

Glossary of Botanical Terms   269

The Sir Harold Hillier Gardens and Arboretum

The Sir Harold Hillier Gardens and Arboretum, in the heart of the Hampshire countryside near Romsey, contains one of the most complete collections of trees and shrubs in the British Isles.

The collection was begun in 1953 by Sir Harold Hillier, in the grounds of his family home. Sir Harold was a dedicated plantsman and avid plant collector, who travelled the world indulging his love for rare and unusual plants, and the later years of his life were spent achieving his great ambition of creating a unique and special collection of plants from all temperate regions of the globe.

In 1977, keen to secure the long-term future of his life's work, he gifted the gardens in trust to Hampshire County Council. They have been open to the public since 1978, when they were officially opened by HRH The Queen Mother.

Sir Harold created a plantsman's paradise which now holds nine National Collections, including Cotoneasters, Oaks, Pines and Hazels. The breadth of the collections, with over 36,000 plants of 11,000 different sorts, means that there is something to see all year round, earning the Hillier Gardens the reputation as 'the garden for all seasons'.

In mid-winter, the witch hazels never

(*Opposite*): Part of the North-west Slope and Three-acre Paddock which drop down to the Ditch, photographed in the mid-1960s. (*Above*): A similar view, taken nearly thirty years later

fail to delight, with their strange flowers and sweet scent. As winter turns to spring, the Gardens become a kaleidoscope of colour, as cherries, magnolias, camellias, azaleas and rhododendrons all vie for attention. Summer interest is provided by a succession of flowering shrubs, which bloom vigorously until autumn days bring a change of pace and colour, as leaves turn colour and berries ripen.

This wealth of trees and shrubs is explained to visitors by a current interest sheet, which is updated each week and highlights a trail around the Gardens for visitors to follow, looking at plants at their best. This is available free to visitors on entry, as are other trail leaflets.

Guided walks with members of staff are also a regular feature at the Gardens, with walks every Wednesday and Sunday afternoon in both May and October, when colour is superb. A yearly calendar of events gives full details of all the walks, practical workshops and other activities taking place throughout the year.

The elegant Jermyns House, once the Hillier family home, is now a visitor centre, with tearooms, an exhibition area, a classroom and toilets.

The Sir Harold Hillier Gardens and Arboretum, Jermyns Lane, Ampfield, Near Romsey, HAMPSHIRE SO51 0QA
Telephone: (0794) 68787
Fax: (0794) 68027

Curator: Barry R. Phillips Dip Hort Kew, MI Hort

Open:
March-November
10.30am-5pm weekdays
10.30am-6pm weekends and Bank Holidays
December-February
10.30am-dusk weekdays and Sundays, excluding first Sunday after Christmas

Admission Charge
REGRET NO DOGS

Preface

In an era when gardening books, many of dubious authenticity and doubtful value, tumble like secondhand confetti from the publishers' presses, *Hillier's Manual of Trees & Shrubs*, first published in 1971 and now in its sixth edition, stands out as a classic that will hold its own among the great reference works on gardening for many decades, and perhaps centuries, to come. Both amateur and professional gardeners regard it as an essential aid to their hobby or profession and many, as I do myself, take a copy on every visit to a garden or nursery to use as a *vade mecum*, which accurately presents concise but detailed information on the widest range of trees and shrubs known and grown in the northern hemisphere. It is, in short, indispensable.

Today, with inflation outstripping even that most rampant of climbers *Fallopia baldschuanica* in growth, and economic pressures battering the horticultural trade on all sides, it is clearly, if regrettably, impracticable for any one nursery to stock permanently the enormous range of trees and shrubs for which the name of Hillier is known throughout the gardening world. Among the 9,000 or more items described in the *Manual* are some which, although fascinating to the botanist and collector, have little general garden appeal. Many hundreds of others, excellent garden plants in their own right, are scarcely known and seldom available from other sources.

It is, therefore, a very great pleasure to provide this preface for a new, completely revised and updated edition of this complementary publication, *The Hillier Colour Dictionary of Trees & Shrubs*, which describes over 2,500 trees, shrubs, climbers and conifers carefully selected for their garden value and illustrates in colour over 600 of the plants included. These have been chosen with particular care to ensure that they represent the best available species and cultivars for garden decoration. The information provided is neatly distilled from the descriptions in the *Manual* and together with the very wide range of colour illustrations, unmatched in any other comparable work, provides both the beginner and the enthusiast with an invaluable reference and guide.

As an ardent believer in the need to conserve our garden plants, it is particularly pleasing to find included many uncommon plants which should, in my view, be more widely grown for their beauty and aesthetic appeal but which, through lack of publicity, are in danger of being lost.

This new edition of the *Colour Dictionary* should, through its illustrations, descriptions and other helpful information, stimulate all those interested in woody plants, and seems destined once again to become as indispensable as the *Manual*.

CHRISTOPHER D. BRICKELL, CBE, BSc (Hort) VMH
Director General of The Royal Horticultural Society

Introduction

In 1864, after having gained a knowledge and love of plants in some of the leading horticultural establishments of his day, Edwin Hillier bought a small nursery business and florist's shop in the centre of Winchester.

Gradually the business expanded, more land was acquired and the range of plants increased. Regular deliveries of flowers and plants were made by horse and cart to the great houses and estates in and around the ancient city, and as the Hillier reputation for quality began to spread, greater use of the nearby railway was made to despatch plants further afield.

Edwin Hillier's two sons, Edwin Lawrence and Arthur Richard and, in turn, Edwin's son, Harold, continued the tradition, and through their particular dedication to woody plants raised the firm to international pre-eminence, with a range of plants running into thousands and a complex of nurseries covering around 800 acres in Hampshire.

In 1938 a Royal Warrant of Appointment was granted to Hillier and Sons as Nurserymen to HRH The Prince of Wales. Later in the same year this was replaced when the present Queen Mother granted hers as Nurserymen and Seedsmen. Her Majesty Queen Elizabeth granted a similar Warrant in 1983, adding to that which already existed.

In 1977 Hillier and Sons became Hillier Nurseries, but the change in name had no effect on the family's ambition – to grow the widest possible selection of woody plants for today's gardener, and to introduce new and interesting trees and shrubs into cultivation. Indeed, the family's commitment to the introduction, identification and conservation of trees and shrubs is evidenced by the fact that around 200 cultivars, subspecies or varieties have been raised, selected or named by Hillier Nurseries.

In 1983 Harold Hillier received the accolade of Knighthood from Her Majesty Queen Elizabeth the Queen Mother, and thus became Sir Harold Hillier, CBE, FLS, VMH. As President of the Hillier organisation he travelled many thousands of miles during his notional

'retirement', obtaining new specimens and sharing his knowledge with plantsmen in the UK and overseas, until his death in 1985.

In a memorial tribute to Sir Harold, the Lord Aberconway, President Emeritus of the Royal Horticultural Society, said, 'The words on Christopher Wren's tomb in St Paul's Cathedral could equally come to mind for Harold as one walks around Britain's gardens – *If you seek his memorial, look around you.*'

Harold Hillier founded the Hillier Arboretum in 1952, when he acquired Jermyns House. His desire was to create an arboretum and gardens which would become a definitive and comprehensive legacy of temperate-zone woody plants, providing a priceless conservation and education 'bank'. In 1976 the gardens and arboretum were transferred to a charitable trust administered by Hampshire County Council, and now contain over 11,000 different plants, many of them rare in the wild or in cultivation, in the 160 acre grounds – a gardeners' and botanists' paradise.

Today, the family tradition is being upheld by Harold's two sons, John and Robert Hillier, and each year sees enhancement of the Hillier reputation – in 1992 the Nurseries were proud to be awarded their 47th consecutive Chelsea Gold Medal. Since the small beginnings in 1864 much has changed in the day to day running of the Nurseries, with an increasing degree of mechanisation, the use of modern materials, chemicals and fertilisers, increasing production of container-grown plants, computerisation of production schedules and stock control, and even the adoption of 'space-age' horticultural techniques, such as clonal selection.

One thing, however, remains constant – a total dedication to producing a wide range of quality plants which will bring pleasure and an element of environmental stability in an ever-changing world.

How to Use the Dictionary

For ease of reference, the dictionary is divided into three sections: Trees and Shrubs, Climbers, and Conifers. The plants in each section are then listed in strict alphabetical order, by GENERA, in bold capital letters, like this:
ACER

Immediately after the generic name the FAMILY to which that genus belongs is shown in **bold type,** with a capital initial, followed by one or more abbreviations or symbols (as listed on page 9) and, perhaps, a common name, enclosed in double inverted commas, like this:

ACER – Aceraceae		SS-I T "Maples"
genus	family	range from small shrubs to large trees commonly called Maples

Next you will find a paragraph in *italic* type, describing the general characteristics of the genus and its broad requirements in terms of soil and situation, where these are important. There may also be a guide to pruning (see page 33) where pruning requirements are common to the whole or most of the genus.

Below each generic description, there then follows a descriptive list of individual species, subspecies or varieties, and cultivars.

SPECIES
These appear in bold type, with a small initial letter.
eg in the **ACER** section,
– campestre
indicates the species **campestre** of the genus.

SUBSPECIES AND VARIETIES
Wild varieties and subspecies are shown in bold type with small initial letter, following the species to which they belong, so, under the genus **BETULA** and the species **utilis**, you will find the variety **jacquemontii** listed like this:
– – var. **jacquemontii**

Subspecies (subsp.) are treated in the same way.

CULTIVARS
Garden varieties and selected forms from the wild maintained in cultivation normally follow the species to which they belong. They are shown in bold type with a capital initial, and in single inverted commas. Thus, under the genus **ACER,** species **campestre** the cultivar **'Postelense'** appears like this:
– – **'Postelense'**

CLONES
A clone is a group of plants derived originally from a single plant and maintained in cultivation true to type by vegetative propagation. Most of the cultivars described in this book are clonal in origin.

HYBRIDS
Hybrids between two or more species, forms, etc are normally given a collective Latin name, shown as for a species, but preceded by a multiplication sign, eg under the genus **ABELIA**, you will find
– × **grandiflora**

Sometimes, a group of hybrids is given a collective English name – eg **RHODODENDRON – Vanessa.** Within these groups, selected plants are often named as cultivars, eg
– – **'Pastel'**

Where no collective name is available for a hybrid the cultivar name immediately follows that of the genus, eg
CISTUS
– **'Silver Pink'**

INTERGENERIC HYBRIDS

Natural (sexual) hybrids between species of two different genera are shown in bold capitals, preceded by a multiplication sign, followed by the names of the parents, italicised and in parenthesis, like this:

× **MAHOBERBERIS** (*Mahonia* × *Berberis*)

Names of graft hybrids which have originated artificially as a result of grafting species of two different genera are preceded by a 'plus' sign, and names of the parents are similarly linked, thus:

+ **LABURNOCYTISUS**
(*Laburnum* + *Cytisus*)

GROUPS

When a number of plants within a species share certain characteristics, they are often recognised as a **group**, eg *Acer palmatum* Dissectum group. Groups such as this often contain named cultivars.

SYNONYMS

Plant names can and do change for a variety of reasons. Names by which plants were formerly known, or which are not accepted in this book, are shown in parenthesised italics after the accepted name

eg **COTONEASTER**
– **dammeri** (*C. humifusus*)

Where the abbreviation hort. follows a synonym, it indicates that the plant in question is often known by this name in gardens

eg **EUONYMUS**
– **planipes** (*E. sachalinensis* hort.)

COMMON NAMES

Frequently used common names are given in double inverted commas after the botanical names to which they relate

eg **ARBUTUS**
– **unedo** "Killarney Strawberry Tree"

The more familiar common names are also included alphabetically among the genera, and cross referenced to the appropriate botanical name

eg **"LILAC"** see *Syringa*

AWARDS

Many plants of particular merit are given awards by the Royal Horticultural Society. The most important of these are given at the end of the relevant plant descriptions, and are described in the key to abbreviations and symbols (page 13).

HEIGHTS

The ultimate height of a tree will depend upon many factors (including soil, aspect and local climate), and may take many years to attain. The abbreviations used in this book relate to a scale devised to give British gardeners the probable height range of each plant growing under average conditions:

Trees

LT - Large tree growing to over 18m (over 60ft)
MT - Medium tree, growing to 10–18m (35–60ft)
ST - Small tree, growing to 4.5–10m (15–35ft)

Shrubs

LS - Large shrub, growing to over 3m (over 10ft)
MS - Medium shrub, growing to 1.5–3m (5–10ft)
SS - Small shrub, growing to 1–1.5m (3–5ft)
DS - Dwarf shrub, growing to 0.3–0.6m (1–2ft)
PS - Prostrate shrub, creeping habit

FLOWERING PERIODS

Flowering periods will inevitably vary according to locality and from year to year, depending upon the vagaries of the season. Those given in this book should therefore be taken as approximate.

PRUNING

Advice on pruning, and the key to the pruning symbols used in the text, will be found on pages 33–34.

Symbols and Abbreviations

Plants not marked are suitable for most situations.

(E)	Evergreen	+	Chimera (graft hybrid)
♠	Spreading tree	ST	Small tree (eventual height 4.5–9m)
♣	Conical tree	MT	Medium tree (eventual height 10–18m)
♥	Broadly columnar tree		
!	Columnar (fastigiate) tree	LT	Large tree (eventual height over 18m)
♠	Weeping tree		
hort.	Name used in horticultural (garden) context	PS	Prostrate (creeping) shrub
		DS	Dwarf shrub (0.3–0.6m)
Hdg	Suitable for hedging or	SS	Small shrub (1–1.5m)
(1.0m)	edging (figure in brackets indicates recommended planting distance)	MS	Medium shrub (1.5–3m)
		LS	Large shrub (over 3m)
†	Not recommended for exposed positions without some protection	Cl	Self clinging
		○	Thrives in full sun
⟋	Will not tolerate alkaline or chalky conditions	◑	Thrives in partial shade
		●	Thrives in dense shade
×	Hybrid origin	GC	Suitable for use as ground cover

Royal Horticultural Society Awards (followed by year of award)

Many plants have been given awards by the Royal Horticultural Society, but the criteria and procedures vary considerably according to the type of award.

Award of Garden Merit (AGM) –

Subjects for this award are recommended to the Council by the appropriate plant committee on the basis of their assessment as valuable garden plants. Gardens of all sizes are included, from the smallest to the largest.

The plant should be:
- excellent for ordinary garden decoration or use in the open or under protection
- of good constitution
- available in the horticultural trade

The plant should not:
- be particularly susceptible to any pest or disease
- require highly specialised growing conditions
- be subject to an unreasonable degree of reversion

During 1992 the Committees have been reassessing all the plants to which the award had already been granted and have made further recommendations. At the time of going to press the Committees covering the plants in this *Dictionary* had had their list ratified by the Council, with the exception of *Rosa*. In this edition of the *Dictionary*, any AGM awards preceding the 1993 list have been disregarded other than for *Rosa*.

First Class Certificate (FCC) – instituted 1859
Award of Merit (AM) – instituted 1888
Recommendations for these awards are made by the appropriate committee to the RHS council, usually after viewing as a cut specimen in a vase, occasionally as a specimen plant. Judgement is therefore 'as seen' on the day, in an 'exhibition' context.
FCCT and AMT
Recommendations are again made to the RHS council, by the appropriate committee, but only after trials at the RHS Gardens, Wisley.
Cory Cup The Reginald Cory Cup, awarded to the raiser of the best deliberately raised hybrid of that year.
At the time of going to press, the whole system of RHS awards is under review.

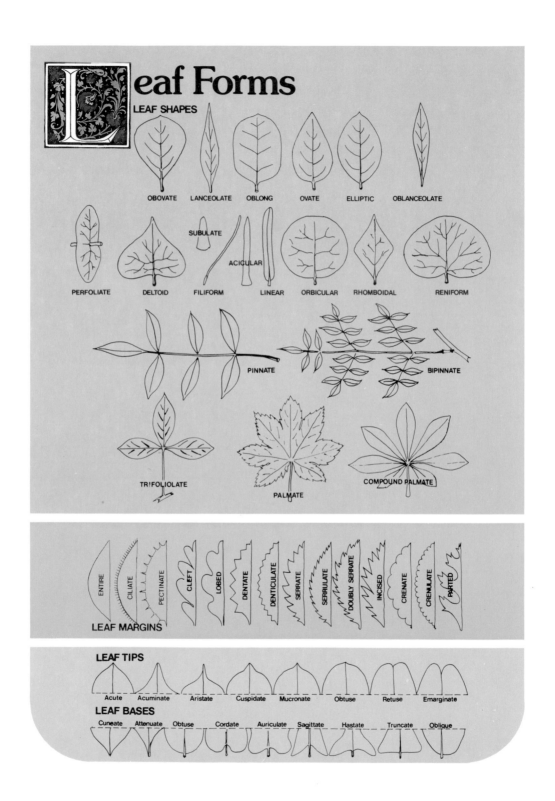

Leaf Forms

LEAF SHAPES

OBOVATE LANCEOLATE OBLONG OVATE ELLIPTIC OBLANCEOLATE

SUBULATE

ACICULAR

PERFOLIATE DELTOID FILIFORM LINEAR ORBICULAR RHOMBOIDAL RENIFORM

PINNATE BIPINNATE

TRIFOLIOLATE PALMATE COMPOUND PALMATE

LEAF MARGINS

ENTIRE CILIATE PECTINATE CLEFT LOBED DENTATE DENTICULATE SERRATE SERRULATE DOUBLY SERRATE INCISED CRENATE CRENULATE PARTED

LEAF TIPS

Acute Acuminate Aristate Cuspidate Mucronate Obtuse Retuse Emarginate

LEAF BASES

Cuneate Attenuate Obtuse Cordate Auriculate Sagittate Hastate Truncate Oblique

Inflorescences

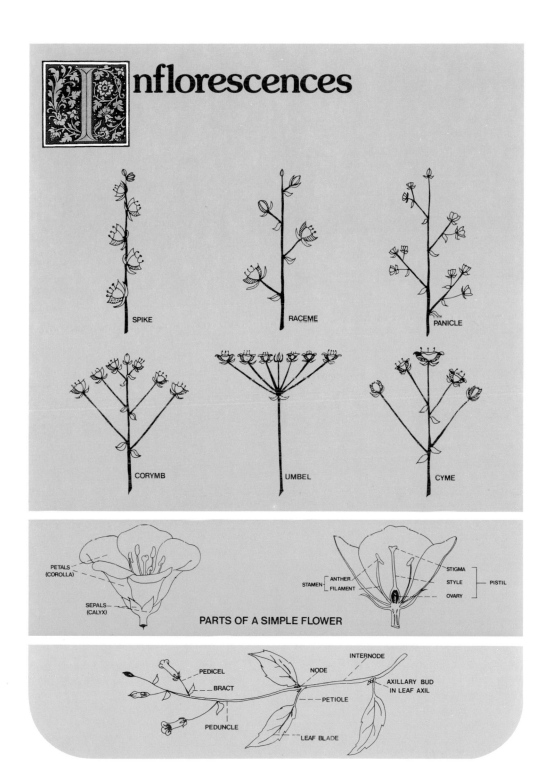

SPIKE

RACEME

PANICLE

CORYMB

UMBEL

CYME

PETALS (COROLLA)

SEPALS (CALYX)

STAMEN — ANTHER, FILAMENT

STIGMA

STYLE

OVARY

PISTIL

PARTS OF A SIMPLE FLOWER

PEDICEL

BRACT

NODE

INTERNODE

AXILLARY BUD IN LEAF AXIL

PETIOLE

PEDUNCLE

LEAF BLADE

Understanding Plant Names and Classification

Plant names can sometimes appear difficult to understand and even harder to pronounce! The reason is that, because plants are international, we have to stick to agreed 'Codes' to meet the needs of many countries.

Two codes are internationally accepted –the 'International Code of Botanical Nomenclature' covering wild plants, and the 'International Code of Nomenclature for Cultivated Plants', for cultivars.

As man's knowledge of plant variations and plant relationships expands, so the re-classification of many plants inevitably results. This, together with the remorseless application of the 'Rule of Priority' (ie standardisation on the earliest legitimate name known for a plant) means a number of imposed changes in the names of plants which may have been familiar to us.

For various reasons, not all changes are accepted in this book, but much attention has been paid to appending and cross-referencing synonyms for 'accepted' names.

This is described more fully in the section 'How to Use the Dictionary' (commencing on page 11) as are the other main factors in plant nomenclature and classification.

Botanical names are latinised so that they can be accepted the world over, to avoid further translation and the confusion which can so easily arise in national or even regional differences in 'common names'.

Fortunately, one does not have to be a devoted Latin scholar to gain a reasonable grasp of the more commonly used elements of botanical names and their meanings – and as these become more familiar, so we learn more about the plants they describe.

Don't be put off by a long name. It's the beauty and interest of the plant that matters.

GENERIC NAMES

These are always nouns. Their origins and meanings are occasionally obscure, but the majority are derived from older names in Greek, Latin, Arabic and other languages.

Some generic names are based on characters in Greek mythology, eg
DAPHNE named after the river god's daughter
ANDROMEDA named after the daughter of Cepheus and Cassiope
PHYLLODOCE name of a sea nymph; whilst others commemorate people, such as botanists, patrons, etc, eg
BUDDLEJA named after Rev. Adam Buddle
DEUTZIA named after J. Deutz
ESCALLONIA named after Signor Escallon
FUCHSIA named after Leonard Fuchs
LONICERA named after Adam Lonicer

SPECIFIC EPITHETS

The names used to describe species are varied and fall into four main categories, namely:

A   Names which indicate the origin of the plant, eg continent, country, region, etc.
B   Names that describe the habitat of a plant (where it grows in the wild), eg, in woods, or mountains, by rivers, etc.
C   Names that describe a plant or a particular feature, such as size, habit, leaf shape, colour of flower, etc.
D   Names which commemorate people, eg botanists, plant collectors, patrons, famous horticulturists, etc.

Here is a selection of the most commonly used names (specific epithets) and their meanings.

Names describing Habit

arborea(um) (us)	tree-like
fastigiata(um) (us)	erect, the branches
fruticosa(um) (us)	shrubby
horizontale(is)	horizontally spreading
humile(is)	low growing
major(us)	greater
minor(us)	lesser
nana(um) (us)	dwarf
pendula(um) (us)	pendulous, weeping
procera(um) (us)	very tall, high
procumbens	procumbent, creeping
prostrata(um) (us)	prostrate, hugging the ground
repens	creeping and rooting
suffruticosa(um) (us)	woody at base

Names describing Habitat

alpina(um) (us)	alpine, of the Alps or growing in alpine regions
arvense(is)	of fields or cultivated land
aquatica(um) (us)	of water, or growing by water
campestre(is)	of plains or flat areas
littorale(is)	of sea shores
maritima(um) (us)	by the sea
montana(um) (us)	of mountains
palustre(is)	of swamps or marshes
rivulare(is)	of streams and brooks
rupestre(is)	of rocks or cliffs
sylvatica(um) (us)	of woods

Names which are Geographical

atlantica(um) (us)	of the Atlas Mountains (North Africa)
australe(is)	southern
boreale(is)	northern
californica(um) (us)	of California
capense(is)	of the Cape (South Africa)
europaea(um) (us)	of Europe
himalaica(um) (us)	of the Himalaya
hispanica(um) (us)	of Spain
japonica(um) (us)	of Japan
lusitanica(um) (us)	of Portugal
nipponica(um) (us)	of Japan
occidentale(is)	western
orientale(is)	eastern
sinense(is)	of China

Names describing Leaves

angustifolia(um) (us)	narrow-leaved
arguta(um) (us)	sharp
coriacea(um) (us)	coriaceous, leathery
crassifolia(um) (us)	thick-leaved
crenata(um) (us)	with shallow, rounded teeth
decidua(um) (us)	deciduous, dropping its leaves
glabra(um) (us)	glabrous, without hairs
glutinosa(um)	sticky
heterophylla(um) (us)	variable-leaved
hirsuta(um) (us)	hairy
incana(um) (us)	grey-downy
integerrima(um) (us)	without teeth
laciniata(um) (us)	cut into narrow pointed lobes
laevigata(um) (us)	smooth and polished
lanceolata(um) (us)	lance shaped
latifolia(um) (us)	broad-leaved
macrophylla(um) (us)	large-leaved
maculata(um) (us)	spotted, blotched
marginata(um) (us)	margined
microphylla(um) (us)	small-leaved
molle(is)	soft
nitida(um) (us)	shining
ovata(um) (us)	egg-shaped
parvifolia(um) (us)	small-leaved
picta(um) (us)	painted, coloured
pinnata(um) (us)	pinnate
platyphylla(os) (um) (us)	broad-leaved
reticulata(um) (us)	net-veined
rotundifolia(um) (us)	round-leaved
sempervirens	always green, evergreen
serrata(um) (us)	saw-toothed
splendens	glittering, shining
tomentosa(um) (us)	covered with a short dense pubescence
variegata(um) (us)	variegated, two coloured
velutina(um) (us)	velvety

Names describing Flowers

(flora(um) (us) = flower)

campanulata(um) (us)	bell-shaped
floribunda(um) (us)	free-flowering
grandiflora(um) (us)	large-flowered
macropetala(um) (us)	large petalled
nudiflora(um) (us)	naked, without leaves
nutans	nodding
paniculata(um) (us)	flowering in panicles
parviflora(um) (us)	small-flowered

pauciflora(um) (us)	few-flowered
polyantha(um) (us)	many-flowered
racemosa(um) (us)	flowers in racemes
spicata(um) (us)	flowers in spikes
stellata(um) (us)	starry
triflora(um) (us)	flowers in threes
umbellata(um) (us)	flowers in umbels
uniflora(um) (us)	one-flowered

Names describing Colours

alba(um) (us)	white
argentea(um) (us)	silvery
aurantiaca(um) (us)	orange
aurea(um) (us)	golden
bicolor	two coloured
carnea(um) (us)	flesh-coloured
caerulea(um) (us)	blue
cinerea(um) (us)	ash grey
coccinea(um) (us)	scarlet
concolor	of the same colour
discolor	two-coloured
ferruginea(um) (us)	rusty brown
flava(um) (us)	pale yellow
glauca(um) (us)	sea-green
lactea(um) (us)	milk white
lilacina(um) (us)	lilac
lutea(um) (us)	yellow
nigra(um) (us)	black
punicea(um) (us)	crimson
purpurea(um) (us)	purple
rosea(um) (us)	rose-coloured
rubra(um) (us)	red
sanguinea(um) (us)	blood red
tricolor	three-coloured
variegata(um) (us)	variegated – two-coloured
versicolor	variously coloured, or changing colour
violacea(um) (us)	violet
viride(is)	green

Names describing Aromas and Scents

aromatica(um) (us)	aromatic
citriodora(um) (us)	lemon-scented
foetida(um) (us)	strong-smelling, unpleasant
fragrans	fragrant
fragrantissima(um) (us)	most fragrant
graveolens	smelling unpleasantly
odorata(um) (us)	sweet-scented
odoratissima(um) (us)	sweetest-scented
moschata(um) (us)	musk-scented
suaveolens	sweet-scented

Names alluding to Other Plants

bignoniodes	Bignonia-like
jasminea	Jasmine-like
liliiflora(um) (us)	Lily-flowered
pseudoplatanus	False Plane
salicifolia(um) (us)	Willow-leaved
tulipifera(um) (us)	Tulip-bearing

Names which are Commemorative

delavayi	after the Abbé Delavay
harryana(um) (us)	after Sir Harry Veitch
henryana(um) (us)	after Dr Augustine Henry
hookeri	after Sir Joseph Hooker
thunbergii	after Carl Peter Thunberg
williamsiana(um) (us)	after Mr J.C. Williams
willmottiana(um) (us)	after Miss Ellen Willmott
wilsoniae	after Mr E.H. Wilson

Miscellaneous Names

affine(is)	related (to another species)
alata(um) (us)	winged
amabile(is)	lovely
ambigua(um) (us)	doubtful (identity?)
amoena(um) (us)	charming, pleasant
bella(um) (us)	pretty
commune(is)	common, occurring in plenty
confusa(um) (us)	confused (identity?)
dulce(is)	sweet
edule(is)	edible
florida(um) (us)	free-flowering
formosa(um) (us)	handsome, beautiful
hybrida(um) (us)	hybrid
insigne(is)	outstanding
intermedia(um) (us)	intermediate
media(um) (us)	middle, midway between
officinale(is)	of the shop (herbal)
praecox	early
pulchella(um) (us)	beautiful
speciosa(um) (us)	showy
sativa(um) (us)	sown, planted or cultivated
utile(is)	useful
vernale(is)	spring
vulgare(is)	common

Choosing Trees and Shrubs

Reasons for choosing trees and shrubs can appear to be almost as many and varied as the range of plants available.

Personal taste plays an important role, as do factors such as whether the plants are required for a public or private place, a small or large garden, or for their effect in a particular season.

At the end of this section, you will find tables designed to give you clues to selecting trees and shrubs for particular purposes or with certain characteristics.

The suggestions are by no means exhaustive. They are simply intended as a guide – or perhaps, just a reminder – of trees and shrubs suitable for some of the many different soils, situations and conditions found in the British Isles and other temperate regions – and even within one site.

In the majority of cases, the tables list complete genera, leaving the pleasure of final selection to the reader, by browsing through the detailed descriptions of plants within a particular genus. In some cases, however, certain species or forms 'break the rules' of their genus by proving to have marked characteristics or tolerance of conditions which differ from those of most of their close relatives – and thus offer prospects of success in conditions in which other plants of the same genus might fail. Thus, you will find some plants listed more specifically in the tables.

When thinking about planting new trees and shrubs, it makes good sense to take a walk around the area in which you live, visiting public parks or private gardens which may be open to the public at different seasons, and even looking over fences, making notes of those subjects which appear to do well. If yours is a chalk-soil district, for instance, you probably won't find any rhododendrons or azaleas, whereas shrubs such as the potentillas, with their long flowering season, will probably thrive.

The three main factors controlling the growth of a plant (and, consequently, its selection for the garden) are soil, situation and hardiness.

Most of us think of soil as being either clay, sandy or chalky, and wet or dry, but there are obviously many degrees of these conditions. Many shrubs which are weak and miserable in a shallow soil over chalk will grow well in a deep soil over chalk.

THE IMPORTANCE OF SOIL pH

The pH scale is a means of measuring the acid or alkaline reaction of the soil. A pH reading of seven is neutral. Soils rich in lime are said to be alkaline, and show progressive readings above seven on the scale, whilst readings below this figure indicate progressive acidity.

Simple proprietary soil testing kits are readily available, and are a worthwhile investment. A kit may well cost appreciably less than a single tree or shrub, and a few minutes spent in using it may save an expensive disappointment by warning you to steer clear of a particular plant, or indicating how conditions for it might be improved.

Most ornamental plants thrive best in soils with a pH between 5.7 and 6.7, but, happily, one can find cultivated trees and shrubs which will tolerate the most extreme conditions at either end of the scale. For example, some species in the family Ericaceae will flourish in soils with a pH as low as 4, whereas some members of the Oleaceae, Rosaceae and other families will thrive in limy soils with readings as high as 8.5.

In some cases (Holly, Beech, Yew, etc) plants have a very wide range of tolerance to both acidity and alkalinity – from, say, pH3.6 to above 8.

The relationship between soil pH and plant growth is extremely complex, and secondary factors certainly play an important part in a plant's reaction. Hard and fast rules are therefore difficult, and one may well find, for example, that a Rhododendron will do well in one type of soil with a pH of 6.5 (slightly acid) but may fail in a different type of soil with the same reading.

The most profound influence of pH on plant growth is its effect on the availability of soil chemical elements to the plant. In the pH range between 5.7 and 6.7 the greatest number of nutrients are in a soluble state, the state in which they can most easily be absorbed.

As the pH rises, such important major elements as nitrogen, phosphorus and potassium gradually become less available and minor elements such as iron become increasingly unobtainable. As the pH decreases and the soil becomes more acid, availability of the three major elements again decreases, and the important minor element, calcium, is deficient. At the same time, other minor elements such as iron, manganese and aluminium become only too readily available, giving rise to toxic symptoms.

The choice of worthwhile trees and shrubs is so vast that, as a rule, there is not much point in struggling to grow subjects in soils which are really unsuitable. However, excessively acid soils may be improved by adding chalk or limestone, whilst the pH of alkaline soils may be lowered by applying iron sulphate, ammonium sulphate or flowers of sulphur.

Gardeners wishing to grow acid-loving plants on alkaline soils can often achieve satisfactory results by applying the missing elements in chelated form – as iron sequestrene .

WHAT IS HARDINESS?

The hardiness of plants is something about which the gardener is always wondering – and frequently baffled!

Why is it that trees which thrive in the harshness of Northern Europe, Russia or Siberia may fail in the comparatively warmer and apparently kinder conditions of southern England? One answer is that our treacherous springs, with mild spells followed by sharp frosts, trick these unsuspecting trees into early growth, only to cut them back, again and again, until the tree is exhausted and dies. Plants from the milder countries, such as New Zealand or Chile are not so easily fooled. They wait for the more settled weather of late spring before making their move.

As most experienced gardeners know to their cost, few plants may confidently be described as being sure to withstand any condition in any part of Britain. Conversely it is surprising (and encouraging) just how many 'suspect' subjects may be grown with very little protection.

It is known and accepted that in general the milder, moister areas of western Britain are more hospitable to tender plants than the often colder or drier areas of central and eastern regions. What is not always appreciated is that many tender subjects may be (and are) grown in central, eastern and northern gardens where careful positioning or sheer good luck has provided adequate protection.

Fortunately, a combination of legislation, advancing technology and increasing environmental awareness has decreased the volume of atmospheric pollution in industrial and urban areas – and lessened the extent to which it affects the well-being of plants. It is happily rarer nowadays to find leaves coated with grime, soil defiled by sulphur dioxide or evergreens which have become wholly or partly deciduous because of chemical 'burn'.

As a result, it is encouraging to see town gardens which contain as many beautiful and interesting plants as those in rural areas. Indeed, the microclimate in some favoured town situations enables successful cultivation of a number of exotic plants which are less likely to succeed in the harsher climate of nearby country districts.

Trees

Key to symbols & abbreviations

□   Suitable for conditions or having marked characteristics listed in column headings

■   Suitable for extreme conditions or having indicated characteristic to an intense degree

S   Semi-evergreen

Figures in 'Flowering time' column indicate months (ie 1 = January, and so on)

	CLAY	DRY	CHALK	MOIST/BOGGY	COLD EXPOSED INLAND	COASTAL	EVERGREEN (S=Semi)	DECIDUOUS	LARGE	MEDIUM	SMALL	WEEPING HABIT	UPRIGHT NARROW HABIT	RED OR PURPLE FOLIAGE	GOLD OR YELLOW FOLIAGE	GREY OR SILVER FOLIAGE	VARIEGATED FOLIAGE	AROMATIC FOLIAGE	AUTUMN COLOUR	BOLD ARCHITECTURAL FOLIAGE	ORNAMENTAL BARK	ORNAMENTAL FRUIT	FLOWERING TIME	FRAGRANT FLOWERS	HEDGING/SCREENING	SOUTHWEST WALLS	SHADE TOLERANT
ACACIA ("Wattle") ✗ †		□						□			□				□								1/2	□	□		
ACER campestre & cultivars ("Field Maple")	□	□	■		□			□			□								□						□		
ACER capillipes & other "Snake Barks"	□	□						□			□								□		□	□					
ACER griseum ("Paper Bark Maple")	□	□						□			□								■		□						
ACER negundo & cultivars ("Box Elder")	□	□	■					□		□					□		□										
ACER platanoides & cultivars ("Norway Maple")	□	□	■		□	□		□	□					□	□		□		□				1				
ACER pseudoplatanus & cultivars ("Sycamore")	□	□	■		□	□		□	□					□	□		□		□								
ACER rubrum & cultivars ("Red Maple")								□	□	□			■						■								
ACER saccharinum & cultivars ("Silver Maple")	□	□						□	□			□							□								
AESCULUS ("Horse Chestnut")	□	■						□	□	□										□			5/6		□		
AILANTHUS altissima ("Tree of Heaven")	□	□	□					□	□											□	□						
ALNUS ("Alder")	■		■	□	□	□		□	□														3				
AMELANCHIER ("Snowy Mespilus")	□							□			□								■				4/5				
ARBUTUS ("Strawberry Tree")		□			□	□					□										□	□	10/11				
BETULA ("Birch")	□	□	□	□	□			□	□	□						□			□		□						
CARAGANA ("Pea Tree")	□	□	□		□			□			□				□								5/6				
CARPINUS ("Hornbeam")	□		■	□	□			□	□										□							□	
CARYA ("Hickory")	□							□	□										□								
CASTANEA ("Sweet Chestnut") ✗		□				□		□	□										□				7				
CATALPA ("Bean Tree")	□	□						□		□					□					□			7				
CELTIS ("Hackberry")	□	□						□		□																	
CERCIDIPHYLLUM								□				□															
CERCIS ("Judas Tree")		□	■					□			□												5				
CLADRASTIS	□		□					□		□													6/7	□			
CORNUS ("Dogwood")	□		□					□			□								□				5/6/7				
CORYLUS colurna ("Turkish Hazel")	□		□		□			□					□									□					
COTONEASTER	□	□	□				S	□			□								□			□	6				
CRATAEGUS ("Thorn")	■		■	■	□			□			□								□			■	5		□	□	

21

Species	CLAY	DRY	CHALK	MOIST/BOGGY	COLD EXPOSED INLAND	COASTAL	EVERGREEN (S=Semi)	DECIDUOUS	LARGE	MEDIUM	SMALL	WEEPING HABIT	UPRIGHT NARROW HABIT	RED OR PURPLE FOLIAGE	GOLD OR YELLOW FOLIAGE	GREY OR SILVER FOLIAGE	VARIEGATED FOLIAGE	AUTUMN COLOUR	BOLD ARCHITECTURAL FOLIAGE	AROMATIC FOLIAGE	ORNAMENTAL FRUIT	ORNAMENTAL BARK	FLOWERING TIME	FRAGRANT FLOWERS	HEDGING/SCREENING	SOUTHWEST WALLS	SHADE TOLERANT
DAVIDIA ("Pocket Handkerchief Tree")			☐					☐		☐													5				
EMBOTHRIUM ("Chilean Fire Bush") ↙				☐				☐			☐												5/6				
EUCALYPTUS ("Gum")	☐	☐					☐		☐	☐	☐					☐						☐					
EUCRYPHIA ↙				☐			☐																7/8/9	☐			
FAGUS ("Beech")			■		☐			☐	☐																☐		
FRAXINUS ("Ash")	■	☐	■		☐			☐	☐												☐		5/6				
GLEDITSIA		☐	☐					☐	☐						☐						☐	☐					
GYMNOCLADUS		☐	☐					☐	☐										☐	☐							
HALESIA ("Snowdrop Tree") ↙				☐				☐		☐													5				
IDESIA								☐		☐									☐		☐		6				
ILEX ("Holly")	■	☐	☐			☐	☐			☐	☐						☐				☐				☐		☐
JUGLANS ("Walnut")			☐					☐	☐											☐	☐						
KOELREUTERIA ("Pride of India")		☐	☐					☐													☐		7/8				
LABURNUM	☐		■		☐			☐			☐	☐											6	☐			
LIGUSTRUM ("Privet")	☐	☐					☐			☐	☐						☐						8				
LIQUIDAMBAR ↙	☐			☐				☐	☐	☐				☐				■									
LIRIODENDRON ("Tulip Tree")	☐	☐						☐	☐						☐			☐					6/7				
MAGNOLIA (Some ↙)	☐	☐	☐					☐			☐												2/5 & 8/9	☐		☐	
MALUS ("Flowering Crabs")	☐		■		☐			☐			☐	☐		☐							☐		4/5	☐			
MORUS ("Mulberry")			■					☐		☐											☐						
NOTHOFAGUS ("Southern Beech") ↙				☐				☐	☐	☐								☐									
NYSSA ↙				☐				☐										■									
OSTRYA ("Hop Hornbeam")			☐					☐		☐	☐							☐									
PARROTIA			☐					☐		☐								■			☐						☐
PAULOWNIA		☐	☐					☐	☐										☐				5			☐	
PHELLODENDRON ("Amur Cork Tree")	☐	☐						☐											☐	☐	☐						
PHILLYREA	☐	☐				☐	☐				☐												5				
PLATANUS ("Plane")	☐							☐	☐									☐				☐					
POPULUS ("Poplar")	■	☐	☐	☐	☐			☐	☐						☐	☐				☐							
PRUNUS ("Almond", "Cherry", "Peach", "Purple Leaf Plum")	☐		■					☐			☐	☐	☐	☐							☐	☐	2/12	☐	☐		
PTEROCARYA	☐			☐	☐			☐	☐										☐				6				
PYRUS ("Pear")	☐	☐	☐					☐			☐	☐				☐		■					4				
QUERCUS ("Oak")	☐	☐	☐			☐	☐	☐	☐	☐								☐									☐
RHUS ("Sumach")		☐						☐			☐							☐	☐								

(continued)

	CLAY	DRY	CHALK	MOIST/BOGGY	COLD EXPOSED INLAND	COASTAL	EVERGREEN	DECIDUOUS	LARGE	MEDIUM	SMALL	WEEPING HABIT	UPRIGHT NARROW HABIT	RED OR PURPLE FOLIAGE	GOLD OR YELLOW FOLIAGE	GREY OR SILVER FOLIAGE	VARIEGATED FOLIAGE	AUTUMN COLOUR	BOLD ARCHITECTURAL FOLIAGE	AROMATIC FOLIAGE	ORNAMENTAL FRUIT	ORNAMENTAL BARK	FLOWERING TIME	FRAGRANT FLOWERS	HEDGING/SCREENING	SOUTHWEST WALLS	SHADE TOLERANT
ROBINIA ("False Acacia")		☐	☐					☐	☐	☐			☐		☐								6		☐		
SALIX ("Willow")	■		☐	■	☐			☐	☐	☐		☐			☐							☐	3				
SASSAFRAS ✗			☐					☐										☐		☐							
SOPHORA			☐			☐		☐	☐				☐														
SORBUS ("Mountain Ash/Whitebeam")	☐		☐		☐	☐		☐		☐			☐		☐			☐			☐		5/6		☐		
STUARTIA ✗			☐					☐							☐			☐			☐		7/8				
STYRAX ("Snowbell")			☐					☐			☐												6		☐		
TETRADIUM			■					☐											☐	☐							
TILIA ("Lime")	☐		☐					☐	☐													☐	7/9		☐		
TOONA			☐					☐	☐													☐	6		☐		
TRACHYCARPUS	☐	☐	☐			☐	☐			☐									☐				6				
ZELKOVA			☐					☐	☐													☐					

Conifers as Trees

	CLAY	DRY	CHALK	MOIST/BOGGY	COLD EXPOSED INLAND	COASTAL	EVERGREEN	DECIDUOUS	LARGE	MEDIUM	SMALL	WEEPING HABIT	UPRIGHT NARROW HABIT	GOLD OR YELLOW FOLIAGE	GREY OR SILVER FOLIAGE	VARIEGATED FOLIAGE	AUTUMN COLOUR	AROMATIC FOLIAGE	ORNAMENTAL CONES	ORNAMENTAL BARK	HEDGING/SCREENING	SHADE TOLERANT
ABIES ("Silver Firs")	☐		☐	☐	☐		☐		☐	☐			☐	☐					☐	☐		
ARAUCARIA ("Monkey Puzzle")	☐		☐	☐			☐		☐	☐			☐						☐			
CALOCEDRUS ("Incense Cedar")	☐		■	☐			☐		☐	☐			☐	☐		☐		☐				
CEDRUS ("Cedar")	☐		☐				☐		☐	☐					☐				☐			
CHAMAECYPARIS lawsoniana & cultivars ("Lawson Cypress")	☐	☐	■	☐			☐		☐	☐		☐	☐	☐	☐	☐					☐	
CHAMAECYPARIS nootkatensis ("Nootka Cypress")	☐	☐	☐	☐			☐		☐			☐	☐						☐			
CHAMAECYPARIS obtusa & cultivars ("Hinoki Cypress")	☐	☐	☐	☐			☐			☐	☐		☐	☐		☐						
CHAMAECYPARIS pisifera & cultivars ("Sawara Cypress")	☐	☐					☐		☐				☐	☐		☐						
CRYPTOMERIA ("Japanese Cedar")	☐		☐	☐			☐		☐				☐							☐		
CUNNINGHAMIA ("Chinese Fir")	☐		☐				☐		☐				☐									

23

Conifers / Trees

	CLAY	DRY	CHALK	MOIST/BOGGY	COLD EXPOSED INLAND	COASTAL	EVERGREEN	DECIDUOUS	LARGE	MEDIUM	SMALL	WEEPING HABIT	UPRIGHT NARROW HABIT	GOLD OR YELLOW FOLIAGE	GREY OR SILVER FOLIAGE	VARIEGATED FOLIAGE	AUTUMN COLOUR	AROMATIC FOLIAGE	ORNAMENTAL CONES	ORNAMENTAL BARK	HEDGING/SCREENING	SHADE TOLERANT
× CUPRESSOCYPARIS ("Leyland Cypress")		□	□	□	□		□		□												□	
CUPRESSUS ("Cypress")	□	■	■		□	□	□		□		□		□	□	□	□		□			□	
GINKGO ("Maidenhair Tree")	□	□	□		□			□	□				□	□			□					
JUNIPERUS ("Juniper")	□	■	■	□	□	□	□			□	□		□	□	□	□		□				
LARIX ("Larch")	□	□	□	□	□			□	□	□							□					
METASEQUOIA ("Dawn Redwood")	□	□		■				□	□				□				□				□	
PICEA ("Spruce")	□		□	□	□		□		□	□	□	□		□	□				□		□	
PINUS ("Pine")	□	■	■		□	□	□		□	□	□		□	□	□			□	□		□	
PSEUDOTSUGA ("Douglas Fir") ∠	□			□	□		□		□									□				□
SEQUOIA ("Californian Redwood")		□		□	□		□		□											□		
SEQUOIADENDRON ("Wellingtonia")	□		□		□		□		□		□									□		
TAXODIUM ("Swamp Cypress") ∠	■			■				□	□	□							□					
TAXUS ("Yew")	□	□	■		□	□	□			□	□		□	□	□	□				□	□	□
THUJA ("Arborvitae")	□	□	■		□	□	□			□	□		□	□	□	□	□	□			□	
THUJOPSIS	□	□	■		□	□	□			□	□			□	□	□				□		
TSUGA ("Hemlock")	□		□	□	□		□		□		□								□			□

Shrubs

	CLAY	DRY	CHALK	MOIST/BOGGY	COLD EXPOSED INLAND	COASTAL	EVERGREEN (S=Semi)	DECIDUOUS	LARGE	MEDIUM	SMALL	DWARF	GROUND COVER	RED OR PURPLE FOLIAGE	GOLD OR YELLOW FOLIAGE	GREY OR SILVER FOLIAGE	VARIEGATED FOLIAGE	AUTUMN COLOUR	BOLD ARCHITECTURAL FOLIAGE	AROMATIC FOLIAGE	ORNAMENTAL FRUIT	ORNAMENTAL BARK	FLOWERING TIME	FRAGRANT FLOWERS	HEDGING/SCREENING	NORTH/EAST WALLS	SOUTHWEST WALLS	SHADE TOLERANT
ABELIA	□		□			S		□		□	□				□								6/9	□		□		
ABELIOPHYLLUM		□	□					□			□						□						2	□		□		
ABUTILON		□	□					□		□							□						5/9					
ACER japonicum, palmatum & cultivars ("Japanese Maples")	□							□			□			□				■	□									□
AESCULUS ("Horse Chestnut")	□		■					□	□									□	□				5/7					

	CLAY	DRY	CHALK	MOIST/BOGGY	COLD EXPOSED INLAND	COASTAL	EVERGREEN (S=Semi)	DECIDUOUS	LARGE	MEDIUM	SMALL	DWARF	GROUND COVER	RED OR PURPLE FOLIAGE	GOLD OR YELLOW FOLIAGE	GREY OR SILVER FOLIAGE	VARIEGATED FOLIAGE	AUTUMN COLOUR	BOLD ARCHITECTURAL FOLIAGE	AROMATIC FOLIAGE	ORNAMENTAL FRUIT	ORNAMENTAL BARK	FLOWERING TIME	FRAGRANT FLOWERS	HEDGING/SCREENING	NORTH/EAST WALLS	SOUTH-WEST WALLS	SHADE TOLERANT
ALOYSIA ("Lemon Plant") †		☐	☐					☐												☐			8				☐	
AMELANCHIER ("Snowy Mespilus")	☐		☐					☐	☐									☐					4/5					
ANDROMEDA ✗				☐			☐			☐													5/6					☐
ARALIA	☐		☐					☐	☐								☐	☐					7/9					
ARBUTUS ("Strawberry Tree")			☐			☐	☐		☐												☐	☐	10/11					
ARCTOSTAPHYLOS ✗		☐					☐					☐									☐		4/5					☐
ARONIA ("Chokeberry")	☐		☐					☐										☐			☐		4					
ARTEMISIA		☐					☐					☐				☐												
ARUNDINARIA ("Bamboo")	☐		☐	☐			☐					☐							☐									☐
ATRIPLEX			☐		☐	☐	S				☐					☐												
AUCUBA	☐		■				☐				☐						☐											☐
AZARA				☐			☐																3	☐		☐		
BALLOTA		☐	☐				☐					☐				☐							7					
BERBERIS ("Barberry")	☐	☐	■		☐		☐	☐	☐	☐	☐	☐	☐	☐				☐			☐		4		☐			
BUDDLEJA	☐	☐	■		☐			☐			☐		☐			☐	☐						5/6 & 8/9	☐			☐	
BUPLEURUM	☐	☐	☐	☐			☐		☐														7					
BUXUS ("Box")	☐	☐	☐					☐		☐	☐	☐					☐								☐			☐
CALLICARPA			☐					☐		☐	☐							☐			☐		8					
CALLISTEMON ("Bottle Brush")		☐				☐	☐			☐									☐				7				☐	
CALLUNA ("Ling") ✗		☐		☐	☐		☐				☐	☐		☐	☐								7/10					
CALYCANTHUS ("Allspice")	☐		☐					☐		☐										☐			7					
CAMELLIA ✗			☐				☐			☐													2/5		☐	☐	☐	
CARAGANA ("Pea Tree")	☐	☐	☐	☐	☐			☐			☐												5					
CARPENTERIA			☐				☐			☐													7				☐	
CARYOPTERIS		☐	☐					☐			☐					☐				☐			8					
CASSINIA		☐	☐			☐	☐					☐	☐										7					
CEANOTHUS ("California Lilac")		☐	☐			☐	☐			☐		☐											5 & 8				☐	
CERATOSTIGMA ("Plumbago")		☐	☐					☐				☐						☐					8/10					
CERCIS ("Judas Tree")		☐	■					☐	☐														5					
CHAENOMELES ("Japonica")	☐	☐	☐		☐			☐			☐										☐		3/4			☐	☐	
CHIMONANTHUS ("Winter Sweet")			☐					☐		☐													1	☐		☐		
CHIONANTHUS ("FringeTree")			☐					☐		☐											☐		6/7	☐				
CHOISYA ("Mexican Orange")	☐		☐				☐			☐							☐			☐			5/6	☐		☐	☐	☐
CISTUS ("Sun Rose")		☐	■				☐			☐						☐							6/7					
CLERODENDRUM	☐		☐					☐	☐									☐	☐		☐		8/9	☐				
CLETHRA ✗				☐				☐		☐								☐				☐	7/8	☐				
CLIANTHUS ("Lobster's Claw") †		☐	☐				☐			☐													6				☐	
COLLETIA		☐	☐				☐			☐													7/8				☐	

25

	CLAY	DRY	CHALK	MOIST/BOGGY	COLD EXPOSED INLAND	COASTAL	EVERGREEN (S=Semi)	DECIDUOUS	LARGE	MEDIUM	SMALL	DWARF	GROUND COVER	RED CR PURPLE FOLIAGE	GOLD OR YELLOW FOLIAGE	GREY OR SILVER FOLIAGE	VARIEGATED FOLIAGE	AUTUMN COLOUR	BOLD ARCHITECTURAL FOLIAGE	AROMATIC FOLIAGE	ORNAMENTAL FRUIT	ORNAMENTAL BARK	FLOWERING TIME	FRAGRANT FLOWERS	HEDGING/SCREENING	NORTH/EAST WALLS	SOUTH/WEST WALLS	SHADE TOLERANT
COLUTEA ("Bladder Senna")	☐	☐	■			☐		☐		☐	☐							☐			☐		6/8					
COMPTONIA ("Sweet Fern") ✓				☐				☐			☐							☐					3					
CONVOLVULUS		☐	☐			☐					☐					☐							5					
CORNUS ("Dogwood")	☐	☐	☐	☐		☐		☐	☐	☐		☐	☐		☐		☐	☐			☐	☐	2/5/6					☐
COROKIA		☐	☐		☐	☐	☐			☐	☐					☐							5/6					
CORONILLA		☐	☐			☐	☐				☐					☐					☐		5/7	☐		☐		
CORYLOPSIS	☐		☐					☐		☐								☐					3/4	☐				☐
CORYLUS ("Hazel")	☐	☐	☐					☐	☐					☐	☐						☐		2					☐
COTINUS ("Smoke Tree")		☐	☐					☐		☐				■				☐					6/7					
COTONEASTER	☐	☐	☐		☐	☐	☐	☐	☐	☐	☐							☐			☐		6		☐	☐		☐
CRINODENDRON ✓				☐		☐	☐			☐													5			☐	☐	
CYTISUS ("Broom")	☐	☐	☐			☐		☐		☐	☐	☐											5/7				☐	
DABOECIA ("Irish Heath") ✓				☐			☐				☐	☐											6/8					
DANAE ("Alexandrian Laurel")	☐			☐			☐				☐										☐							☐
DAPHNE			☐			☐	☐	☐			☐						☐				☐		2/6	☐		☐		
DECAISNEA		☐	☐	☐				☐	☐	☐									☐		☐		5				☐	
DENDROMECON		☐	☐			☐	☐				☐							☐					5/10				☐	
DESFONTAINIA ✓				☐			☐				☐												7/9			☐		
DEUTZIA	☐	☐	■	☐				☐		☐	☐												6/7					
DIERVILLA	☐	☐	☐	☐				☐			☐				☐								6/7					
DIPELTA			☐					☐	☐	☐													5	☐				
DIPTERONIA	☐							☐	☐										☐								☐	
DISANTHUS ✓ ○	☐		☐					☐		☐								■					10					
DISTYLIUM	☐					☐	☐			☐													4					☐
DORYCNIUM		☐	☐			☐					☐					☐					☐		8/9					
DRIMYS			☐				☐		☐														4/5	☐		☐		☐
EDGEWORTHIA			☐					☐			☐												3					
ELAEAGNUS	☐	☐	☐		☐	☐	☐	☐	☐	☐					☐		☐				☐		5/6 & 10	☐	☐			☐
ENKIANTHUS ✓				☐				☐		☐								■					5					☐
ERICA, tall forms ("Heath") ✓		☐		☐		☐	☐			☐	☐				☐								3/5					
ERICA carnea, erigena, terminalis and × darleyensis		☐	☐			☐	☐				☐	☐	☐		☐								4/5 & 9					
ERICA, others ✓	☐	☐		☐		☐	☐				☐	☐			☐								6/10					
ERIOBOTRYA ("Loquat")	☐		☐				☐												☐						☐	☐		
ESCALLONIA		☐	☐			☐	☐			☐	☐												6/7		☐			
EUONYMUS	☐	☐	■			☐				☐	☐				☐			☐			☐		5/6		☐			☐
EURYOPS		☐	☐			☐					☐					☐							4/5				☐	
EXOCHORDA	☐	☐	☐					☐		☐	☐												5					
FABIANA			☐			☐	☐			☐	☐												5/6					
× FATSHEDERA	☐	☐	☐			☐	☐			☐									☐							☐		☐

	CLAY	DRY	CHALK	MOIST/BOGGY	COLD EXPOSED INLAND	COASTAL	EVERGREEN (S=Semi)	DECIDUOUS	LARGE	MEDIUM	SMALL	DWARF	GROUND COVER	RED OR PURPLE FOLIAGE	GOLD OR YELLOW FOLIAGE	GREY OR SILVER FOLIAGE	VARIEGATED FOLIAGE	AUTUMN COLOUR	BOLD ARCHITECTURAL FOLIAGE	AROMATIC FOLIAGE	ORNAMENTAL FRUIT	ORNAMENTAL BARK	FLOWERING TIME	FRAGRANT FLOWERS	HEDGING/SCREENING	NORTH/EAST WALLS	SOUTH/WEST WALLS	SHADE TOLERANT
FATSIA	□		□			□	□		□										□				10					□
FORSYTHIA	□		■		□			□	□								□						3/4			□		
FOTHERGILLA ✗	□			□				□			□							■					4	□				
FREMONTODENDRON †		□	□					□	□														6/8				□	
FUCHSIA								□			□	□	□										7/9				□	
GARRYA	□						□		□														1/2			□		
× GAULNETTYA ✗				□	□		□				□										□		5/6					□
GAULTHERIA ✗				□			□					□	□								□		5/6	□				□
GENISTA ("Broom")	□	□	□					□		□	□	□											5/9					
GREVILLEA ✗ †		□					□					□	□										6/7				□	
GRINDELIA		□					□				□												6/10				□	
GRISELINIA †						□	□										□								□			
HAKEA	□	□					□			□													4/5					
× HALIMIOCISTUS ("Sun Rose")		□	■			□	□					□				□							5/9					
HALIMIUM ("Sun Rose")		□	□			□	□					□	□			□							5/6					
HAMAMELIS ("Witch Hazel")	□			□				□	□									■					12/3	□				
HEBE ("Veronica")			■			□	□			□	□	□				□							6/10					
HEDYSARUM		□						□			□												7/9					
HELIANTHEMUM ("Rock Rose")		□	■				□					□	□			□							5/9					
HELICHRYSUM		□	□				□					□				□				□			7					
HIBISCUS	□		■					□		□													7/10					
HIPPOPHAE ("Sea Buckthorn")	□	□	■			□		□	□							□					□							
HOHERIA		□	□					□	□														6/7	□		□		
HOLODISCUS	□	□	■					□	□							□							7					
HYDRANGEA	□			□				□		□	□												6/9			□	□	□
HYPERICUM	□		■				□				□	□	□										6/10			□	□	□
ILEX ("Holly")	□	□	□		□	□	□		□								□				□				□			□
ILLICIUM				□			□													□			5/6				□	
INDIGOFERA	□		■					□		□													6/9				□	
ITEA ilicifolia	□						□			□													8	□		□	□	
JASMINUM ("Jasmine")	□							□														□	11/12 & 6/7	□		□	□	□
KALMIA ✗				□			□						□									□	4/6					
KERRIA	□		■					□									□					□	4/5			□		
KOLKWITZIA ("Beauty Bush")	□	□	■					□	□														5/6					
LAURUS ("Sweet Bay")	□	■	■			□	□								□					□					□			
LAVANDULA ("Lavender")		■	■				□					□				□				□			7	□				
LAVATERA	□	□				□				□													6/10					
LEPTOSPERMUM							□				□									□			5/6				□	
LESPEDEZA	□	□						□		□													8/9					
LEUCOTHOE ✗				□			□					□		□	□								5/8					□

27

	CLAY	DRY	CHALK	MOIST/BOGGY	COLD EXPOSED INLAND	COASTAL	EVERGREEN (S=Semi)	DECIDUOUS	LARGE	MEDIUM	SMALL	DWARF	GROUND COVER	RED OR PURPLE FOLIAGE	GOLD OR YELLOW FOLIAGE	GREY OR SILVER FOLIAGE	VARIEGATED FOLIAGE	AUTUMN COLOUR	BOLD ARCHITECTURAL FOLIAGE	AROMATIC FOLIAGE	ORNAMENTAL FRUIT	ORNAMENTAL BARK	FLOWERING TIME	FRAGRANT FLOWERS	HEDGING/SCREENING	NORTH/EAST WALLS	SOUTHWEST WALLS	SHADE TOLERANT
LEYCESTERIA		☐	☐			☐		☐		☐											☐	☐	6/9					
LIGUSTRUM ("Privet")	☐	☐	■			☐		☐		☐							☐				☐		6/9		☐			☐
LINDERA ✗				☐				☐		☐								■										
LOMATIA ✗				☐			☐			☐													7			☐		
LONICERA ("Honeysuckle")	☐	☐	■			☐		☐		☐											☐		1/3 & 5/6					☐
LUCULIA							S			☐													12	☐				
MAGNOLIA	☐	☐	☐	☐		☐		☐	☐										☐				7/9 & 3/4	☐				
MAHONIA	☐	☐	■				☐			☐	☐								☐		☐		11/12/4	☐				☐
MELIANTHUS			☐				☐			☐						☐			☐				6/7					
MENZIESIA ✗				☐				☐			☐												5					
MYRICA	☐							☐		☐										☐	☐		4/5					
MYRTUS ("Myrtle") †		☐	☐			☐	☐			☐							☐			☐			7/8	☐				☐
NANDINA ("Sacred Bamboo")		☐	☐				☐			☐				☐				☐					6/7					
NEILLIA	☐		■					☐		☐													5/6					
OLEARIA ("Daisy Bush")	☐	☐	■			☐	☐			☐						☐							5/8	☐	☐			
ONONIS		☐	■					☐				☐											6/7					
OSMANTHUS	☐	☐	☐				☐			☐	☐												4/5 & 9	☐				
OZOTHAMNUS		☐	☐				☐			☐	☐					☐							7	☐				
PACHYSANDRA	☐		☐	☐			☐					☐	☐										2/3					☐
PAEONIA ("Tree Paeony")			■					☐		☐									☐				5/6					
PARAHEBE		☐	☐				☐				☐	☐											7/8					
PARROTIA	☐	☐		☐				☐	☐									☐				☐	3					
PERNETTYA	☐	☐		☐			☐				☐										☐		5/6					
PEROVSKIA		☐	☐			☐		☐			☐					☐				☐			8/9					
PHILADELPHUS ("Mock Orange")	☐	☐	■					☐		☐					☐								6/7	☐				☐
PHILLYREA		☐	☐				☐			☐													5	☐				☐
PHLOMIS		☐	☐				☐				☐					☐							6					
PHORMIUM							☐			☐				☐			☐		☐				7/9					
PHOTINIA	☐	☐					☐			☐				☐							☐		5/6		☐			
PHYGELIUS ("Cape Figwort")			☐	☐							☐												7/9				☐	
× PHYLLIOPSIS			☐	☐			☐					☐											5/6 & 11					
PHYLLOSTACHYS ("Bamboo")		☐	☐				☐	☐														☐						
PHYSOCARPUS	☐	☐		☐				☐		☐					☐								6					
PIERIS ✗				☐			☐			☐				☐									3/5			☐		
PIPTANTHUS ("Evergreen Laburnum")		☐	☐				S			☐													5				☐	
PITTOSPORUM	☐	☐	☐			☐	☐			☐	☐						☐						5/6	☐	☐			
POLYGALA ✗				☐			☐				☐	☐											4/6					

	CLAY	DRY	CHALK	MOIST/BOGGY	COLD EXPOSED INLAND	COASTAL	EVERGREEN (S=Semi)	DECIDUOUS	LARGE	MEDIUM	SMALL	DWARF	GROUND COVER	RED OR PURPLE FOLIAGE	GOLD OR YELLOW FOLIAGE	GREY OR SILVER FOLIAGE	VARIEGATED FOLIAGE	AUTUMN COLOUR	BOLD ARCHITECTURAL FOLIAGE	AROMATIC FOLIAGE	ORNAMENTAL FRUIT	ORNAMENTAL BARK	FLOWERING TIME	FRAGRANT FLOWERS	HEDGING/SCREENING	NORTH/EAST WALLS	SOUTHWEST WALLS	SHADE TOLERANT
PONCIRUS ("Bitter Orange")	☐	☐	☐					☐		☐											☐	☐	5	☐				
POTENTILLA	☐	■	■		☐	☐		☐		☐	☐					☐							6/11		☐			☐
PRUNUS	☐	☐	■		☐		☐	☐	☐								■	☐			☐	☐	3/6					
PSEUDOWINTERA							☐																					☐
PTELEA ("Hop Tree")	☐							☐			☐				☐								6	☐				
PTEROSTYRAX	☐		☐					☐															6/7	☐				
PUNICA ("Pomegranate") †		☐						☐		☐													9/10				☐	
PYRACANTHA ("Firethorn")	☐	☐	■		☐	☐	☐			☐											☐		6		☐	☐	☐	☐
RHAMNUS ("Buckthorn")	☐	☐	■		☐	☐	☐	☐		☐												☐						☐
RHAPHIOLEPIS		☐	☐			☐	☐					☐											6				☐	
RHODODENDRON ✗	☐			☐			☐		☐	☐	☐	☐	☐										1/8	☐	☐			☐
RHODODENDRON AZALEA, deciduous ✗	☐							☐		☐	☐							☐					5/6	☐				☐
RHODODENDRON AZALEA, evergreen ✗	☐		☐		☐		☐			☐	☐							☐					4/5					☐
See also charts 'Choosing Rhododendrons' page 32																												
RHODOTYPOS	☐	☐	■					☐			☐										☐		5/7					
RHUS ("Sumach")	☐	☐	■			☐		☐	☐									■	☐					☐				
RIBES ("Currants" and "Gooseberries")	☐	☐	■	☐		☐	☐	☐		☐	☐		☐		☐			☐					2/5					
ROMNEYA ("Tree Poppy")		☐	☐		☐			☐		☐						☐							7/10	☐				
ROSA ("Rose species")	☐	☐	☐		☐			☐	☐	☐											☐		5/7	☐	☐			
ROSE ("Shrub Roses")	☐		☐					☐		☐											☐		6/9	☐	☐	☐		
ROSMARINUS ("Rosemary")		☐	■		☐		☐			☐										☐			5				☐	
RUBUS ("Brambles")	☐	■	☐	☐	☐	☐	☐	☐		☐	☐		☐								☐	☐	5/8					☐
RUSCUS ("Butcher's Broom")	☐	☐	☐	☐			☐			☐											☐							☐
RUTA ("Rue")		☐	☐				☐				☐					☐				☐			6/8					
SALIX ("Willow")	■		☐	■				☐	☐	☐	☐		☐									☐	2/3					
SALVIA		☐	☐		S			☐		☐	☐		☐										8/9				☐	
SAMBUCUS ("Elder")	☐	☐	■	☐				☐	☐						☐						☐		6				☐	
SANTOLINA ("Cotton Lavender")		☐	☐		☐	☐	☐				☐					☐				☐			7					
SARCOCOCCA ("Christmas Box")	☐	■	☐				☐			☐											☐		2	☐				☐
SASA ("Bamboo")	☐		☐	☐			☐			☐																	☐	☐
SENECIO	☐	☐	■		☐	☐	☐			☐	☐		☐			☐							6/7					
SENNA	☐	☐	☐				S	☐															8/9			☐		
SKIMMIA	☐	☐	☐				☐				☐										☐	☐	4/5	☐				☐
SOPHORA	☐	☐	☐				☐			☐													2/4				☐	
SORBARIA	☐	☐	■	☐	☐			☐										☐					6/8					
SPARTIUM ("Spanish Broom")	☐	☐	■		☐	☐		☐		☐												☐	6/8	☐				
SPIRAEA	☐	☐	■	☐	☐			☐		☐	☐				☐			☐					4/8					
STACHYURUS	☐	☐	☐					☐		☐													8					

29

Shrubs (continued)

	CLAY	DRY	CHALK	MOIST/BOGGY	COLD EXPOSED INLAND	COASTAL	EVERGREEN (S=Semi)	DECIDUOUS	LARGE	MEDIUM	SMALL	DWARF	GROUND COVER	RED OR PURPLE FOLIAGE	GOLD OR YELLOW FOLIAGE	GREY OR SILVER FOLIAGE	VARIEGATED FOLIAGE	AUTUMN COLOUR	BOLD ARCHITECTURAL FOLIAGE	AROMATIC FOLIAGE	ORNAMENTAL FRUIT	ORNAMENTAL BARK	FLOWERING TIME	FRAGRANT FLOWERS	HEDGING/SCREENING	NORTH/EAST WALLS	SOUTHWEST WALLS	SHADE TOLERANT
STAPHYLEA ("Bladder Nut")		□	□					□	□												□		5/6					
STEPHANANDRA		□	□					□		□	□	□					□					□	6					
SYCOPSIS		□	□				□			□	□												2/3					
SYMPHORICARPOS		□	■	□	□			□		□			□				□								□			□
SYRINGA ("Lilac")		□	■					□	□	□													5/6	□				
TAMARIX ("Tamarisk")		□	□			□		□		□													3 & 7/9					
TELOPEA ("Waratah") ✗			□	□			□			□	□												6					
TEUCRIUM		□	□								□	□					□						6/8			□		
TIBOUCHINA		□	□					□		□													6/11			□		
TROCHODENDRON ✗		□	□				□			□	□												5/6					□
ULEX ("Gorse")		■	□			□	□			□	□												3/5 & 8/10	□				
VACCINIUM ✗		□	□								□	□						□			□							
VIBURNUM		□	□					□		□		□									□		11/3 & 4/6	□	□			□
VINCA ("Periwinkle")		□	□				□						□				□						4/6					
VITEX ("Chaste Tree")		□	□					□		□									□				9/10				□	
WEIGELA	□	□	■					□		□	□			□	□								5/6					
XANTHOCERAS	□	□	□					□		□													5					
XANTHORHIZA		□	□					□		□					□			□					3/4					
YUCCA		□	□				□			□									□		□		7/8					
ZENOBIA ✗			□					□															6/7					

Conifers as Shrubs

	CLAY	DRY	CHALK	MOIST/BOGGY	COLD EXPOSED INLAND	COASTAL	EVERGREEN	LARGE	MEDIUM	SMALL	DWARF	GROUND COVER	UPRIGHT, NARROW	GOLD OR YELLOW FOLIAGE	GREY OR SILVER FOLIAGE	VARIEGATED FOLIAGE	AUTUMN COLOUR	AROMATIC FOLIAGE	ORNAMENTAL CONES	SHADE TOLERANT
ABIES ("Silver Fir")	□		□	□			□			□	□		□	□					□	
CEDRUS ("Cedar")		□	■				□		□	□			□						□	
CHAMAECYPARIS lawsoniana & cultivars ("Lawson Cypress")	□		■	□			□			□			□							
CHAMAECYPARIS obtusa & cultivars ("Hinoki Cypress")	□		□	□			□			□						□				
CHAMAECYPARIS pisifera & cultivars ("Sawara Cypress")	□		□	□			□			□				□						□
CHAMAECYPARIS thyoides & cultivars ("White Cypress")	□		□	□			□			□									□	□

	CLAY	DRY	CHALK	COASTAL	EVERGREEN (S=Semi)	DECIDUOUS	VIGOROUS	MEDIUM	GROUND COVER	TWINING	SELF CLINGING	RED OR PURPLE FOLIAGE	GOLD OR YELLOW FOLIAGE	VARIEGATED FOLIAGE	AUTUMN COLOUR	ORNAMENTAL FRUIT	BOLD ARCHITECTURAL FOLIAGE	FLOWERING TIME	FRAGRANT FLOWERS	NORTH/EAST WALLS	SOUTH/WEST WALLS	SHADE OF TOLERANT
CRYPTOMERIA ("Japanese Cedar")	□		□	□				□									□					
JUNIPERUS ("Juniper")	□		■	□												□					□	
PICEA ("Spruce")	□		□	□									□									
PINUS ("Pine")	□		■	□									□									
TAXUS ("Yew")	□		■	□									□								□	
THUJA ("Arborvitae")	□		■	□									□			□			□			
TSUGA ("Hemlock")	□		□	□				□					□									

Climbers

	CLAY	DRY	CHALK	COASTAL	EVERGREEN (S=Semi)	DECIDUOUS	VIGOROUS	MEDIUM	GROUND COVER	TWINING	SELF CLINGING	RED OR PURPLE FOLIAGE	GOLD OR YELLOW FOLIAGE	VARIEGATED FOLIAGE	AUTUMN COLOUR	ORNAMENTAL FRUIT	BOLD ARCHITECTURAL FOLIAGE	FLOWERING TIME	FRAGRANT FLOWERS	NORTH/EAST WALLS	SOUTH/WEST WALLS	SHADE OF TOLERANT
ACTINIDIA	□	□	□			□	□			□						□	□	7/8	□	□		
AKEBIA	□	□			S		□			□							□	4		□	□	
AMPELOPSIS	□	□				□		□			□				□					□		
ARISTOLOCHIA	□	□				□				□							□	6		□	□	
ASTERANTHERA					□			□	□									6				
BERBERIDOPSIS					□													7/8		□		
CAMPSIS ("Trumpet Vine")			□			□	□				□							8/9			□	
CELASTRUS						□	□			□						□				□		
CLEMATIS	□	□	□			□	□	□		□								4/10		□	□	
DECUMARIA	□	□	□		□			□			□							5		□	□	□
DREGEA	□	□	□		S					□								6/8				□
FALLOPIA ("Russian Vine")	■	■	□			□	■		□									7/9		□		
HEDERA ("Ivy")	■	□	□	□	□			□	□		□		□	□								■
HOLBOELLIA	□	□			□			□		□								4/5	□	□	□	
HUMULUS ("Hop")	□	□	□			□	□			□			□									
HYDRANGEA, climbing	□	□	□			□		□			□							6		□		□
JASMINUM ("Jasmine")	□	□	□			□		□		□								8/9	□	□	□	
LAPAGARIA			□		□					□								6/10		□		
LONICERA ("Honeysuckle")	□	□	□	□	□	□		□		□						□		5/10	□	□	□	
PARTHENOCISSUS	□	□	□			■	□				■				□					□		
PASSIFLORA ("Passion Flower") †	□	□	□			□				□						□		6/9			□	
PILEOSTEGIA	□	□	□		□			□			□							8/9		□		
RUBUS ("Bramble")	□	■	□			□			□											□		
SCHISANDRA						□				□								5 & 8/9		□		
SCHIZOPHRAGMA	□	□				□					□							7		□	□	
SENECIO		□	□		S													9/11			□	
SOLANUM	□	□	■		S		□											7/10			□	
SOLLYA	□	□	□					□	□									6/10			□	
STAUNTONIA	□	□	□		□			□								□	□	5	□			
TRACHELOSPERMUM	□	□	□		□					□							□	7/8	□	□		
VITIS ("Vines")	□	□	□			□	□			□					□	□	□			□		
WISTERIA	□	□	□			□	□			□								5/6	□		□	

Choosing Rhododendrons

The genus RHODODENDRON is so vast that the range of choice can sometimes appear to be overwhelming.

The table below, based upon a representative selection of species and hybrids, has been designed to facilitate selection by three main factors – height, colour and flowering period.

Names commencing with a small initial letter are those of species; those starting with a capital letter (with or without quotation marks) are hybrids.

Figures following the names indicate the flowering period (depending on location and season). A figure 1 represents January, and so on.

Information on relative hardiness and other characteristics is incorporated within individual plant descriptions.

TALL

REDS
- 'Bagshot Ruby' 5–6
- 'Britannia' 5–6
- 'Cynthia' 5–6
- 'Fusilier' 5–6
- 'Isabel Pearce' 5–6
- 'Kluis Sensation' 5–6
- *mallotum* 3–4
- Nobleanum 1–3

YELLOWS
- 'Beatrice Keir' 4–5
- 'Crest' 5–6
- *falconeri* 4–5
- Jalisco 'Elect' 6–7
- *macabeanum* 3–4
- 'Tortoiseshell Champagne' 6–7

PINKS
- 'Alice' 5–6
- 'Betty Wormald' 5–6
- *fortunei* subsp. *discolor* 6–7
- 'Lady Clementine Mitford' 6–7
- 'Lem's Monarch' 5–6
- Loderi 'Pink Diamond' 5–6
- Loderi 'Venus' 4–5
- Nobleanum 'Venustum' 12–1
- *orbiculare* 3–4
- Vanessa 'Pastel' 5–6

WHITES
- *auriculatum* 7–8
- 'Beauty of Littleworth' 5–6
- Carita 'Charm' 3–4
- *decorum* 5–6
- 'Gomer Waterer' 6–7
- 'Lodauric Iceberg' 7–8
- Loderi 'King George' 4–5
- 'Loder's White' 5–6
- 'Marinus Koster' 5–6
- 'Mrs P.D. Williams' 6
- 'Polar Bear' 7–8
- 'Sappho' 5–6
- 'Seven Stars' 5–6
- 'Sir Charles Lemon' 2–6
- 'Snow Queen' 5–6

BLUES
- *augustinii* 'Electra' 4–5
- 'Fastuosum Flore Pleno' 5–6
- 'Lavender Girl' 5–6
- 'Purple Splendour' 5–6
- 'Susan' 5–6

MEDIUM

REDS
- *cinnabarinum* Conroy 5–6
- Cinnkeys 5–6
- 'Dopey' 5–6
- 'Elizabeth' 4–5
- Fabia 5–6
- 'May Day' 5–6
- 'Morning Red' 5–6
- 'The Honourable Jean Marie de Montague' 5–6
- 'Titian Beauty' 5–6
- 'Vulcan' 5–6
- 'W.F.H' 5–6
- 'Windlesham Scarlet' 6

YELLOWS
- 'Bo-peep' 3–4
- 'Hotei' 5–6
- *lutescens* 'Bagshot Sands' 3–4
- 'Queen Elizabeth II' 5–6
- 'Unique' 4–5
- 'Yellow Hammer' 3–4

PINKS
- 'Anna Rose Whitney' 5–6
- 'Bashful' 4–5
- 'Brocade' 4–5
- 'Christmas Cheer' 3–4
- *davidsonianum* 4–5
- 'Pink Cherub' 5–6
- 'Praecox' 2–3
- 'Souvenir de Dr S. Endtz' 5–6
- 'Vintage Rosé' 6
- 'Winsome' 5–6

WHITES
- 'Arthur Stevens' 5–6
- Cilpinense 3–4
- 'Hydon Hunter' 5–6
- 'Lem's Cameo' 5–6
- 'Mrs A.T. de la Mare' 5–6
- 'Mr Charles E. Pearson' 5–6
- 'Percy Wiseman' 5–6
- *quinquefolium* (azalea) 4–5
- *roxieanum* Oreonastes 4–5
- *yakushimanum* 'Koichiro Wada' 5–6

BLUES
- 'Emasculum' 4–5
- 'P.J. Mezitt' 3–4
- 'Penheale Blue' 4–5
- Russautinii 5–6
- 'Saint Merrin' 5–6
- 'Saint Tudy' 4–5

DWARF

REDS
- *calostrotum* 'Gigha' 5–6
- 'Elisabeth Hobbie' 4–5
- 'Gartendirektor Glocker' 5–6
- 'Jenny' 5–6
- 'Red Carpet' 4–5
- 'Scarlet Wonder' 5–6

YELLOWS
- 'Curlew' 4–5
- 'Golden Torch' 5
- 'Patty Bee' 3–4
- 'Princess Anne' 5–6

PINKS
- 'Anna Baldsiefen' 3–4
- 'Bow Bells' 4–5
- 'Doc' 5–6
- 'Ginny Gee' 4–5
- 'Hydon Dawn' 5–6
- 'Pink Pebble' 5–6
- *racemosum* 'Forrest's Dwarf ' 3–4
- 'Razorbill' 4–5
- 'Surrey Heath' 5–6
- 'Temple Belle' 4–5
- 'Tessa Roza' 2–3
- *williamsianum* 4–5

WHITES
- 'Arctic Tern' 5–6
- 'Bric-a-brac' 3–4
- 'Dora Amateis' 4–5
- 'Ptarmigan' 3–4
- 'Snow Lady' 5–6

BLUES
- 'Caroline Allbrook' 5–6
- *impeditum* 4–5
- 'Moerheim' 5–6
- *polycladum* Scintillans (FCC form) 4–5
- *russatum* 4–5
- 'Sapphire' 4–5
- 'Silver Cloud' 5–6

Pruning Garden Shrubs and Climbers

Although the methods and times of pruning are (and will probably remain) a controversial subject, there are some useful guidelines which can confidently be recommended.

The aim of pruning should primarily be to remove any dead, diseased, weak or straggly growth. This ensures a healthy open framework within which air can circulate freely.

The majority of trees and shrubs need little further pruning provided due regard was paid to their ultimate height and spread when they were sited. It is better to thin out and transplant trees and shrubs if they were placed too close together initially, than to clip them all round every year as a means of restriction.

However, others, particularly shrubs which tolerate frequent clipping such as Yew (*Taxus*), Bay (*Laurus*), Box (*Buxus*), etc, may be formed, if desired, into hedges, arches, or examples of the topiarist's art. Annual or bi-annual removal of old flowering wood encourages many shrubs to produce a greater number of flowers.

'Dead-heading' reduces competition for nutrients between developing seeds and the rest of the plant, so that further flowering and a better flush of vegetative growth is often encouraged. New basal growth can be stimulated in plants such as Laurel, Yew, Holly, some Rhododendrons, Cotoneaster and Viburnums, which have become bare at the base, by cutting back hard into the old wood in April. Similarly, brightly coloured new shoots of shrubs such as *Cornus alba* are induced by cutting the old shoots near to the ground in winter or early spring.

Large cuts should always be coated with a bituminous dressing or a proprietary wound sealant.

SHRUB TYPES AND PRUNING KEY

Throughout this book, abbreviated guides to pruning have been incorporated in the generic descriptions, or appended to the descriptions of individual types wherever this is thought to be helpful or the need for pruning is significant. **A capital letter** indicates the general extent to which pruning may be required, as defined below:

A   In general, little pruning required

B   Cut back to within two or three buds/15–30cm (6–12in) of ground level

C   On young or semi-mature plants, cut back each flowering shoot *as soon as the blossoms have faded*, leaving one or two young shoots at the base of each

D   Cut out as much old wood as possible *during the winter*, consistent with leaving last year's growth for the following year's flowering

E   Shorten back side shoots of current season's growth to within five or six buds during August or September

A small letter in parenthesis gives supplementary pruning information and/or details of method, as follows:

(a)   To increase size, a framework of old wood may be built up, in which case prune to within two or three buds of the old wood

(b)   If damaged by frost or straggly in habit, cut back to sound wood

(c)   As (b), but damage may be so severe as to require cutting back to ground level

(d)   Where grown as a foliage shrub, may be cut to within a bud or two of ground level to maintain compact growth

(e) Makes a small tree. Attend to formation in the early stages by preventing crossing or touching branches and lopsided growth

(f) Restrict growth as desired

(g) Occasionally, thin out older wood and unproductive shoots to encourage new basal growths

(h) If vigorous, leave unpruned for one season

(i) Remove seed pods immediately after flowering

(j) Remove seed pods and weaker shoots immediately after flowering

(k) Remove suckers (understock), preferably during the dormant season

(l) Trim lightly after flowering to retain compact growth

A figure (1–12) indicates the month of the year when the work should be carried out.

Thus, for example, cultivars of *Buddleja davidii* carry the pruning guide B(a)4 in the main text, most Forsythias are classified A (g) 1, 2, 3, and Wisterias E (f) 8 and 11.

Trees and Shrubs

A

ABELIA – Caprifoliaceae SS-LS ○
Graceful shrubs with tubular flowers,
abundant summer-autumn. A (b) 5
– chinensis MS ○
Fragrant flowers, white flushed rose, freely
produced July–August. AM 1976. A (b) 5
– 'Edward Goucher' SS Semi-(E) ○
Lilac pink flowers freely produced July-
September. AGM 1993. A (b) 5

ABELIA 'Edward Goucher'

– floribunda MS Semi-(E) ○ †
Abundant cherry red flowers up to 5cm long
in June. Best against a warm wall. AGM
1993. A (b) 5
– × grandiflora SS-MS Semi-(E) ○
Pink and white flowers, continuously
July–September. AGM 1993. A (b) 5
– – 'Francis Mason' SS ○
Golden-yellow foliage. Scented flowers, white
flushed rose. AGM 1993. A (b) 5

ABELIA × grandiflora

– schumannii SS ○
Prolonged display of abundant lilac pink
flowers, blotched with orange during late
summer and autumn. AM 1926. A (b) 5
– triflora LS ○
Clusters of fragrant flowers white, flushed
rose produced in threes, June. Erect habit. AM
1959. A (b) 5

ABELIOPHYLLUM – Oleaceae SS ◑
Monotypic genus
– distichum SS ◑
Scented star-shaped flowers, white, flushed
pink, produced February on bare stems. Slow
growth. AM 1937 FCC 1944

ABUTILON – Malvaceae SS-LS ○
Elegant shrubs for south wall. Bell or
saucer-shaped flowers over long period.
– 'Ashford Red' MS ○ †
Apple green leaves. Large bell-shaped flowers
of deep crushed strawberry. AGM 1993

ABUTILON 'Kentish Belle'

– **'Kentish Belle'** SS-MS ○
Arching branches bear drooping, bell-shaped flowers with red calyx and apricot petals flushed red, summer-autumn. South wall. AM 1968 AGM 1993. A (b) 5
– **megapotamicum** SS-MS ○
Attractive, pendulous, bell-shaped flowers with red calyces, yellow petals and purple anthers, summer-autumn. South wall. AM 1949 AGM 1993. A (b) 5

ABUTILON megapotamicum

– – **'Variegatum'** MS ○
As above. Leaves green mottled yellow. AM 1988
– × **milleri 'Variegatum'** MS ○ †
Profuse, bell-shaped orange flowers are borne in summer and autumn or continuously in mild weather. Leaves boldly mottled with yellow. South wall or conservatory. AM 1988. A (b) 5

ABUTILON × suntense 'Jermyns'

– × **suntense** MS-LS ○
Abundant, saucer-shaped flowers 3-5cm, and vine-shaped grey 'felted' leaves. We recommend the following:
– – **'Jermyns'** MS-LS ○
Clear dark mauve flowers. AGM 1993
– – **'White Charm'** MS ○
White flowers.
– **vitifolium** LS ○
Saucer-shaped flowers, 3-5cm, and vine-shaped felted grey leaves. The following clones are in cultivation:
– – **'Tennant's White'** LS ○
Pure white flowers, freely borne. AGM 1993. A (b) 5
– – **'Veronica Tennant'** LS ○
Abundant large mauve flowers. AGM 1993. A (b) 5

ABUTILON vitifolium 'Tennant's White'

ACACIA – Leguminosae LS-ST (E) ○ †
"Wattle"
Yellow blossom winter-spring. Only hardy in the mildest areas – elsewhere requiring full sun and shelter. Most are intolerant of alkaline soils.
– **baileyana** LS (E) ○ † "Cootamundra Wattle"
Leaves glaucous. Abundant bright yellow flowers in racemes winter and spring. AM 1927 FCC 1936 AGM 1993
– – **'Purpurea'** LS (E) ○ †
Young foliage deep purple turning to blue-green.
– **dealbata** LS (E) ○ † "Mimosa" "Silver Wattle"
Dainty silvery green fern-like leaves. Clusters of scented, fluffy golden balls, winter-spring. AM 1935 FCC 1971 AGM 1993. A (c) 5

"ACACIA, FALSE" see *Robinia pseudoacacia*

ACACIA dealbata

ACER – Aceraceae SS-LT "Maples"
Extensive, variable genus, mostly easy to grow and hardy. Leaves noted for rich autumn colours. Flowers inconspicuous, except where indicated otherwise. Stems often attractively striated.
– **campestre** MT ♀ Hdg (0.5m) "Field or Hedge Maple"
Foliage turns clear yellow occasionally flushed red, in autumn. AGM 1993
– – **'Postelense'** MT ♀
Young leaves golden, striking in spring.
– – **'Pulverulentum'** MT ♀
Leaves attractively mottled and blotched white.
– **capillipes** ST ♀
'Snakebark' with silvery-green striations.

Young growths coral red. Leaves tinted red in autumn. AM 1975 AGM 1993
– **cappadocicum** MT-LT ♀
Elegant habit. Leaves turn butter-yellow in autumn.
– – **'Aureum'** MT ♀ ◑
Young foliage red, turning golden yellow. AGM 1993
– – **'Rubrum'** LT ♀
Striking blood-red young foliage, turning through green to red and gold by autumn. AGM 1993
– **carpinifolium** ST ⚲ "Hornbeam Maple"
Leaves similar to native Hornbeam, turning gold and brown in autumn.
– **circinatum** LS ○ "Vine Maple"
Leaves almost circular, turning orange and red in autumn. Flowers plum red and white produced in April. AGM 1993

ACER davidii 'George Forrest'

ACER cappadocicum 'Aureum'

ACER griseum

– **davidii** ST ♥
'Snakebark' with attractive green and white striations. Green fruits, suffused red, hang along branches in autumn. Following clone is recommended.
– – **'George Forrest'** ST ♥
 Excellent form. Vigorous spreading branches. Large dark green leaves with red stalks, variously autumn tinted. AM 1975 (for fruit) AGM 1993
– **ginnala** LS-ST ♥
Vigorous. Bright green, 3-lobed leaves, turning fiery red in autumn. AGM 1993

ACER ginnala

– **griseum** ST ♥ "Paperbark Maple"
Attractive bark, peels revealing cinnamon-coloured underbark. Trifoliolate leaves have glorious fiery autumn tints. AM 1922 AGM 1993
– **grosseri** var. **hersii** (*A. hersii*) ST ♥
Leaves with or without lobes. Marbled bark. Yellow racemes of flowers followed by conspicuous seed. Red autumn colour. AGM 1993
– **hersii** see *A. grosseri* var. *hersii*
– **japonicum** LS-ST ♥
Usually a large shrub with soft green leaves and autumn colour. Natural shelter from cold winds is desirable. The following clones are recommended:
– – **'Aconitifolium'** ('Laciniatum') ('Filicifolium') LS

ACER japonicum 'Vitifolium'

Leaves deeply lobed and cut, turning ruby crimson in autumn. AGM 1993
– – **'Aureum'** see *A. shirasawanum* 'Aureum'
– – **'Vitifolium'** LS
Large, fan-shaped leaves which turn brilliant red in autumn. FCC 1974 (for autumn foliage) AGM 1993
– **lobelii** LT ♥
Distinctive columnar habit. Rich green palmately lobed leaves turning yellow in autumn.
– **maximowiczianum** (*A. nikoense*) ST-MT ♥ "Nikko Maple"
Trifoliolate leaves. Fiery autumn tints. FCC 1971
– **negundo** MT-MT ♥ "Box Elder"
Bright green, pinnate leaves, normally 3-5 separate leaflets. Fast growing. We offer:

ACER negundo 'Elegans'

– – **'Elegans'** ('Elegantissimum') MT 🌳
Leaves irregularly margined bright yellow,
fading to cream. FCC 1898
– – **'Flamingo'** ST 🌳
Leaves variegated with a pink margin which
changes to white. Shoots bloomy. AGM 1993
– – **'Variegatum'** ('Argenteovariegatum')
MT 🌳
Leaves irregularly margined white.
– – **violaceum** MT 🌳
Young shoots purple with white bloom.
Long reddish pink flower tassels in spring. AM
1975 when shown by us in flower. AGM
1993
– **nikoense** see *A. maximowiczianum*
– **palmatum** LS-ST 🌳 "Japanese Maple"
Elegant habit. 5 or 7 lobed, bright green
leaves, turning orange/red in autumn. Many
cultivars with beautiful autumn colour.
Natural shelter from cold winds is
desirable.
– – **'Asahi-Zuru'** LS
Leaves attractively blotched with white,
sometimes all pink or white when young.
– – **Atropurpureum** group MS
Brilliant purple summer foliage turning rich
crimson purple in autumn.

ACER palmatum Atropurpureum

– – **'Beni Maiko'** SS
Young leaves brilliant red turning pink then
greenish-red.
– – **'Beni Shichihenge'** SS
Blue-green deeply lobed leaves margined
pinkish-white or nearly all bright orange pink.
– – **'Bloodgood'** LS
Deep reddish-purple leaves turn brilliant red in
autumn when fruits are an added attraction.
AGM 1993

– – **'Burgundy Lace'** ST
Wine-red leaves deeply cut into slender lobes.
AGM 1993
– – **'Butterfly'** MS
Upright branches bear deeply cut, grey-green,
cream and pink-margined leaves becoming
red tinged in autumn. AGM 1993
– – **'Chitoseyama'** MS
Deep cut green/bronze leaves. Rich autumn
colour. Becomes mound-like with age. AGM
1993
– – **'Corallinum'** DS
Young stems coral pink. Small 5-lobed leaves,
bright shrimp pink when young, turning to
pale mottled green. Slow growth.
– – **coreanum** see 'Koreanum'
– – **'Crimson Queen'** (Dissectum group) SS
Leaves deeply divided into finely cut lobes
coloured a long-lasting, deep reddish purple.
AGM 1993
– – **'Deshojo'** MS
Upright habit with brilliant-red young leaves
cut into slender lobes, later bright green.
– – **Dissectum** group SS-MS
Group of clones with deeply cut and finely
divided fern like leaves. Mushroom shaped,
ultimately dense rounded habit.
– – **'Dissectum'** SS
Soft green leaves, turning red in autumn,
occasionally yellow. AGM 1993
– – **'Dissectum Atropurpureum'** SS
Bronze-purple leaves. Red in autumn.
– – **Elegans** group (Heptalobum group)
Includes forms with relatively large leaves.
Generally with 7 lobes, finely doubly
serrate.

ACER palmatum 'Dissectum'

ACER palmatum 'Dissectum Atropurpureum'

ACER palmatum 'Elegans'

– – **'Elegans'** LS
Fresh green, attractive, deeply toothed leaves,
up to 13cm long.
– **'Garnet'** (Dissectum group) SS
Large, deep garnet-red leaves with finely cut
lobes. Vigorous. AGM 1993
– – **'Heptalobum Elegans Purpureum'** see
'Hessei'
– – **'Hessei'** (Elegans group) ('Heptalobum
Elegans Purpureum') LS
Large, deep bronze-crimson leaves
– – **'Inaba Shidare'** (Dissectum group) SS
Large, deeply divided, red-purple leaves on
red stalks turn crimson in autumn. Vigorous.
AGM 1993
– – **'Kagiri Nishiki'** ('Roseomarginatum') MS
Pale green leaves with an irregular coral-pink
margin. FCC 1865
– – **'Karasugawa'** MS
Leaves deeply lobed, pink when young, later
mottled and streaked pink and white.

– – **'Koreanum'** (coreanum) MS-LS
Leaves crimson in autumn, longer lasting than
most. AGM 1993
– – **'Linearilobum'** ('Scolopendrifolium') MS
Green leaves divided into long narrow lobes.
AM 1896 AGM 1993
– – **'Osakazuki'** (Elegans group) LS
Green leaves change through various shades
to brilliant flame scarlet in autumn.
Spectacular. AGM 1993

ACER palmatum 'Osakazuki'

– – **'Red Pygmy'** SS
Reddish-purple leaves deeply cut into, long
slender lobes. AGM 1993
– – **'Ribesifolium'** ('Shishigashira') LS
Distinct upright form, but with a broad
crown. Slow growing. Dark green leaves
turning old-gold in autumn.
– – **'Seiryu'** (Dissectum group) LS
Upright branches bear deeply cut, bright
green leaves, red-tinged when young, turning
orange-yellow splashed crimson in autumn.
AGM 1993
– – **'Senkaki'** ('Sangokaku') LS "Coral Bark
Maple"
Conspicuous coral-red branches, particularly
effective in winter. Leaves colouring soft
yellow in autumn. AM 1950 AGM 1993
– – **'Shishio Improved'** LS
Deeply lobed leaves, crimson when young.
– – **'Trompenburg'** LS
Leaves deep purple-red turning green then
red in autumn. Narrow lobes have margins
rolled under the leaf.
– **pensylvanicum** ST ♣
Young stems pale green with white
striations. Large 3-lobed leaves turn to

ACER palmatum 'Senkaki'

ACER platanoides 'Columnare'

buttercup-yellow in autumn. Not good on shallow chalk soils. AGM 1993

– – 'Erythrocladum' ST ♥
Delightful form. Juvenile shoots shrimp-pink with pale striations, conspicuous in winter. AM 1976 FCC 1977

– pentaphyllum ST ♥ †
Green leaves, glaucous beneath with 5 linear-lanceolate segments on elongated scarlet leaf stalks. Handsome and rare.

– platanoides LT ♥ "Norway Maple"
Magnificent, fast growing. Green leaves, turn buttercup-yellow, occasionally red, in autumn. Conspicuous yellow flowers in clusters on naked stems from April make this one of the most outstanding large trees in the British landscape. AM 1967 AGM 1993

– – 'Columnare' LT ♦
Erect form with closely packed branches

– – 'Crimson King' LT ♥
Striking form with deep crimson-purple leaves. AGM 1993

– – 'Crimson Sentry' MT ♦
Narrow form with red-purple leaves.

– – 'Deborah' MT ♥
Brilliant red young leaves turn to dark green. An improvement on 'Schwedleri'.

ACER platanoides 'Crimson King'

– – 'Drummondii' MT-LT ♥
Leaves with broad, creamy-white margins. Elegant. AM 1956 AGM 1993

– – 'Emerald Queen' LT ♥
Vigorous form with dark glossy green leaves. Upright when young.

– – 'Globosum' ST
Short branches forming a dense globular crown which glows golden in autumn.

– – **'Schwedleri'**
(AGM 1993) see under **'Deborah'**
– **pseudoplatanus** LT ♥ "Sycamore"
Magnificent green leaved tree, tolerant of
virtually all conditions and soils other than
waterlogged sites.
– – **'Atropurpureum'** ('Purpureum Spaethii')
LT ♥
Form with purple undersides to leaves. AGM
1993
– – **'Brilliantissimum'** ST ♥
Spectacular. Delightful, shrimp-pink young
foliage. Slow grower. AM 1925 AGM 1993
– – **'Erectum'** ('Fastigiatum') LT ♦
Strongly ascending branches.
– – **'Leopoldii'** MT ♥
Variegated foliage, initially yellowish-pink
then green with yellow and pink splashes and
speckles. FCC 1865 AGM 1993
– – **'Nizetii'** LT ♥
Leaves with yellow, pink and white markings,
purple beneath.
– – **'Worleei'** MT ♥ "Golden Sycamore"
Beautiful soft golden leaves, turning green in
high summer. AGM 1993
– **rubrum** LT ♥ ✗ "Red Maple" "Canadian
Maple"

Dark green, palmate leaves with bluish green
undersides, turning red or scarlet in autumn.
Rarely colours well on chalk. AM 1969
– – **'October Glory'** MT ♥
Brilliant red autumn colour over a long period.
AM 1988 AGM 1993
– – **'Red Sunset'** MT ♥
Upright form with particularly brilliant autumn
colour.
– – **'Scanlon'** MT ♥
Rich autumn hues. Excellent for smaller
gardens and restricted spaces. AGM 1993
– – **'Schlesingeri'** MT ♥
Early autumn colour of deep scarlet. AM 1976

ACER rubrum 'Schlesingeri'

– **rufinerve** MT ♥
Snake bark. Older stems and trunk green with
white striations. 3-lobed leaves turn scarlet
and yellow in autumn. AGM 1993
– **saccharinum** LT ♥ "Silver Maple"
A remarkably fast growing tree with large,
deeply five-lobed leaves, silvery beneath.
Good autumn colour. AGM 1993
– – **Laciniatum** group MT-LT ♥
Graceful trees with gently drooping branches
and finely and deeply cut leaves.
– – **'Lutescens'** LT ♥
Orange-yellow young leaves turn to soft
yellow-green.
– – **'Pyramidale'** ('Fastigiatum') LT ♦
Upright growing form.
– **saccharum** LT ♥ "Sugar Maple"
5-lobed leaves turn crimson, orange or gold in
a good autumn.
– **shirasawanum 'Aureum'** (*A. japonicum*
'Aureum') ST ♥
Slow-growing tree with attractive soft yellow
leaves. FCC 1884 AGM 1993

ACER pseudoplatanus 'Brilliantissimum'

ACER

– 'Silver Vein' ST ♥
Perhaps the most spectacular snake bark maple. The large leaves turn yellow in autumn.
– triflorum ST ♥
Dark brown furrowed bark. Trifoliolate leaves, glaucous beneath; consistently brilliant autumn colour. Rare and slow growing .
– wilsonii LS-ST
Generally 3-lobed leaves, shrimp-pink when young, changing to coral and finally soft green.
– × zoeschense MT ♥
5-lobed leaves of dark green, tinged purple.

AESCULUS – Hippocastanaceae "Horse Chestnut" MT-LT ♥
Ornamental late spring/early summer flowering. Leaves compound, palmate, flowers in erect racemes. Easy cultivation. Any soil.
– × carnea MT-LT ♥ "Red Horse Chestnut"
Magnificent deep pink 'candles' up to 20cm long in May. We recommend:
– – 'Briotii' MT-LT ♥
More compact form. Flowers a richer shade of rose-pink. AM 1965 AGM 1993

AESCULUS × carnea 'Briotii'

– flava (*A. octandra*) MT-LT ♥ "Sweet Buckeye"
Flowers creamy-yellow with red markings. Leaves normally have good autumn colour. AGM 1993

– hippocastanum LT ♥ "Common Horse Chestnut"
Impressive, especially in May with erect panicles of white flowers. "Conkers" produced in autumn. AGM 1993
– – 'Baumannii' ('Flore Pleno') LT ♥
Double white form, does not set seed, therefore of no attraction to stone-throwing boys. AGM 1993
– indica LT ♥ "Indian Horse Chestnut"
Superb tree with slender panicles of pink flushed flowers up to 40cm long, June-July. AM 1922 FCC 1933 AGM 1993
– – 'Sydney Pearce' LT ♥
Dark olive green leaves. Free flowering, with large panicles with petals white marked yellow and tinged pink. AM 1967
– × mutabilis LS-ST
Flowers red and yellow May-June. We recommend the form:
– – 'Induta' ('Rosea Nana') LS-ST ♥
Delightful apricot flowers with yellow markings in early summer.
– × neglecta MT ♥
Leaves attractively coloured in autumn. Panicles of pale yellow flowers, May-June. The following form is recommended:
– – 'Erythroblastos' MT ♥ ◑
Young leaves delightful shrimp pink, changing pale yellow/green and finally orange and yellow in autumn. Slow grower. AM 1962 AGM 1993
– parviflora MS
Panicles of white flowers with red anthers, freely produced July-August. Good autumn leaf colour. AM 1955 AGM 1993
– pavia LS-ST ♥ "Red Buckeye"
Crimson flowers in panicles June. AGM 1993 We recommend the selected form:

AESCULUS pavia 'Atrosanguinea'

– – **'Atrosanguinea'** LS-ST ♀
Beautiful form with deep crimson flowers,
June.
– **turbinata** LT ♀ "Japanese Horse Chestnut"
Fast growing with large leaves colouring in
autumn. Long panicles of creamy flowers with
red markings, June.

AILANTHUS – Simaroubaceae LT ♀
*Elegant, fast growing. Tolerant of most soils
and conditions – including industrial pollution.*
– **altissima** (*A. glandulosa*) LT ♀ "Tree of
Heaven"
Large, ash-like leaves to 1m long. Reddish
"key"-like fruits in conspicuous bunches on
female trees. AM 1953 AGM 1993

ALBIZIA – Leguminosae LS-ST ♀ ○
*Mimosa-like, attractive foliage and fluffy
heads of flowers.*
– **julibrissin** LS-ST ○
Deeply divided fern-like foliage. Pink flowers
in summer. We commend the following form:
– – **'Rosea'** LS-ST ○
Dense heads of deep rose-pink flowers.
Withstands severe frosts.

"ALMOND" see *Prunus dulcis*

ALNUS – Betulaceae MS-LT "Alder"
*Tolerant of most soils, except shallow chalk.
Ideal for damp sites. Often bear attractive
catkins .*
   cordata MT ♠ "Italian Alder"
Fresh green glistening foliage. Attractive
cone-shaped fruiting heads. Grows rapidly –
even on chalk. AM 1976 FCC 1987 AGM
1993
– **glutinosa** MT ♀ "Common Alder"
Smooth grey bark. Sticky young growths.
Leaves green and shiny, retained until late
autumn. Yellow catkins in March.
– – **'Imperialis'** MT ♠
Attractive form with finely cut feathery leaves.
AM 1973 AGM 1993
– **incana** ST ♀ "Grey Alder"
Oval to round leaves with grey undersides.
Extremely hardy; ideal for cold wet situations.
Fast growth.
– – **'Aurea'** ST
Young shoots and foliage yellow. Catkins red
tinted. Bright orange wood in winter. Slow
growth.
– – **'Pendula'** ST ♠
Weeping branches and grey-green foliage
forming a dense mound. Bright catkins in
January.

ALNUS glutinosa 'Imperialis'

– × **spaethii** MT ♀
Large, green leaves. Showy catkins. AGM
1993

ALOYSIA – Verbenaceae MS
*Aromatic shrubs, only the following
commonly grown:*
– **triphylla** (*Lippia citriodora*) MS † ○ "Lemon
Plant"
Lemon-scented, lanceolate leaves. Tiny, pale
purple flowers, August. Best on a south-
facing wall in most areas. The aromatic leaves
can be used as a flavouring or to make
refreshing drinks.

AMELANCHIER – Rosaceae MS-ST
"Snowy Mespilus" "June Berry"
*Beautiful genus with abundant racemes of
white flowers in spring. Often rich autumn
colour. Best in lime-free soils.* A (E) 2
– **'Ballerina'** LS-ST ♀
Bronze young leaves turn red and brown in
autumn. Fragrant, large white flowers very
profusely borne. AGM 1993
– **canadensis** see *A. lamarckii*
– × **grandiflora** LS
A North American hybrid of which we
recommend the following:
– – **'Robin Hill'**
Compact and upright with bronze young
leaves. Pale pink flowers open from deeper
buds and turn to white.
– **lamarckii** (*A. canadensis* hort.) ST ♀
Silky, coppery-red young leaves, turning
scarlet in autumn. Clusters of starry flowers in
lax racemes. Often grown as *A. canadensis*.
AGM 1993. A (E) 2

AMELANCHIER lamarckii

ANDROMEDA – Ericaceae DS-SS (E) ✓ ●
Slender-stemmed shrubs for damp acid soils or rock garden.
– **polifolia** DS (E) ✓ ● "Bog Rosemary"
Narrow glaucous green leaves, white beneath. Terminal clusters of soft pink flowers, May-June. We recommend the form:
– – **'Major'** SS (E) ✓ ●
Broader leaves. Taller.

"ANGELS TRUMPET" see *Brugmansia*

ANTHYLLIS – Leguminosae DS-SS ○
Sun-loving shrubs or herbs. The following species is in cultivation.
– **hermanniae** DS ○
Abundant, small pea flowers, yellow with orange markings on standards, produced June-July.

ARALIA – Araliaceae LS-ST ○
Handsome, large compound leaves. Hardy but prefer some shelter to protect leaves.
– **elata** LS ○ "Japanese Angelica Tree"
Huge, "Angelica"-like leaves, forming ruffs at ends of branches. Crowned by large branched heads of white flowers in early autumn. AM 1959 AGM 1993
– – **'Aureovariegata'** LS
Leaflets margined and splashed yellow, turning silver-white later in summer.
– – **'Variegata'** LS
Leaflets margined creamy white, turning silver-white later in summer. AM 1902 AGM 1993
– **sieboldii** see *Fatsia japonica*

ARBUTUS – Ericaceae ST-MT ♥ (E)
"Strawberry trees"
Ornamental evergreens with dark green leathery leaves. Clusters of white, pitcher-

ARALIA elata

ARBUTUS unedo 'Rubra'

shaped flowers followed by strawberry-like fruits.
– × **andrachnoides** ST ♥ (E)
Attractive peeling cinnamon red bark. Flowers late autumn and winter. Lime tolerant and hardy. AM 1953 AGM 1993

– **menziesii** MT ♀ (E) ✗ "Madrona"
Flowers in conspicuous panicles late spring, followed by orange yellow fruits. AM 1926 AGM 1993
– **unedo** ST ♀ (E) "Killarney Strawberry Tree"
Gnarled trunk with brown shredding bark. Flowers and fruit borne simultaneously late autumn. Lime tolerant. FCC 1933 AGM 1993
– – **'Rubra'** ST ♀ (E)
More compact form with pink flushed flowers and abundant fruit. AM 1925 AGM 1993

ARCTOSTAPHYLOS – Ericaceae PS-ST (E)
✗ ○
Variable genus allied to Rhododendrons and needing similar conditions.
– **manzanita** MS (E) ✗
Sea-green leaves. Dark reddish brown stems. Spikes of pink/white pitcher-shaped flowers. FCC 1923
– **uva-ursi** PS (E) ✗ GC "Red Bearberry"
Creeping alpine with small white, pink-tinged flowers. Red fruits.

ARONIA – Rosaceae SS-MS
White flowers in spring, followed by red or black berries. Bright autumn foliage. Not for shallow chalk.
– **arbutifolia** MS "Red Chokeberry"
Bright red fruits and brilliant autumn foliage.
– – **'Brilliant'**
The best form, selected for its particularly attractive fruits.

ARTEMISIA – Compositae MS-SS ○
Attractive grey or green foliage. Aromatic.
– **abrotanum** SS "Lad's Love"
"Southernwood"
Grey-green, sweetly aromatic, finely cut

ARTEMISIA 'Powis Castle'

leaves. Upright habit.
– **'Powis Castle'** SS GC ○
Compact, spreading habit, finely cut, silvery grey, aromatic leaves.

ARUNDINARIA – Gramineae DS-LS (E)
Clump-forming or spreading bamboos. The spreading species are useful for ground cover or screens, depending on their size.
– **anceps** see *Sinarundinaria anceps*
– **auricoma** (*A. viridistriata*) SS-MS (E)
Erect, slender, purplish-green canes forming small patches. Leaves dark green, striped rich yellow. AM 1972 AGM 1993

ARUNDINARIA auricoma

ARUNDINARIA fortunei

– **fortunei** (*A. variegata*) SS (E)
Dense, tufted species with erect, zig-zag, pale
green canes. Leaves dark green striped with
white. AGM 1993
– **'Gauntlettii'** see *A. humilis* 'Gauntlettii'
– **hindsii** MS (E)
Vigorous, thicket-forming habit with erect
olive-green canes and thickly clustered sea-
green leaves.
– **humilis** SS (E)
Thicket-forming with slender canes. We
recommend:
– – **'Gauntlettii'** (*A.* 'Gauntlettii') SS (E) GC
Compact, less rampant form good for ground
cover.
– **japonica** see *Pseudosasa japonica*
– **murielae** see *Thamnocalamus spathaceus*
– **nitida** see *Sinarundinaria nitida*
– **pumila** DS (E) GC
Dense carpets of slender, purplish canes.
– **pygmaea** DS (E) GC
Wide-spreading, carpet-forming species with
slender stems.
– **simonii** LS (E)
Vigorous clump-forming species with erect,
olive-green canes, bloomed when young.
Luxuriant foliage. Makes a good screen.
– **spathiflora** see *Thamnocalamus
spathiflorus*
– **vagans** see *Sasa ramosa*
– **variegata** see *A. fortunei*
– **viridistriata** see *A. auricoma*

"ASH" see *Fraxinus*

"ASPEN" see *Populus tremula*

ASTERANTHERA ovata see under
CLIMBERS

ATRIPLEX – Chenopodiaceae MS Semi-
(E) ○
*Striking silvery-grey foliage. Thrives on saline
soil. Excellent seaside plant.*
– **halimus** MS Semi-(E) ○ "Tree Purslane"
Silvery-grey leaves.

AUCUBA – Cornaceae SS-MS (E)
*Handsome rounded shrubs with glossy green
or variegated leaves. Male and female
(berrying) forms. Suitable for almost all soils
and situations. Poisonous.*
– **japonica** MS (E)
 Wild type with green leaves. FCC 1864. We
recommend selected forms:

AUCUBA japonica 'Crotonifolia'

– – **'Crotonifolia'** ('Crotonoides') MS (E)
 Large leaves boldly speckled gold. Male.
AGM 1993
– – **'Gold Dust'** MS (E)
Leaves boldly speckled gold. Female.
– – **'Golden King'** MS (E)
Similar to 'Crotonifolia' but with more striking
variegation. Male.
– – **'Hillieri'** MS (E)
Large, glossy, dark green leaves. Pointed
fruits. Female.
– – **'Lance Leaf'** MS (E)
Glossy, green, lance-shaped leaves. Male
– – **'Longifolia'** MS (E)
Long, bright green leaves. Female. FCC 1864
AGM 1993
– – **'Nana Rotundifolia'** SS (E)
Small, rich green leaves, toothed in upper half.
Sea-green stems. Free berrying, female form.
– – **'Rozannie'** MS (E)
Large red fruits freely borne. Dark green
leaves. Female.
– – **'Salicifolia'** MS (E)
Narrow leaved, free berrying, female form.
– – **'Variegata'** MS (E) ('Maculata')
 Yellow blotched leaves. Female. FCC 1865

AZALEA and × **AZALEODENDRON** see
under *Rhododendron*

AZARA – Flacourtiaceae LS-ST (E) †
*Attractive leaves and fragrant flowers, early
spring. Best against a wall.*
– **microphylla** ST (E) †
Dainty, dark green leaves. Vanilla scented,
yellow flowers in clusters, early spring. FCC
1872 AGM 1993

B

BALLOTA – Labiatae DS ○
Sub-shrubs for sunny, well-drained sites.
– pseudodictamnus DS ○
Leaves orbicular-cordate, whole shrub greyish-white, woolly. Flowers lilac-pink, July. AGM 1993

"BAMBOOS" see *Arundinaria, Chusquea, Indocalamus, Phyllostachys, Pseudosasa, Sasa, Shibataea, Sinarundinaria* and *Thamnocalamus*

"BARBERRY" see *Berberis*

"BAY" see *Laurus nobilis*

"BEAUTY BUSH" see *Kolkwitzia amabilis*

"BEECH" see *Fagus*

"BEECH, SOUTHERN" see *Nothofagus*

BERBERIS – Berberidaceae DS-LS
Variable genus with evergreen and deciduous members. Spring flowers from pale yellow to orange. Showy fruits. Many have brilliant autumn foliage. Easy cultivation, any soil not waterlogged. Poisonous
– 'Bountiful' SS
Spreading habit. Clusters of coral red berries on arching branches in autumn.
– buxifolia MS Semi-(E)
Early flowers, followed by grape-like purple blue berries. AM 1961. We recommend:
– – 'Nana' DS (E)
Dense, mound like habit. Slow growing.
– darwinii MS (E) Hdg (0.5m)
Glossy dark green, three pointed leaves. Spectacular deep-yellow flowers in racemes April-May. Purplish-blue berries. AGM 1930 FCC 1967 AGM 1993
– dictyophylla (*B. dictyophylla* 'Albicaulis') MS
Red young stems, clothed in white bloom. Leaves white beneath – good autumn colour. Large, single, red berries with white bloom. AGM 1993
– × frikartii SS (E)
Compact shrubs with attractive glossy foliage. We recommend:
– – 'Amstelveen' SS (E)
Dense, mound-like habit. Yellow flowers. AGM 1993

BERBERIS darwinii

BERBERIS 'Goldilocks'

– – 'Telstar' SS (E)
Compact habit with arching branches and glossy green leaves, glaucous beneath. Yellow flowers in spring. AGM 1993
– gagnepainii SS (E) Hdg (0.5m)
Dense habit. Makes excellent impenetrable hedge. Narrow undulate leaves. Black berries with blue bloom.
– georgei MS
Yellow flowers in May followed by profuse hanging clusters of conspicuous bright crimson berries. AM 1979 FCC 1985
– 'Goldilocks' LS (E)
Vigorous and upright with dark, glossy green leaves. Profuse clusters of golden-yellow flowers in spring. FCC 1991 AGM 1993

49

– hypokerina SS (E) ⚊
Thicket of purple stems. Holly-like leaves, silver beneath up to 10cm long. Dark blue berries with white bloom. AM 1932
– × interposita SS (E)
Dense mound of arching stems. Vigorous. Spiny, glossy dark green leaves. We recommend:
– – 'Wallich's Purple' SS (E)
Bronze-red young leaves turn to glossy green.
– × irwinii and cultivars see under *Berberis × stenophylla*
– julianae MS (E)
Dense habit. Spiny stems and stiff, narrow leaves, copper tinted when young. Yellow, slightly scented flowers in axillary clusters.
– linearifolia MS (E)
Erect habit. Glossy, dark green, spineless leaves. Orange-red flowers, early spring and sometimes autumn. FCC 1931

BERBERIS linearifolia 'Jewel'

BERBERIS × stenophylla

– – 'Jewel' MS (E)
Conspicuous flowers, scarlet in bud, opening bright orange. AM 1978
– – 'Orange King' MS (E)
Form with larger rich orange flowers.
– × lologensis LS (E)
Leaves variable, entire and spiny on same plant. Apricot yellow flowers. A lovely shrub. AM 1931
– – 'Apricot Queen' LS (E)
Large, bright orange flowers profusely borne. Broadly upright habit. AGM 1993
– × media 'Parkjuweel' SS Semi-(E) ○
Clusters of small yellow flowers in spring. Dense, prickly habit. Leaves almost spineless, colouring well in autumn (occasionally lasting until spring). AGM 1993
– – 'Red Jewel' SS Semi-(E)
Dark green leaves turn to deep red-purple. AGM 1993
– × ottawensis MS
Oval or rounded green leaves and drooping clusters of red berries. We recommend the form:
– – 'Superba' ('Purpurea') MS
Vigorous form with rich purple foliage. Flowers yellow, followed by red berries. AM 1979 AGM 1993
– panlanensis see *B. sanguinea* 'Panlanensis'
– 'Rubrostilla' SS
Large, showy, coral-red, oblong berries. FCC 1916 AGM 1993
– sanguinea 'Panlanensis' MS (E) Hdg (0.5m)
Compact, neat habit. Spiny, sea-green, linear leaves.
– × stenophylla MS (E) Hdg (0.5m)
Long, arching branches. Golden-yellow flowers, April-May. FCC 1864 AGM 1993
– – 'Claret Cascade' MS (E)
Flowers rich orange flushed red, foliage tinged purple
– – 'Corallina Compacta' DS (E)
Coral-red buds, opening yellow. AGM 1993
– – 'Irwinii' SS (E)
Deep yellow flowers.
– temolaica MS
Vigorous, striking shrub. Glaucous young growths, shoots dark purple-brown and glaucous with age. Egg-shaped, red, bloomy berries.
– thunbergii SS Hdg (0.5m)
Compact growth. Bright red berries and brilliant autumn foliage. FCC 1890 AGM 1993
– – Atropurpurea group SS Hdg (0.5m)
Reddish-purple foliage, becoming richer in colour towards winter. AM 1926

BERBERIS × stenophylla 'Corallina Compacta'

BERBERIS thunbergii 'Rose Glow'

– – **'Atropurpurea Nana'** DS Hdg (0.4m)
Dwarf form with purple foliage, ideal for rock gardens or dwarf hedge. AGM 1993
– – **'Aurea'** SS
Yellow leaves, turning pale green by late summer.
– – **'Bagatelle'** DS
Compact, bun-shaped habit with purple foliage. AGM 1993
– – **'Green Carpet'** SS
Low, spreading habit with arching branches. Leaves red in autumn.
– – **'Harlequin'** SS
Similar to 'Rose Glow' but with more strikingly variegated, smaller leaves. AM 1978
– – **'Helmond Pillar'** SS
Narrow, upright habit, foliage rich purple.
– – **'Red Chief'** SS
Rich wine-red foliage on upright branches. AGM 1993
– – **'Rose Glow'** SS
Young leaves purple, mottled silver-pink and bright rose, later becoming purple. AGM 1993
– **valdiviana** LS (E)
Elegant, distinctive plant. Large leathery, almost spineless leaves. Saffron-yellow flowers in slender drooping racemes followed by blue-black berries. AM 1939
– **verruculosa** MS (E)
Slow growing, compact habit. Warty stems with small, glossy, dark green leaves, white beneath. Golden-yellow flowers. AM 1911 AGM 1993
– **wilsoniae** SS
Dense, mound-like habit. Small, sea-green leaves, turning attractive colours in autumn. Coral-red berries. FCC 1907 AGM 1993

BERBERIS verruculosa

BERBERIS wilsoniae

BETULA – Betulaceae SS-LT "Birch"
Many noteworthy for stem colour and beautiful yellow autumn leaves. Good on most soils, but do not attain full height on shallow chalk.
– **albo-sinensis** var. **septentrionalis** MT ♠
Shining orange-brown bark with a pink and grey "bloom". AGM 1993
– **alleghaniensis** (*B. lutea*) MT ♀
Attractive peeling bark of amber or golden brown. Rich yellow autumn leaves.
– **costata** see *B. ermanii* 'Grayswood Hill'
– **ermanii** LT ♠
Peeling, creamy-white bark, tinted pink,

BETULA ermanii 'Grayswood Hill'

BETULA utilis var. jacquemontii 'Jermyns'

branches orange brown.
– – **'Grayswood Hill'** LT ♠
A form with striking white bark and good, yellow autum colour. Previously listed as *B. costata*. AGM 1993
– **'Fetsowii'** MT ♀
Graceful habit. Chalk-white, peeling bark.
– **jacquemontii** see *B. utilis* var. *jacquemontii*
– **'Jermyns'** see *B. utilis* 'Jermyns'
– **nigra** ST ♀ "River Birch"
Shaggy bark. Diamond shaped, soft green leaves. Excellent for damp, but not waterlogged, ground. AGM 1993
– **papyrifera** LT ♀ "Paper Birch" "Canoe Birch"
White, papery bark. Yellow autumn leaf colour.
– – var. **kenaica** MT ♀
White bark, tinged orange.
– **pendula** (*B. verrucosa*) MT ♠ " Common Silver Birch"
White bark and rough warty shoots. Drooping branchlets with diamond-shaped leaves. AGM 1993
– – **'Dalecarlica'** LT ♀ "Swedish Birch"
Slender tree with gracefully drooping branchlets. Deeply cut, long pointed leaves. AGM 1993
– – **'Fastigiata'** MT ❢
Form with erect stiff habit.
– – **'Purpurea'** MT ♀ "Purple Leaf Birch"
Ornamental, slow growing form with purple leaves. FCC 1874
– – **'Tristis'** LT ♀
Graceful, drooping branches, forming a narrow symmetrical head. AGM 1993
– – **'Youngii'** ST ♠ "Young's Weeping Birch"
Broad, mushroom-headed habit. Branches ultimately reaching the ground. AGM 1993
– **platyphylla** var. **szechuanica** see *B. szechuanica*
– **pubescens** MT ♀ "Common White Birch"
Thrives in all soils, especially damp locations. White bark and smooth downy shoots.
– **szechuanica** (*B. platyphylla* var. *szechuanica*) MT ♠
Vigorous growth with blue-green, sharply toothed leaves yellow in autumn. Chalk-white bark.
– **utilis** MT ♀ "Himalayan Birch"
A variable species of which we recommend:
– – var. **jacquemontii** (*B. jacquemontii*) MT
This name includes trees with white bark. We offer the following selected forms:
– – – **'Doorenbos'** MT ♠
Striking white, peeling bark creamy when newly exposed. AGM 1993
– – – **'Jermyns'** (*B.* 'Jermyns') MT ♠

BETULA pendula 'Youngii'

Creamy-white peeling bark, orange-brown or coppery on smaller branches and good yellow autumn colour. Very long catkins in spring. AGM 1993
– – **'Silver Shadow'** MT ♦
Dazzling white stems and large, drooping leaves. Long catkins. AGM 1993
– **verrucosa** see *Betula pendula*

"BIRCH" see *Betula*

"BITTER NUT' see *Carya cordiformis*

"BLACKTHORN" see *Prunus spinosa*

"BLADDER NUT" see *Staphylea*

"BLADDER SENNA" see *Colutea*

"BLUEBERRY" see *Vaccinium*

"BOTTLEBRUSH" see *Callistemon*

"BOX" see *Buxus*

"BOX ELDER" see *Acer negundo*

"BRAMBLE" see *Rubus*

"BROOM" see *Cytisus* and *Genista*

"BROOM, BUTCHER'S" see *Ruscus aculeatus*

"BROOM, SPANISH" see *Spartium junceum*

BRUGMANSIA – Solanaceae LS † ○
"Angel's Trumpets"
Tree-like shrubs with large, pendulous trumpet flowers. For mild areas or conservatory. Poisonous.
– × **candida 'Grand Marnier'** LS † ○
Large, hanging, peach-coloured flowers ending in long, pointed lobes. AGM 1993
– **sanguinea** (*Datura sanguinea*) LS † ○
Long, orange-red trumpets in May and June and large, hairy leaves. AGM 1993
– **suaveolens** (*Datura suaveolens*) LS † ○
Large, fragrant, white trumpets are borne throughout summer. AGM 1993

BRUGMANSIA suaveolens 'Flore Pleno'

– – **'Flore Pleno'** LS † ○
A form with double flowers.

"BUCKEYE" see *Aesculus*

"BUCKTHORN" see *Rhamnus*

"BUCKTHORN, SEA" see *Hippophae rhamnoides*

BUDDLEJA – Loganiaceae MS-LS ○
"Butterfly Bush"
Opposite leaves except Buddleja alternifolia. Generally flowering July to September. Thriving in virtually all soils.
– **alternifolia** LS ○

Narrow, dark green, alternate leaves on arching branches. Fragrant, lilac flowers, June. AM 1922 AGM 1993

– – **'Argentea'** MS ○

Leaves covered in silky hairs, giving a silvery sheen.

– **colvilei** LS ○

Dark green leaves. Large tubular flowers in terminal drooping panicles, June. Vigorous. FCC 1896. We recommend the form:

– – **'Kewensis'** LS ○

Rich red flowers. AM 1947

– **crispa** MS-LS ○

Leaves and stems covered in white felt. Scented flowers lilac with orange throat, in terminal panicles, September. AM 1961

– **davidii** MS ○

Fragrant flowers in long racemes are very attractive to butterflies. Best when pruned hard in March. AM 1898. We recommend:

– – **'Black Knight'** MS ○

Dark violet flowers. AGM 1993. B (a) 4

– – **'Dartmoor'** MS ○

Broad panicles of magenta flowers. AM 1973 FCC 1990 AGM 1993. B (a) 4

– – **'Empire Blue'** MS ○

Flowers rich violet blue with orange eye. AGM 1993. B (a) 4

– – **'Harlequin'** MS ○

Leaves variegated creamy white. Reddish-purple flowers. B (a) 4

BUDDLEJA davidii 'Harlequin'

– – **'Royal Red'** MS ○

Red-purple flowers in huge panicles. AM 1950 AGM 1993. B (a) 4

– – **'White Cloud'** MS ○

Pure white flowers in dense panicles. B (a) 4

– **fallowiana** MS ◑

White woolly stems and leaves. Pale lavender, fragrant flowers in large panicles. Requires shelter. B (a) 4

BUDDLEJA globosa

BUDDLEJA 'Lochinch'

– – var. **alba** MS ◑

Creamy-white flowers with orange eye. AM 1978 AGM 1993. B (a) 4

– **globosa** MS ○ "Orange Ball Tree"

Sweetly scented, orange ball-like inflorescences, May. AGM 1993. A (g) 5

– **'Lochinch'** MS ○

Grey, pubescent young shoots, leaves later green, white beneath. Flowers scented, violet-blue, orange eye. AM 1993

– **'Pink Delight'** MS ○

Long panicles of bright pink flowers. Grey-green leaves. AM 1988 AGM 1993. B (a) 4

BUPLEURUM fruticosum

BUDDLEJA 'Pink Delight'

– × **weyeriana** MS ○
Ball-shaped heads of flowers in long panicles
on the young wood in summer. We
recommend the form:
– – **'Golden Glow'** LS ○
Interrupted spikes of mauve flowers, suffused
yellow. AM 1981

BUPLEURUM – Umbelliferae
*Generally sub shrubs and herbs. The
following is the only woody species in open
cultivation in Britain.*
– **fruticosum** MS (E) ○
Sea-green foliage. Yellow flowers, July to
September. Excellent for exposed coastal sites.
AM 1979

"BUTCHER'S BROOM" see *Ruscus
aculeatus*

BUXUS – Buxaceae DS-LS (E)
*Thriving in most soils. Many forms useful for
hedging.*
– **microphylla** DS (E)
Dense rounded habit. Narrow, oblong leaves.
– **sempervirens** LS (E) Hdg (0.6m) "Common
Box"
Dense mass of small dark green leaves. Also
available as specimens trimmed to ball,
pyramid and other shapes. AGM 1993
– – **'Elegantissima'** SS (F)
Dense dome-shaped habit. Leaves have
irregular creamy-white margin. Slow grower.
AGM 1993
– – **'Latifolia Maculata'** MS (E)
Bright yellow young growth becomes dark
green blotched yellow. Dense habit. AGM
1993
– – **'Suffruticosa'** DS (E) "Edging Box"
Rounded, shiny, green leaves. Used as low
formal edging to paths and flower beds. AGM
1993

C

"CABBAGE TREE" see *Cordyline*

CAESALPINIA – Leguminosae LS † ○
Spectacular inflorescenses. Bright yellow flowers with clusters of scarlet stamens, in erect racemes.
– japonica LS † ○
Prominent spines. Acacia-like soft green leaves. Flowers, 20 to 30 to a raceme, June. FCC 1888

CALCEOLARIA – Scrophulariaceae SS (E) † ○
Requires well drained position. "Pouch-like" flowers in terminal panicles.
– integrifolia SS (E) † ○
Large yellow flowers late summer. AGM 1993
– violacea see *Jovellana violacea*

"CALICO BUSH" see *Kalmia latifolia*

CALLICARPA – Verbenaceae MS
Leaves have soft rose-madder autumn colour. Small pink flowers. Conspicuous lilac/purple fruits, freely produced when several shrubs planted in group.
– bodinieri MS ◑
Foliage rose-purple in autumn. We recommend:
– – 'Profusion' MS ◑
Pale pink flowers and bronze young foliage. Very free-fruiting form with purple-violet berries. FCC 1992 AGM 1993

CALLICARPA bodinieri

CALLISTEMON – Myrtaceae MS (E) † ○
"Bottle Brush"
Flowers in cylindrical spikes with long showy stamens. Not for shallow chalk.
– citrinus MS (E) † ○
Vigorous, spreading habit. Narrow leaves, lemon-scented when crushed. We recommend the form:
– – 'Splendens' MS (E) † ○
Graceful shrub. Brilliant scarlet flowers throughout summer. AM 1926 AGM 1993
– salignus MS (E) † ○
Narrow willow-like leaves. Pale yellow flowers. One of the hardiest. AM 1948 AGM 1993

CALLUNA – Ericaceae DS (E) ✗
Genus of a single species with many forms.
– vulgaris DS (E) ✗ "Heather" "Ling"
Many forms cultivated, varying in habit, foliage and flower colour. Flowering times are as follows:
Early – July-August
Mid – August-September
Late – October-November
C (e) 9 or 10
We recommend the following:
– – 'Blazeaway' DS (E) ✗
Green foliage, turning rich red in winter. Lilac mauve flowers. Mid. 50cm.
– – 'County Wicklow' ('Camla')
Spreading. Double shell-pink flowers. Mid. AMT 1969 FCCT 1961 AGM 1993
– – 'Elsie Purnell' DS (E) ✗
Double, silvery-pink flowers deeper in bud. Mid to Late. 60-80cm. AMT 1963 AGM 1993

CALLISTEMON citrinus 'Splendens'

CALLUNA vulgaris 'Elsie Purnell'

– – **'Gold Haze'** DS (E) ✗
Bright gold foliage. White flowers. Mid.
50cm. AMT 1961 FCCT 1963 AGM 1993
– – **'Golden Feather'** DS (E) ✗
Golden, feathery foliage, orange in winter.
50cm. AMT 1965 FCCT 1967
– – **'H. E. Beale'** DS (E) ✗
Long racemes of bright rose, double flowers.
Mid-Late. 60cm. FCC 1943
– – **'J. H. Hamilton'** DS (E) ✗
Large pink, double flowers. Early. 25cm. AM
1935 AMT 1960 FCCT 1961 AGM 1993
– – **'Joy Vanstone'** DS (E) ✗
Golden foliage, turning rich orange in winter.
Orchid-pink flowers. Mid. 50cm. AMT 1971
AGM 1993
– – **'Kinlochruel'** DS (E) ✗
Bright green foliage. Profuse, double white
flowers. Mid. 25cm. AM 1980 FCC 1982
AGM 1993
– – **'Peter Sparkes'** DS (E) ✗
Long racemes of double pink flowers. Mid-
late. 50cm. AM 1958 FCCT 1962

Colourful foliage of CALLUNA among dwarf conifers

CALLUNA vulgaris 'Gold Haze'

– – **'Robert Chapman'** DS (E) ✓
Golden foliage, turning orange, then red. Soft
purple flowers. Mid. 30-60cm. AMT 1962
AGM 1993
– – **'Silver Queen'** DS (E) ✓
Silver-grey foliage. Pale mauve flowers. Mid.
60cm. AGM 1993
– – **'Sir John Charrington'** DS (E) ✓
Yellow foliage tinged red in summer and
winter. Flowers lilac-pink. Early. 40cm. AMT
1970 AGM 1993
– – **'Sister Anne'** DS (E) ✓
Mounds of grey foliage. Pink flowers. Mid.
10cm. AGM 1993
– – **'Tib'** DS (E) ✓
Double rosy red flowers. Early. 30-60cm. AMT
1960 FCCT 1962 AGM 1993
– – **'Wickwar Flame'** DS (E) ✓
Bright orange and yellow foliage turns copper
and gold in winter. Mauve-pink flowers.
30cm. AGM 1993

CALYCANTHUS – Calycanthaceae MS
"Allspice"
*Aromatic shrubs with red-brown flowers.
Summer–early autumn. Easy cultivation.*
– **floridus** MS "Carolina Allspice"
Reddish-purple, fragrant flowers. Undersides
of leaves downy. Rare.

CAMELLIA – Theaceae SS-LS (E) ✓ ○ or ◑
*Beautiful hardy spring-flowering shrubs. Acid
or neutral peat soil. Light shade or sheltered*

*sunny position – avoid early-morning spring
sunshine, which can damage frost-covered
flowers. Ideal for tubs or cool greenhouse.
Flower form:*
*Single – single row of up to 8 petals,
conspicuous stamens*
*Semi-double – two or more rows of petals,
conspicuous stamens*
*Anemone – one or more rows of large petals,
central convex mass of petaloids and stamens.*
*Paeony – convex mass of petals, petaloids and
sometimes stamens.*
*Double – imbricated petals, stamens in
concave centre*
*Formal double – many rows of fully
imbricated petals, no stamens*
Flower diameter:
Small – 5 to 7.5cm
Medium – 7.5 to 10cm
Large – 10 to 12.5cm
Very large – 12.5cm+
– **'Charlean'** LS (E) ✓ ◑
Orchid-pink, medium to large, semi-double
with yellow anthers.
– **'Cornish Snow'** MS (E) ✓ ◑
Masses of white flowers along branchlets. AM
1948 AGM 1993
– **'Inspiration'** MS (E) ✓ ◑
Large, semi-double, deep pink flowers. AM
1954 FCCT 1979 AGM 1993

CAMELLIA 'Inspiration'

– **japonica** LS (E) ✓ ◑ "Common Camellia"
Parent of many cultivars. Majority are MS,
flowering within range Feb to mid-May. Size
and colour depend on age, season and
conditions. We recommend the following:

CAMELLIA japonica 'Adolphe Audusson'

– – **'Adolphe Audusson'** MS (E) ✄ ◑
Blood red, conspicuous stamens; large, semi-double. Vigorous, compact. AM 1934 FCC 1956 AGM 1993
– – **'Alba Plena'** ('Alba Grandiflora') MS (E) ✄◑
White; large, formal double. Erect, bushy. AM 1948
– – **'Ballet Dancer'** MS (E) ✄ ◑
Cream, shading to coral pink at the edges. Medium, full paeony form. Compact, upright habit. AM 1976 AGM 1993
– – **'Bob's Tinsie'** MS (E) ✄ ◑
Brilliant red, small, anemone form. Compact, upright habit. AGM 1993
– – **'Chandleri Elegans'** see 'Elegans'

CAMELLIA japonica 'Elegans'

– – **'Clarise Carleton'** MS (E) ✄ ◑
Red, large to very large, semi-double. Vigorous, upright habit.
– – **'Devonia'** MS (E) ✄ ◑
White; medium, single. Vigorous, erect. AM 1900
– – **'Donckelaeri'** MS (E) ✄ ◑
Red, sometimes with white marbling; large, semi-double. Slow, bushy. AM 1960 AGM 1993
– – **'Elegans'** ('Chandleri Elegans') MS (E) ✄◑
Deep peach; very large, anemone. Spreading form. AM 1953 FCC 1958 AGM 1993
– – **'Gloire de Nantes'** MS (E) ✄ ◑
Rose pink; large, semi-double. Erect, compact. AM 1956 AGM 1993
– – **'Grand Prix'** MS (E) ✄ ◑
Brilliant red, very large, semi-double with irregular petals. AGM 1993
– – **'Grand Slam'** MS (E) ✄ ◑
Brilliant, dark red. Large to very large semi-double to anemone form. Vigorous, open, upright habit. AM 1975 AGM 1993
– – **'Guilio Nuccio'** MS (E) ✄ ◑
Coral pink; very large, semi-double. Vigorous. Erect. AM 1962 AGM 1993
– – **'Hakurakuten'** MS (E) ✄ ◑
White; large, semi-double to loose paeony form. Vigorous. Erect. AM 1977 AGM 1993
– – **'Jupiter'** MS (E) ✄ ◑
Scarlet blotched white sometimes; medium, single to semi-double, conspicuous stamens. Vigorous, erect. AM 1953 AGM 1993
– – **'Lady Clare'** MS (E) ✄ ◑
Deep, clear peach pink; large, semi-double. Vigorous spreading. AM 1927 AGM 1993
– – **'Lady Vansittart'** MS (E) ✄ ◑
White striped rose-pink; medium, semi-double. Bushy.
– – **'Latifolia'** MS (E) ✄ ◑
Soft rose-red; medium, semi-double. Vigorous, bushy.
– – **'Lavinia Maggi'** MS (E) ✄ ◑
White-pale pink with dark rose stripes; large, formal double. FCC 1862 AGM 1993
– – **'Magnoliiflora'** MS (E) ✄ ◑
Blush pink; medium, semi-double. Compact. AM 1953 AGM 1993
– – **'Margaret Davis'** MS (E) ✄ ◑
White streaked rose-red with vermilion edge, medium, paeony form. AM 1984
– – **'Mars'** MS (E) ✄ ◑
Turkey red; large, semi-double. Conspicuous stamens. Open, loose growth. AGM 1993
– – **'R. L. Wheeler'** LS (E) ✄ ◑
Rose-pink; very large, semi-double-anemone

CAMELLIA japonica 'Lavinia Maggi'

CAMELLIA japonica 'Rubescens Major'

CAMELLIA japonica 'Tricolor'

form. Vigorous. AM 1959 FCC 1975 AGM 1993

– – **'Rubescens Major'** MS (E) ✗ ◑
Crimson, dark veins large double. Bushy. AM 1959 AGM 1993

– – **'Sieboldii'** see 'Tricolor'

– – **'Silver Anniversary'** MS (E) ✗ ◑
White, large, semi-double with irregular petals and golden stamens.

– – **'Souvenir de Bahaud Litou'** MS (E) ✗ ◑
Light pink; large formal double. Vigorous erect. AGM 1993

– – **'Tricolor'** ('Sieboldii') MS (E) ✗ ◑
White-streaked carmine; medium, semi-double. AGM 1993

– **'Leonard Messel'** LS (E) ✗ ◑
Rich clear pink; large, semi-double. Dark green leaves. AM 1958 FCC 1970 AGM1993

– **reticulata** LS (E) ✗ ◑
Rose-pink, large single flowers trumpet-shaped before opening. Produced freely late winter-early spring. AM 1944. We recommend the following selected clones which require a conservatory except in mild areas:

– – **'Captain Rawes'** ('Semi-plena') LS (E) † ✗ ◑
Carmine pink; very large, semi-double. FCC 1963 AGM 1993

– – **'Robert Fortune'** ('Pagoda') ('Flore Pleno') LS (E) † ✗ ◑
Dark crimson; large, double. Compact. FCC 1865

– **sasanqua** MS (E) ✗ ◑
Small, fragrant usually white flowers produced winter-early spring. Require wall protection. FCC 1892. We recommend the following forms:

– – **'Crimson King'** MS (E) ✗ ◑
Red; small, single. AGM 1993

– – **'Narumi-gata'** MS (E) ✗ ◑
Creamy-white, pink towards margins; large, fragrant. AM 1953 AGM 1993

– **'Tristrem Carlyon'** MS (E) ✗ ◑
Rose-pink, medium, paeony form. Vigorous, upright habit. AM 1977

– × **williamsii** MS (E) ✗ ◑
Best camellia for general planting. Free flowering over long period from November to May. We recommend the following cultivars:

– – **'Anticipation'** MS (E) ✍ ◑
Deep rose, large, paeony form. Upright habit.
AMT 1974 FCCT 1975 AGM 1993
– – **'Brigadoon'** MS (E) ✍ ◑
Rose-pink, medium, semi-double. Compact,
upright habit. AMT 1974 AGM 1993
– – **'China Clay'** MS (E) ✍ ◑
White, medium, semi-double. Open habit.
AM 1976 AGM 1993
– – **'Daintiness'** MS (E) ✍ ◑
Salmon-pink, large, semi-double. Open habit.
AM 1986 AGM 1993
– – **'Debbie'** MS (E) ✍ ◑
Clear pink, large, semi-double. AM 1971
AGM 1993
– – **'Donation'** LS (E) ✍ ◑
Orchid pink; large, semi-double. Erect
vigorous. AM 1941 AM 1952 FCCT 1974
AGM 1993
– – **'E. T. R. Carlyon'** MS (E) ✍ ◑
White, medium, semi-double to rose form
double. Vigorous, upright habit.

– – **'Glenn's Orbit'** MS (E) ✍ ◑
Deep orchid pink, large, semi-double to loose
paeony form. Vigorous, upright habit. AM
1962 AMT 1976
– – **'J. C. Williams'** MS (E) ✍ ◑
Phlox pink; medium, single. FCC 1942 AMT
1977 AGM 1993
– – **'Jury's Yellow'** MS (E) ✍ ◑
White with wavy petals and a central mass of
creamy-yellow petaloids. Medium, anemone
form.
– – **'Mary Christian'** MS (E) ✍ ◑
Clear pink; small, single. AM 1942 AGM 1993
– – **'Rose Parade'** MS (E) ✍ ◑
Deep rose pink, medium, single. Compact,
upright habit. AGM 1993
– – **'St. Ewe'** MS (E) ✍ ◑
Rose pink; medium, single. AM 1947 FCCT
1974 AGM 1993

CANTUA – Polemoniaceae SS (E) † ○
*Small S. American genus. The following
species is cultivated:*
– **buxifolia** (*C. dependens*) "Magic Tree" SS
(E) † ○
Tubular cherry red flowers in drooping
corymbs. April. Semi-(E) in mild areas.
Requires sheltered wall. AM 1905

CAMELLIA × williamsii 'Donation'

CAMELLIA × williamsii 'E. T. R. Carlyon'

CARAGANA arborescens 'Lorbergii'

CARAGANA – Leguminosae SS-ST
Yellow pea flowers, early summer. Compound leaves, often spiny.
– **arborescens** ST ❦ "Pea Tree"
Shrubby habit. Flowers in May. Succeeds in exposed situations and most soils.
– – **'Lorbergii'** LS
Graceful form with very narrow leaflets. AGM 1993

CARPENTERIA – Philadelphaceae MS (E)
○
Monotypic genus, native of California, best as a wall shrub in sunny position.
– **californica** MS (E) ○
Large white flowers with golden anthers, July. FCC 1888. A (b) 5. We recommend:

CARPENTERIA californica

CARPINUS betulus 'Fastigiata'

– – **'Bodnant'**
A very hardy form with large flowers. AGM 1993

CARPINUS – Carpinaceae ST-MT ❦
"Hornbeams"
Hardy trees for any fertile soil. Produce clusters of hop-like fruits.
– **betulus** MT ❦ Hdg (0.5m) "Common Hornbeam"
Characteristic grey fluted bark. Strongly ribbed and toothed leaves turn yellow in autumn. As a hedge, leaves retained into winter, like beech. AGM 1993
– – **'Fastigiata'** ('Pyramidalis') MT ❦
Narrow as a young tree, broadening with age. AGM 1993
– – **'Frans Fontaine'** MT ❦
Similar to 'Fastigiata' but retains its narrow habit with age.

CARYA – Juglandaceae MT-LT ❦ "Hickory"
Large compound leaves turn clear yellow in autumn. Grey trunks attractive in winter. Fast growing, but best planted small.
– **cordiformis** (*C. amara*) LT ❦ "Bitter Nut"
Thin brown scaly bark. Characteristic yellow winter buds. Best "Hickory" for general planting. AM 1989 AGM 1993
– **ovata** MT ❦ "Shagbark Hickory"
Leaves of 5 pointed leaflets, the 3 upper ones large. Rich yellow autumn colour. AGM 1993

CARYA ovata

CARYOPTERIS – Verbenaceae SS ○
Aromatic leaves. Blue flowers late summer. Well drained soil. Ideal for chalk.
– × **clandonensis** SS ○
A variable hybrid of which we recommend the following form:
– – **'Heavenly Blue'** SS ○

CARYOPTERIS × clandonensis 'Heavenly Blue'

Attractive deep blue flowers over a long period, August to September. Compact habit. AGM 1993. A (b) (g) 5

CASSIA obtusa see *Senna × floribunda*

CASSINIA – Compositae SS-MS (E) ○
Heath-like shrubs requiring well drained soil,

CASSINIA fulvida

– **fulvida** (*Diplopappus chrysophyllus*) SS (E) ○
Small massed leaves have golden appearance. Flowers white, July. Young growth sticky.
– **vauvilliersii** SS (E) ○
Slightly taller than *C. fulvida* with larger leaves, dark green. The following is the best form:
– – var. **albida** SS (E) ○
White hoary leaves and stems.

CASSIOPE – Ericaceae PS-DS (E) ⟋ ◑
Shrublets needing moist peaty soil. White bell flowers in spring.
– **'Muirhead'** DS (E) ⟋ ◑
Characteristic curved forked shoots. Small

CASTANEA sativa

nodding flowers. AM 1953 FCC 1962 AGM 1993

CASTANEA – Fagaceae LT ♥ "Chestnuts"
Long lance-shaped serrated leaves. Small white flowers in slender racemes. Moderately lime-tolerant but chlorotic on shallow chalk.
– **sativa** LT ♥ "Sweet Chestnut" "Spanish Chestnut"
Pale yellow catkins, July. Hot summers necessary for worthwhile crop of edible nuts. Old trees develop characteristic grooved, spiralling bark. Fast growing. AGM 1993
– – **'Albomarginata'** LT ♥
Leaves have creamy white margins. AM 1964
– – **'Marron de Lyon'** LT ♥
Nuts borne at early age – best fruiting clone.

CATALPA – Bignoniaceae MT ♥
Large leaves. Foxglove-like flowers in conspicuous panicles (on older trees) late summer. All well drained soils.
– **bignonioides** MT ♥ "Indian Bean Tree"
Large heart-shaped leaves. White, yellow and purple marked flowers July and August. AM 1933 AGM 1993
– – **'Aurea'** ST ♥ "Golden Indian Bean Tree"
Large velvety soft yellow leaves. AM 1974 AGM 1993
– × **erubescens** MT ♥
Broad ovate leaves. Small numerous flowers late July, similar to *C. bignonioides*. We recommend the form:

CATALPA bignonioides

CEANOTHUS arboreus 'Trewithen Blue'

CATALPA bignonioides 'Aurea'

– – 'Purpurea' MT ♠
Young leaves and shoots dark, almost black-purple, becoming dark green with age. AM 1970 AGM 1993
– fargesii MT ♠
Lilac pink flowers with reddish brown spots and yellow staining, 7 to 15 together in corymbs. AM 1973. We recommend the form:
– – f. duclouxii MT ♠
Leaves less hairy with conspicuous tapered lobes. AM 1934

CEANOTHUS – Rhamnaceae PS-LS ○
"Californian Lilacs"
Variable genus incorporating evergreen and deciduous members. Mainly blue flowers. Require shelter and good drainage. Not for shallow chalk.

– arboreus MS (E) † ○
Large leaved species. Deep blue flowers, spring, in large panicles. We recommend the form:
– – 'Trewithen Blue' MS (E) † ○
Slightly scented deep blue flowers in large panicles. AGM 1993. A (b) 5
– 'Autumnal Blue' MS (E) ○
Abundant deep blue flowers late summer and autumn. Hardy. AM 1930 AGM 1993. A (b) 5
– 'Blue Mound' DS (E) ○
Dense mound-like habit. Mid-blue flowers, May-June. AGM 1993
– 'Burkwoodii' MS (E) † ○
Rich dark blue flowers summer and autumn. AM 1930 AGM 1993. A (b) 5
– 'Cascade' MS (E) † ○
Bright blue flowers in long-stalked clusters, spring. AM 1946 AGM 1993. A (b) 5

CEANOTHUS 'Cascade'

CEANOTHUS 'Delight'

– 'Concha' MS (E) ○
Profuse deep blue flowers in spring from red
buds. Arching branches. AM 1986 FCC 1992
– 'Delight' MS (E) ○
Rich blue spring flowers in long panicles.
Hardy. AM 1933 AGM 1993. A (b) 5
– 'Gloire de Versailles' MS ○
Powder blue flowers in large panicles, summer
and autumn. FCC 1872 AGM 1993. B (a) 4
– 'Henri Desfosse' MS ○
Violet blue flowers in panicles, summer. AM
1926. B (a) 4
– impressus 'Puget Blue' see *C.* 'Puget Blue'
– 'Italian Skies' MS (E) † ○
Vigorous with deep blue flowers late spring.
Small, dark green leaves. A (b) 5
– papillosus LS (E) † ○
Rich blue flowers late spring. Long narrow
sticky leaves. We recommend the form:
– – subsp. **roweanus** LS (E) † ○
Darker blue flowers. A (b) 5
– 'Perle Rose' MS ○
Rose carmine flowers, summer. B (a) 4

– prostratus PS (E) ○ "Squaw Carpet"
Creeping form. Bright blue flowers, spring.
AM 1935
– 'Puget Blue' (*C. impressus* 'Puget Blue') MS
(E) ○
Very profuse deep blue flowers in late
spring. Compact and vigorous with small,
dark green leaves. AM 1971 AGM 1993.
A (B) 5
– 'Southmead' MS (E) ○
Rich blue flowers, May–June. Small oblong
leaves, dark glossy green above. AM 1964
AGM 1993. A (b) 5
– thyrsiflorus LS (E) ○
Bright blue flowers, early summer. Hardy. AM
1935. We recommend:
– – var. **repens** PS (E) GC ○ "Creeping Blue
Blossom"
Light blue flowers. Vigorous, mound-forming.
AGM 1993. A (b) 5
– 'Topaz' MS ○
Light indigo blue flowers, summer. AM 1961
AGM 1993. B (a) 4
– × veitchianus MS (E) ○
Deep blue flowers, May-June. Hardy. A (b) 5

CEDRELA sinensis see *Toona sinensis*

CERATOSTIGMA - Plumbaginaceae DS-
SS ○ "Hardy Plumbago"
*Blue flowers, early autumn. Dry, well drained
soils.*
– griffithii SS ○
Deep blue flowers. Often conspicuous red
autumnal tints.
– willmottianum SS ○
Rich blue flowers July to autumn. Red-tinted
foliage in autumn. AM 1917 AGM 1993

CERATOSTIGMA willmottianum

CEANOTHUS 'Gloire de Versailles'

CERCIDIPHYLLUM japonicum

CERCIDIPHYLLUM – Cercidiphyllaceae
MT

Elegant, autumn colouring trees. Flowers insignificant. Moist, well drained soils.

– japonicum MT ♀
Slightly pendulous branches. Bright green leaves turn smoky-pink or yellow in autumn and evict pungent aroma of burnt sugar. AGM 1993

CERCIS siliquastrum

– – var. **magnificum** (*C. magnificum*) MT ♀
Smoother bark and larger leaves than *C. japonicum*. Yellow autumn leaves. Rare. AGM 1993

– – **'Pendulum'** MT ♠
Rare weeping form with long, hanging branches.

CERCIS – Leguminosae LS-ST ○
Distinctive foliage. Pea-flowers in spring. Usually low branched large shrubs, though attaining tree-size after many years. Good drainage.

– canadensis ST ♀
Pale pink flowers May-June. We recommend:

– – **'Forest Pansy'** ST ♀
Magnificent new introduction. Deep reddish-purple foliage, retaining colour throughout the season. AGM 1993

– siliquastrum ST ♀ "Judas Tree"
Branches laden with clusters of rosy lilac flowers, May. Conspicuous red seed pods July onwards. Legendary tree from which Judas hanged himself. AGM 1993

– – **'Alba'** ST ♀
White flowers. AM 1962

– – **'Bodnant'** ST ♀
Deep purple flowers. FCC 1944

CESTRUM – Solanaceae MS (E) † ○
Shrubs for warm wall or conservatory.

– 'Newellii' MS (E) † ○
Large orange-red flowers. FCC 1876 AM 1951 AGM 1993

– parqui MS (E) ○
Yellow-green flowers very fragrant at night. Can be almost herbaceous. AM 1990 AGM 1993

CHAENOMELES – Rosaceae DS-LS ○ or ◑
"Japonica"
Saucer-shaped flowers in spring, followed by yellow quinces. Easy growing in open or against a wall. Prune wall-grown shrubs only. C4/E9

– speciosa (*C. lagenaria*) (*Cydonia speciosa*) MS ○ or ◑ "Japonica"
With spreading, branched habit. Many forms of varying flower colour are in cultivation, of which we recommend the following:

– – **'Moerloosei'** MS ○ or ◑
Pink and white. AM 1957 AGM 1993

– – **'Nivalis'** MS ○ or ◑
Large pure white.

– × superba SS-MS ○ or ◑
Vigorous habit. We recommend the following forms:

CHAENOMELES × superba 'Crimson and Gold'

CHAENOMELES speciosa 'Moerloosei'

– – **'Crimson and Gold'** MS ○ or ◑
Crimson petals and golden anthers. AM 1979
AGM 1993
– – **'Knap Hill Scarlet'** MS ○ or ◑
Bright flame, profuse spring – early summer.
AM 1961 AGM 1993
– – **'Nicoline'** SS ○ or ◑

CHAENOMELES × superba 'Pink Lady'

Scarlet. Spreading. AGM 1993
– – **'Pink Lady'** SS ○ or ◑
Rose pink. Spreading. AGM 1993
– – **'Rowallane'** MS ○ or ◑
Large blood-red, spreading habit. AGM 1993

CHAMAEROPS – Palmae SS (E) † ○
A genus of a single species:
– **humilis** SS (E) † ○ "Dwarf Fan Palm"
Miniature palm with fan-shaped leaves rarely
higher than 1.5m. Hardy in mild areas. AGM
1993

"CHASTE TREE" see *Vitex agnus-castus*

"CHERRY" see *Prunus*

"CHERRY, CORNELIAN" see *Cornus mas*

CHAENOMELES × superba 'Rowallane'

CHIMONANTHUS praecox

"CHERRY, KOREAN HILL" see *Prunus verecunda*

"CHESTNUT, HORSE" see *Aesculus hippocastanum*

"CHESTNUT, SPANISH" see *Castanea sativa*

"CHILEAN FIRE BUSH" see *Embothrium*

CHIMONANTHUS – Calycanthaceae MS ○ "Winter Sweet"
Best against sunny wall. Any well drained soil – good on chalk
– **praecox** (*C. fragrans*) (*Calycanthus praecox*) MS ○
Pale waxy yellow flowers, purple at centre on bare branches, winter. Sweetly scented. E2
– – **'Grandiflorus'** MS ○
Deeper yellow flowers with red centre. AM 1928 FCC 1991 AGM 1993
– – **'Luteus'** MS ○
Large clear waxy yellow flowers, opening later. AM 1948 FCC 1970 AGM 1993

CHIONANTHUS – Oleaceae LS ○ "Fringe Tree"
White flowers with strap-shaped petals produced abundantly June-July, on older plants. Easy cultivation.
– **retusus (FORREST FORM)** LS ○ "Chinese Fringe Tree"
Handsome shrub. Flowers followed by damson-like fruits. FCC 1885

CHOISYA – Rutaceae MS (E) ○ or ●
Small genus of attractive shrubs.
– **'Aztec Pearl'** MS ○
Fragrant white flowers pink tinged as they open in late spring and again late summer to

CHOISYA 'Aztec Pearl'

autumn. Leaves with slender, aromatic leaflets. AM 1990 AGM 1993. A (b) 5
– **ternata** MS (E) ○ or ● "Mexican Orange Blossom"
Rounded habit. Glossy dark green leaves, aromatic when bruised. White sweetly scented flowers late spring - early summer. FCC 1880 AGM 1993. A (b) 5
– – **'Sundance'** SS ○
Young leaves bright yellow. AGM 1993

"CHOKEBERRY, RED" see *Aronia arbutifolia*

CHUSQUEA – Gramineae
Distinguished from other bamboos by the solid stems.
– **culeou** LS (E)
Rare bamboo forming broad, dense clumps. Deep olive-green canes bear dense clusters of slender, short, leafy branches along their entire length. AM 1974 AGM 1993

CISTUS – Cistaceae DS-MS (E) ○ "Sun Roses"

CHOISYA ternata

Except otherwise stated, white flowers June-July. Ideal for rock gardens, dry banks. Resent frost, but wind and salt tolerant. Good on chalk.
– × **aguilari** SS (E) † ○
Very large flowers. Vigorous. We recommend the form:
– – **'Maculatus'** SS (E) † ○
Flowers have ring of crimson blotches in centre. AM 1936 AGM 1993
– × **corbariensis** SS (E) ○
Crimson tinged buds, opening white. Hardy. AGM 1993
– × **cyprius** MS (E) ○
Large flowers with crimson basal blotches. Hardy. AMT 1925 AGM 1993
– × **dansereaui** (*C.* × *lusitanicus*) SS (E) ○
Large flowers with crimson basal blotches. We recommend:
– – **'Decumbens'** DS (E) ○ GC
Wide spreading form. AGM 1993

CISTUS × pulverulentus

CISTUS × dansereaui 'Decumbens'

– **ladanifer** MS (E) † ○ "Gum Cistus"
Large flowers with chocolate basal stain, frilled petals. Upright habit with dark green lance-shaped leaves. AGM 1993
– **laurifolius** MS (E) ○
Flowers with yellow centres. Dark green leathery leaves. Erect habit. Hardy. AGM 1993
– × **lusitanicus** see *C.* × *dansereaui*
– **palhinhae** SS (E) † ○
Large pure white flowers. Glossy, sticky leaves. Distinctive. AM 1944 AGM 1993
– **'Peggy Sammons'** MS (E) ○
Pale pink flowers. Grey-green leaves. Erect habit. AGM 1993
– **populifolius** SS (E) ○
Flowers white with central yellow blotches. Leaves small, hairy and poplar-like. Erect habit. AM 1930. We recommend the form:
– – var. **lasiocalyx** SS (E) ○
Large, wavy flowers with inflated calyx. AGM 1993
– × **pulverulentus** (*C.* 'Sunset') DS (E) † ○
Bright cerise flowers. Sage-green wavy leaves. AGM 1993
– × **purpureus** SS (E) † ○
Reddish shoots and narrow leaves. Large rosy-crimson flowers with chocolate basal blotches. AMT 1925 AGM 1993
– **'Silver Pink'** SS (E) ○
Silver-pink flowers in long clusters. Very hardy. AM 1919
– × **skanbergii** SS (E) † ○
Dense habit with narrow grey-green leaves. Clear pink flowers. AGM 1993

CITRUS – Rutaceae ST Semi-(E) † ○
Grown for their fruits. In this country require sunny wall or conservatory. White flowers, when produced.

CISTUS × purpureus

CISTUS 'Silver Pink'

– **'Meyer's Lemon'** LS Semi-(E) † ○
Large dark-green elliptic leaves. Fragrant
flowers. Large fruits. AM 1982

CLADRASTIS – Leguminosae MT ❀
Ornamental trees with pinnate leaves.
Fragrant flowers in panicles – not on young
trees.
– **lutea** MT ❀ "Yellow Wood"
Long hanging panicles of white flowers, June.
Leaves turn yellow in autumn. AM 1924 AGM
1993
– **sinensis** MT ❀ "Chinese Yellow Wood "
Soft green compound leaves. White, pink-
tinged flowers July. AM 1923 AM 1938

CLEMATIS see climbers

CLERODENDRUM – Verbenaceae MS-LS
Valuable late summer and autumn flowering
shrubs.
– **bungei** MS ◑
Semi-woody, suckering. Large heart-shaped
leaves. Dense corymbs of fragrant rosy-red
flowers August-September. AM 1926 AGM
1993
– **trichotomum** LS ○
Fragrant star-like flowers August-September.
China-blue berries in crimson calyces follow.
FCC 1893. We recommend:

CLERODENDRUM trichotomum

– – var. **fargesii** LS ○
Smooth stems and leaves. Fruits usually more
freely produced. AM 1911 AGM 1993

CLETHRA – Clethraceae MS ✗
Fragrant, white flowers July-August.
– **alnifolia** MS ✗ "Sweet Bush"
Scented flowers in terminal racemes, August.
We recommend the selected forms:

CLETHRA alnifolia 'Paniculata'

– – **'Paniculata'** MS ✎
Flowers in terminal panicles. AM 1956 AGM 1993
– – **'Rosea'** MS ✎
Buds and flowers, pink-tinged. Glossy leaves.
– **barbinervis** MS ✎
Long racemes of flowers. Autumn leaf colour red and yellow. AM 1985 AGM 1993
– **delavayi** LS ✎
Deep green leaves and spreading racemes of elegant, cup-shaped flowers tinged pink in bud. FCC 1927 AGM 1993
– **fargesii** MS ✎
Long pure-white panicles of flowers, July. Rich yellow autumn leaf colour. AM 1924

CLEYERA – Theaceae MS (E) ✎
A small genus of trees and shrubs related to Camellia.
– **fortunei** see *C. japonica* 'Tricolor'
– **japonica** MS-LS (E) ✎
Variable shrub with glossy leaves and small white flowers in spring. We recommend:
– – **'Tricolor'** (*C. fortunei*) (*Eurya fortunei*) LS (E) ✎
Leathery blunt-tipped leaves – dark glossy green with grey marbling. Margins cream, sometimes flushed deep pink.

CLIANTHUS – Leguminosae MS † ○
Require well drained soil. For sheltered sunny position or conservatory. Suitable for training on a south-facing wall.
– **puniceus** MS Semi-(E) † ○ "Lobster's Claw"
Pinnate leaves. Distinctive claw-like flowers bright-red, in pendulous racemes, early summer. AM 1938 AGM 1993
– – **'Flamingo'**
A form with deep rose-pink flowers.
– – **'White Heron'**
Flowers pure white flushed green.

CLIANTHUS puniceus

COLLETIA – Rhamnaceae SS-MS
Spiny shrubs. Fragrant flowers, late summer and autumn.
– **armata** see *C. hystrix*
– **hystrix** (*C. armata*) MS
Stout rounded spines. Small white pitcher-shaped flowers smother branches. AM 1973. We recommend:
– – **'Rosea'** MS
Flower buds pink. AM 1972
– **cruciata** see *C. paradoxa*
– **paradoxa** (*C. bictoniensis*) (*C. cruciata*) SS
Branchlets comprised of flat triangular spines. Pitcher-shaped white flowers. Slow growing. AM 1959

COLLETIA hystrix 'Rosea'

COLUTEA arborescens

COLUTEA – Leguminosae MS-LS "Bladder Sennas"
Pinnate leaves. Pea-flowers throughout summer. Inflated seed pods.
– **arborescens** LS
Yellow flowers. Vigorous.

COMPTONIA – Myricaceae SS ✗ ○
Monotypic genus:
– **peregrina** SS ✗ ○ "Sweet Fern"
Frond-like narrow leaves. Small brown catkins, spring. Aromatic, suckering shrub.

CONVOLVULUS – Convolvulaceae
Large genus composed mainly of perennials. The following shrubby species is cultivated.

CONVOLVULUS cneorum

– **cneorum** SS (E) † ○ GC
Silky silver leaves. Large pink and white funnel-shaped flowers, May. Needs well drained sunny site. AM 1977 AGM 1993

CORDYLINE – Agavaceae ST (E) † ♥
Distinctive trees or shrubs. Only the following species is commonly grown.
– **australis** ST (E) † ♥ "Cabbage Tree"
Single trunk with stout ascending branches, dense mass of sword-like leaves. Small fragrant creamy flowers in panicles early summer. AM 1953 AGM 1993
– – **'Purpurea'** ('Atropurpurea') ST (E) † ♥
Purple leaves.
– – **'Sundance'** ST (E) † ♥
Mid ribs and leaf bases attractively flushed with deep pink.
– – **'Torbay Dazzler'** ST (E) † ♥
Leaves with a bright creamy-white margin, slightly pink flushed in the centre.

CORNUS – Cornaceae SS-MT "Dogwoods"
Extensive genus, containing many valuable garden plants.
– **alba** MS "Red barked Dogwood"
Forms thicket of stems – young ones red in winter. Good autumn leaf colour. Tolerant of wet soils. B (a) 4

CORNUS alba 'Elegantissima'

– – **'Aurea'** MS
Soft yellow leaves. B (a) 4
– – **'Elegantissima'** MS
Leaves with white margins and mottling. AGM 1993. B (a) 4
– – **'Kesselringii'** MS
Purplish-black stems. B (a) 4
– – **'Sibirica'** ('Atrosanguinea') MS
"Westonbirt Dogwood"

CORNUS alba 'Spaethii'

CORNUS 'Eddie's White Wonder'

Bright crimson winter shoots. AM 1961 AGM 1993. B (a) 4

– – 'Sibirica Variegata' MS
Leaves with broad, creamy-white margin. Winter shoots deep red. B (a) 4

– – 'Spaethii' MS
Golden margined leaves. FCC 1889 AGM 1993. B (a) 4

– alternifolia LS-ST
Horizontal spreading branches. Alternate small leaves, sometimes colouring in autumn. We recommend:

– – 'Argentea' ('Variegata') MS
Small leaves with creamy margins. Dense habit. AGM 1993

– canadensis PS ✗ ◑ GC "Creeping Dogwood "
Herbaceous species. Makes thick carpet, white flowers in summer. Bright red fruits. AM 1937 AGM 1993

– controversa ST ❦
Layered branches with broad heads of cream flowers May. Small black fruits. Purple-red autumn foliage. AM 1984

– – 'Variegata' ST ❦
Silver variegated leaves. AGM 1993

– 'Eddie's White Wonder' LS-ST
Large white flower heads in spring. Brilliant orange, red and purple autumn colour. AM 1972 FCC 1977 AGM 1993

– florida LT-ST North American "Flowering Dogwood". Flowers have 4 conspicuous white bracts, May. Colourful autumn foliage. Not for shallow chalk. AM 1951

– – 'Apple Blossom' LS
Pale pink flower bracts.

– – 'Cherokee Chief' LS
Deep rose-red flower bracts. AGM 1993

– – 'Cloud Nine' LS
Large white bracts. Free-flowering even when young.

– – 'First Lady' MS
Leaves attractively margined with yellow, colouring well in autumn.

– – 'Welchii' ('Tricolor') MS
Green leaves variegated cream flushed rose. In autumn turn bronzy-purple edged deep rose.

– – 'White Cloud' MS
Free flowering, pure white bracts. Bronzed foliage.

CORNUS controversa 'Variegata'

CORNUS florida 'Cherokee Chief'

CORNUS kousa var chinensis

– kousa LS
Conspicuous white bracts, June. Strawberry-like fruits. Leaves colour in autumn. FCC 1892 AM 1958. We recommend:
– – var. chinensis LS
Taller, more open form. Larger leaves. FCC 1924 AM 1959 AM 1975 AGM 1993
– – 'Gold Star' MS
Leaves blotched with golden yellow, turning red and purple in autumn.

– – 'Satomi' LS
Bracts deep pink. Leaves deep red-purple in autumn. AM 1991 AGM 1993
– mas LS "Cornelian Cherry"
Small yellow flowers, before leaves, February. Edible cherry-like red fruits. Red-purple autumn foliage. AM 1929 AGM 1993
– – 'Aurea' LS
Leaves suffused yellow.
– – 'Variegata' MS
Conspicuous white leaf margins. Free fruiting. AGM 1993
– 'Norman Hadden' ST ♀ Semi-(E)
Flowering dogwood with profuse, creamy-white bracts in June turning deep pink in July. Conspicuous red strawberry-like fruits hang in autumn. AM 1974 AGM 1993

CORNUS 'Norman Hadden'

– nuttallii MT ♀
Flowers with large white bracts, occasionally flushed pink, May. Yellow (occasionally red) autumn foliage. Not for shallow chalk. FCC 1920 AM 1971
– – 'Colrigo Giant'
Vigorous, upright form with large leaves and large white bracts.
– – 'Portlemouth'
A form with very large flower heads and red autumn colour.
– officinalis LS-ST
Exfoliating bark. Yellow flowers before leaves, February. Red fruits. Rich autumn foliage. AM 1970
– sanguinea MS "Common Dogwood"
Greenish red stems. Black fruits. Purple autumn foliage.
– – 'Winter Beauty' ('Winter Flame')
Young shoots bright orange-yellow and red in winter.
– stolonifera MS
Suckering shrub forming dense thickets of

CORNUS stolonifera 'Flaviramea'

stems. We recommend the forms:
– – **'Flaviramea'** MS
Young shoots yellow to olive-green. Good on wet soils. AM 1985 AGM 1993. B (d) 4
– – **'White Gold'** SS
Leaves with a white margin.

COROKIA – Cornaceae SS-MS (E) ○
Small star-like yellow flowers. Orange fruits.
– **cotoneaster** SS (E) ○ "Wire-netting bush"
Stiff intertwined branchlets. Small dark green leaves, white felted beneath. AM 1934
– × **virgata** MS (E) ○
Erect habit. Floriferous and free fruiting. AM 1934. We recommend:
– **'Red Wonder'**
Berries deep red.
– – **'Yellow Wonder'**
Berries bright yellow.

CORONILLA – Leguminosae MS ○
Bright yellow pea-flowers produced freely through the season.

CORONILLA valentina subsp. glauca

– **emerus** MS ○
Flower clusters in leaf axils. Slender seed pods, articulated, like a scorpion's tail.
– **glauca** see *C. valentina* subsp. *glauca*
– **valentina** SS (E) † ○
A small shrub of which we recommend the following forms:
– – **'Citrina'** MS (E) †
Flowers pale lemon-yellow. AM 1989 AGM 1993
– – subsp. **glauca** (*C. glauca*) MS (E) † ○
Glaucous leaves. Flowers mainly April, but intermittently throughout year. Requires a warm wall. AM 1957 AGM 1993
– – **'Variegata'** MS (E) † ○
Conspicuous creamy variegation to leaves. AGM 1984

CORREA – Rutaceae SS (E) † ○
For mildest areas or cool greenhouse. Abundant flowers late winter.
– × **harrisii** SS (E) † ○
Rose scarlet flowers. AM 1977 AGM 1993

CORYLOPSIS – Hamamelidaceae SS-LS
Drooping racemes of fragrant primrose yellow flowers before leaves, spring.
– **pauciflora** SS ✓
Bristle-toothed leaves, pink when young. Cowslip-scented flowers in short racemes, March. FCC 1893 AGM 1993
– **spicata** MS
Narrow racemes of bright yellow flowers with dark purple anthers. AM 1897
– **veitchiana** LS
Large racemes of flowers with conspicuous brick-red anthers. AM 1912 FCC 1974 AGM 1993
– **willmottiae** MS
Leaves often purple or reddish-purple when young. Dense racemes of flowers. AM 1912 FCC 1965 AGM 1993. We recommend:

CORYLOPSIS pauciflora

CORYLOPSIS

CORYLOPSIS willmottiae 'Spring Purple'

– – **'Spring Purple'** MS
Plum purple young growths.

CORYLUS – Corylaceae MS-LT "Hazels"
Many cultivated for their nuts. Any soils. Will tolerate bleak sites.
– **avellana** LS "Hazel"
Long yellow "lambs' tails", February. Leaves yellow in autumn. Good for screening.
– – **'Aurea'** MS ◑
Soft yellow leaves.
– – **'Contorta'** MS "Corkscrew Hazel" "Harry Lauder's Walking Stick"
Unusual twisted branches. Showy catkins, February. AM 1917 AGM 1993
– **colurna** LT ❦ "Turkish Hazel"
Striking bark with corky corrugations. AGM 1993

– **maxima** LS "Filbert"
Large rounded heart-shaped leaves. Large nuts. We recommend the form:
– – **'Purpurea'** ('Atropurpurea') LS "Purple-leaf Filbert"
Rich purple leaves. AM 1977 AGM 1993

COTINUS – Anacardiaceae LS-ST
The "Smoke Trees". Distinctive inflorescences. Rich autumn leaf colour.
– **coggygria** (*Rhus cotinus*) LS "Venetian Sumach" "Smoke Tree"
Smooth, rounded, green leaves. Fawn plume-like inflorescences June-July turn grey by late summer. AGM 1993
– – **'Flame'** see *C.* 'Flame'
– – **'Royal Purple'** LS
Deep wine-purple leaves, reddening towards autumn. AGM 1993
– – **'Velvet Cloak'** LS
Leaves a long-lasting deep red-purple until autumn when they turn bright red.
– **'Flame'** (*C. coggygria* 'Flame') LS
Rounded leaves brilliant orange-red in autumn. Large pink flower plumes in summer. AGM 1993
– **'Grace'** LS
Large soft purple leaves turn brilliant trans-lucent red in late autumn. Large pink plumes

CORYLUS avellana 'Contorta'

COTINUS 'Grace'

COTINUS 'Flame'

COTONEASTER conspicuus 'Decorus'

in summer. AM 1983 FCC 1990 AGM 1993
– **obovatus** (*C. americanus*) (*Rhus cotinoides*)
ST
Leaves colour brilliantly in autumn. AM 1904
AM 1976 AGM 1993

COTONEASTER – Rosaceae PS-ST
Variable genus evergreen and deciduous.
Bright autumn colour of leaf or fruit. Almost
all soils and conditions.
– **adpressus** DS GC
Small leaves scarlet in autumn. Bright red
fruits. Spreading habit. AGM 1993
– – var. **praecox** see *C. nanshan*
– **bullatus** LS
Large, conspicuously corrugated leaves
colour well in autumn. Large bright-red fruits.
AGM 1993

– **cochleatus** (*C. microphyllus* var. *cochleatus*)
PS (E) GC
Small, rounded leaves on spreading shoots,
studded with deep pink fruits in autumn.
AM 1930 AGM 1993
– **conspicuus** MS (E)
Arching branches. Small leaves. White
flowers smother branches early summer.
Abundant bright-red fruits. Spreading habit.
AM 1933
– – **'Decorus'** DS (F)
Free fruiting. FCC 1953 AGM 1993
– – **'Highlight'** MS (E)
Dense mound of arching shoots. Large
orange-red fruits.
– **'Coral Beauty'** SS (E) GC
Glossy green leaves. Orange-red fruits. Wide
spreading.
– **'Cornubia'** (Watereri Group) LS-ST Semi-(E)
Long leaves. Profuse large red fruits weigh
down branches. AM 1933 FCC 1936 AGM
1993
– **dammeri** (*C. humifusus*) PS (E)
Leaves to 4cm long. Long trailing shoots.
Sealing wax-red fruits. AGM 1993

COTONEASTER bullatus

COTONEASTER 'Cornubia'

COTONEASTER horizontalis 'Variegatus'

COTONEASTER integrifolius

– – **'Variegatus'** DS GC
Small cream variegated leaves, suffused red in autumn. AGM 1993
– **'Hybridus Pendulus'** ST ♠
Glossy leaves. Abundant brilliant red fruits on hanging branches autumn and winter. AM 1953
– **integrifolius** DS (E) GC
Dense habit with small, glossy leaves and extra large, deep pink fruits. Commonly grown as *C. microphyllus*. AGM 1993
– **'John Waterer'** see *C.* × *watereri* 'John Waterer'
– **lacteus** MS (E) Hdg (0.5m)
Large oval leathery leaves grey beneath. Late ripening clusters of red fruits last beyond Christmas. AM 1935 AGM 1993
– **microphyllus** see under *C. integrifolius*
– – var. **cochleatus** see *C. cochleatus*
– **nanshan** (*C. adpressus* var. *praecox*) (*C. praecox*) DS GC
Arching branches bear large, orange-red fruits. Glossy, rounded leaves turn bright red in autumn.

COTONEASTER 'Hybridus Pendulus'

– **floccosus** (*C. salicifolius* var. *floccosus*) MS (E)
Distinctive glossy narrow leaves, woolly white beneath on slender drooping stems. Abundant small red berries. AM 1920
– **franchetii** MS Semi-(E)
Very graceful habit. Sage-green foliage. Ovoid orange-scarlet fruits.
– – var. **sternianus** see *C. sternianus*
– **frigidus** LS-ST
Large broad elliptic leaves, large heavy clusters of crimson fruits, autumn and winter. Spreading habit. AM 1966
– **glaucophyllus** f. **serotinus** see *C. serotinus*
– **'Gnom'** (*C. salicifolius* 'Gnom') DS (E) GC
Forming a dense, low mound with prostrate branches and small, narrow, glossy green leaves. Red fruits usually sparse.
– **horizontalis** PS GC
Spreading "herring-bone" branches. Rich autumn coloured leaves and fruit. Excellent wall shrub. FCC 1897 AGM 1993

COTONEASTER 'Rothschildianus'

78

– **'Pink Champagne'** (Watereri group) LS (E)
Slender arching branches. Narrow leaves.
Abundant, small yellow fruits, become pink-
tinged.
– **praecox** see *C. nanshan*
– **'Rothschildianus'** (Watereri group) LS (E)
Light green leaves. Creamy-yellow fruit
clusters. Spreading habit when young. AGM
1993
– **salicifolius** var. **floccosus** see *C. floccosus*
– – **'Gnom'** see *C. 'Gnom'*
– **serotinus** (*C. glaucophyllus* f. *serotinus*) LS
(E)
Tree-like habit with leathery leaves. Profuse,
small white flowers in July followed by
persistent, small orange-red fruits during
winter. FCC 1919 AGM 1993
– **simonsii** MS Semi-(E) Hdg (0.5m)
Large scarlet fruits. Erect growing. AGM 1993
– **'Skogholm'** DS (E) GC
Small leaves. Large, coral-red obovoid berries.
Wide spreading.
– **splendens** (*C. splendens* 'Sabrina') (*C.*
'Sabrina') MS
Arching shoots bear small leaves which turn
red in late autumn and winter. Profuse bright
orange berries. AM 1950 AGM 1993
– **sternianus** (*C. franchetii* var. *sternianus*) MS
Sage-green leaves, silver-white beneath.
Abundant fruits. AM 1939 AGM 1993
– × **watereri** LS-ST Semi-(E)
Variable hybrids. Long leaves. Profuse red or
orange-red berries. Strong vigorous growth.
AM 1951. We recommend:
– – **'John Waterer'** LS Semi-(E)
Spreading branches. Abundant bunches of
red fruits, autumn. AM 1951 AGM 1993

"CRAB APPLE" see *Malus*

CRATAEGUS – Rosaceae LS-ST-MT
"Thorns"
*Attractive autumn leaf colour. Generally white
flowers, red fruits. Tolerant of most soils and
conditions, even windswept coastal areas.*
– × **carrierei** see *C.* × *lavallei* 'Carrierei'
– **laciniata** (*C. orientalis*) ST ❦
Deeply cut downy leaves, grey beneath. Large
fruits, coral- or yellowish-red. AM 1933 FCC
1970
– **laevigata** (*C. oxyacantha*) ST ❦
May-flowering species similar to *C. monogyna*
and including several ornamental flowering
trees.
– – **'Paul's Scarlet'** ('Coccinea Plena') ST ❦
Double scarlet flowers. FCC 1867 AGM 1993
– – **'Plena'** ST ❦

CRATAEGUS laevigata 'Paul's Scarlet'

White, double flowers.
– – **'Rosea Flore Pleno'** ST ❦
Double, pink flowers. AGM 1993
– × **lavallei 'Carrierei'** (*C.* × *carrierei*) ST ❦
Long, shiny dark green leaves. Orange-red
persistent fruits. AM 1924 AGM 1993
– **monogyna** MT ❦ Hdg (0.5) "Common
Hawthorn" "May" "Quick"
Strongly fragrant flowers. Mass of red "haws"
in autumn.

CRATAEGUS prunifolia

– – **'Biflora'** ('Praecox') ST ♛ "Glastonbury Thorn"
Earlier leafing. Occasionally flowers during winter.
– – **'Stricta'** ('Fastigiata') ST ♛
Erect branches.
– – **'Variegata'** ST ♛
Leaves splashed and mottled creamy-white.
– **oxyacantha** see *C. laevigata*
– **pinnatifida** ST ♛
Large conspicuously lobed leaves. Crimson fruits. We recommend the form:
– – var. **major** ST ♛
Rich red autumn leaves. Glossy crimson fruits. FCC 1886
– **prunifolia** ST ♛
Glossy oval leaves, colour well in autumn, persistent showy fruits. AGM 1993
– **tanacetifolia** ST ♛ "Tansy-leaved Thorn"
Grey, downy leaves. Usually thornless. Large yellow fruits like small apples. AM 1976

CRINODENDRON – Elaeocarpaceae LS
(E) † ⚹ ◑
Attractive shrubs for mild areas.
– **hookerianum** (*Tricuspidaria lanceolata*) LS
(E) † ⚹ ◑
Dense habit. Long, narrow, deep-green leaves. Crimson "lantern" flowers on long stalks, hang along branches May-June. FCC 1916 AGM 1993
– **patagua** LS (E) † ⚹
Fast-growing with oval, glossy green leaves on reddish shoots. White bell-shaped flowers in summer. AM 1984

"CUCUMBER TREE" *see Magnolia acuminata*

"CURRANT, FLOWERING" *see Ribes*

CRINODENDRON hookerianum

"CURRY PLANT" see *Helichrysum italicum* subsp. *serotinum*

CYDONIA japonica see *Chaenomeles speciosa*

CYDONIA maulei see *Chaenomeles japonica*

CYTISUS – Leguminosae PS-LS ○
"Brooms"
Typical pea-shaped flowers – yellow unless stated otherwise. Poisonous.
Pruning: Trim young plants after flowering to maintain compact growth.
Shorten long growths on mature bushes immediately after flowering.
– **battandieri** LS ○
Silky grey leaves. Pineapple scented flowers in cone-shaped clusters, July. Excellent for a high wall. AM 1931 FCC 1934 AGM 1993
– – **'Yellow Tail'** LS ○
Long spikes of flowers.
– × **beanii** DS ○
Golden yellow flowers, May. FCC 1955 AGM 1993
– **'Boskoop Ruby'** SS ○
Rounded habit with profuse, deep crimson

CYTISUS battandieri

CYTISUS 'Burkwoodii'

flowers. AGM 1993
– **'Burkwoodii'** MS ○
 Cerise flowers, wings deep crimson edged yellow, May-June. AMT 1973 AGM 1993
– **'C. E. Pearson'** MS ○
Flowers creamy-yellow flushed crimson and flame, May to June.
– **'Cottage'** DS ○
Upright habit with profuse, creamy-yellow flowers similar to those of *C. × kewensis.*
– **'Hollandia'** SS ○
Cream flowers cerise on the back with deeper wings. AGM 1993
– **'Johnson's Crimson'** MS ○
Clear crimson flowers. AMT 1972 FCCT 1973

CYTISUS × praecox 'Allgold'

CYTISUS × kewensis

– × **kewensis** DS ○
Mass of cream flowers, May. Semi-prostrate habit. AGM 1993
– – **'Niki'** DS ☋
A form with golden-yellow flowers.
– **'Killiney Red'** MS ○
Rich red flowers, darker velvety wings, May-June.
– **'La Coquette'** MS ○
Flowers with rose-red and yellow standard, orange-red wings and pale yellow keel. AMT 1972
– **'Lena'** SS ○
Compact, with red and yellow flowers freely borne. FCCT 1974 AGM 1993
– **'Lord Lambourne'** MS ○
Pale cream standard, dark red wings, May-June. AM 1927
– **'Luna'** SS ○
Large creamy-yellow and red flowers with rich yellow wings. AMT 1972 FCCT 1974 AGM 1993
– **'Minstead'** MS ○
Small white flowers, tinged lilac, darker on wings May-June. AM 1949 AGM 1993
– **'Mrs Norman Henry'** MS ○
Profuse small, lilac flowers with deep pink wings, May-June. AMT 1972
– **multiflorus** MS ✗ ○ "White Spanish Broom"
Small white flowers, May-June. Erect habit. AMT 1974 AGM 1993
– **nigricans** (*carlieri*) SS
Long terminal racemes of flowers continuously late summer.
– **'Porlock'** LS Semi-(E) † ○
Racemes of fragrant butter-yellow flowers, April-May. AM 1931 FCC 1990 AGM 1993
– × **praecox** SS ○ "Warminster Broom"
A tumbling mass of rich cream flowers, May. We offer the original form now named 'Warminster'. AGM 1993
– – **'Albus'** SS ○
White flowers.
– – **'Allgold'** SS ○
Arching sprays of bright yellow flowers. FCCT 1974 AGM 1993

CYTISUS scoparius 'Dragonfly'

– **purpureus** DS ○ "Purple Broom"
Lilac-purple flowers, May. AM 1980
– – **Albus** group DS ○
White flowers.
– – **'Atropurpureus'** DS ○
Deep purple flowers. AGM 1993
– **scoparius** MS ○ "Common Broom"
Rich butter-yellow flowers, May. Not suitable for shallow chalk.
– – **'Andreanus'** MS ○
Flowers marked with brown-crimson. FCC 1890 FCCT 1973 AGM 1993
– – **'Cornish Cream'** MS ○
Cream flowers. AM 1923 FCCT 1973 AGM 1993
– – **'Dragonfly'** MS ○
Deep yellow standard, crimson wings, May-June. Strong growing.
– – **'Fulgens'** MS ○
Orange yellow flowers with crimson wings, June. Dense, compact habit.
– – **'Golden Sunlight'** MS ○
Rich yellow flowers. Strong growing. AMT 1973
– **'Windlesham Ruby'** MS ○
Dark mahogany-crimson flowers.
– **'Zeelandia'** SS ○
Standard lilac and cream, wings pinkish and creamy, May-June. FCCT 1974 AGM 1993

D

DABOECIA – Ericaceae DS (E) ✓ ○
Dwarf, heath-like shrubs related to Erica.
– cantabrica DS (E) ✓ ○ "Connemara Heath"
Long racemes, rose-purple flowers June to November. We recommend the following forms:
– – 'Alba' DS (E) ✓ ○
White flowers.
– – 'Atropurpurea' DS (E) ✓ ○
Dark rose-purple flowers.
– – 'Bicolor' DS (E) ✓ ○
Flowers white, rose-purple, or striped – often all on same raceme. AGM 1993
– – 'Praegerae' DS (E) ✓ ○
Rich pink flowers. AMT 1970

"DAISY BUSH" see *Olearia*

DANAE – Ruscaceae SS (E) ●
Monotypic genus. Hermaphrodite flowers in terminal racemes.
– racemosa (*Ruscus racemosus*) SS (E) ●

"Alexandrian Laurel"
Arching sprays of narrow, glossy leaves. Orange berries. AM 1933 AGM 1993

DAPHNE – Thymelaeaceae PS-MS ○ or ◑
Generally fragrant, evergreen and deciduous shrubs. Ideal for rock garden. Good drainage and loamy soil necessary. Poisonous.
– bholua 'Gurkha' MS ○
Richly scented, purplish-rose flowers. December to February. Black fruits. AGM 1993
– – 'Jacqueline Postill' MS Semi-(E) ○
Larger flowers than 'Gurkha' offset by dark green leaves. FCC 1991 AGM 1993
– blagayana DS ◑
Terminal clusters of fragrant, creamy-white flowers, March-April. Whitish fruits. Best in deep leaf mould. FCC 1880
– × burkwoodii SS Semi-(E) ○
Clusters of very fragrant, pale pink flowers borne in May-June and usually again in

Grouped DABOECIA

DAPHNE bholua 'Jacqueline Postill'

DAPHNE × burkwoodii

DAPHNE × napolitana

October. AGM 1993. The two common forms of this hybrid, 'Albert Burkwood' (AM 1935) and 'Somerset' (AM 1937 FCC 1980) are very similar.
– – **'Carol Mackie'** ('Variegata') DS Semi-(E) ○
Leaves margined with golden-yellow, later creamy white.
– **cneorum** PS (E) ◑
Clusters of richly scented, rose-pink flowers, April-May. Brownish-yellow fruits.
– – **'Eximia'** PS (E) ◑
Larger leaves and flowers. Crimson buds opening rose-pink. AM 1938 FCC 1967 AGM 1993
– – **'Variegata'** PS (E) ◑
Leaves margined cream. Vigorous.
– **collina** DS (E) ○
Blunt, deep green leaves. Terminal clusters of fragrant rose-purple flowers, May. AM 1938 FCC 1984 AGM 1993
– – var. **neapolitana** see D. × napolitana
– **dauphinii** see D. × hybrida
– × **hybrida** (D. dauphinii) SS (E) ○
Very fragrant, reddish purple flowers, late autumn through winter.
– **longilobata** SS Semi-(E) ○
Slender-stemmed shrub with narrow leaves. White flowers in summer are followed by red berries. We recommend:
– – **'Peter Moore'** DS Semi-(E) ○
Grey-green leaves conspicuously margined with creamy white.

– × **mantensiana 'Manten'** DS (E) ○
Clusters of fragrant, deep rose-purple and lilac flowers April-May and again summer and autumn. Dense, rounded habit.
– **mezereum** SS ○
Scented purple-red flowers, February-March before leaves. Red, poisonous berries. Good on chalk.
– – f. **alba** SS ○
White flowers. Clear amber fruits.
– × **napolitana** (D. collina var. neapolitana) DS (E) ○
Compact habit with dark green leaves. Clusters of fragrant, rose-pink flowers April to June. AM 1984 AGM 1993
– **odora** (D. indica hort.) SS (E) ○
Very fragrant purple-pink flowers, winter-early spring. We recommend:
– – f. **alba** SS (E) ○
White flowers.

DAPHNE mezereum

DAVIDIA involucrata

– – **'Aureomarginata'** SS (E) ○
Leaves with creamy-white margins.
– **pontica** SS (E) ◑
Bright green, glossy leaves. Spidery yellow-green flowers, April-May. Blue-black fruits. AM 1977 AGM 1993
– **retusa** DS (E) ○
Fragrant deep rose-purple flowers, May-June. AM 1927 AGM 1993
– **'Somerset'** see under *D.* × *burkwoodii*
– **tangutica** DS (F) ○
Terminal clusters of fragrant flowers, white, tinged purple on inside, rose-purple outside, March-April. AM 1929 AGM 1993
– **'Valerie Hillier'** DS (E) ○
Clusters of fragrant, pale pink flowers almost continuously May to autumn. Spreading habit with glossy leaves.

DAPHNIPHYLLUM – Daphniphyllaceae LS (E)
Large rhododendron-like leaves. Inconspicuous flowers.
– **macropodum** LS (E)
Pale green leaves, glaucous beneath. Clusters of pungent, pink and green flowers, late spring. FCC 1888 FCC 1987

DATURA see *Brugmansia*

DAVIDIA – Davidiaceae MT ❦
Hardy trees for all fertile soils. Small inconspicuous flowers in May, each accompanied by two large conspicuous white bracts.

– **involucrata** MT ❦ "Pocket Handkerchief Tree" "Dove Tree" "Ghost Tree"
Heart-shaped leaves, felted beneath. Conspicuous handkerchief-like bracts. AM 1972 AGM 1993
– – var. **vilmoriniana** MT ❦
The most commonly grown form with leaves smooth beneath. FCC 1911 AGM 1993

DECAISNEA – Lardizabalaceae MS
Requires moist well-drained soil.
– **fargesii** MS
Pinnate leaves 0.6-1.0m long. Yellowish green flowers in racemes. Metallic blue "broadbean" pods.

DENDROMECON – Papaveraceae LS (E) † ○
Entire green leaves. Poppy-like yellow flowers.
– **rigida** LS (E) † ○
Rigid, narrow glaucous leaves. Buttercup-yellow flowers intermittently over long period. AM 1913

DESFONTAINIA – Potaliaceae MS (E) † ✗ ◑
Small holly-like leaves. Tubular flowers. Not for shallow chalk.
– **spinosa** MS (E) † ✗ ◑
Scarlet flowers with yellow mouth, late summer. AM 1931 AGM 1993

DESMODIUM penduliforum see *Lespedeza thunbergii*

DEUTZIA – Philadelphaceae MS
Attractive June-flowering shrubs for all fertile soils. D (h) 2 or (b) 5

DESFONTAINIA spinosa

DEUTZIA × hybrida 'Strawberry Fields'

– **chunii** MS
Flowers with pink petals, white inside, reflexed, displaying golden anthers. Produced in panicles along branches, July. We recommend:
– – **'Pink Charm'** MS
Conspicuous pink flowers.
– **compacta** SS
Sweetly scented white flowers, pink in bud, in wide corymbs, July.
– – **'Lavender Time'** MS
Lilac flowers, turning pale-lavender.
– × **elegantissima** MS
Fragrant, rose-tinted flowers, in paniculate corymbs. AM 1914. We recommend:
– – **'Rosealind'** MS
Deep carmine-pink flowers. AM 1972 AGM 1993
– × **hybrida** MS
Profusely flowering hybrids of which we recommend:
– – **'Magicien'** MS
Large flowers with pink-tinted, white-edged petals. Prominent purple streak on reverse.
– – **'Mont Rose'** MS
Profuse rose-pink flowers, tinted darker. AGM 1993

– – **'Strawberry Fields'** MS
Large, deep crimson flowers, white flushed pink inside.
– **longifolia** MS
Long narrow leaves. Clusters of flowers, June-July. AM 1912. We recommend the form:
– – **'Veitchii'** MS
Rich lilac-pink tinted flowers. AM 1912 FCC 1978 AGM 1993
– **'Magicien'** see *D.* × *hybrida* 'Magicien'

DEUTZIA × hybrida 'Magicien'

– **monbeigii** MS
Small leaves, white beneath. Mass of star-like, small white flowers; late. AM 1936
– **'Mont Rose'** see *D. × hybrida* 'Mont Rose'
– **pulchra** MS
White flowers in racemes, resembling drooping spikes of lily-of-the-valley.
– × **rosea** SS
Bell-shaped, pink flowers on arching branches. We recommend the form:
– – **'Carminea'** SS
Rose-carmine flushed flowers. AGM 1993
– **setchuenensis** MS
Corymbs of small starry white flowers July-August. AM 1945.
– – var. **corymbiflora** MS
Form with broader leaves. One of the most beautiful flowering shrubs. AM 1945 AGM 1993

DIERVILLA – Caprifoliaceae SS
Yellow, two-lipped, tubular flowers. Easy cultivation.
– × **splendens** SS
Bushy, spreading habit. Bright, sulphur-yellow, tubular flowers in summer.

DIPELTA – Caprifoliaceae LS
Tall shrubs with funnel-shaped flowers, resembling Weigela.
– **floribunda** LS
Fragrant pink flowers with yellow throat produced abundantly in May. AM 1927

DIPTERONIA – Aceraceae LS
Pinnate leaves. Clusters of winged seeds.
– **sinensis** LS
Inconspicuous flowers. Large clusters of pale green fruits turning red. AM 1922

DISANTHUS – Hamamelidaceae MS ✗
Monotypic genus. Moist well-drained soil.
– **cercidifolius** MS ✗ ◑
Leaves colour claret and crimson in autumn. Tiny purplish flowers October. AM 1936 FCC 1970 AGM 1993

DISTYLIUM – Hamamelidaceae LS-ST (E) ◑
Shiny leathery leaves. Flowers in racemes.

DISANTHUS cercidifolius

– **racemosum** LS (E) ◑
Wide spreading, slow. Flowers with no petals, conspicuous red stamens, April.

"DOGWOOD" see *Cornus*

DORYCNIUM – Leguminosae DS ○
Sub-shrubs and herbs. Well-drained situation in most soils.
– **hirsutum** DS ○
Silvery, hairy plant. Pink-tinged, white, pea flowers on erect stems, late summer-autumn. Red-tinged fruit pods.

"DOVE TREE" see *Davidia involucrata*

DRIMYS – Winteraceae LS (E) † ◑
Handsome shrubs for sheltered situations – ideal against a wall.
– **colorata** see *Pseudowintera colorata*
– **lanceolata** (*D. aromatica*) LS (E) † ◑
Narrow upright habit. Dark green leaves bronze when young, purple-red shoots. Creamy-white flowers April-May. AM 1926
– **winteri** LS (E) † ◑ "Winter's Bark"
Large leathery leaves. Fragrant ivory flowers in loose umbels, May. AM 1971

EDGEWORTHIA – Thymelaeaceae SS
Small genus related to Daphne.
– **chrysantha** (*E. papyrifera*) SS
Fragrant, yellow flowers in terminal
clusters, covered by silky hairs on outside.
AM 1961
– – f. **rubra** SS
A striking form with bright orange-red
flowers. AM 1982

ELAEAGNUS – Elaeagnaceae MS-LS ○
*Fast-growing deciduous and evergreen. Very
resilient – ideal shelter belts for exposed and
maritime areas. Abundant small fragrant
flowers. Not for shallow chalk.*
– **angustifolia** LS ○ "Oleaster"
Spiny shrub with silver-grey willow-like leaves.
Fragrant flowers, June. Silvery amber fruits.
AM 1978. We recommend:
– – var. **caspica** LS ○
Young leaves very silvery. Fragrant yellow
flowers early summer. AGM 1993
– **commutata** MS ○ "Silver Berry"
Silver leaves and small egg-shaped fruits.
Flowers, May. AM 1956

ELAEAGNUS commutata

– × **ebbingei** LS (E) ○
Large leaves, silvery beneath. Silvery scaly
flowers, autumn. Orange, silver-speckled
fruits, spring.

ELAEAGNUS × ebbingei 'Gilt Edge'

– – **'Gilt Edge'** LS (E) ○
Leaves margined golden yellow. AM 1971
FCC 1987 AGM 1993
– – **'Limelight'** LS (E) ○
Leaves with a broad central blotch of deep
yellow.
– **macrophylla** LS (E) ○
Silvery, round leaves, becoming green.
Flowers autumn. AM 1932
– **pungens** LS (E) ○
Shiny green leaves, dull white speckled
with brown scales beneath. Flowers,
autumn. We recommend:
– – **'Goldrim'** MS (E) ○
Dark green leaves with bright yellow margin.
– – **'Maculata'** MS (E) ○ Hdg (0.5)
Golden central splash to leaves. FCC 1891
AGM 1993
– **umbellata** LS ○
Leaves silvery beneath. Yellow-brown
shoots. Flowers, May-June. Small orange
fruits. AM 1933

"ELDER" see *Sambucus*

"ELDER, BOX" see *Acer negundo*

"ELM" see *Ulmus*

ELSHOLTZIA – Labiatae SS ○
*Aromatic sub-shrubs. Late flowering. Any
fertile soil.*
– **stauntonii** SS ○
Leaves smell of mint when crushed.
Abundant lilac-purple flowers in panicles,
August-October.

EMBOTHRIUM – Proteaceae LS (E) ✗ ❶
Spectacular flowering shrubs. Deep moist well-drained soil.
– **coccineum** LS Semi-(E) ✗ ❶ "Chilean Fire Bush"
Vigorous, upright and tree-like. Profusion of brilliant orange-scarlet flowers, May-early June. AM 1928
– – **Lanceolatum** group LS Semi-(E) ✗ ❶
Form with linear-lanceolate leaves. Hardy.
– – **'Norquinco Form'** LS Semi-(E) ✗
Profuse red flowers densely cover the shoots. AGM 1993

EMBOTHRIUM coccineum Lanceolatum group

ENKIANTHUS – Ericaceae MS-LS ✗ ❶
Distinctive shrubs with outstanding autumn leaf colour. Drooping flowers, cup or urn-shaped, produced May.
– **campanulatus** MS ✗ ❶
Cup-shaped flowers, sulphur-bronze produced abundantly. Autumn foliage yellow through shades to red. AM 1890 AGM 1993
– – **Albiflorus** group MS ✗ ❶
Flowers creamy white with faint pink flush on the lobes.
– – **'Red Bells'** MS ✗ ❶

ENKIANTHUS campanulatus

Compact, columnar habit. Profuse flowers richly streaked with red.
– **cernuus** var. **rubens** MS ✗ ❶
Deep red, fringed flowers. Brilliant autumn colour of red-purple over a long period. AM 1930 FCC 1992 AGM 1993
– **chinensis** see under *E. deflexus*
– **deflexus** LS ✗ ❶
Flowers yellow and red with darker veins, in umbels. Leaves generally with red petioles, good autumn colour. Has been confused with *E. chinensis.*
– **perulatus** MS ✗ ❶
Urn shaped, compact habit, small, pendulous white flowers freely borne, with the leaves, spring. Scarlet autumn colour. AM 1979 AGM 1993

"EPAULETTE TREE" see *Pterostyrax hispida*

ERICA – Ericaceae DS-LS (E) "Heath"
Conspicuous colourful corollas. A prolonged show of flowers can be obtained by planting different species and varieties. Generally lime-hating. C(l)
– **arborea** LS (E) ✗ "Tree Heath"
Fragrant, white, globular flowers, early spring. We recommend:
– – **'Albert's Gold'** MS (E) ○
Foliage bright yellow. AGM 1993
– – var. **alpina** LS (E) ✗
Brighter green foliage. Hardier. AM 1962 AGM 1993
– **australis** MS (E) ✗ "Spanish Heath"
Rose-purple flowers, April-May. AM 1935 FCC 1962 AGM 1993. We recommend:
– – **'Mr. Robert'** MS (E) ✗
White flowers. AM 1929 AGM 1993

ERICA arborea var. alpina

– – **'Riverslea'** MS (E) ⚹
Fuchsia-purple flowers. AM 1946 AGM 1993
– **carnea** DS (E) GC
Rosy-red flowers through winter. Numerous cultivars, all lime tolerant. Flowering season:
Early November-December
Mid January-March
Late April
Height 15-23cm
We recommend the following:
– – **'Ann Sparkes'** DS (E)
Golden foliage. Rich purple flowers. AMT 1971 AGM 1993

ERICA carnea 'Myretoun Ruby'

– – **'December Red'** DS (E)
Deep green foliage. Rose-red flowers. Mid to late. AMT 1966
– – **'Eileen Porter'** DS (E)
Carmine-red flowers, October to April. Dark corollas with pale calyces. AM 1956
– – **'Foxhollow'** DS (E)
Yellow foliage, tinged red in winter. Pale pink flowers. AGM 1993
– – **'Loughrigg'** DS (E)
Dark green foliage. Rose-purple flowers, Mid. AMT 1966 AGM 1993
– – **'Myretoun Ruby'** DS (E)
Dark green foliage. Large, deep rose-pink flowers. FCC 1988 AGM 1993

ERICA lusitanica

– – **'Pink Spangles'** DS (E)
Profuse pink flowers in winter. AGM 1993
– – **'Praecox Rubra'** DS (E)
Deep rose-red. Early-Mid. AMT 1966 FCCT 1968 AGM 1993
– – **'Ruby Glow'** DS (E)
Bronzed foliage. Rich dark-red flowers, late. AMT 1967
– – **'Springwood Pink'** DS (E)
Clear rose-pink flowers. Mid. AMT 1964
– – **'Springwood White'** DS (E)
Superb white, urn-shaped flowers. Mid. FCCT 1964 AGM 1993
– – **'Winter Beauty'** DS (E)
Rose-pink flowers. December onwards. AM 1922

– **ciliaris** DS (E) ✗ "Dorset Heath"
Large rose-red flowers July-October. We
recommend the forms:
– – **'Mrs. C. H. Gill'** DS (E) ✗
Dark green foliage. Clear red flowers. Up to
30cm. AGM 1993
– – **'Stoborough'** DS (E) ✗
Long racemes of white flowers. 50-60cm.
AGM 1993
– **cinerea** DS (E) ✗ "Bell Heather"
Purple flowers, June-September. Wiry stems.
Generally 23-30cm. We recommend the
following forms:
– – **'Alba Minor'** DS (E) ✗
White flowers. 15cm. AMT 1967 FCCT 1968
AGM 1993
– – **'Atrosanguinea Smith's Variety'** DS (E)
✗
Dark foliage. Intense scarlet flowers. 15cm.
– – **'C. D. Eason'** DS (E) ✗
Deep pink. FCCT 1966 AGM 1993
– – **'Eden Valley'** DS (E) ✗
Lilac-pink, paler at base. 15cm. AM 1933
AGM 1993
– – **'Golden Hue'** DS (E) ✗
Golden foliage turning red in winter. 50cm.
AGM 1993
– – **'Pink Ice'** DS (E) ✗
Compact, with bright green foliage and pale
pink flowers. AMT 1968 FCCT 1971 AGM
1993
– – **'Velvet Night'** DS (E) ✗
Blackish-purple flowers. AGM 1993
– × **darleyensis** DS (E)
Flowering throughout winter. Lime tolerant,
but not for shallow chalk. 50-60cm high. We
recommend the clones:
– – **'Arthur Johnson'** DS (E)
Magenta flowers in long sprays. AM 1952
AGM 1993
– – **'George Rendall'** DS (E)
Rich pink flowers.
– – **'Silberschmelze'** ('Molten Silver') DS (E)
Sweetly scented white flowers. AMT 1968
– **erigena** (*E. hibernica*) (*E. mediterranea*) SS
(E)
Fragrant rose-red flowers, March-May. Lime
tolerant but not for shallow chalk.
– – **'Brightness'** SS (E)
Bronze-red buds opening rose-pink. 0.6-1.0m.
AM 1972
– – **'Irish Dusk'** SS (E)
Compact habit with dark green foliage.
Flowers salmon-pink. 45cm. AGM 1993
– – **'W. T. Rackliff'** SS (E)
Dark green foliage. Pure white flowers with
brown anthers. 1-1.2m. AM 1972 AGM 1993

– **hibernica** see *E. mediterranea*
– **lusitanica** LS (E) ✗ "Portugal Heath" "Tree
Heath"
With pale green, plumose stems. Fragrant
white flowers, pink in bud, December
onwards. AM 1972 FCC 1977 AGM 1993
– **mediterranea** see *E. erigena*
– **terminalis** MS (E) "Corsican Heath"
Rose-coloured flowers late summer, fading
brown and remaining throughout winter.
Good on chalk. AGM 1993
– **tetralix** DS (E) ✗ "Cross-leaved Heath"
Rose-coloured flowers June-October. 20-
50cm. We recommend the forms:

ERICA tetralix 'Alba Mollis'

– – **'Alba Mollis'** ('Mollis') DS (E) ✗
Grey foliage. White flowers. AM 1927 AGM
1993
– – **'Con Underwood'** DS (E) ✗
Grey-green foliage. Crimson flowers. AGM
1993
– – **'L. E. Underwood'** DS (E) ✗
Silver-grey foliage. Pale-pink flowers,
terracotta in bud.
– **vagans** DS (E) ✗ "Cornish Heath"
Flowers in long sprays, July-October. We
recommend:
– – **'Lyonesse'** DS (E) ✗
White flowers, protruding brown anthers.
0.5-1.0m. AM 1928 AGM 1993

– – **'Mrs. D. F. Maxwell'** DS (E) ✗
Deep cerise. 50cm. AM 1925 FCCT 1970
AGM 1993
– – **'St. Keverne'** ('Kevernensis') DS (E) ✗
Clear rose-pink flowers. 50cm. AM 1914
FCCT 1971
– – **'Valerie Proudley'** DS (E) ✗
Golden-yellow foliage. White flowers. AMT
1971 AGM 1993
– × **veitchii** MS (E) ✗
A "Tree Heath", the following clone is in
cultivation:
– – **'Exeter'** MS (E) ✗
Bright green foliage. Plumes of fragrant
white flowers, spring. AM 1905 AGM 1984

ERIOBOTRYA – Rosaceae LS-ST (E)
Small genus of which we recommend:
– **japonica** LS (E) "Loquat"
Leathery, corrugated leaves up to 30cm long.
Pungent, hawthorn-like flowers, after a hot
summer, intermittently Nov-April. Occasionally
globe or pear-shaped yellow fruits produced.
Best against a wall. AGM 1993

ERYTHRINA – Leguminosae S-T † ○
*Large genus. Trifoliolate leaves and prickly
stems.*
– **crista-galli** MS † ○ "Coral Tree"
Waxy, deep scarlet, "Sweet Pea" flowers,
summer. Requires sunny wall and winter
protection. AM 1954 FCC 1987 AGM 1993

ESCALLONIA – Escalloniaceae SS-LS (E)
*Useful shrubs tolerating lime and drought.
Most withstand salt-laden winds. Good
hedges and windbreaks. Small leaves and
abundant small flowers, summer-autumn.
Generally A (b) 5 or C7*
– **'Apple Blossom'** MS (E)
Pink and white flowers. Slow. AM 1946 AGM
1993

ESCALLONIA 'Donard Seedling'

ERIOBOTRYA japonica

– **'Crimson Spire'** see *E. rubra* 'Crimson Spire'
– **'Donard Radiance'** MS (E)
Large, glossy leaves. Large chalice-shaped
flowers, rose-red. Strong growth. AM 1954
AGM 1993
– **'Donard Seedling'** MS (E)
Large leaves. White flowers, pink in bud.
Vigorous. AM 1916
– **'Iveyi'** LS (E) †
Large, glossy leaves. Large panicles of white
flowers, autumn. Vigorous. AM 1926 AGM
1993
– **'Langleyensis'** MS (E)
Arching branches. Small leaves. Rose-pink
flowers. AM 1897 AGM 1993

ESCALLONIA 'Langleyensis'

– **macrantha** see *E. rubra* var. *macrantha*
– **'Peach Blossom'** MS (E)
Clear peach-pink flowers. Slow growth. AGM
1993
– **'Pride of Donard'** MS (E)
Dark, glossy leaves. Large, bright rose, bell-

ESCALLONIA rubra 'Crimson Spire'

shaped flowers, June onwards. AGM 1993
– **punctata** see *E. rubra*
– **rubra** MS (E)
Leaves aromatic when bruised. Red flowers in panicles, July. We recommend:
– – **'Crimson Spire'** MS (E)
Dark glossy green leaves. Bright crimson flowers. Vigorous and upright. AGM 1993
– – var. **macrantha** (*E. macrantha*) LS (E) Hdg (0.5m)
Glossy, aromatic leaves. Rose-crimson flowers. Excellent for coast.

EUCALYPTUS – Myrtaceae ST-LT (E) ♀ or ♂ "Gum Tree"
Fast-growing trees noted for their attractive stems and leaves and unusual white flowers. Leaves of mature trees often completely different from those of saplings. Will tolerate a variety of soils – not shallow chalk, except E. parvifolia. Best spring-planted as young pot-grown plants.
– **coccifera** LT (E) ♀ "Tasmanian Snow Gum"
Patchwork grey and white bark. Silvery-grey adult leaves. AM 1953 AGM 1993
– **dalrympleana** MT (E) ♂
Cream, brown and grey patchwork bark. Grey-green adult leaves are bronzed when young. Fast growth. AM 1953 AGM 1993

– **gunnii** LT (E) ♀
Sage-green, sickle-shaped, adult leaves. Silver-blue, rounded juvenile foliage, for floral art. AM 1950 AGM 1993
– **niphophila** see *E. pauciflora* subsp. *niphophila*
– **parvifolia** MT (E) ♀
Narrow, blue-green adult leaves. Smooth grey bark. Tolerant of chalk. AGM 1993
– **pauciflora** ST (E) ♀ "Cabbage Gum"
White trunk. Adult leaves sickle-shaped, up to 20cm. We offer:

EUCALYPTUS pauciflora subsp. niphophila

– – subsp. **niphophila** (*E. niphophila*) ST (E) ♀ "Snow Gum"
Attractive grey, green and cream "Python's Skin" bark. Scimitar-shaped, grey-green adult leaves. Slow growth. AM 1977 AGM 1993

EUCRYPHIA – Eucryphiaceae LS-MT ☺
Highly ornamental. White flowers with conspicuous stamens July-September, when mature. Prefers moist loam with shade at roots, preferably non-calcareous.
– **glutinosa** LS ☺
Glossy, dark green, pinnate leaves turning orange and red in autumn. Abundant flowers, July-August. FCC 1880 FCC 1976 AGM 1993
– × **intermedia** ST (E) ♂
Leaves varying, single to trifoliolate. Mass of small flowers, August-September. Fast growing. We recommend the form:

– – **'Rostrevor'** ST (E) ▼
Fragrant flowers crowd the slender branches.
AM 1936 FCC 1973 AGM 1993
– **milliganii** (*E. lucida* var. *milliganii*) SI ▼ (E)
† ◑
Small, glossy, dark green leaves. Miniature
cup-shaped flowers freely borne, June-July.
Narrow habit. AM 1978
– × **nymansensis** MT (E) ▼
Dark green leaves, simple and compound on
the same plant. We recommend the form:
– – **'Nymansay'** MT (E) ▼
Flowers, 6cm across, crowd branches August-
September. Rapid growth. AM 1924 FCC
1926 AGM 1993

EUONYMUS alatus

– – **'Compactus'** SS
Dense, compact form – makes a good low
hedge. AGM 1993
– **europaeus** LS "Spindle"
Green-stemmed shrub. Abundant, rosy-red.
fruit capsules. Brilliant autumn foliage.
– – **'Red Cascade'** MS
Branches weighed down in autumn by mass
of fruits as the leaves turn red. AM 1949
AGM 1993

EUCRYPHIA × nymansensis 'Nymansay'

EUONYMUS europaeus 'Red Cascade'

EUODIA daniellii see *Tetradium daniellii*
– **hupehensis** see *Tetradium daniellii*

EUONYMUS – Celastraceae PS-LS
Evergreen or deciduous shrubs. Flowers,
green or purplish, early summer. Often showy
fruits, persisting into winter. Suitable for most
soils, particularly chalk.
– **alatus** MS
Broad, corky wings on the branchlets.
Excellent autumn leaf colour. Slow growth.
AGM 1993

– **fortunei** PS (E) GC
Trailing or climbing evergreen. Small, pale
green flowers. Pink fruits. We recommend:
– – **'Coloratus'** PS (E) GC
Leaves tinged purple in winter.
– – **'Emerald Gaiety'** SS (E) GC
Upright and spreading. Leaves margined
white. AGM 1993
– – **'Emerald 'n' Gold'** SS (E) GC
Dwarf bushy habit. Bright golden variegated
leaves, tinged bronzy-pink in winter. AM
1979 AGM 1993

EUONYMUS fortunei 'Emerald 'n' Gold'

– – 'Harlequin' DS (E) GC
Low, compact, spreading habit. Small leaves
heavily speckled with white.
– – 'Silver Queen' MS (E)
Green foliage, variegated creamy-white,
tinted rose in winter. Compact habit. AM
1977 AGM 1993
– hamiltonianus subsp. **sieboldianus 'Coral
Chief'** LS
Profuse, pale-pink fruits open to show red
seeds in autumn when leaves turn pale
yellow. Upright habit.
– japonicus LS (E)
Glossy green, leathery leaves. Extremely versa-
tile – tolerant of salt spray and smog. AM 1976
– – 'Duc d'Anjou' LS
Leaves pale green with a dark green central
blotch.
– – 'Latifolius Albomarginatus'
('Macrophyllus Albus') LS (E)
Conspicuous white margins to leaves, which
are larger and broader than the type. AGM
1993
– – 'Macrophyllus Albus' see 'Latifolius
Albomarginatus'

EUONYMUS fortunei 'Silver Queen'

– 'Marieke' SS (E)
Leaves margined with bright yellow. An
improvement on 'Ovatus Aureus'.
– – 'Microphyllus Pulchellus' ('Microphyllus
Aureus') SS (E)
Small leaves, variegated with gold.
– – 'Microphyllus Variegatus' SS (E)
Small leaves with white margins.
– – 'Ovatus Aureus' (AGM 1993) see
'Marieke'
– planipes (*E. sachalinensis* hort.)
Rich autumn leaf colour. Large scarlet fruits.
AM 1954 AGM 1993

EUPHORBIA – Euphorbiaceae DS-SS (E)
*A large and diverse genus of which the
following hardy, sub-shrubby members
are grown. All have poisonous and irritant
sap.*
– amygdaloides SS
The common native "Wood Spurge" of which
we recommend:
– – var. robbiae DS (E) ● "Mrs Robb's
Bonnet"
Rosettes of glossy green leaves and heads of
greenish-yellow flowers effective over a long
period during late winter and spring. AM
1968 AMT 1975 AGM 1993
– characias SS (E) ○
Narrow, blue-green leaves clustered on

EUPHORBIA characias

EXOCHORDA × macrantha 'The Bride'

upright stems. Flowerheads with conspicuous yellow-green bracts and red-purple glands during spring and summer. AGM 1993
– – subsp. **wulfenii** (*E. wulfenii*) SS (E) ○
Glands in the inflorescence yellowish-green. AM 1905 FCC 1988 AGM 1993
– **robbiae** see *E. amygdaloides* var. *robbiae*
– **wulfenii** see *E. characias* subsp. *wulfenii*

EURYOPS – Compositae DS-SS (E) ○
Conspicuous, yellow, daisy flowers. Require well drained soil.
– **acraeus** (*E. evansii* hort.) DS (E) ○

Small, narrow, silvery-grey leaves. Canary-yellow flowers, freely borne May-June. AM 1952
– **pectinatus** SS (E) ○
Downy, grey shoots and leaves. Rich yellow flowers May-June. AGM 1993

EXOCHORDA – Rosaceae LS
Long arching branches. Conspicuous racemes of large paper-white flowers, May. Not suitable for shallow chalk soils. D2 or 7
– **korolkowii** (*E. albertii*) LS
Vigorous. Best species for chalk. AM 1894.
– × **macrantha** LS
Abundant large flowers, late spring. AM 1917. We recommend the form:
– – **'The Bride'** SS
Weeping habit making a low dense mound. Free flowering. AM 1973 FCC 1985 AGM 1993

F

FABIANA – Solanaceae SS-MS (E) ○
Heath-like shrub. Requires moist, well drained soil. Will not tolerate shallow chalk soil.
– imbricata MS(E) † ○
Abundant, tubular white flowers along branches, June. AM 1934. We recommend:

FABIANA imbricata

– – 'Prostrata' SS (E) † ○
Mound-like habit. Small, pale-mauve tinted flowers, May-June.
– – f. violacea MS (E) † ○
Lavender-mauve flowers. FCC 1932 AGM 1993

FAGUS – Fagaceae ST-LT "Beech"
Small genus containing several beautiful large, hardy trees. Important for timber, windbreaks and hedges.
– engleriana MT ♠
Glaucous, sea-green foliage. Rare.
– sylvatica LT ♥ "Common Beech" Hdg (0.5m)
Large, noble tree. Leaves turning golden-copper in autumn. Requires well drained soil. Tolerates most soils, including chalk. When trimmed as hedge retains brown leaves through winter. AGM 1993
– – 'Albovariegata' LT ♥
Leaves margined and streaked with white.
– – 'Aspleniifolia' (var. *heterophylla*) LT ♥
"Fern-leaved Beech" "Cut-leaved Beech"

FAGUS sylvatica 'Dawyck Gold' and 'Dawyck Purple'

Graceful tree with narrow leaves, variously cut and lobed. AGM 1993
– – 'Aurea Pendula' ST ♠ ◑
Pendulous branches. Golden yellow leaves.
– – 'Cockleshell' MT ♦
Small, rounded leaves.
– – 'Dawyck' ('Fastigiata') LT ♦ "Dawyck Beech"
Slender tree, broadening in maturity. AGM 1993
– – 'Dawyck Gold' MT ♦ "Golden Dawyck"
Form with golden young leaves. AGM 1993
– – 'Dawyck Purple' MT ♦ "Purple Dawyck"
Form with purple leaves. FCC 1973 AGM 1993
– – 'Fastigiata' see 'Dawyck'
– – var. heterophylla see 'Aspleniifolia'
– – 'Pendula' LT ♠ "Weeping Beech"
High, arching and weeping branches. AGM 1993
– – 'Purple Fountain' MT ♠
Tree of slender habit with purple leaves and weeping branches. AGM 1993
– – Purpurea group LT ♥ "Purple Beech"

Covers a number of forms with purplish leaves, see also 'Riversii'.
– **'Purpurea Pendula'** ST ♠ "Weeping Purple Beech"
Mushroom-headed. Dark purple leaves.
– – **'Purpurea Tricolor'** LT ♥
('Roseomarginata')
Purple leaves with irregular pale-pink margins.
– – **'Riversii'** LT ♥ "Purple Beech"
Large dark-purple leaves. AGM 1993
– – **'Rohanii'** MT ♦
"Fern-leaved Beech" with purple leaves.
– – **'Zlatia'** MT ♥
Soft yellow leaves, turning green by late summer. Slow growing.

× **FATSHEDERA** (*Fatsia* × *Hedera*) –
Araliaceae SS (E) GC
Tolerant of pollution and salt winds. For all soils. Taller if trained on a wall.
– **lizei** SS (E) GC
Large, leathery, palmate leaves. Loose habit. Round heads of small white flowers, autumn. AGM 1993

× FATSHEDERA lizei

– – **'Annemieke'** SS (E)
Leaves with a central blotch of bright yellow-green.
– – **'Variegata'** SS (E)
Greyish-green leaves, irregularly margined with white. AGM 1993

FATSIA – Araliaceae LS (E) ◑
A monotypic genus, succeeding in all well drained soils.
– **japonica** (*Aralia sieboldii*) MS-LS (E) ◑
Large polished, dark green, palmate leaves. Panicles of milk-white, globular flowerheads, October. Excellent for seaside gardens. FCC 1966 AGM 1993
– – **'Variegata'** MS (E) ◑
Lobes of leaves white at tips. FCC 1868 AGM 1993

FATSIA japonica

FEIJOA – Myrtaceae LS (E) † ○
Summer flowering, monotypic genus.
– **sellowiana** LS (E) † ○
Grey-green leaves. Flowers have fleshy red and white petals, and long crimson stamens. Large egg-shaped berries after a hot summer. Edible petals and fruit are aromatic. AM 1927
– – **'Variegata'** LS (E) † ○
Cream and white variegated leaves. AM 1969

FICUS – Moraceae LS-ST
Large variable genus; evergreen and deciduous. Very few hardy in this country.
– **carica** LS-ST ♥ "Common Fig"
Handsome, lobed leaves and edible fruits in autumn. Best against a sunny wall. Irritant sap. We recommend:
– – **'Brown Turkey'**
The best outdoor fig, popular for its brown-purple fruits.

"FIG, COMMON" see *Ficus carica*

"FIRETHORN" see *Pyracantha*

FORSYTHIA – Oleaceae MS-LS
Generally golden-yellow flowers cover branches, early spring. Very hardy and easy to grow.
– **'Golden Nugget'** MS
Vigorous with large, golden-yellow flowers.
– × **intermedia** MS
Vigorous. Flowers late March-April. AM 1894. A (g) 1,2,3. We recommend the forms:
– – **'Fiesta'** MS
Leaves with a bold central blotch of gold. Compact with golden-yellow flowers.

FORSYTHIA × intermedia 'Lynwood'

FOTHERGILLA major

– – 'Lynwood' MS
Abundant large flowers with broad petals. AM
1956 FCC 1966 AGM 1993. A (g) 1,2,3
– suspensa LS
Rambling habit. Flowers on slender stalks
March-April. AGM 1993. C2 or 3, wall shrubs.

FOTHERGILLA – Hamamelidaceae DS-
MS ⚬
Conspicuous bottle brush-like flower spikes,
spring. Rich autumn leaf colour.
– gardenii DS ⚬
Erect, scented inflorescences – clusters of white
stamens, April-May.
– major (*F. monticola*) MS ⚬
Conspicuous white flower clusters before
leaves. Rich autumn leaf colour. AM 1927 FCC
1969 AGM 1993

FRAXINUS – Oleaceae ST-LT "Ash"
Fast-growing trees with pinnate leaves. Tolerate
wind, salt and atmospheric pollution. All soils.
– americana LT ♥ "White Ash"
Fast growing. We recommend:
– – 'Autumn Purple' LT ♦
Dark green leaves turn red-purple in autumn.
– angustifolia LT ♥
Glabrous slender pointed leaflets. Brown
winter buds. Fast growing. We recommend:
– – 'Raywood' (*F. oxycarpa* 'Raywood') LT ♥
"Claret Ash"
Small leaves turn plum-purple in autumn. AM
1978 AGM 1993
– excelsior LT ♥ "Common Ash"
Valuable timber tree. Black winter buds. AGM
1993. Named clones include:
– – 'Jaspidea' MT ♥ "Golden Ash"
Yellowish branches and golden young shoots.
Leaves clear-yellow in autumn. Vigorous. AGM
1993

FRAXINUS excelsior 'Pendula'

– – 'Pendula' MT ♠ "Weeping Ash"
Mound-like form with weeping branches.
AGM 1993
– – 'Westhof's Glorie' LT ♥
Strong growing form. Glossy dark green leaves
open late. AGM 1993
– mariesii (Ornus Sect.) ST ♥
Beautiful "Flowering Ash". Creamy-white
flowers in panicles, June. Slow growing. AM
1962
– ornus (Ornus Sect.) MT ♥ "Manna Ash"
"Flowering Ash"
Abundant white flowers in panicles, May.
AGM 1993
– oxycarpa 'Raywood' see *F. angustifolia*
'Raywood'

– **pennsylvanica** MT ♥ "Red Ash"
Downy shoots, large leaves. Winter buds
brown. Fast growth. We recommend the
following:
– – **'Summit'** MT ♦
Glossy leaves turn golden in autumn.
– **velutina** MT ♥ "Arizona Ash"
Leaves and shoots coated in grey, velvety
down. Winter buds brown.

FREMONTODENDRON (*Fremontia*) –
Sterculiaceae LS (E) † ○
*Conspicuous flowers with colourful calyx.
Require good drainage. Good on chalk.
Irritant foliage.*
– **'California Glory'** LS (E) † ○
Yellow flowers up to 5cm. South-facing wall.
FCC 1967 AGM 1993

FREMONTODENDRON 'California Glory'

"FRINGE TREE, CHINESE" *retusus* see
Chionanthus

FUCHSIA – **Onagraceae** DS-MS
*Flowers freely borne, summer-autumn. Red
sepals unless stated otherwise. All well-
drained soils.* B or (a) or (b) 4
– **'Alice Hoffman'** SS
Purple tinged leaves. Small flowers, calyx
scarlet, petals white.
– **'Blue Gown'** DS
A dwarf, floriferous plant of compact
habit. Corolla double, deep purple, calyx
scarlet.
– **'Chillerton Beauty'** SS
Medium flowers. Calyx white, tinged rose,
soft-violet petals. AMT 1977 AGM 1993
– **'Corallina'** SS
Scarlet and violet flowers. Spreading. AGM
1993

FUCHSIA 'Madame Cornelissen'

– **'Garden News'** SS
Large double flowers with pale pink sepals
and magenta-rose corolla.
– **'Genii'** DS
Small flowers with cerise sepals and reddish-
purple petals. Leaves lime-yellow.
– 'Lady Thumb' DS
Bushy habit. Semi-double flowers with light-
red calyx and white, red-veined petals. FCCT
1977 AGM 1993
– 'Lena' SS
Semi-double flowers with pale pink calyx and
rosy-magenta petals flushed pink. AMT 1962
AGM 1993
– **'Madame Cornelissen'** MS †
Large flowers; red calyx, white petals. AM
1941 AMT 1965 FCCT 1978 AGM 1993
– **magellanica** MS
Long slender flowers; calyx scarlet, petals
violet. We recommend:
– – **'Alba'** see var. *molinae*
– – **'Aureovariegata'** SS
Leaves margined with bright yellow.
– – var. **gracilis** MS
Small flowers, scarlet and violet. AMT 1978
AGM 1993
– – var. **molinae** ('Alba') MS
Shorter flowers, white tinged mauve. AM
1932
– – **'Sharpitor'** SS
Leaves grey-green with a white margin.
Flowers white with faint mauve tinge.
– – **'Variegata'** (*F. gracilis* 'Variegata') SS
Green leaves, margined creamy yellow, tinged

FUCHSIA 'Mrs Popple'

FUCHSIA magellanica 'Variegata'

pink. Small scarlet and purple flowers. AMT 1975 AGM 1993
– – **'Versicolor'** SS
Grey-green leaves, rose-tinted when young, variegated creamy-white when mature. AMT 1965 AGM 1993
– **'Margaret Brown'** DS
Large flowers; crimson and magenta.
– **'Mrs Popple'** SS
Large flowers; scarlet and violet. Protruding crimson stamens and style. AM 1934 AMT

1962 AGM 1993
– **'Mrs W. P. Wood'** SS
Profuse small flowers with pale pink sepals and white corolla. AGM 1993
– **'Pixie'** SS
Flowers with carmine sepals and mauve-purple corolla veined carmine. Foliage yellow-green.
– **'Prosperity'** SS
Vigorous upright habit to 1m. Flowers very large, double; corolla white veined pink, calyx deep rose pink. One of the most spectacular hardy fuchsias. AGM 1993
– **'Riccartonii'** LS
Scarlet calyx, broad violet petals. AMT 1966 FCCT 1977 AGM 1993
– – **'Rose of Castile Improved'** SS
Flowers large with sepals white tinged pink and deep violet corolla.
– **'Tennessee Waltz'** DS
Sepals scarlet, corolla rich purple-violet. Spreading habit. AMT 1978
– **'Tom Thumb'** DS
Abundant flowers; rose-scarlet and violet. AMT 1938 FCCT 1962 AGM 1993

"FURZE" see *Ulex europaeus*

G

GARRYA – Garryaceae LS (E)
Leathery leaves. Dioecious; ornamental catkins. Withstand atmospheric pollution and coastal spray. All well-drained soils.
– elliptica LS (E)
Male plant has magnificent grey-green catkins. January-February. Female has clusters of purple-brown fruits. AM 1931 AGM 1993 (male form). We recommend the form:
– – 'James Roof' LS (E)
Vigorous, male form with extra long catkins. AM 1974 AGM 1993

GARRYA elliptica 'James Roof'

× **GAULNETTYA – Ericaceae** DS-SS (E) ✗ GC
Hybrid origin (Gaultheria × Pernettya) (× Gaulthettya)
– wisleyensis SS (E) ✗ GC
We recommend the following clones:
– – 'Pink Pixie' DS (E) ✗ GC
White pitcher-shaped flowers, tinged pink, May. Purplish-red fruits. AM 1976
– – 'Wisley Pearl' SS (E) ✗ GC
Dull, dark-green leaves. Large ox-blood-red fruits, autumn and winter. AM 1939

GAULTHERIA – Ericaceae PS-SS (E) ✗
Mainly tufted shrubs. White urn-shaped flowers, late spring, early summer.

– cuneata DS (E) ✗
Compact habit. Narrow oblanceolate leaves. White fruits. Smell of 'Germolene' when crushed. AM 1924 AGM 1993
– procumbens PS (E) ✗ GC "Checker-berry"
Creeping carpet of dark green leaves. Bright-red fruits. AGM 1993

GAULTHERIA procumbens

– shallon SS (E) ✗
Broad, leathery leaves. Pinkish white flowers. Clusters of dark-purple fruits. Vigorous.

"GEAN" see *Prunus avium*

GENISTA – Leguminosae DS-LS ○
Allied to Cytisus. *Generally have yellow flowers. Lime-tolerant, succeed in acid or neutral soils.*
– aetnensis LS ○ " Mount Etna Broom"
Slender, nearly leafless shoots. Flowers freely borne, July. FCC 1938 AGM 1993
– hispanica SS ○ GC "Spanish Gorse"
Mass of flowers, May-June. Ideal for dry banks.
– lydia DS GC ○
Slender drooping branchlets. Abundant golden flowers May-June. AM 1937 FCC 1957 AGM 1993
– pilosa DS GC ○
Cascades of golden flowers, May.
– tenera LS
Profusely flowering shrub of which we recommend:

GENISTA tenera 'Golden Shower'

GENISTA lydia

GENISTA hispanica

GLEDITSIA triacanthos 'Sunburst'

– – **'Golden Shower'** LS
Masses of brilliant yellow, fragrant flowers on arching branches, June. AGM 1993
– **tinctoria** SS ○ "Dyer's Greenweed"
Flowers in long terminal racemes, June-September. We recommend the form:
– – **'Plena'** DS ○
Double flowers, freely borne. Excellent rock garden shrub. AGM 1993
– – **'Royal Gold'** SS ○
Mass of flowers throughout summer. AGM 1993

"GHOST TREE" see *Davidia involucrata*

GLEDITSIA – Leguminosae MT-LT ○
Delightful foliage trees. Trunk and branches generally barbed with vicious spines. Seeds in flattened pods. All well-drained soils.

Tolerates atmospheric pollution.
– **triacanthos** LT ○ ♥ "Honey Locust"
Feathery, green leaves, yellow in autumn. Long, shining, brown seed pods.
– – **'Elegantissima'** LS-ST ♥ ○
Compact, bushy habit with large fern-like leaves. Slow.
– – **'Ruby Lace'** MT ♥
Young foliage deep bronze-red.
– – **'Shademaster'** LT ♥ ○
Thornless, with ascending branches and dark green leaves.
– – **'Sunburst'** MT ♥
Spineless stems. Bright-yellow young foliage. AGM 1993

"GOLDEN RAIN" see *Laburnum*

"GORSE, COMMON" see *Ulex europaeus*

"GORSE, SPANISH" see *Genista hispanica*

GREVILLEA – Proteaceae MS (E) † ╱ ○
Flowers like those of Honeysuckle, but smaller, produced over long period. Good drainage essential.

103

– **juniperina** MS (E) † ⚹ ○
Bright green, needle-like leaves. We
recommend:
– – **'Sulphurea'** (*G. sulphurea*) MS (E) † ⚹ ○
Clusters of bright yellow flowers. AM 1974
AGM 1993
– **rosmarinifolia** MS (E) † ⚹ ○
Deep green, needle-like leaves. Crimson
flowers in long terminal racemes. AM 1932
AGM 1993
– **sulphurea** see *G. juniperina* 'Sulphurea'

GRINDELIA – Compositae SS (E) ○
Small genus. We recommend the following:
– **chiloensis** (*G. speciosa*) SS (E) ○
Narrow hoary leaves. Cornflower-like, yellow
flowers on tall thick stems, June-October. AM
1931

GRISELINIA – Cornaceae MS-LS (E) †
*Densely leafy shrubs, ideal for hedging.
Insignificant flowers.*
– **littoralis** LS (E) † Hdg (0.50m)
Leathery apple-green leaves. All soils. Ideal
coastal hedge plant. AGM 1993
– – **'Dixon's Cream'** MS (E) † ◑
Leaves splashed and mottled creamy
white.

GRISELINIA littoralis 'Dixon's Cream'

– – **'Variegata'** MS (E) † ◑
White-margined leaves. AM 1978

"GUELDER ROSE" see *Viburnum opulus*

"GUM TREE" see *Eucalyptus*

GYMNOCLADUS – Leguminosae MT ♀
Pod-bearing trees with bipinnate leaves.
– **dioica** (*G. canadensis*) MT ♀ "Kentucky
Coffee Tree"
Large compound leaves, pink-tinged when
unfolding, clear-yellow in autumn. Whitish-
grey young twigs.

H

HAKEA – Proteaceae MS-LS (E) ○
Ideal shrubs for sunny, arid sites. Not good on chalk.
– **lissosperma** (*H. sericea* hort.) LS (E) ○
Dense, upright habit with needle-like leaves. Clusters of showy white flowers April-May.
– **sericea** see *H. lissosperma*

HALESIA – Styracaceae LS-ST ♥ ∕
Delightful small trees producing snowdrop-like flowers along branches, before leaves, May. Small, green, winged fruits.
– **carolina** (*H. tetraptera*) ST ♥ ∕ "Snowdrop Tree"
White, nodding flowers in clusters of 3 or 5. Pear-shaped, winged fruits. AM 1954 FCC 1980
– **diptera** ST ♥ ∕
More shrubby and less free-flowering than *H. carolina*. AM 1948. We recommend the form:
– – var. **magniflora** LS ∕
Larger flowers, 2 to 3cm long. AM 1970
– **monticola** ST ♥ ∕ "Mountain Snowdrop Tree"
Larger tree with larger flowers and fruit than *H. carolina*. AM 1930. We recommend:
– – **'Rosea'** ST ♥ ∕
Flowers of delicate blush-pink. FCC 1984
– – var. **vestita** ST ♥ ∕
Superb form with even larger flowers, white, sometimes rose-tinted. AM 1958 AGM 1993

HALESIA monticola var. vestita

× HALIMIOCISTUS (*Halimium* × *Cistus*) – Cistaceae DS (E) ○
Attractive hybrids requiring good drainage.
– **'Ingwersenii'** (*Helianthemum clusii*) DS (E) ○
Pure white flowers, over a long period.
– **sahucii** DS (E) ○
Linear leaves. Pure white flowers, May-September. AGM 1993
– **wintonensis** DS (E) † ○
Grey foliage. Pearly-white flowers, stained yellow at petal bases, with maroon pencilled zone. AM 1926 AGM 1993

× HALIMIOCISTUS wintonensis

– – **'Merrist Wood Cream'** DS (E) † ○
Flowers pale creamy-yellow blotched crimson-maroon. AGM 1993

HALIMIUM – Cistaceae DS-SS (E) ○
Low spreading shrubs for a sunny, well-drained site.
– **lasianthum** (*Cistus formosus*) SS (E) ○
Greyish leaves. Golden-yellow flowers with dark basal-blotches, May. AM 1951 AGM 1993
– **ocymoides** (*Helianthemum algarvense*) DS (E) ○
Grey leaves. Bright yellow flowers with black-brown basal markings. AGM 1993
– – **'Susan'** DS (E)
Broad-leaved form of compact habit. AGM 1993

HALIMODENDRON – Leguminosae DS
One species. Suitable for all well-drained soils. Best given full sun.

HALIMIUM ocymoides

– **halodendron** MS "Salt Tree" ○
Spiny shrub with silvery leaves. Abundant
purple-pink pea flowers, June-July.

HAMAMELIS – Hamamelidaceae MS-LS
Delightful, fragrant, winter flowering shrubs.
Spidery yellow or reddish flowers, December-
March, before leaves. Good autumn leaf
colour.
Flower size:
Large – over 3cm across
Medium – 2 to 3cm across
Small – up to 2cm across
– × **intermedia** LS
Medium to large flowers. Following clones are
recommended:
– – **'Arnold Promise'** LS
Vigorous with large, bright yellow flowers.
AGM 1993
– – **'Diane'** LS
Coppery-red flowers. Rich autumn leaf colour.
AM 1969 AGM 1993
– – **'Jelena'** ('Copper Beauty') LS
Dense clusters of large flowers, yellow, suf-
fused coppery red – appearing orange. Flame
autumn leaf colours. AM 1955 AGM 1993
– – **'Sunburst'** LS
Large, pale yellow flowers. Leaves yellow in
autumn. Strongly upright habit.
– – **'Winter Beauty'** LS
Flowers large with long, orange-yellow petals
tinged red towards the base.
– **mollis** LS "Chinese Witch Hazel"
Large, golden, broad-petalled flowers, Decem-
ber-March. Strong, sweet scent. Yellow autumn
leaves. FCC 1918 AGM 1993 (to vegetatively
propagated clones only). See 'Jermyn's Gold'

HAMAMELIS × intermedia 'Jelena'

– – **'Jermyns Gold'** LS
Golden yellow, fragrant flowers. An
outstanding form previously grown as *H.*
mollis. AGM 1993
– – **'Pallida'** LS
Dense clusters of large, sulphur-yellow
flowers. AM 1932 FCC 1958 AGM 1993

HAMAMELIS mollis 'Pallida'

– **vernalis** MS "Ozark Witch Hazel"
Abundant small flowers, January-February,
pale yellow to red. Heavily scented. Good
autumn leaf colour. We recommend the form:
– – **'Sandra'** MS
Purplish young leaves, turning green, purple
beneath, flame autumn colour. Cadmium-
yellow flowers. AM 1976 AGM 1993

"HAWTHORN" see *Crataegus monogyna*
and *C. laevigata*

"HAZEL" see *Corylus*

HAMAMELIS vernalis 'Sandra'

"HEATHER" see *Calluna, Daboecia & Erica*

HEBE (*Veronica* in part) – **Scrophulariaceae**
DS-MS (E) ○
*Useful genus of variable species, invaluable
for industrial and coastal areas. Useful for
hedging, and ground cover. All well drained
soils. Generally white flowers, spring to
autumn flowering. A (b) 5*
– **albicans** DS (E) ○
Dense, rounded habit. Glaucous leaves. AGM
1993

HEBE albicans

– **'Alicia Amherst'** ('Veitchii') ('Royal Purple ')
SS (E) † ○
Long racemes of deep-purple flowers, late
summer. AGM 1993

– × **andersonii** MS (E) † ○
Long racemes of soft-mauve flowers, fading
to white, August-September. Vigorous.
– – **'Variegata'** MS (E) † ○
Leaves margined and splashed cream.
– **armstrongii** see under *H. ochracea*
– **'Autumn Glory'** SS (E) ○
Glossy, green leaves, tinged purple. Intense
violet flowers, continuously June-October.
– **'Blue Clouds'** SS (E) ○
Wisteria-blue flowers in long spikes through
summer. Dark, glossy green leaves turn purple
in winter. AGM 1993
– **brachysiphon** (*H. traversii* hort.) SS (E) ○
Rounded habit. Abundant flowers, June-July.
– – **'White Gem'** see *H.* 'White Gem'
– **'Carl Teschner'** see *H.* 'Youngii'
– **'Carnea Variegata'** SS (E) † ○
Long racemes of rose-pink flowers May-
September. Leaves grey-green margined
creamy-white.
– **cupressoides** SS (E) ○
Distinctive, dense, rounded habit. Long
slender branches resemble a *Cupressus*. Pale-
blue flowers, June-July. FCC 1894. We
recommend:
– – **'Boughton Dome'** DS (E) ○
Dwarf form of dense habit with green foliage.
FCC 1982 AGM 1993
– **'Emerald Green'** DS (E) ○
Compact, bun-shaped habit with small,
glossy leaves. White flowers in summer.
AGM 1993
– × **franciscana** SS (E) ○
Excellent hybrid. We recommend the clones:
– – **'Blue Gem'** SS (E) ○
Compact, dome shape. Racemes of bright
blue flowers. Extremely hardy. FCC 1869
AGM 1993
– – **'Variegata'** SS (E) ○
Broad, creamy leaf margins. AGM 1993
– **'Gloriosa'** ('Pink Pearl') SS (E) † ○
Compact habit. Long racemes of bright pink
flowers.
– **'Great Orme'** SS (E) ○
Compact. Long, tapering racemes of bright
pink flowers. Fairly hardy. AGM 1993
– **hulkeana** SS (E) ○
Loose habit. Glossy, green leaves. Panicles of
soft lavender-blue flowers, May-June. FCC
1882 AGM 1993
– × **kirkii** MS (E) ○
Long, slender racemes of white flowers.
Narrow, pointed leaves.
– **'La Seduisante'** ('Diamant') SS (E) ○
Large racemes of bright-crimson flowers. AM
1897 AGM 1993

HEBE 'Great Orme'

HEBE hulkeana

HEBE 'Midsummer Beauty'

– **macrantha** DS (E) † ○
Leathery, toothed leaves. Flowers up to 2cm across. AM 1952 AGM 1993
– **'Marjorie'** SS (E) ○
Long racemes of pale violet and white flowers, July-September. Very hardy.

– **'Midsummer Beauty'** SS (E) ○
Light green leaves, reddish beneath. Long racemes of lavender flowers throughout summer. Moderately hardy. AM 1960 FCCT 1975 AGM 1993
– **'Mrs Winder'** MS (E) ○
Purple foliage. Bright-blue flowers. Moderately hardy. AM 1978 AMT 1982 AGM 1993
– **ochracea** SS (E) ○
Ochre-yellow, "whipcord" foliage. Tiny flowers July-August. Often grown as *H. armstrongii*. AMT 1982
– – **'James Stirling'** DS (E) ○
Stout shoots bear bright ochre-gold foliage. AMT 1982 AGM 1993
– **'Pewter Dome'** DS (E) ○
Dome-shaped, spreading habit with grey-green leaves and flowers in short spikes. AGM 1993
– **pimeleoides 'Glaucocaerulea'** DS (E) ○
Small, glaucous-blue leaves. Pale lavender flowers June-July. Upright habit.
– – **'Quicksilver'** DS (E) ○
Tiny, silvery-blue leaves, low, spreading habit. AGM 1993
– **pinguifolia 'Pagei'** (*Veronica pageana*) PS (E) ○ GC
Small, glaucous-grey leaves. Abundant, small white flowers, May. AM 1958 AMT 1982 AGM 1993
– **'Purple Queen'** SS (E) † ○
Large racemes of purple flowers. AM 1893
– **'Purple Tips'** ('Tricolor') SS (E) † ○
Grey-green leaves with darker veins. Margins yellowish white, flushed purple when young. Long racemes of magenta flowers, turning white in time.
– **rakaiensis** (*H. subalpina hort.*) DS (E) ○
Dense, rounded habit. Small, pale-green leaves. Flowers, June-July. AMT 1982 AGM 1993
– **recurva** ('Aoira') SS (E) ○
Open, rounded habit. Narrow leaves, glaucous above. Slender racemes of flowers. We offer:
– – **'Boughton Silver'** DS (E) ○
Compact with silvery-blue leaves. AGM 1993
– **'Red Edge'** DS (E) ○
Dense habit with blue-grey leaves edged with red in winter. Flowers lilac fading to white in summer. AGM 1993
– **'Rosie'** DS (E) ○
Profuse spikes of clear pink flowers with purple anthers, borne over a long period, summer and autumn. The best dwarf pink *Hebe*.
– **salicifolia 'Spender's Seedling'** see *H. 'Spender's Seedling'*

HEBE pinguifolia 'Pagei'

HEBE rakaiensis

– **'Simon Delaux'** SS (E) † ○
Rounded habit. Large racemes of crimson
flowers. AGM 1993
– **'Spender's Seedling'** (*H. salicifolia*
'Spender's Seedling') SS (E) ○
Fragrant, white flowers, abundant. AM 1954
AMT 1982 AGM 1993
– **subalpina** see *H. rakaiensis*
– **traversii** see *H. brachysiphon*
– **'Tricolor'** see 'Purple Tips'
– **'White Gem'** (*H. brachysiphon* 'White
Gem') DS (E) ○
Compact habit with profuse white flowers in
summer.
– **'Youngii'** (*H.* 'Carl Teschner') DS (E) ○ GC
Mound-like habit. Small leaves and violet,
white-throated flowers June-July. AM 1964

HEDYSARUM – Leguminosae SS ○
*Large genus, easy cultivation. We
recommend:*
– **multijugum** SS ○
Sea-green, pinnate leaves. Racemes of rosy-
purple pea flowers, summer. Lax habit. AM
1898

HEBE 'Youngii'

HELIANTHEMUM – Cistaceae DS (E) ○
"Rock Rose" "Sun Rose"
*Green and grey-leaved plants. Abundant,
brilliant flowers, throughout summer. Ideal for
dry, sunny positions.*

HELIANTHEMUM on scree beds at the Hillier Arboretum

– **'Ben Fhada'** DS (E) ○ GC
Golden-yellow with orange centre; grey-green
foliage.
– **'Ben Hope'** DS (E) ○ GC
Carmine with deep orange centre; grey-green
foliage.
– **'Ben Ledi'** DS (E) ○ GC
Bright tyrian rose with dark green foliage.
– **'Ben More'** DS (E) ○ GC
Bright, rich orange with darker centre; dark
green foliage.
– **'Ben Nevis'** DS (E) ○ GC
Deep buttercup-yellow with bronze-crimson
centre; green foliage. AM 1924 AMT 1924
– **'Cerise Queen'** DS (E) ○ GC
Scarlet, double; green foliage.

– **'Fire Dragon'** DS (E) ○ GC
Neat growth. Flame-orange flowers. Grey-green foliage. AGM 1993
– **'Golden Queen'** DS (E) ○ GC
Green foliage. Golden flowers.
– **'Henfield Brilliant'** DS (E) ○ GC
Bright orange with grey-green foliage. AGM 1993
– **'Jubilee'** DS (E) ○ GC
Green foliage. Drooping, double, primrose-yellow flowers. AMT 1970 AGM 1993
– **'Mrs C. W. Earle'** DS (E) ○ GC
Dark-green foliage. Double, scarlet flowers with yellow bases. AGM 1993
– **'Praecox'** DS (E) ○ GC
Grey foliage. Bright yellow flowers.
– **'Raspberry Ripple'** DS (E) ○ GC
Deep reddish-pink with white-tipped petals; foliage dark green.
– **'Red Orient'** see 'Supreme'
– **'Rose of Leeswood'** DS (E) ○ GC
Rose-pink, double; foliage green.
– **'Supreme'** ('Red Orient') DS (E) ○ GC
Grey-green foliage. Crimson flowers.
– **'The Bride'** DS (E) ○ GC
Creamy-white with bright yellow centre; silver-grey foliage. AM 1924 AMT 1924 AGM 1993
– **'Wisley Pink'** DS (E) ○ GC
Soft pink flowers on grey foliage. AGM 1993
– **'Wisley Primrose'** DS (E) ○ GC
Grey-green foliage. Primrose-yellow flowers, deeper centre. AMT 1970 AGM 1993
– **'Wisley White'** DS (E) ○ GC
Pure white with golden anthers and grey leaves.

HELICHRYSUM – Compositae DS-SS (E) ○

Attractive foliage, often aromatic. Bright yellow flowers. Well drained, poor soil.
– **italicum** (*H. rupestre* hort.) DS (E) ○
Long, narrow, grey leaves. Clusters of flowers, summer. AGM 1993
– – subsp. **serotinum** (*H. serotinum*) DS (E) ○ "Curry Plant"
Narrow, sage-green leaves with curry-like smell. Heads of yellow flowers in midsummer. AGM 1984
– **ledifolium** see *Ozothamnus ledifolius*
– **rosmarinifolium** see *Ozothamnus rosmarinifolius*
– **serotinum** see *H. italicum* subsp. *serotinum*
– **splendidum** (*H. triliniatum*) SS (E) ○
Silvery-grey leaves, with three longitudinal ridges. Everlasting flowers keep colour into the following year. AGM 1993

HELICHRYSUM splendidum

HESPEROYUCCA whipplei see *Yucca whipplei*

HIBISCUS – Malvaceae MS ○

Late summer, early autumn flowering shrubs.
– **sinosyriacus** MS ○
Vigorous. Sage-green leaves. Large trumpet-shape flowers, September-October, until the frosts. Rounded open habit. We recommend the clones:

HIBISCUS sinosyriacus 'Autumn Surprise'

– – **'Autumn Surprise'** MS ○
White petals have an attractively feathered cerise base.
– – **'Lilac Queen'** MS ○
White, lilac-tinted petals, garnet red at base.
– **syriacus** MS ○
Trumpet-shaped flowers, successively July-October. Compact upright habit. We recommend the following clones:

HIBISCUS syriacus 'Woodbridge'

HIBISCUS syriacus 'Blue Bird'

– – **'Blue Bird'** ('Oiseau Bleu') MS ○
Single, violet-blue flowers, darker eye. AM
1965 AGM 1993
– – **'Diana'** MS ○ .
Large, single, pure-white flowers. AGM 1993
– – **'Hamabo'** MS ○
Large, single, blush flowers, crimson eye.
AGM 1993
– – **'Helene'** MS ○
Large flowers, white streaked deep pink with
feathered maroon base.
– – **'Pink Giant'** MS ○
Large flowers, clear pink with a feathered,
deep red eye. AGM 1993
– – **'Red Heart'** MS ○
White flowers with a conspicuous red centre.
AGM 1993
– – **'Russian Violet'** MS ○
Large, lilac-pink flowers with a deep red
centre.
– – **'Woodbridge'** MS ○
Large, single, rose-pink flowers, carmine eye.
AM 1937 AGM 1993

"HICKORY" see *Carya*

HIPPOPHAE – Elaeagnaceae LS-ST ○
*Silvery or sage-green, willowy leaves. Female
plants have orange berries. Good maritime
windbreak.*

HIPPOPHAE rhamnoides

– **rhamnoides** MS ○ "Sea Buckthorn"
Silvery leaves. Berries last through to following
February. Plant in groups to ensure pollination
of females. AM 1944 AGM 1993

HOHERIA – Malvaceae LS ○ or ◑
*Variable genus, some evergreen, which
require protection. White flowers, mid-late
summer.*
– **glabrata** LS ○
Mass of fragrant, almost translucent, flowers,
June-July. AM 1911 FCC 1946 AGM 1993
– **'Glory of Amlwch'** LS Semi-(E) ○
Leaves retained in mild winters. Large flowers
smothering stems, summer. AM 1960 AGM
1993
– **populnea** LS (E) † ◑
Flowers in dense clusters, late summer-
autumn. AM 1912. We recommend:
– – **'Alba Variegata'** LS (E) † ◑
Dark-green leaves, irregularly margined
creamy-white. AM 1976

HOHERIA glabrata

– sexstylosa LS (E) † ◑
Green, lanceolate leaves. Flowers borne freely.
Hardier than *H. populnea*. FCC 1924 AM
1964 AGM 1993

"HOLLY" see *Ilex*

HOLODISCUS – Rosaceae LS
Spiraea-like shrubs. Finely divided leaves.
Feathery flower panicles, July. Hardy.
– discolor (*Spiraea discolor*) LS ○
Greyish-white leaves, tomentose beneath.
Creamy-white flowers. AM 1978

"HONEY LOCUST" see *Gleditsia triacanthos*

"HONEYSUCKLE" see *Lonicera*

"HOP HORNBEAM" see *Ostrya carpinifolia*

"HORNBEAM" see *Carpinus*

"HORSE CHESTNUT" see *Aesculus
hippocastanum*

HYDRANGEA – Hydrangeaceae DS-LS ◑
or ○
*Attractive summer-autumn flowering shrubs
with generally dome-shaped or flattened
heads. Easy cultivation, but resent dryness at
roots. Pruning for all (except H. paniculata) A
(g) 10 or 4*
– arborescens SS ◑
Flowers with conspicuous, creamy, marginal
ray florets, July-September. We recommend
the following:
– – 'Annabelle' ◑
Large, hemispherical heads of white, nearly all
sterile, flowers. AM 1978 AGM 1993

– aspera MS ◑
Large leaves. Pale blue flowers with lilac-pink
or white ray florets, June-July.
– – subsp. sargentiana (*H. sargentiana*) MS ◑
Large, bluish flowers with white ray florets,
July-August. Large, velvety leaves and hairy
shoots. AM 1912 AGM 1993
– – Villosa group (*H. villosa*) MS ◑
Large, lilac-blue flowers with serrated,
margined sepals. Leaves and stems hairy. AM
1950 AGM 1993
– 'Ayesha' ('Silver Slipper') SS ◑
Distinctive shrub. Glossy, green leaves.
Greyish-lilac-pink, flattened flower heads,
with thick cup-shaped florets. AM 1974 AGM
1993
– heteromalla LS ◑
Dark green leaves, whitish beneath. White
flowers with conspicuous ray florets. AM
1978. We recommend:
– – 'Bretschneideri' LS ◑
A form with peeling brown bark and broad
lacecaps. AGM 1993
– – 'Jermyns Lace' LS ◑
Vigorous with large leaves, bark of 2nd year
shoots peeling. Very large heads of white
flowers over a long period in summer, the
outer sterile florets ageing to pink. Named
here from a plant in the Sir Harold Hillier
Gardens and Aboretum received as *H.
xanthoneura* var. *wilsonii*.
– involucrata SS ◑
Blue or rosy-lilac flowers, margined with white
or tinted ray florets.
– – 'Hortensis' SS ◑
Double, creamy-white florets, tinted pink in
the open. AM 1956 AGM 1993
– macrophylla DS-LS ◑
Large group incorporating the **HORTENSIAS**
and the **LACECAPS**:
HORTENSIAS "Mop-headed hydrangeas"
Large globular heads of sterile florets, pink, red,

HYDRANGEA macrophylla 'Altona'

white, blue or combination. A hydrangea colourant is necessary in alkaline soils to retain blue shades. Excellent maritime plants, also thrive in inland sheltered gardens. We recommend:

– – **'Alpenglühen'** SS ◑
Large heads of crimson florets.
– – **'Altona'** SS ◑
Rose-coloured, large florets. Blues well if treated. AM 1957 AGM 1993
– – **'Ami Pasquier'** DS ◑
Deep red. AM 1953 AGM 1993
– – **'Europa'** SS ◑
Deep pink, large florets. AGM 1993

HYDRANGEA macrophylla 'Ami Pasquier'

– – **'Générale Vicomtesse de Vibraye'** SS ◑
Vivid rose. Blues well if treated. AM 1947 AGM 1993
– – **'King George'** SS ◑
Rose pink. Large florets with serrated sepals. AM 1927
– – **'Madame Emile Mouillère'** SS ◑
White, with pink or blue centre. Large florets with serrated sepals. AM 1910 AGM 1993
– – **'Nigra'** SS ◑
Rose-pink or sometimes blue; black stems. FCC 1895 AGM 1993
– – **'Parzival'** SS ◑
Crimson-pink to purple or blue. AM 1922 AGM 1993
– – **'Westfalen'** SS ◑
Vivid crimson or violet. AM 1958 AGM 1993
LACECAPS
Large corymbs of fertile flowers, ringed by sterile, coloured ray florets. Similar requirements to **HORTENSIAS.** We recommend:
– – **'Blue Wave'** MS ◑
Blue, fertile flowers with large ray florets, varying pink to blue. Beautiful gentian-blue in suitable soils. AM 1956 FCC 1965 AGM 1993

HYDRANGEA macrophylla 'Blue Wave'

HYDRANGEA paniculata 'Grandiflora'

-- **'Geoffrey Chadbund'** SS ◑
Brick-red on alkaline or neutral soils. AGM 1993

-- **'Lanarth White'** MS ◑
Bright blue or pink fertile flowers, ringed with white ray florets. AM 1949 AGM 1993

-- **'Mariesii'** SS ◑
Rosy-pink flowers, very large ray florets. Rich blue in suitable soils. FCC 1881

-- **'Tricolor'** MS ◑
Pale pink to white flowers. Variegated leaves of green, grey and pale yellow. FCC 1882 AGM 1993

-- **'White Wave'** ('Mariesii Alba') SS ◑
Pink or blue fertile flowers, pearl-white ray florets. AM 1948 AGM 1993

- **paniculata** MS-LS ○
Dense, terminal panicles of both fertile and large, creamy sterile florets, late summer-autumn. AM 1964. B (a) 4. We recommend the forms:

-- **'Everest'** LS ○
Large, dense heads of fully sterile florets, white turning pink. AM 1990

-- **'Grandiflora'** LS ○
Massive panicles of sterile florets, white, turning to pink. FCC 1869 AGM 1993

-- **'Praecox'** LS ○
Smaller panicles of dentated, ray florets, early July. AM 1956 FCC 1973 AGM 1993

-- **'Tardiva'** LS ○
More numerous ray florets, September-October. Short, stiff, erect branches.

- **'Unique'** LS ○
Larger panicles than *H. paniculata* 'Grandiflora'. AM 1990 AGM 1993

- **petiolaris** see under CLIMBERS

- **'Preziosa'** see *H. serrata* 'Preziosa'

- **quercifolia** MS ○
White flowers. Superb autumn leaf colour. AM 1928 AGM 1993

-- **'Snow Queen'** MS ○
Large, dense, upright heads of white, sterile florets.

-- **'Snowflake'** MS ○
Large heads of double flowers.

- **sargentiana** see *H. aspera* subsp. *sargentiana*

- **serrata** (*H. macrophylla* subsp. *serrata*) DS ◑
Flattened corymbs of white or blue flowers; pink, white or blue ray florets, sometimes crimson in autumn. We recommend the forms:

-- **'Bluebird'** (*H. acuminata* 'Bluebird') SS ◑
Slightly dome-shaped corymbs of blue, fertile flowers, ringed by large red-purple ray florets – sea-blue on acid soil. AM 1960 AGM 1993

HYDRANGEA serrata 'Preziosa'

-- **'Grayswood'** SS ◑
Blue fertile flowers, white ray florets, turning rose, then crimson. AM 1948 AGM 1993

-- **'Preziosa'** SS ◑
Globular heads of rose-pink, florets, reddish-purple in autumn. Purplish-red stems. Leaves tinged purple when young. AM 1963 FCC 1964 AGM 1993

-- **'Rosalba'** SS ◑
White ray florets, turning crimson. Large leaves. AM 1939 AGM 1993

- **serratifolia** see under CLIMBERS

- **villosa** see *H. aspera* Villosa group

HYPERICUM – Guttiferae DS-MS
Abundant yellow flowers, summer and autumn. Almost all well drained soils.

- **androsaemum** DS "Tutsan"
Small flowers over a long period, conspicuous anthers. Berry-like capsules, red turning black, autumn.

- **beanii 'Gold Cup'** see *H.* × *cyathiflorum* 'Gold Cup'

HYDRANGEA aspera Villosa group (HYDRANGEA villosa)

HYPERICUM 'Hidcote'

– **calycinum** DS (E) GC "Rose of Sharon"
Large leaves. Large golden flowers. Excellent
in dry and in shady places. AM 1978
– × **cyathiflorum** SS
Hybrid of which we recommend the form:
– – **'Gold Cup'** (*H. beanii* 'Gold Cup') SS
Deep yellow, cup-shaped flowers 6cm across.
– **forrestii** SS
Leaves have rich autumn colour. Abundant
saucer-shaped flowers, summer and autumn.
AM 1922 AGM 1993
– **'Hidcote'** (*H. patulum* 'Hidcote') MS Semi-
(E)
Compact habit. Abundant, large saucer-
shaped flowers, July-October. AM 1954 AGM
1993
– **kouytchense** SS Semi-(E)
Golden-yellow flowers with conspicuous
stamens, June-October. Bright red long-styled
capsules. AGM 1993
– × **moserianum** DS GC
Arching, reddish stems. Flowers with
conspicuous reddish anthers, July-October.
FCC 1891 AGM 1993

HYPERICUM × moserianum 'Tricolor'

– – **'Tricolor'** DS ◑
Leaves variegated pink, white and green. AM
1896
– **'Rowallane'** MS Semi-(E) †
Rich golden flowers, to 7.5cm wide. Graceful
habit. AM 1943 AGM 1993

I

IDESIA – Flacourtiaceae MT ♀
Monotypic. Dioecious. Prefers neutral to acid soil.
– polycarpa MT ♀
Large ovate leaves. Terminal panicles of small yellowish-green flowers, summer on older trees. Bunches of red berries, autumn, on female trees. AM 1934

ILEX – Aquifoliaceae DS-MT
Variety of forms, many evergreen. Generally dioecious. Great variety of leaf and berry. Many withstand industrial pollution and maritime exposure. Some make excellent hedges. Poisonous foliage and berries.
A (f) 5 (all evergreens)
– × altaclerensis LS-ST (E) Hdg (0.5m)
Vigorous growth. Large leaves. Tolerant of maritime and industrial atmosphere. Good hedges and screens. We recommend several forms:

– – 'Belgica Aurea' ('Silver Sentinel') ST (E) ♦
Erect habit. Deep green leaves, mottled grey and pale-green, with creamy margin. Few spines. Female. AM 1985 AGM 1993
– – 'Camelliifolia' LS (E)
Pyramidal habit. Long, generally spineless, shiny, dark green leaves, reddish-purple when young. Purple stems. Large fruit. AGM 1993
– – 'Golden King' LS (E)
Broad, green, almost spineless leaves, with golden margin. Female. AM and FCC 1898 AGM 1993
– – 'Lawsoniana' LS (E)
Generally spineless leaves with central yellow splash. Female. FCC 1894 AGM 1993
– – 'Silver Sentinel' see 'Belgica Aurea'
– – 'Wilsonii' LS (E)
Dome-shaped habit. Prominently veined, spiny leaves. Female. FCC 1899 AGM 1993
– aquifolium MT (E) ♀ Hdg (0.5m)
"Common Holly"
Spiny, glossy dark-green leaves. Male and female forms. Excellent hedges. Tolerant of most conditions. Variety of clones. AGM 1993
– – 'Amber' LS (E)
Large bronze-yellow fruits. FCC 1985

ILEX × altaclerensis 'Golden King'

ILEX aquifolium 'Argentea Marginata'

– – **'Argentea Marginata'** LS (E) "Broad-leaved Silver Holly"
Leaves margined white. We recommend the female form. AGM 1993
– – **'Argentea Marginata Pendula'** ST (E) ♠
"Perry's Silver Weeping Holly"
Strongly weeping branches. Leaves margined white. Free fruiting.
– – **'Ferox Argentea'** MS (E) "Silver Hedgehog Holly"
Creamy-white margins and spines. Purple twigs. Male. AM 1988 AGM 1993

ILEX aquifolium 'Ferox Argentea'

– – **'Ferox Aurea'** MS (E) "Gold Hedgehog Holly"
Leaves with golden central splash. Male.
– – **'Flavescens'** ('Clouded Gold') LS (E) "Moonlight Holly"
Leaves suffused yellow-old gold. Female.
– – **'Golden Milkboy'** ('Aurea Mediopicta Latifolia') MS (E)
Flattened, spiny green leaves, with central golden splash. Male. AGM 1993
– – **'Golden Milkmaid'** LS (E)
Large, spiny leaves with central golden blotch. Female with red berries.
– – **'Golden Queen'** ('Aurea Regina') MS (E)
Green or reddish young shoots. Dark green

ILEX aquifolium 'Pyramidalis Fructu Luteo'

spiny leaves, shaded grey and pale green, margined yellow. Male. AGM 1993
– – **'Green Pillar'** MT (E) ♦
Dark green spiny leaves. Female. AGM 1993
– – **'Handsworth New Silver'** LS (E)
Purple stems. Leaves mottled grey, broad creamy-white margin. Female. AGM 1993
– – **'J. C. van Tol'** ('Polycarpa') LS (E)
Glossy, dark green, almost spineless leaves. Abundant red berries. AGM 1993
– – **'Madame Briot'** LS (E)
Purple stems. Spiny green leaves, mottled and margined dark yellow. Female. AGM 1993
– – **'Polycarpa'** see 'J. C. van Tol'
– – **'Pyramidalis'** MT (E) ♥
Conical when young, broadening in maturity. Bright green leaves. Abundant fruit. AM 1989 AGM 1993
– – **'Pyramidalis Fructu Luteo'** MT (E) ♥
Abundant bright yellow fruits. Perhaps the best yellow-fruited holly. AM 1985 AGM 1993
– – **'Silver Milkmaid'** ('Silver Milkboy') ('Argentea Mediopicta') LS (E)
Dark green spiny leaves, with central cream blotch. Female. FCC 1985 AGM 1993
– **cornuta** MS (E)
Unusual rectangular leaves, generally 5-spined. Large red berries. Slow. We recommend:
– – **'Burfordii'** SS (E)
Glossy leaves with single terminal spine. Free fruiting.

ILEX aquifolium 'Silver Milkmaid'

– **crenata** SS (E)
Tiny leaves. Small, shiny black berries. Slow.
We recommend the forms:
– – **'Convexa'** SS (E)
Free fruiting. Excellent low hedge. AGM 1993
– – **'Golden Gem'** DS (E)
Yellow leaves. AGM 1993
– **kingiana** (*I. insignis*) (*I. nobilis*) ST (E) ♥ †
Leathery, few-spined leaves – very spiny on
young plants. Large red fruits. AM 1964
– × **koehneana** LS (E)
Purple-tinged young shoots. Glossy dark
green leaves. Large red berries on female
plants. We recommend the form:
– – **'Chestnut Leaf'** (*castaneifolia* hort.)
Thick, yellowish-green leaves, with strong
spines. Female with red berries. AGM 1993
– **latifolia** ST (E) ♥
Huge, glossy dark green leaves, oblong with
serrated margins. We grow a female selection
with abundant scarlet berries. AM 1952
(foliage and fruit) AM 1977 (flowers)
– **'Lydia Morris'** MS (E)
Compact pyramidal habit. Glossy, strongly
spiny leaves. Large red berries.
– × **meserveae** MS (E)
The "Blue Hollies". Evergreen shrubs more
suited to the small garden than common
holly. We recommend:
– – **'Blue Prince'** MS (E)
Stems tinged purple, bright glossy green
leaves. Male.
– – **'Blue Princess'** MS (E)
Bushy habit with purple shoots and dark blue-
green, softly spiny leaves. Red berries. AM
1992 AGM 1993
– **pernyi** LS (E)
Small, almost triangular, spined leaves. We
grow a female form with small, bright red
fruits. FCC 1908

INDIGOFERA potaninii

– **verticillata** LS ✗
Deciduous. Purple-tinged leaves, yellow in
autumn. Bright red fruits. AM 1962. Male and
female selections are available.

ITEA ilicifolia

ILLICIUM – Illiciaceae MS (E) ◑
Aromatic shrubs with unusual many-petalled flowers.
– **anisatum** (*I. religiosum*) MS (E) ◑
Thick, fleshy, glossy leaves. Pale yellow flowers, spring. AM 1930
– **henryi** MS (E) ◑
Shiny, leathery leaves. Bright rose flowers.

"INDIAN BEAN TREE" see *Catalpa bignonioides*

INDIGOFERA – Leguminosae SS-MS ○
Pinnate leaves. Racemes of flowers in leaf axils of growing shoots, all summer and autumn. All soils. Excellent on dry sites. A (b) 4·
– **amblyantha** MS ○
Dense racemes of pink flowers over a long period during summer. AGM 1993
– **heterantha** (*I. gerardiana*) SS ○
Bright purple-pink flowers. AM 1977 AGM 1993

– **potaninii** MS ○
Clear pink flowers continuously June to September.

INDOCALAMUS – Gramineae MS (E)
Small genus of bamboos of which we recommend:
– **tessellatus** (*Sasa tessellata*) SS (E)
Dense thickets of slender, arching, bright green canes. Shining green leaves up to 60cm, largest of all hardy bamboos.

ITEA – Iteaceae SS-MS ◑
Unusual evergreen and deciduous shrubs. Summer flowering.
– **ilicifolia** MS (E) ◑
Lax, holly-like shrub. Drooping racemes of fragrant, greenish-white flowers, late summer. AM 1911 FCC 1988 AGM 1993

JASMINUM – Oleaceae MS "Jasmine"
"Jessamine"
*More or less deciduous. Green stems. Bright
yellow flowers. All soils. For climbing species
see under CLIMBERS.*
– humile MS Semi-(E)
Semi-climbing growth. Trifoliolate leaves.
Terminal clusters of flowers, June-July. We
recommend the form:
– – 'Revolutum' *(J. revolutum)* MS (E)
Deep green leaves, with 5 to 7 leaflets.
Slightly scented flowers, in cymose clusters,
summer. AM 1976 AGM 1993
– nudiflorum MS "Winter Jasmine"
Bright yellow flowers on naked green
branches, November-February. Excellent
against walls. AGM 1993. C2 or 3

JASMINUM nudiflorum

"JERUSALEM SAGE" see *Phlomis fruticosa*

JOVELLANA – Scrophulariaceae DS-SS
† ◖
Attractive shrubs flowering June-July.
– violacea *(Calceolaria violacea)* SS (E) †
◖
Small neat leaves. Pale violet flowers with
darker markings. AM 1930 AGM 1993

"JUDAS TREE" see *Cercis siliquastrum*

JUGLANS regia

JUGLANS – Juglandaceae LT ❦ "Walnuts"
*Often large, pinnate leaves. Generally fast
growing, all soils, but site where late frosts
unable to damage emerging foliage.*
– ailantifolia *(J. sieboldiana)* MT ❦
Large handsome leaves, up to 1m long.
– elaeopyren *(J. microcarpa var. major)* MT ❦
Vigorous, conical when young. Bold, pinnate
leaves turn clear yellow in autumn.
– microcarpa var. **major** see *J. elaeopyren*
– nigra LT ❦ "Black Walnut"
Deeply furrowed bark. Large leaves. Large
round fruits. AGM 1993
– regia LT ❦ "Common Walnut"
Slow growing, valuable timber tree. Clones
which will fruit at an early age are also
available. AGM 1993
– – 'Laciniata' MT ❦ "Cut-leaved Walnut"
Deeply cut leaflets. Pendulous branchlets. AM
1960

"JUNE BERRY" see *Amelanchier*

K

KALMIA – Ericaceae DS-MS ⚘ ◑
Conspicuous saucer-shaped flowers, spring-early summer. Moist soil for maximum flowering. Poisonous.
– angustifolia DS (E) ⚘ ◑
Spreading habit. Leaves in twos or threes. Rose-red flowers, June. We recommend the form:
– – 'Rubra' DS (E) ⚘ ◑
Deep green foliage. Rich rosy flowers over a long period.
– latifolia MS (E) ⚘ ◑ "Calico Bush"
Rhododendron-like shrub with shiny leaves. Clusters of bright pink flowers, June. AGM 1993

– – 'Clementine Churchill' MS (E) ⚘ ◑
Form with red flowers. AM 1952
– – 'Ostbo Red' MS (E) ⚘ ◑
Bright red buds open to pale pink. AGM 1993

KALOPANAX – Araliaceae ST ❀
Monotypic genus, with 5-7 lobed leaves, over 30cm across in young plants.
– pictus (*K. septemlobus*) (*Acanthopanax ricinifolius*) ST ❀
Branches and suckers bear stout prickles. Clusters of white flowers in flattish heads, autumn.

KALMIA latifolia

"KENTUCKY COFFEE TREE" see
Gymnocladus dioica

KERRIA – Rosaceae SS-MS ○
Monotypic genus. Suckering shrub with alternate leaves and yellow flowers, April-May. May be thinned and pruned after flowering.
– japonica MS ○
Green stems. Arching branches. Rich yellow, buttercup-like flowers.
– – 'Golden Guinea' MS ○
Large, single, golden flowers. AGM 1993
– – 'Pleniflora' ('Flore Pleno') MS ○
Double flowered form. Taller and more vigorous than type. AM 1978 AGM 1993

KERRIA japonica 'Pleniflora'

– – 'Variegata' ('Picta') SS ○
Spreading habit. Creamy-white variegated leaves. Flowers single.

KOELREUTERIA – Sapindaceae MT ☙
Long pinnate leaves. Large panicles of small yellow flowers, July-August. All soils.
– paniculata MT ☙ "Pride of India" "China-tree" "Golden rain-tree"
Flowers followed by bladder-like fruits. Leaves turn yellow, autumn. AM 1932 AGM 1993

KOLKWITZIA – Caprifoliaceae MS ○
Monotypic genus. Graceful, twiggy bush, with peeling brown stems. Delightful fox-glove-like flowers. D (h) 2 or 7
– amabilis MS ○ "Beauty Bush"
Drooping branches laden with soft pink, yellow-throated flowers, May-June. AM 1923. We recommend:
– – 'Pink Cloud' MS ○
Superb pink-flowered seedling.'Rosea' is a similar clone. FCC 1963 AGM 1993

KOELREUTERIA paniculata

KOLKWITZIA amabilis

L

+ LABURNOCYTISUS (*Laburnum + Cytisus*)
– Leguminosae ST ♥
Graft hybrid (chimera) with laburnum as the core, enclosed by broom.
– adamii ST ♥
Branches bear either yellow laburnum flowers or clusters of purple broom. Also intermediate coppery-pink flowers produced.

LABURNUM – Leguminosae ST ♥
"Golden Rain"
Yellow pea flowers in drooping racemes, late spring-early summer. All parts are poisonous. All soils; particularly good on dry chalk.
– × watereri ST ♥
Glossy leaves. Long slender racemes, June. We recommend the form:
– – 'Vossii' ST ♥
Free flowering, long racemes. Produces little seed. AGM 1993

"LABURNUM, EVERGREEN" see *Piptanthus laburnifolius*

"LAUREL, ALEXANDRIAN" see *Danae racemosa*

"LAUREL, COMMON" or **"CHERRY"** see *Prunus laurocerasus*

"LAUREL, PORTUGAL" *see Prunus lusitanica*

LAURUS – Lauraceae LS (E)
Small, yellow, dioecious flowers, April. Shiny black fruits on female trees. All well-drained soils.
– nobilis LS (E) ○ Hdg (0.5m) "Sweet Bay" "Bay Laurel"
Dense, pyramidal habit. Glossy dark green, wavy margined leaves – aromatic when crushed, used for flavouring. Excellent coastal hedge. AGM 1993
– – 'Aurea' LS (F) ◐
Golden-yellow leaves. AGM 1993

"LAURUSTINUS" see *Viburnum tinus*

LAVANDULA – Labiatae DS-SS (E) ○
"Lavender"
Aromatic shrubs. Excellent maritime plants,

LABURNUM × watereri 'Vossii'

good dwarf hedging. All well-drained soils. (j) 8 or (c) 3. *Spring pruning preferable.*
angustifolia (*L. spica*) SS (E) ○ "Old English Lavender"
Flowers on long stems in dense spikes. AMT 1962. Several clones are recommended:
– – 'Alba' SS (E) ○
Robust. Long, narrow grey-green leaves. White flowers, late July.
– – 'Grappenhall' SS (E) ○
Robust. Broad grey-green leaves. Lavender-blue flowers, late July.
– – 'Hidcote' SS (E) ○
Compact. Narrow, grey leaves. Violet flowers, early July. AM 1950 FCCT 1963 AGM 1993
– – 'Munstead' DS (E) ○
Compact. Narrow, green leaves. Lavender-blue flowers, early July. AMT 1963
– – 'Nana Alba' DS (E) ○
Compact. Broad, grey-green leaves. White flowers, early July.

– – **'Rosea'** SS (E) ○
Compact. Narrow, green leaves. Soft pink
flowers, early-mid July.
– – **'Twickel Purple'** DS (E) ○
Broad, grey-green leaves. Lavender-purple
flowers from early July. AMT 1961 AGM 1993
– – **'Vera'** SS (E) ○ "Dutch Lavender"
Robust. Broad, grey leaves. Lavender-blue
flowers, early July. AMT 1962 AGM 1993
– **lanata** DS (E) † ○
White-woolly leaves and stems. Fragrant,
bright violet flowers, July-September. AGM
1993
– **spica** see *L. angustifolia*
– **stoechas** DS (E) ○ "French Lavender"
Narrow leaves. Dark purple flowers in terminal
heads, summer. AM 1960 AGM 1993
– – var. **leucantha** DS (E) ○
A form with white flowers.
– – subsp. **pedunculata** "Butterfly Lavender"
"Papillon Lavender" DS (E) ○
Densely clustered flowers in long-stalked
heads. AM 1981 AGM 1993

LAVATERA – Malvaceae MS ○
*Palmate leaves. Hollyhock-like flowers. All
soils. Excellent for coastal sites.*
– **maritima** (*L. bicolor*) SS (E) † ○
White-woolly shoots and grey-hairy, rounded
leaves. Pale pink flowers blotched red, summer
to autumn.
– **thuringiaca** ○
Grey-downy subshrub producing abundant
large flowers over a long period during
summer and autumn. AM 1912. We
recommend:
– – **'Barnsley'** MS ○
Pale pink becoming white with a conspicuous
red eye. AM 1986 AGM 1993
– – **'Burgundy Wine'** MS ○
Deep purplish pink.
– – **'Candy Floss'** MS ○
Very pale pink.
– – **'Ice Cool'** SS ○
Pure white.
– – **'Pink Frills'** SS ○
Masses of deep pink, frilly-edged, semi-double
flowers.
– – **'Rosea'** (*L. olbia* 'Rosea') MS ○
Large, pale pink flowers. AM 1920 AGM 1993

"LAVENDER" see *Lavandula*

"LAVENDER, PAPILLON" see *Lavandula
stoechas* subsp. *pendunculata*

"LEMON PLANT" see *Aloysia triphylla*

LAVATERA thuringiaca 'Barnsley'

LEONOTIS – Labiatae SS † ○
*Small genus of herbs and shrubs. The
following need a warm wall in mild areas or a
conservatory.*
– **leonurus** SS † ○ "Lion's Ear"
Dense whorls of bright orange-scarlet flowers
5cm long in late autumn. AM 1982

LEPTOSPERMUM – Myrtaceae MS (E) ○
*Small leaves. Generally white flowers May-
June. Well drained neutral or acid soil.*
– **cunninghamii** see *L. lanigerum*
– **humifusum** (*L. scoparium* var. *prostratum*
hort.) PS (E) ○
Carpet of reddish stems and small leathery
leaves. Small flowers on older plants. Very
hardy. AGM 1993

LEPTOSPERMUM lanigerum

– **lanigerum** (*L. cunninghamii*) MS (E) ○
Long silvery leaves, bronzing towards autumn.
Hardier than most. AGM 1993
– – **'Silver Sheen'** MS (E) ○
A form with attractive silvery-grey foliage on
reddish stems. A very hardy form flowering
over a long period in summer.
– **scoparium** MS (E) † ○ "Manuka" "Tea-
tree"
Flowers single, white. AM 1972
This species has given rise to many forms, the
best of which are the following:
– – **'Keatleyi'** MS (E) † ○
Young shoots and leaves, silky crimson. Large,
soft pink flowers. AM 1961 AGM 1993
– – **'Kiwi'** DS (E) † ○
Deep pink flowers and bronze foliage. Dense
habit. AGM 1993
– – **'Nichollsii'** MS (E) † ○
Dark purplish-bronze foliage. Large carmine
red flowers. AGM 1993

LESPEDEZA thunbergii

LEPTOSPERMUM scoparium 'Nichollsii'

– – var. **prostratum** see *L. humifusum*
– – **'Red Damask'** MS (F) † ○
Deep red, double, persistent flowers. AM
1955 AGM 1993

LESPEDEZA – Leguminosae SS ○ "Bush
Clover"
*Trifoliolate leaves. Abundant racemes of pea-
flowers, late summer.*
– **thunbergii** (*L. sieboldii*) (*Desmodium
penduliflorum*) SS ◑
Arching stems. Huge panicles of rose-purple
flowers, September. FCC 1871 FCC 1987
AGM 1993

LEUCOTHOE – Ericaceae SS ∠
*Attractive summer-flowering shrubs. Some
members evergreen.*
– **fontanesiana** SS (E) ∠ GC
Arching stems. Leathery leaves, tinged red or

bronze-purple in winter. Pendant, white
pitcher flowers, May. AM 1972 AGM 1993.
We recommend:
– – **'Rainbow'** ('Multicolor') SS (E) ∠ GC
Leaves variegated yellow, pink and cream.
– – **'Rollissonii'** SS (F) ∠ GC
A selection with narrow leaves. AM 1981
AGM 1993

LEYCESTERIA formosa

– – **'Scarletta'** SS (E) ✗ GC
Arching stems bear bright, glossy green leaves turning deep red-purple in winter.

LEYCESTERIA – Caprifoliaceae MS ○
Hollow-stemmed shrubs. All fertile soils.
– **formosa** MS ○ "Flowering Nutmeg"
"Pheasant Berry"
White flowers in drooping panicles of claret-red bracts, June-September. Shiny, reddish-purple berries. B3

LIGUSTRUM – Oleaceae DS-ST ♥ "Privets"
Evergreen or semi-evergreen, for all soils.
Generally white flowers. Fast growing.
Poisonous.
– **chenaultii** LS Semi-(E)
Narrow, lance-shaped leaves. Flowers in large panicles, late summer.
– **japonicum** LS (E) "Japanese Privet"
Shiny, olive-green, camellia-like foliage. Large panicles of flowers, late summer. Excellent for screening. AGM 1984

LIGUSTRUM lucidum 'Excelsum Superbum'

– – **'Aureum'** MS ○ "Golden Privet"
Rich yellow leaves, generally green centred.
AM 1977 AGM 1993
– **quihoui** MS
Large flower panicles, August-September. Elegant habit. AM 1980 AGM 1993
– **vulgare** MS Hdg (0.5m) "Common Privet"
Conspicuous shiny black fruits in long clusters, autumn.

"LILAC" see *Syringa*

"LIME" see *Tilia*

LINDERA – Lauraceae MS ✗ ◑
Aromatic shrubs. Small unisexual flowers.
Attractive leaves.

LIGUSTRUM japonicum

– – **'Rotundifolium'** ('Coriaceum') DS (E)
Round, leathery, black-green leaves. Compact habit. Slow.
– **lucidum** ST (E) ♥
Shiny, long-pointed, large leaves. Large panicles of flowers, autumn. AM 1965 AGM 1993. We recommend:
– – **'Latifolium'** ST (E) ♦
Large, broad and glossy leaves.
– – **'Excelsum Superbum'** ST (E) ♥
Leaves variegated creamy-white and deep yellow. AGM 1993
– **ovalifolium** LS (E) Hdg (0.5m) "Oval-leaf Privet"
Commonly grown species. Useful for hedging. Loses leaves in cold areas.

LINDERA benzoin

– **benzoin** (*Benzoin aestivale*) MS ✗ ◐ "Spice Bush"
Leaves turn clear yellow, autumn. Yellowish green flowers. Red berries on female plants.
– **obtusiloba** MS ✗ ◐
Large ovate or obovate leaves, butter-yellow with rich pink tints in autumn. Mustard-yellow flowers, early spring. AM 1952 AGM 1993

"LING" see *Calluna*

"LION'S EAR" see *Leonotis leonurus*

LIPPIA citriodora see *Aloysia triphylla*

LIQUIDAMBAR – Hamamelidaceae ST-LT ♥ ✗
Generally 5-lobed, maple-like leaves, colouring richly in autumn. Insignificant flowers. Prefer moist, well drained soil. Not for shallow chalk.
– **formosana** ST ♥ ✗
Leaves tinted red in spring and again in autumn. We recommend:
– – **Monticola** group ST ♥ ✗
Very hardy form with large 3-lobed leaves, colouring well in autumn. AM 1958
– **styraciflua** LT ♥ ✗ "Sweet Gum"
Handsome tree. Glossy, maple-like leaves turn shades of crimson and purple in autumn.
– – **'Lane Roberts'** LT ♥ ✗
Reliable rich black crimson-red autumn leaf colour. AGM 1993

LIQUIDAMBAR styraciflua 'Lane Roberts'

– – **'Moonbeam'** MT ♥
Pale, creamy-yellow leaves turn red, yellow and purple in autumn.
– – **'Silver King'** ST ♦
Leaves margined with creamy-white, flushed with pink in late summer and autumn.
– – **'Variegata'** MT ♥ ✗
Leaves striped and mottled with yellow.
– – **'Worplesdon'** LT ♥
Leaves with long, narrow lobes, turning orange and yellow in autumn. AM 1987 AGM 1993

LIRIODENDRON – Magnoliaceae MT-LT ♥ "Tulip Tree"
Fast-growing trees for all fertile soils – including chalk. Distinctive lobed leaves turn clear yellow, in autumn.
– **tulipifera** LT ♥ "Tulip Tree"
Tulip-shaped flowers, yellowish-green with orange internal markings, June-July – not on young trees. AM 1970 AGM 1993

LIRIODENDRON tulipifera

– – **'Aureomarginatum'** MT ♥
Leaves margined yellow or greenish-yellow. AM 1974 AGM 1993
– – **'Fastigiatum'** ('Pyramidale') MT ♦
Columnar form, ideal for limited spaces. AGM 1993

LITHOCARPUS – Fagaceae ST (E) ♥ ✗
Evergreen trees related to Quercus.
– **henryi** (*Quercus henryi*) ST (E) ♥ ✗
Very long, lanceolate, slender pointed leaves. Slow. A remarkable hardy tree.

LITHODORA – Boraginaceae DS ○
Low-growing, blue-flowered plants. Ideal for rock garden.
– **diffusa** (*Lithospermum diffusum*) PS (E) ✗ ○
Forms a large mat, smothered in flowers, late spring-early summer. Not for shallow chalk. We recommend:

LIRIODENDRON tulipifera 'Fastigiatum'

– – **'Heavenly Blue'** PS (E) ✗ ○
Delightful blue flowers. AM 1909

LITHOSPERMUM diffusum see *Lithodora diffusa*

"LOBSTER'S CLAW" see *Clianthus puniceus*

LOMATIA – Proteaceae SS-LS (E) ✗ ◑
Attractive flower and foliage shrubs, excellent for floral art. Not for shallow chalk.
– **ferruginea** LS (E) † ✗ ◑
Large, deep green, fern-like leaves. Rust coloured velvety stems. Buff and scarlet flowers. AM 1927
– **myricoides** (*L. longifolia*) MS (E) ✗ ◑
Long, narrow, toothed leaves. Fragrant white flowers, July. AM 1955
– **silaifolia** SS (E) ✗ ◑
Finely divided leaves. Large panicles of creamy-white flowers, July.

"LOMBARDY POPLAR" see *Populus nigra* 'Italica'

LOMATIA myricoides

LONICERA nitida 'Baggesen's Gold'

"LONDON PLANE" see *Platanus* × *hispanica*

LONICERA – Caprifoliaceae DS-MS
Shrubby honeysuckles. Flowers in pairs, followed by completely or partially fused berries. All soils. For climbing species see CLIMBERS.
– **nitida** MS (E) Hdg (0.25m)
Dense habit. Small leaves. Useful for hedging. We recommend the clones:

– – **'Baggesen's Gold'** MS (E)
Yellow leaves, turning yellow-green in
autumn. AGM 1993
– – **'Ernest Wilson'** MS (E) Hdg (0.25m)
Arching branches. Tiny ovate leaves. This is
the form commonly used for hedging. AM
1911
– **pileata** DS Semi-(E) GC
Small, bright green leaves. Clusters of
translucent violet berries. AM 1910

LONICERA pileata

– × **purpusii** MS Semi-(E)
Vigorous. Cream-coloured, fragrant flowers,
winter. AM 1971. A (g) 3 or 7. We
recommend:
– – **'Winter Beauty'** MS Semi-(E)
Free flowering over a long period. AM 1992
AGM 1993. A (g) 3 or 7
– **pyrenaica** SS ○
Small sea-green leaves. Cream and pink

LONICERA × purpusii 'Winter Beauty'

funnel-shaped nodding flowers. May-June.
Orange-red berries. AM 1928. A (g) 3 or 7
– **setifera** MS
Bristly stems. Clusters of fragrant, tubular pink
and white flowers on bare stems, winter-early
spring. AM 1980. A (g) 3 or 7
– **syringantha** SS
Small leaves. Fragrant, tubular, soft lilac
flowers, May-June. A (g) 3 or 7

"LOQUAT" see *Eriobotrya japonica*

LUCULIA – Rubiaceae MS † ○
*Delightful shrubs for conservatory or mildest
gardens.*
– **gratissima** MS Semi-(E) † ○
Fragrant almond-pink flowers, winter. AM
1938 AGM 1993

LUPINUS – Leguminosae MS ○
Shrubby lupins.
– **arboreus** MS (E) ○ "Yellow Tree Lupin"
Scented, normally yellow flowers in dense
racemes, throughout summer. Fast growth.
AGM 1993

LYONOTHAMNUS – Rosaceae ST (E) ❦ † ✓
Monotypic genus.
– **floribundus** subsp. **aspleniifolius** ST (E) ❦ †
✓
Chestnut brown and grey shreddy bark.
Glossy, green, fern-like leaves, grey, hairy
beneath. Slender spiraea-like panicles of
creamy-white flowers, early summer.

M

MAACKIA – Leguminosae ST ♥
Slow-growing trees related to Cladrastis.
– amurensis (*Cladrastis amurensis*) ST♥
Pinnate leaves, white flowers tinged pale
slate-blue, in upright racemes, July-August.

"MADRONA" see *Arbutus menziesii*

MAGNOLIA – Magnoliaceae MS-LT
*Variety of forms, some evergreens. Include
magnificent flowering varieties. Require good
drainage, plenty of moisture. Very tolerant of
heavy clay and atmospheric pollution. Shelter
early-flowering kinds from cold winds and
spring frosts. Flowers of deciduous species
produced before leaves, unless stated
otherwise.*

MAGNOLIA campbellii

– acuminata LT ♥ "CucumberTree"
Vigorous. Greenish, metallic blue and yellow
flowers with leaves, May-June. Cucumber-like
fruit clusters.
– – var. subcordata (*M. cordata*) ST ♥
Soft canary-yellow flowers produced in
summer with leaves, and again autumn.
– 'Betty' MS ✗ ○
Large flowers 20cm across, purplish-red
outside, white within. AGM 1993
– campbellii LT ♥ ✗ "Pink Tulip Tree"
Large goblet-shaped flowers opening like

water lilies, February-March. Deep rose-pink
petals outside, paler within. Flowers not
produced until approximately twenty years
old. Colour variation from white to deep rose-
purple. FCC 1903
– – Alba group LT ♦ ✗
White flowers. Vegetatively propagated.
– – 'Charles Raffill' LT ♥ ✗
Vigorous. Large flowers, deep rose in bud
opening rose-purple outside, white flushed
marginally, pinkish-purple within. AM 1963
FCC 1966 AGM 1993
– – 'Darjeeling' LT ♥ ✗
Dark rose-coloured flowers.
– – 'Ethel Hillier' MT ♥ ✗
Vigorous. Very large white flowers, tinged
pink at the base on outside.
– – 'Kew's Surprise' LT ♥ ✗
Large rich pink flowers. FCC 1967
– – 'Lanarth' MT ♥ ✗
Very large "water-lily" flowers, cyclamen-
purple with darker stamens. FCC 1947
– – subsp. mollicomata (*M. mollicomata*) MT
♥ ✗
Very large pink to rose-purple "water-lily"
flowers, produced at ten to fifteen years of
age. FCC 1939
– cordata see *M. acuminata* var. *subcordata*
– cylindrica LS ✗ ○
Elegant white cup-shaped flowers, April.
Cylindrical fruits. AM 1963 AGM 1993
– dawsoniana MT ♥ ✗
Long leathery leaves, glaucous beneath. Large
pale-rose flowers, suffused purple outside,
spring – on mature trees. AM 1939
– delavayi LS (E) † ○
Huge sea-green leaves, glaucous beneath.
Slightly fragrant, creamy-white flowers up to
20cm across, late summer-early autumn. Best
against a wall. FCC 1913
– denudata (*M. conspicua*) LS ✗ ○ "Yulan"
"Lily Tree"
Pure white, cup-shaped fragrant flowers with
thick fleshy petals, early spring. FCC 1968
AGM 1993
– 'Elizabeth' ST ♦ ✗
Fragrant, pale primrose-yellow flowers open
before the leaves in spring. AGM 1993
– 'Galaxy' MT ♦ ✗
Large flowers before the leaves, white inside,

MAGNOLIA grandiflora 'Exmouth'

MAGNOLIA 'Heaven Scent'

MAGNOLIA liliiflora 'Nigra'

richly streaked deep carmine-pink outside.
– grandiflora LS (E) ○
Leathery, glossy leaves, often rust coloured
beneath. Huge, fragrant creamy-white flowers
up to 25cm across, summer-autumn. Excellent
wall shrub. We recommend the forms:
– – 'Exmouth' LS (E) ○
Very large flowers at an early age. AGM 1993
– – 'Little Gem' LS (E) ○
Narrow, upright habit with smaller leaves and
flowers.
– – 'St Mary' LS (E) ○
Flowers freely when young. Leaves wavy-
edged and brown-felted beneath.
– – 'Samuel Sommer' LS (E) ○
A very hardy form with huge flowers borne
from an early age.
– 'Heaven Scent' MT ♀ ✗
Large white, goblet-shaped flowers, streaked
rose-purple on outside, spring. AGM 1993
– hypoleuca MT ♀ ✗
Very large obovate leaves. Fragrant, creamy-
white flowers with central ring of red
stamens, June. Attractive large fruit clusters.
FCC 1893 AGM 1993
– 'Iolanthe' ST ♀ ✗
Large, cup-shaped flowers, deep rose-pink
outside, creamy-white within borne from an
early age. AGM 1993
– 'Jane' MS ✗
Fragrant, cup-shaped flowers red-purple
outside, white within Compact, upright

habit. AGM 1993
– 'Kewensis' ST ♠
Slender habit. White flowers 6cm long, April.
AM 1952
– liliiflora MS ✗ ○
Wide spreading habit. Slender tulip-like
flowers, creamy-white inside, flushed purple
outside, late April-June and recurrently
summer. We recommend:
– – 'Nigra' (*M.* × *soulangeana* 'Nigra') MS ✗
○
More compact. Dark vinous-purple flowers,
creamy-white stained purple within over a
long period during spring and summer. AM
1907 FCC 1981 AGM 1993
– × loebneri 'Leonard Messel' LS ○
Lilac-pink flowers, deeper in bud, strap-like
petals. AM 1955 FCC 1969 AGM 1993
– – 'Merrill' LS ○
Large white, fragrant flowers, freely borne.
FCC 1979 AGM 1993

– **macrophylla** ST ♥ ✓
Enormous leaves sometimes exceeding 0.6m length. Very large, ivory-coloured, fragrant flowers with central purple blotch, early summer. FCC 1900

– **'Peppermint Stick'** MT ♥ ✓
Upright habit. White, narrowly goblet-shaped flowers, flushed pale purple at base. AGM 1993

– **salicifolia** ST ♦ ✓
Narrow willow-like leaves. Fragrant, white, narrow-petalled flowers, April. Leaves, bark and wood lemon-scented when bruised. AM 1927 FCC 1962 AGM 1993

– **sargentiana** MT ♥ ✓
Leathery leaves. Huge, rose-pink, water-lily-like flowers, paler pink inside produced April-May on mature specimens. FCC 1935. We recommend:

– – var. **robusta** MT ♥ ✓
Longer narrower leaves. Rose-crimson flowers, paler inside. Larger fruits. FCC 1947

– **'Sayonara'** ST ♥ ✓
Superb large white globular flowers. AM 1990 AGM 1993

– **sieboldii** LS ✓ ○
Wide-spreading. Fragrant, cup-shaped, pendent flowers, white with crimson stamens, produced with leaves intermittently May-August. Spectacular crimson fruit clusters. FCC 1894 AGM 1993

– **sinensis** LS ○
Lemon-scented, white nodding flowers, with central red staminal cone, produced with leaves, June. AM 1927 FCC 1931 AGM 1993

– × **soulangeana** LS ✓ ○
Wide spreading. Large tulip-shaped white flowers stained rose-purple at the base, April-early May before the leaves. Flowers when young. Not for shallow chalk. AGM 1993

– – **'Alba Superba'** LS ✓ ○
Fragrant white flowers.

– – **'Brozzonii'** LS ✓ ○
Superb large white, elongated flowers, purple at the base. FCC 1929 AGM 1993

– – **'Lennei'** (*M.* × *lennei*) LS ✓ ○
Vigorous, spreading. Huge goblet-shaped rose-purple flowers, creamy-white stained soft purple inside, April-May and sometimes autumn. FCC 1863 AGM 1993

– – **'Lennei Alba'** LS ✓ ○
Globular ivory-white flowers. AGM 1993

MAGNOLIA × soulangeana 'Lennei'

MAGNOLIA sieboldii

MAGNOLIA × soulangeana 'Rustica Rubra'

– – **'Nigra'** see *M. liliiflora* 'Nigra'
– – **'Picture'** LS ✕ ○
Large leaves. Vinous-purple flowers, white inside. Vigorous, erect habit. AM 1969
– – **'Rustica Rubra'** ('Rubra') LS ✕ ○
Vigorous. Rich rosy-red cup-shaped flowers. AM 1960 AGM 1984
– **sprengeri** MT ❦ ✕
Goblet-shaped, fragrant, rose-carmine flowers, April. We recommend:
– – **'Eric Savill'** MT ❦ ✕
Large, rich deep pink flowers.
– **stellata** MS ○
Slow. Compact, rounded habit. Fragrant, white flowers with strap-like petals, March-April. FCC 1878 AGM 1993. We recommend:
– – **'Water Lily'** MS ○
Larger flowers with more petals. AGM 1993
– **'Susan'** LS ✕ ○
Erect habit. Flowers deep purple in bud, opening white, stained purple, April-June. AGM 1993
– ✕ **thompsoniana** LS ○
Wide spreading. Large, fragrant, parchment-coloured flowers, intermittently through summer even on young plants. AM 1958

MAGNOLIA stellata 'Water Lily'

MAHONIA aquifolium

– ✕ **veitchii** MT ❦ ✕
Very vigorous. Goblet-shaped flowers. The following is a selection from the original cross.
– – **'Peter Veitch'** MT ❦ ✕
White flowers, flushed purple-pink, April. FCC 1921
– **'Wada's Memory'** ST ❦
Abundant, fragrant, white flowers. FCC 1986 AGM 1993
– **wilsonii** (*M. nicholsoniana*) LS ◑
Wide spreading. Pendulous saucer-shaped flowers, white, with crimson stamens, May-June. AM 1932 FCC 1971 AGM 1993

✕ **MAHOBERBERIS** (*Mahonia* ✕ *Berberis*) – **Berberidaceae** SS (E)
Hybrids of distinct appearance, suitable for any soil.
– **'Magic'** SS (E)
Upright habit with glossy, dark-green, spiny leaves. Clusters of yellow flowers in spring.

MAHONIA – **Berberidaceae** DS-MS (E)
Attractive pinnate leaves. Racemes of yellow flowers, winter or spring. Generally, blue-black berries. Most well drained soils, including chalk.
– **aquifolium** SS (E) "Oregon Grape"
Glossy green leaves, sometimes red in winter. Terminal clusters of rich yellow flowers, early spring. Decorative berries.
– – **'Apollo'** DS (E) GC
Large clusters of bright yellow flowers, dark green leaves. Low, spreading habit. AGM 1993

MAHONIA ✕ media 'Charity'

– – **'Atropurpurea'** SS (E)
Rich red-purple leaves, winter-early spring.
– – **'Moseri'** SS (E)
Bronze-red young leaves turn through apple-green to dark green.
– **'Buckland'** see *M. × media* 'Buckland'
– **'Charity'** see *M. × media* 'Charity'
– **fremontii** SS (E) ○
Blue-green leaves with small spiny leaflets. Small flower clusters, May-June. Inflated yellowish or red berries.
– **japonica** MS (E)
Magnificent deep-green leaves. Fragrant, lemon-yellow flowers in long pendulous or lax terminal racemes, late autumn-early spring. AM 1916 AGM 1993
– **'Lionel Fortescue'** see *M. × media* 'Lionel Fortescue'
– × **media** MS (E)
Group of hybrids providing some of the best shrubs for late autumn and early winter flowers. We recommend:
– – **'Buckland'** MS (E)
Long leaves, composed of paired leaflets. Long, lax flower racemes. AM 1992 AGM 1993
– – **'Charity'** MS (E)
Upright. Long spreading and ascending terminal racemes of fragrant flowers, autumn-early winter. AM 1959 FCC 1962 AGM 1993
– – **'Lionel Fortescue'** MS (E)
Bright yellow, fragrant flowers in erect racemes in late autumn and early winter. AM 1975 FCC 1992 AGM 1993
– – **'Underway'** MS (E)
Compact with upright racemes of bright yellow flowers. AM 1992
– – **'Winter Sun'** MS (E)
Erect, dense racemes of fragrant, yellow flowers. AGM 1993
– **'Moseri'** see *M. aquifolium* 'Moseri'

MALUS floribunda

– **nervosa** DS ○
Suckering. Lustrous leaves, often reddening in winter. Flower, May-June. Not good on chalk.
– **pinnata** see *M. × wagneri* 'Pinnacle'
– **trifolioliata** MS (E) ○
Leaves of three spiny, heavily veined leaflets. Flower clusters, spring. Redcurrant-like berries. Best against a sunny wall. We recommend the form:
– – var. **glauca** MS (E) ○
Leaflets conspicuously glaucous above.
– **'Undulata'** see *M. × wagneri* 'Undulata'
– × **wagneri** SS (E)
Hybrids of which we recommend:
– – **'Pinnacle'** (*M. pinnata* hort.) MS (E)
Bright green leaves bronze when young. Large clusters of bright yellow flowers. AGM 1993
– – **'Undulata'** MS (E)
Lustrous, dark green leaves, leaflets having undulate margins. Deep yellow flowers, spring. AM 1971 AGM 1993
– **'Winter Sun'** see *M. × media* 'Winter Sun'

"MAIDENHAIR TREE" see *Ginkgo biloba* under CONIFERS

MALUS – Rosaceae ST-MT ❦ "Flowering Crabs"
Attractive April-May flowering trees. Many have attractive fruits in autumn, some persisting late into winter. For all fertile soils.
– **'American Beauty'** ST ❦
Double, deep red flowers. Bronze-red young foliage turns to bronze-green.
– **coronaria** ST ❦
Strong growing. Large shell-pink, fragrant flowers, late May. Often richly coloured leaves, autumn. We recommend the form :
– – **'Charlottae'** ('Flore Pleno') ST ❦
Large-lobed leaves, colouring in autumn. Large semi-double flowers, violet scented.
– **'Crittenden'** ST ❦
Attractive pale pink flowers. Heavy crops of edible, bright scarlet, persistent fruits. AM 1961 FCC 1971
– **'Evereste'** ST ❦
White flowers open from red buds. Fruits 2.5cm across, orange to orange-yellow. AGM 1993
– **floribunda** ST ❦ "Japanese Crab"
Long arching branches. Crimson flower buds opening white or blush. Small yellow and red fruits. AGM 1993
– **'Golden Hornet'** ST ❦
White flowers. Abundant bright yellow persistent fruits. AM 1949 FCC 1961 AGM 1993

MALUS 'Golden Hornet'

MALUS hupehensis

– **hupehensis** (*M. theifera*) ST ♥
Stiff, ascending branches. Abundant, fragrant, white flowers, soft pink in bud. May-June. Yellow fruits, red tinged. AM 1928 AGM 1993
– **'John Downie'** ST ♥
White flowers. Large, conical, edible fruits bright orange and red. AM 1895 AGM 1993
– **'Katherine'** ST ♥
Dense globular head. Semi-double, pink flowers, fading white. Bright red fruits, flushed yellow. AM 1967 AGM 1993
– **'Pink Perfection'** ST ◑
Large fragrant pink flowers from red buds. Upright habit.
– **'Prince George's'** ST ♥
Light pink, fully double, fragrant flowers, late.
– **'Red Jade'** ST ♠
Weeping branches. Pink and white flowers. Persistent red fruits.

MALUS × robusta 'Red Siberian'

– **'Red Profusion'** ST
Purple leaves and red fruits. Very resistant to scab and mildew.
– **'Red Sentinel'** ST ♥
White flowers. Large clusters of persistent deep red fruits. AM 1959 AGM 1993
– × **robusta** MT ♥
White or pinkish flowers. Cherry-like red or yellow persistent fruits. AM 1957. We recommend:
– – **'Red Siberian'** MT ♥
Red fruits. AGM 1993
– – **'Yellow Siberian'** MT ♥
Yellow fruits. AGM 1993
– **'Royal Beauty'** ST ♠
Slender, hanging shoots bear red-purple leaves. Flowers deep red-purple followed by dark red fruits.
– **'Royalty'** ST ♥
Reddish-purple leaves. Crimson flowers. Dark red fruits.
– **'Rudolph'** ST ♥
Rose-red flowers open from deeper buds. Fruits oblong, orange-yellow and long lasting. Young foliage bronze-red.

MALUS × robusta 'Red Siberian'

– **'Snowcloud'** ST ♥
Large, semi-double white flowers from pale pink buds. Young foliage bronze.
– **theifera** see *M. hupehensis*
– **toringoides** ST ♥
Profuse, creamy-white flowers and small, red and yellow fruits. Deeply lobed leaves colour in autumn. AM 1919
– **transitoria** ST ♥
Slender habit. Creamy-white flowers. Small, rounded yellow fruits. Good autumn leaf colour. AGM 1993

MALUS transitoria

MALUS tschonoskii

– **trilobata** MT ♥
Distinctive erect habit. Maple-like, 3-lobed leaves, tinted in autumn. White flowers. Yellowish fruits, seldom produced.
– **tschonoskii** MT ♦
Erect conical habit. Excellent autumn leaf colour. White flowers, tinged pink. Yellow-green, round fruits, tinged reddish-purple. AM 1962 FCC 1983 AGM 1993
– **'Van Eseltine'** ST ♦
Stiffly erect branches. Semi-double, shell pink flowers white within, rose-scarlet in bud. Yellow fruits.
– **yunnanensis** MT ♥
Ovate, occasionally lobed leaves, colouring well in autumn. White flowers. Deep red fruits. We recommend the form:
– – var. **veitchii** MT ♥
Erect branches. Cordate, lobed leaves. Bright-red fruits. AM 1912

"MANUKA" see *Leptospermum scoparium*

"MAPLE" see *Acer*

"MAY" see *Crataegus monogyna*

MAYTENUS – Celastraceae LS (E) ○
For all well drained soils.
– **boaria** LS (E) ○
Graceful, slender branches. Glossy, narrow finely toothed leaves. Profuse, tiny green flowers in spring.

MAYTENUS boaria

"MEDLAR" see *Mespilus germanica*

MELIANTHUS – Melianthaceae SS (E) † ○
Sub-shrubs, suitable only for very mild areas.
Attractive foliage, unusual flowers.
– **major** SS (E) † ○
Spreading, hollow stems. Deeply serrated,
glaucous, pinnate leaves. Tawny-crimson
tubular flowers in erect terminal racemes,
summer. FCC 1975 AGM 1993

MELIOSMA – Sabiaceae ST ♥
Attractive leaves. White, spiraea-like,
paniculate inflorescences. Prefers deep neutral
soil, although lime tolerant.
– **veitchiorum** ST ♥
Stout branches, large pinnate leaves and
prominent winter buds. Panicles of fragrant
creamy flowers, May. Violet fruits.

MENZIESIA – Ericaceae SS ✗ ◑
Waxy flowers in terminal clusters. Best sited
where protected from late frosts.
– **ciliicalyx** SS ✗ ◑
Hairy leaves. Nodding pitcher-shaped flowers
in clusters, May – colour varies cream to soft
purple. AM 1938. We recommend:
– – var. **purpurea** SS ✗ ◑
Spiny-tipped leaves. Larger flowers of rose-
purple, May-June. Slow.

MENZIESIA ciliicalyx

MESPILUS – Rosaceae ST ♥
A monotypic genus related to Crataegus.
– – **germanica** ST ♥ "Medlar"
Large, hairy leaves, warm russet in autumn.
Large, white flowers, May-June. Brown, edible
fruits. Low spreading habit. We recommend
the clone 'Nottingham'.

"MESPILUS, SNOWY" see *Amelanchier*

"MEXICAN ORANGE BLOSSOM" see
Choisya ternata

"MEYER'S LEMON" see *Citrus* 'Meyer's
Lemon'

MICHELIA – Magnoliaceae LS-ST (E) † ✗
Glossy, dark-green leathery leaves. Flowers
borne in leaf axils.
– **doltsopa** ST Semi-(E) ♥ † ✗
Heavily scented flowers, white and
multipetalled, formed in autumn, opening
spring. AM 1961

MIMULUS – Scrophulariaceae SS (E) † ○
Suitable for sheltered sunny positions. Lime
tolerant.
– **aurantiacus** (*M. glutinosus*) SS (E) † ○
"Shrubby Musk"
Sticky stems. Orange or salmon-yellow
flowers, throughout summer-autumn. AM
1938
– – var. **puniceus** (*M. puniceus*) SS (E) † ○
Small brick red or orange-red flowers.

MITRARIA – Gesneriaceae DS (E) † ◑
Monotypic genus.
– **coccinea** DS (E) † ◑
Spreading habit. Small, glossy leaves. Bright
flame-coloured tubular flowers, late spring-
summer. Not for shallow chalk. AM 1927

"MOCK ORANGE" see *Philadelphus*

"MONKEY PUZZLE" see *Araucaria*
araucana under CONIFERS

MORUS – Moraceae ST ♥ "The Mulberries"
Any well drained soil. Ideal for town or
maritime gardens.
– **alba** ST ♥ "White Mulberry"
Heart-shaped leaves. Sweet, edible fruits,
whitish turning reddish-pink. Silk worms are
fed on the leaves.
– – **'Pendula'** ST ♠
Dense weeping branches hang
perpendicularly, like a curtain. AM 1897

– nigra ST ♀ "Black Mulberry"
Architectural tree, becoming gnarled with
age. Heart-shaped rough leaves, downy
beneath. Edible, purplish-red fruits. AGM
1993

"MRS ROBB'S BONNET" see *Euphorbia
amygdaloides* var. *robbiae*

"MOUNTAIN ASH" see *Sorbus aucuparia*

MUEHLENBECKIA – Polygonaceae GC
*Slender-stemmed creepers or climbers with
tiny flowers. Useful ground cover, or over tree
stumps, etc.*
– – axillaris GC
Prostrate, forming dense carpets of
intertwining, thread-like stems. Small,
rounded leaves.

"MULBERRY" see *Morus*

"MULBERRY, PAPER" see *Broussonetia
papyrifera*

MYRICA – Myricaceae SS-LS ⚥ ◑
Aromatic shrubs. Unisexual flowers.
– gale SS ⚥ ◑ "Sweet Gale" "Bog Myrtle"
Dense habit. Golden-brown male and female
catkins, April-May on separate plants.
Tolerates acid, boggy swamp.

"MYROBALAN" see *Prunus cerasifera*

"MYRTLE" see *Myrtus*

MYRTUS – Myrtaceae PS-ST (E) "Myrtles"
*Aromatic, generally white flowered, shrubs.
Any well drained soil. Excellent for coastal
planting.*
– apiculata see *M. luma*
– communis LS (E) ○ "Common Myrtle"
Aromatic, densely leafy. Profuse flowers, July-
August. Purplish-black berries. AM 1972
– – 'Flore Pleno' LS (E) ○
Double flowers.
– – subsp. tarentina ('Jenny Reitenbach') MS
(E) ○

MYRTUS communis

Compact. Narrow leaves. Abundant flowers,
white berries. AM 1977 AGM 1993
– – 'Variegata' MS (E) ○
Leaves variegated creamy-white.
– luma (*M. apiculata*) ST (E) ♀ †
Attractive, peeling, cinnamon outer bark,
reveals young cream surface beneath.
Flowers, late summer-early autumn. Edible,
sweet red and black fruits. AGM 1993
– – 'Glanleam Gold' LS (E) †
Leaves margined with creamy-yellow, tinged
pink when young.

N

NANDINA – Berberidaceae SS (E) ○
Monotypic genus. Any well drained soil, sheltered position.
– domestica SS (E) ○ "Sacred Bamboo"
Large, compound, green leaves, tinged red, spring and autumn. Small white flowers in large terminal panicles, summer. AM 1897 AGM 1993
– – 'Nana Purpurea' SS (E) ○
Compact habit. Young foliage red-purple throughout season.

NEILLIA – Rosaceae MS
Easy cultivation. For all but very dry soils.
–thibetica *(N. longiracemosa)* MS
Erect, downy stems. Slender-pointed, often 3-lobed leaves. Pink, tubular flowers in terminal racemes, May-June. AM 1931

NANDINA domestica

"NORWAY MAPLE" *see Acer platanoides*

NOTHOFAGUS – Fagaceae MT-LT ⤢
"Southern Beech"
Ornamental, generally fast-growing trees, some evergreen. Small leaves. Like deep, moist, well drained soil – not shallow chalk. Poor wind resisters.
– antarctica MT ⚐ "Antarctic Beech"
Dark-green, glossy, rounded and heart-shaped, serrated leaves, turning yellow in autumn.
– betuloides MT (E) ⚐
Densely leafy. Dark-green, glossy, serrated leaves, ovate or rounded.
– dombeyi MT (E) ⚐
Vigorous. Shiny, dark-green, doubly-toothed leaves. May shed leaves in cold winters.
– nervosa *(N. procera)* LT ⚐
Fast growing. Comparatively large leaves, prominent venation. Generally rich autumn colour.

NEILLIA thibetica

"NEW ZEALAND FLAX" *see Phormium tenax*

– **obliqua** LT ♀ "Roblé Beech"
Elegant and fast growing, branches often
droop gracefully at tips. Leaves larger than
most, uneven at base.

– **procera** see *N. nervosa*

– **solanderi** MT (E) ♀ "Black Beech"
Slender habit. Ascending fan-like branches.
Tiny leaves arranged neatly on wiry
branchlets.

NYSSA – Nyssaceae MT ✓

Noted for fine autumn leaf colour.
Insignificant flowers and fruit. Require moist
soil. Best planted young, as resent
disturbance.

– **sinensis** ST ♀ ✓ ○
Young growths red throughout season.
Leaves turn glorious shades of red, autumn.
FCC 1976 AGM 1993

– **sylvatica** MT ♀ ✓ "Tupelo"
Slow growing, glossy, dark-green leaves turn
rich shades of red, yellow and orange,
autumn. AM 1951 FCC 1968 AGM 1993

– – **'Jermyns Flame'** MT ♀ ✓
Large-leaved selection colouring brilliantly in
autumn.

NOTHOFAGUS obliqua

O

"OAK" see *Quercus*

OLEARIA – Compositae SS-LS (E) ○ "Daisy Bushes" "Tree Daisies"
Daisy-like flower-heads, generally white or cream. Easy growing shrubs for all well drained soils. Excellent on chalk. Wind resistant and tolerant of salt and atmospheric pollution. A (b) 4
– × **haastii** MS (E) ○ Hdg (0.5m)
Rounded habit. Small leaves, white-felted beneath. Abundant, fragrant flower-heads, July-August. Good for hedging. FCC 1873

OLEARIA × haastii

OLEARIA macrodonta

– **'Henry Travers'** (*O. semidentata* hort.) MS (E) † ○
Grey-green leaves, silvery beneath. Large, hanging, aster-like flower-heads, lilac with purple centres, June. AM 1916 AGM 1993
– **macrodonta** MS (E) Hdg (0.5m) "New Zealand Holly"
Strong growing. Sage-green, holly-like leaves, silvery beneath. Fragrant flower-heads, June. "Musky" odour. Excellent for hedging. FCC 1895 AGM 1993. We recommend:
– – **'Major'** MS (E)
Larger leaves and flower-heads.
– **phlogopappa** (*O. gunniana*) (*O. stellulata* hort.) MS (E) † ○ "Tasmanian Daisy Bush"
Narrow, toothed, aromatic leaves. Flower-heads in crowded panicles along stems, May. FCC 1885. We recommend:
– – **splendens** group (*O. stellulata* 'Splendens') SS (E) † ○
Showy flower-heads like Michaelmas Daisies. Available in blue, lavender and rose.
– × **scilloniensis** MS (E) † ○
Rounded, compact habit. Grey leaves. Abundant flower-heads, May. AM 1951 AM 1982 AGM 1993
– **semidentata** see *O.* 'Henry Travers'

"OLEASTER" see *Elaeagnus angustifolia*

ONONIS – Leguminosae SS ○
Trifoliolate leaves. Pea-shaped flowers. Any well drained soil including shallow chalk.
– **fruticosa** SS ○
Compact mound-like habit. Narrow leaflets. Clusters of bright rose-pink flowers throughout summer. AM 1926

"OSIER, COMMON" see *Salix viminalis*

"OSIER, PURPLE" see *Salix purpurea*

OSMANTHUS – Oleaceae MS-LS (E)
Holly-like shrubs. Small, white or cream, generally fragrant flowers. Suit almost all soils.
– **armatus** LS (E)
Dense habit. Thick, rigid leaves, edged with stout, often hooked, spiny teeth. Scented flowers, autumn.

OSMANTHUS × burkwoodii

– × burkwoodii (× *Osmarea burkwoodii*) MS (E)
Compact habit. Lustrous green, toothed leaves. Very fragrant flowers, April–May. AM 1978 AGM 1993
– decorus (*Phillyrea decora*) MS (E)
Dome-shaped. Large, glossy, leathery leaves. Small, fragrant, white flowers – spring. Purplish-black fruits. FCC 1888
– delavayi MS (E)
Slow-growing. Small leaves. Abundant, fragrant, white, jasmine-like flowers, April. AM 1914 FCC 1931 AGM 1993
– heterophyllus (*O. aquifolium*) (*O. ilicifolius*) LS (E)
Slow-growing, dense habit. Glossy, dark green, entire or spiny leaves. Sweetly scented flowers, autumn. FCC 1859. We recommend:
– – 'Goshiki' LS (E)
Spiny leaves conspicuously mottled with yellow, bronze when young.

– – 'Gulftide' LS (E)
Strongly spiny, twisted or lobed leaves. Dense habit. AGM 1993
– – 'Latifolius Variegatus' LS (E)
Silver variegated, broad leaves.
– – 'Purpureus' LS (E)
Young growths purple, changing to green, tinged purple.
– – 'Variegatus' ('Argenteomarginatus') LS (E)
Leaves margined creamy-white. AGM 1993

OSMANTHUS heterophyllus 'Variegatus'

OSMANTHUS delavayi

OZOTHAMNUS rosmarinifolius 'Silver Jubilee'

– **ilicifolius** see *O. heterophyllus*
– **serrulatus** MS (E)
Dense, rounded habit with narrow, glossy green leaves. Fragrant white flowers in spring.

OSTRYA – Carpinaceae ST-MT
"Hornbeam"-like trees with hop-like fruits and good autumn colour.
– **carpinifolia** MT ❦ "Hop Hornbeam"
Toothed leaves, clear yellow in autumn. Long, drooping catkins in spring. AM 1976
– **virginiana** ST ♦
Similar to above but dense, conical habit. Warm yellow autumn colour. Rare.

OXYDENDRUM – Ericaceae LS-ST ✍
A monotypic genus.
– **arboreum** (*Andromeda arborea*) LS-ST ✍
"Sorrel Tree"
Slender, drooping racemes of white flowers at shoot tips, late summer-autumn; crimson and yellow autumn colour. AM 1951 (for autumn colour) AM 1957 (for flowers) FCC 1972

OZOTHAMNUS – Compositae SS-MS (E) ○
Summer-flowering shrubs related to Helichrysum.
– **ledifolius** (*Helichrysum ledifolium*) SS (E) ○
Narrow, aromatic leaves, yellow beneath. Flowers reddish in bud opening white; honey-scented seed heads. AGM 1993
– **rosmarinifolius** (*Helichrysum rosmarinifolium*) MS (E) † ○
Dark green, narrow leaves; white, scented flowers, red in bud. AM 1968. We recommend:
– – **'Silver Jubilee'** MS (E) ○
A distinct form with silvery-grey leaves. AGM 1993

P

PACHYSANDRA – Buxaceae DS ● GC
Dwarf, carpeting shrubs for a moist position.
-- **terminalis** DS (E) ● GC
Toothed leaves clustered at stem tips,
greenish-white flower spikes, February-March.
AGM 1993
– – **'Variegata'** DS (E) ● GC
Leaves variegated white. AGM 1993

PAEONIA – Paeoniaceae MS ○
*The "Tree Paeonies" make handsome
flowering shrubs for any well-drained soil .*
– **delavayi** MS ○
Crimson flowers with golden anthers, May.
Attractive, deeply-cut leaves. AM 1934 AGM
1993
– × **lemoinei** MS ○
Large yellow flowers, May. We recommend
the following cultivars:
– – **'Chromotella'** MS ○
Double, sulphur-yellow.
– – **'Souvenir de Maxime Cornu'**
Fragrant, very large, bright yellow edged with
carmine.
– **lutea** MS ○
Cup-shaped, golden-yellow flowers in May-
June. FCC 1903. We recommend:
– – var. **ludlowii** MS ○
Larger saucer-shaped flowers. AM1954 AGM
1993
– **suffruticosa** MS ○ "Moutan Paeony"
Large flowers up to 15cm across, May.

Various named varieties are offered, generally
semi-double, or double, in shades of pink,
purple, red, white and yellow. Young growth
needs protection from spring frosts.

"PAGODA TREE" see *Sophora japonica*

"PALM, DWARF FAN" see *Chamaerops
humilis*

"PALM, HARDY" see *Trachycarpus fortunei*

PARAHEBE – Scrophulariaceae PS-DS ○
Sub-shrubs, intermediate between Hebe *and*
Veronica.
– **catarractae** DS ○ GC
Small leaved, spreading plant, making low
mounds. Flowers blue, in erect racemes, late
summer. AGM 1993
– – **'Delight**' DS ○ GC
Flowers white, veined heliotrope, produced
over a long period. AGM 1993
– – **'Diffusa'** DS ○ GC
Leaves smaller, flowers white, veined rose-
pink.

PARROTIA – Hamamelidaceae ST ♥
A monotypic genus
– **persica** ST ♥
Large "Beech-like" leaves, crimson and gold
in autumn, flaking bark like the "London
Plane". FCC 1884 AGM 1993

PAEONIA lutea

PAEONIA suffruticosa

144

PARROTIA persica

PERNETTYA mucronata 'Pink Pearl', 'Cherry Ripe' and 'White Pearl'

– – **'Vanessa'** ST ♀
A selected form making a distinct tree with an oval head. Good autumn colour.

PASANIA edulis see *Lithocarpus edulis*

"PASSION FLOWER" see *Passiflora* under Climbers

PAULOWNIA – Scrophulariaceae MT ♀
Large-leaved trees with erect panicles of foxglove-like flowers, in spring.
– **tomentosa** (*P. imperialis*) MT ♀
Fragrant, blue-purple flowers like huge foxgloves. AM 1934 AGM 1993

"PEACH" see *Prunus persica*

"PEAR" see *Pyrus*

"PERIWINKLE" see *Vinca*

PERNETTYA – Ericaceae DS (E) ⚘ GC
Low-growing, densely leafy, shrubs for peaty soils. White flowers and conspicuous berries.

Poisonous.
– **mucronata** DS (E) ⚘ GC
Masses of heath-like white flowers, May-June. Showy marble-like berries in profusion on females. A male is needed for pollination. AM 1961. We recommend:
– – **'Cherry Ripe'** DS (E) ⚘ GC
Berries bright cherry-red. AM 1985
– – **Male** DS (E) ⚘ GC
Proven male plants.
– – **'Pink Pearl'** DS (E) ⚘ GC
Lilac pink berries. AGM 1993
– – **'Sea Shell'** DS (E) ⚘ GC
Berries shell-pink, ripening to rose. AGM 1993
– – **'White Pearl'** DS (E) ⚘ GC
Gleaming white berries.

PEROVSKIA – Labiatae SS ○
Valuable late summer and autumn flowering sub-shrubs.
– **atriplicifolia** SS ○
Grey foliage. Long, narrow panicles of lavender-blue flowers. AM 1928. We recommend:
– – **'Blue Spire'** SS ○
Deeply cut, grey-green leaves. Large panicles of lavender-blue flowers. AM 1962 AGM 1993

PERSICARIA – Polygonaceae PS ○
The following makes an attractive ground cover plant on the rock garden:
– **vacciniifolia** (*Polygonum vacciniifolium*) PS ○
Small, glossy leaves on slender shoots. Bright pink flowers in erect spikes late summer to autumn. AGM 1993

PEROVSKIA atriplicifolia 'Blue Spire'

PHILADELPHUS 'Beauclerk'

PHILADELPHUS 'Manteau d'Hermine'

PHELLODENDRON – Rutaceae MT ♥
Very hardy trees with pinnate leaves, yellow in autumn. Small yellowish-green flowers. Black fruits.
– amurense MT ♥ "Amur Cork Tree"
Bright green leaves with 5–11 leaflets. Older branches corky.

PHILADELPHUS – Philadelphaceae SS-LS
○ "Mock Orange"
Fragrant, white flowers, June -July. D (h) 2
– 'Beauclerk' MS ○
Flowers single, 6cm across with broad petals, cerise centres. AM 1947 FCC 1951 AGM 1993
– 'Belle Etoile' MS ○
Very fragrant, single flowers, 5cm across, maroon centres. AM 1930 AGM 1993
– coronarius MS ○
A commonly cultivated species. Creamy-white, richly scented flowers. We recommend:
– – 'Aureus' MS ◑
Young leaves bright yellow. Foliage tends to burn in hot sun. AM 1983 AGM 1993
– – 'Variegatus' MS ○
Leaves with a creamy-white margin. AGM 1993
– delavayi LS ○
We recommend the following form:
– – 'Nymans Variety' LS ○
The best form with heavily scented flowers to 4cm across, in dense racemes, calyx purple. Vigorous, large-leaved shrub. AM 1935
– 'Innocence' MS ○
Profuse single flowers, leaves heavily blotched

with creamy-yellow.
– 'Manteau d'Hermine' DS ○
Creamy-white, double, fragrant flowers. Compact habit. AM 1956 AGM 1993
– microphyllus SS ○
A dainty plant. Small leaves. Small, richly fragrant, single flowers. FCC 1890
– 'Snowbelle' SS ○
Large, bell-shaped flowers.

146

PHILADELPHUS coronarius 'Aureus'

PHILADELPHUS microphyllus

PHILADELPHUS 'Virginal'

– 'Sybille' SS ○
Flowers single, orange-scented, purple-stained petals. Graceful, arching habit. AM 1954 AGM 1993
– 'Virginal' LS ○
A deservedly popular, vigorous shrub, with richly fragrant, double flowers. FCC 1911 AGM 1993

PHILLYREA – Oleaceae MS-ST (E)
Handsome and useful, hardy evergreens.
– angustifolia MS (E)
We recommend:
– – f. rosmarinifolia MS (E)
Compact habit. Dark green, narrow leaves. Small, fragrant creamy-yellow flowers May-June. Tolerates salt spray.
– decora see *Osmanthus decorus*
– latifolia LS-ST (E) ❦
Elegant olive-like plant. Drooping branches, glossy, dark-green leaves. Small ivory-white flowers, late spring.

PHLOMIS – Labiatae DS-SS (E) ○
Shrubs or sub-shrubs with woolly leaves and conspicuous flowers. A (b) 5
– 'Edward Bowles' SS (E) ○
Large, heart-shaped leaves. Sulphur-yellow flowers, late summer-autumn
– fruticosa SS ○
Bright yellow flowers, late summer-autumn. AM 1925 AGM 1993
– italica DS (E) † ○
White-hairy stems and leaves. Pale-lilac flowers, summer.
– longifolia SS (E)
Woolly young shoots bear bright green, deeply veined leaves. Deep golden flowers in summer.

PHLOMIS fruticosa

PHORMIUM – Agavaceae SS-MS (E) ○
Handsome plants with tufts of sword-like leaves. Fairly hardy in all but coldest areas.
– **'Apricot Queen'** SS (E) ↺
Arching, soft yellow leaves flushed apricot and margined dark green and bronze.
– **cookianum** (*P. colensoi*) MS (E) ○
Differs from *P. tenax* in its smaller stature and lax leaves. AGM 1993
– – **'Cream Delight'** SS (E) ○
Leaves with a broad cream central band and narrower cream stripes towards the margin. AGM 1993
– – **'Tricolor'** SS (E) ○
Leaves conspicuously edged creamy-yellow, with a thin red strip on the margin. AGM 1993
– **'Dark Delight'** SS (E) ○
Broad leaves drooping at the tips, dark bronze-purple with a reddish midrib.
– **'Dazzler'** MS (E) ○
A striking plant. Leaves deep red, rose-red in centre.

PHORMIUM 'Dazzler'

– **'Maori Chief'** SS (E) ○
Leaves variegated scarlet, crimson and bronze, upright with drooping tips.
– **'Maori Queen'** SS (E) ○
Leaves bronze-green striped rose-red, upright with drooping tips.
– **'Maori Sunrise'** SS (E) ○
Leaves arching, pale red to pink with bronze margin. Low-growing.
– **tenax** MS (E) ○
Rigid, sword-like leaves. Flowers bronze-red in panicles up to 4.5m. AGM 1993
– – **'Purpureum'** MS (E) ○
Leaves bronze-purple. AGM 1993
– – **'Sundowner'** MS (E) ○
Leaves bronze-green margined deep rose-red. AM 1978

PHORMIUM tenax

– – **'Variegatum'** MS (E) ○
Leaves margined with creamy-white. FCC 1864 AGM 1993
– **'Yellow Wave'** SS (E) ○
Drooping leaves banded with yellow-green. AM 1977

PHOTINIA – Rosaceae MS-ST
Evergreen and deciduous shrubs and small trees.
– **beauverdiana** ST ♥
Pinkish young leaves. White flowers followed by dark-red fruits. Good autumn colour. AGM 1993
– **davidiana** (*Stranvaesia davidiana*) LS (E)
Vigorous, erect habit. Dark green, leathery leaves; old ones turn bright red, autumn. Crimson fruits in hanging clusters. AM 1928. We recommend:
– – **'Palette'** MS (E)
Leaves blotched and streaked creamy-white, pink-tinged when young.
– × **fraseri** LS (E)
Dark, glossy-green leaves. Attractively coloured when young. We recommend the following forms:
– – **'Red Robin'** LS (E) Young leaves brilliant red. AM 1977 AGM 1993
– – **'Robusta'** LS (E)
Brilliant coppery-red young leaves. AM 1974 AM 1990 AGM 1993
– **glabra** MS (E)
We recommend the following form:
– – **'Rubens'** MS (E)
Young leaves bright, sealing-wax red. Dense habit. AM 1972 FCC 1991
– **'Redstart'** (× *Stranvinia* 'Redstart') LS-ST (E)
A vigorous plant with narrow, glossy green leaves tinted coppery-red when young, a few turning to brilliant scarlet in autumn. Dense

PHOTINIA × fraseri 'Robusta'

PHOTINIA 'Redstart'

clusters of white flowers, June. Yellow-tipped red berries. AGM 1993
– **serratifolia** (*Photinia serrulata*) LS-ST (E) ♥
Glossy, green, coarsely toothed leaves, coppery-red when young. Massive heads of small, white flowers in May.

– **villosa** ST ♥
Small, white flowers, May. Bright red fruits. Leaves scarlet and gold in autumn. AM 1932 AGM 1993

PHYGELIUS – Scrophulariaceae SS (E) ○
South African sub-shrubs with conspicuous tubular flowers during summer and autumn.
– × **rectus** SS (E) ○
Hybrids between the only two species. We recommend the following which were raised in our nurseries:
– – **'Devil's Tears'** SS (E) ○
Deep reddish-pink with orange-red lobes. B4
– – **'Moonraker'** SS (F) ○
Pale creamy-yellow. B4

PHYGELIUS × rectus 'Moonraker'

– – **'Salmon Leap'** SS (E) ○
Salmon-orange with darker lobes. B4
– – **'Winchester Fanfare'** SS (E) ○
Dusky reddish-pink with scarlet lobes. B4

× **PHYLLIOPSIS – Ericaceae** DS (E) ⁄ ●
Hybrid between Phyllodoce *and* Kalmiopsis *which occurred in our nursery.*
– **hillieri 'Pinocchio'** DS (E) ⁄ ●
Small, glossy, green leaves. Conspicuous racemes of small, rich pink flowers are freely produced in spring and again in autumn. AM 1976 FCC 1984

149

PHYLLOSTACHYS – Gramineae MS-LS (E)
*Tall, graceful bamboos, usually less invasive
than* Arundinaria *with zig-zag stems flattened
or grooved on alternate sides.*
– aurea LS (E)
Bright green canes, later creamy-yellow,
forming large clumps. Nodes crowded at the
base. AGM 1993
– bambusoides (*P. quiloi*) LS (E)
Canes shining deep green, becoming deep
yellow-green, then brown. Forms large
clumps.
– – 'Sulphurea' see *P. sulphurea*
– flexuosa LS (E)
Slender, somewhat wavy canes, zig-zag at the
base, bright green at first, darkening with
age. Makes a good screen.
– nigra LS (E) "Black Bamboo"
Graceful, arching canes eventually black or
nearly so when mature. AM 1975 AGM 1993
– – 'Boryana' LS (E)
Luxuriant masses of arching, leafy canes,
green at first, becoming yellow, splashed with
purple.
– – var. henonis LS (E)
Masses of lush, dark green leaves. Tall,
yellow-brown canes. AGM 1993
– quiloi see *P. bambusoides*
– ruscifolia see *Shibataea kumasaca*
– sulphurea (*P. bambusoides* 'Sulphurea') LS
(E)
Clump-forming with rich yellow canes,
sometimes striped with green.

PHYSOCARPUS – Rosaceae MS
A small genus of shrubs related to Neillia. *We
recommend the following:*
– opulifolius MS "Nine Bark"
Three-lobed leaves. Dense clusters of pink-
tinged, white flowers, June. We recommend:

PIERIS 'Flaming Silver'

– – 'Dart's Gold' SS
Compact with bright yellow foliage. AGM
1993

PICRASMA – Simaroubaceae ST ❦
Mainly tropical trees related to Ailanthus. *The
following is completely hardy.*
– quassioides ST ❦
Pinnate leaves, orange and scarlet in autumn.
Small, green flowers. Red, pea-like fruits.

PIERIS – Ericaceae DS-LS (E) ✗ ◑
*Conspicuous, usually white, Lily-of-the-Valley-
like flowers, spring. Often attractive young
foliage.*
– 'Bert Chandler' SS (E) ✗ ◑
Bright salmon-pink young leaves turn to
creamy-yellow then green. AM 1977
– 'Firecrest' LS (E) ✗ ◑
Vigorous with deeply veined, dark green
leaves, bright red when young. Large panicles
of white flowers. AM 1973 AM 1981 AGM
1993
– 'Flaming Silver' SS (E) ✗ ◑
Bright red young leaves become green,
margined silvery-white. AGM 1993
– 'Forest Flame' MS (E) ✗ ◑
Large drooping flower panicles. Young leaves
brilliant red, turning pink, creamy-white, then
green. AM 1973 AGM 1993

PIERIS 'Forest Flame'

– formosa LS (E) ◑
Magnificent shrub. Glossy dark-green,
leathery leaves. White flowers in May. AM
1894. We recommend:
– – 'Jermyns' MS (E) ✗ ◑
Red flower buds throughout winter, opening
white. AM 1959 AGM 1993

– – **'Wakehurst'** LS (E) ✗ ◑
Vivid red young foliage. Glistening white flowers. Vigorous growth. FCC 1930 AGM 1993
– **japonica** MS (E) ✗ ◑
Glossy green leaves, coppery when young. Drooping panicles of white flowers, March-April. FCC 1882. We recommend:
– – **'Blush'** MS (E) ✗ ◑
Flowers rose in bud, opening pale blush-pink. AGM 1993
– – **'Debutante'** DS (E) ✗ ◑
Domed habit with upright panicles of white flowers. AGM 1993
– – **'Flamingo'** MS (E) ✗ ◑
Deep red buds open to deep pink then rose-pink. AM 1981

PIERIS japonica 'White Rim'

PITTOSPORUM 'Garnettii'

– – **'Grayswood'** SS (E) ✗ ◑
Compact with dense, spreading panicles of white flowers. AM 1981 AGM 1993
– – **'Little Heath'** DS (E) ✗ ◑
Dense habit with small, silver-margined leaves. AGM 1993
– – **'Valley Valentine'** MS (E) ✗ ◑
The darkest coloured *Pieris* with deep dusky-red flowers. AGM 1993
– – **'White Rim'** MS (E) ✗ ◑
Leaves margined creamy-white, flushed pink when young. Commonly grown as 'Variegata'. AGM 1993

PIPTANTHUS – Leguminosae LS (E) ○
Only one species is commonly cultivated.
– **nepalensis** (*P. laburnifolius*) LS (E) ○
"Evergreen Laburnum"
Evergreen or semi-evergreen, with trifoliolate leaves and large, bright yellow pea-flowers in May. AM 1960. A (b) 5

PITTOSPORUM – Pittosporaceae SS-ST (E)
Attractive foliage plants excellent for mild coastal areas. Several produce small, fragrant flowers.
– **crassifolium** LS (E) †
Leathery leaves, white-felted beneath. Deep purple flowers. Makes an excellent hedge in coastal areas. We recommend:
– – **'Variegatum'** LS (E) †
Grey-green leaves, margined creamy-white. AM 1977
– **dallii** LS (E)
Rounded habit, leathery matt-green leaves. Reddish-purple shoots and leaf stems. Creamy-white, fragrant flowers in late summer on old plants. Hardy.
– **eugenioides** LS (E) † "Tarata"
Glossy, green, undulate leaves. Pale yellow honey-scented flowers, spring. We recommend the following:
– – **'Variegatum'** LS (E) †
Leaves margined creamy-white. AGM 1993
– **'Garnettii'** LS (E) †
Broadly columnar habit. Grey-green leaves, margined white, marked pink in winter. AGM 1993
– **nigricans** see *P. tenuifolium*
– **tenuifolium** (*P. nigricans*) LS-ST (E) ❢ †
Glossy, pale-green, undulate leaves on black shoots. Small, chocolate-purple, honey-scented flowers, spring. Makes excellent hedge in mild areas. AM 1931 AGM 1993
– – **'Eila Keightley'** ('Sunburst') LS (E) †
Pale-green leaves, conspicuously blotched with yellow.

PITTOSPORUM tenuifolium

PLATANUS × hispanica

PLATANUS orientalis

– – **'Garnettii'** see *P.* 'Garnettii'
– – **'Irene Paterson'** MS (E) †
Young leaves creamy-white, becoming deep
green, marbled white, pink tinged in winter.
AGM 1993
– – **'Purpureum'** LS (E) †
Young leaves pale-green, becoming deep
purple.
– – **'Silver Queen'** LS (E) †
Leaves suffused silvery-grey. AM 1914 AGM
1993
– – **'Sunburst'** see 'Eila Keightley'
– – **'Tom Thumb'** DS (E)
Compact, rounded habit with glossy red-purple
foliage, pale green when young. AGM 1993
– – **'Warnham Gold'** MS (E) †
Young leaves greenish-yellow, becoming
golden yellow. AGM 1993
– **tobira** (*P. chinense*) LS (E) †
Whorls of glossy, bright-green leaves. Con-
spicuous, cream, orange-blossom-scented
flowers in summer. AM 1984 AGM 1993
– – **'Variegatum'** LS (E) †
Leaves with a creamy-white margin.

PLAGIANTHUS – Malvaceae
*Australasian shrubs and trees. We recommend
the following:*
– **regius** (*P. betulinus*) ST ♀
Slender tree with variable leaves. Up to 7.5cm
long. Large, dense panicles of tiny, white
flowers, May.

"PLANE" see *Platanus*

PLATANUS – Platanaceae LT ♀
Large trees with attractive, flaking bark.

– × **hispanica** (*P.* × *acerifolia*) LT ♀ "London
Plane"
Large, palmately lobed leaves and patchwork,
flaking bark. Very tolerant of atmospheric
pollution. AGM 1993
– – **'Suttneri'** MT ♀
Leaves boldly variegated creamy-white.
– **orientalis** LT ♀ "Oriental Plane"
Deeply five-lobed leaves. Attractive flaking
bark. AM 1966 AGM 1993
– – **'Digitata'** LT ♀
Leaves deeply divided into three to five finger-
like lobes.

"PLUMBAGO, HARDY" see *Ceratostigma
willmottianum*

"POCKET HANDKERCHIEF TREE" see
Davidia involucrata

POLYGALA – Polygalaceae PS-SS (E) ✗
*Evergreen shrubs with unusual and colourful
pea-like flowers.*
– **chamaebuxus** DS (E) ✗
Low, mat-forming shrub. Creamy-white,

tipped bright yellow flowers, April-June.
– – var. **grandiflora** DS (E) ✗
Flowers purple and yellow. AM 1896
– **myrtifolia** SS (E) † ✗
Bright purple, pea-like flowers over a long period from spring to autumn. Best in the conservatory.

POLYGONUM vacciniifolium see
Persicaria vacciniifolia

"POMEGRANATE" see *Punica granatum*

PONCIRUS – Rutaceae MS ○
A monotypic genus related to Citrus.
– **trifoliata** (*Citrus trifoliata*) MS ○ "Japanese Bitter Orange"
Stout green stems and spines. Large, white, sweetly-scented, flowers in spring. Fruits like miniature oranges, green, becoming yellow.

PONCIRUS trifoliata

"POPLAR" see *Populus*

POPULUS – Salicaceae MT-LT
Fast-growing trees for nearly all soils, even very wet, but usually not at their best on shallow chalk. Several have scented leaves. Others have attractive catkins.

– **alba** LT ❦ "White Poplar"
Leaves irregularly lobed, white-woolly beneath. Autumn colour yellow. Good in exposed sites and coastal areas. Lime tolerant.
– – **'Pyramidalis'** LT ❢
Resembles the "Lombardy Poplar" in habit, but slightly broader.
– – **'Richardii'** MT ❦
Leaves bright golden-yellow above. AM 1912
– **'Balsam Spire'** (*P. balsamifera* × *P. trichocarpa*) (*P.* 'Tacatricho 32') (*P.* 'TT 32') LT ❦
Very fast growing tree of narrow habit. AGM 1993
– **balsamifera** (*P. tacamahacca*) LT ❦
"Balsam Poplar"
Erect branches. Large sticky buds. Young leaves balsam-scented.
– **balsamifera** × **trichocarpa** see *P.* 'Balsam Spire'
– × **canadensis** MT LT ❦
Strong-growing hybrids good for screening. We recommend:
– – **'Robusta'** LT ❦
Vigorous tree with a straight trunk and open crown. Young leaves coppery-red.
– – **'Serotina Aurea'** MT ❦ "Golden Poplar"
Leaves clear golden-yellow in spring and early summer, becoming greenish-yellow. Golden yellow in autumn. AGM 1993

POPULUS × candicans 'Aurora'

– × **candicans** MT ♀ "Ontario Poplar" "Balm of Gilead Poplar"
Broad-headed tree. Downy twigs and leaves grey-white beneath, strongly balsam-scented when young.
– – **'Aurora'** MT ♀
Young leaves marbled creamy-white, tinged pink. AM 1954
– × **canescens** LT ♀
Commonly planted tree. Lobed leaves, grey-white beneath. Attractive catkins, late winter. Yellow, or occasionally red, autumn colour.
– **lasiocarpa** MT ♀
Magnificent tree with stout shoots and huge leaves up to 30cm long. FCC 1908 AGM 1993
– **nigra** LT ♀ "Black Poplar"
We recommend the following forms:
– – var. **betulifolia** LT ♀ "Manchester Poplar"
Bushy-headed tree. Very tolerant of atmospheric pollution. AGM 1993
– – **'Italica'** LT ❢ "Lombardy Poplar"
Very effective as a tall screen. AGM 1993
– **'Robusta'** see *P.* × *canadensis* 'Robusta'
– **'Serotina Aurea'** see *P.* × *canadensis* 'Serotina Aurea'
– **tacamahacca** see *P. balsamifera*
– **'Tacatricho 32'** see *P.* 'Balsam Spire'
– **tremula** MT ♀ "Aspen"
Prominently toothed leaves which tremble in the breeze. Clear yellow in autumn. Long, grey catkins, late winter. AGM 1993

POPULUS × canadensis 'Serotina Aurea'

– – **'Pendula'** ST ♠ "Weeping Aspen"
Weeping form, particularly effective in winter when laden with purplish-grey catkins.

"PORTUGAL LAUREL" see *Prunus lusitanica*

POTENTILLA – Rosaceae DS-MS
Invaluable plants for a shrub border, flowering over a long period.
– **arbuscula** DS
Large, rich yellow flowers midsummer-late autumn. Sage-green leaves. AM 1925 AMT 1965. We recommend:
– – **'Beesii'** DS
Golden-yellow flowers and silvery foliage. AMT 1966 AGM 1993 ·
– **davurica** DS-SS
Variable white flowered species. We recommend the following forms:
– – **'Abbotswood'** DS
Spreading habit. Dark foliage. Flowers profusely over long period. AMT 1965 AGM 1993
– – **'Manchu'** (*P. fruticosa* var. *mandschurica* hort.) DS GC
Dwarf, spreading habit. Greyish foliage. Continuous flowering. AM 1924

POTENTILLA davurica 'Manchu'

– **'Daydawn'** SS
Flowers peach-pink, suffused cream. AGM 1993
– **'Elizabeth'** SS GC
Dome-shaped bush. Large, rich canary-yellow flowers late spring-autumn. AMT 1965 AGM 1993
– **'Goldfinger'** SS
Compact habit. Large, rich yellow flowers. AGM 1993

POTENTILLA 'Elizabeth'

POTENTILLA parvifolia 'Klondike'

POTENTILLA 'Tangerine'

– **'Goldstar'** DS
Upright habit with large, deep yellow flowers over a long period.
– **'Katherine Dykes'** MS
Dome-shaped, with arching branches. Large, yellow flowers, continuously produced. AM 1944 AGM 1993
– **'Longacre'** DS GC
Dense, mat-forming habit. Large, bright yellow flowers. AMT 1965 AGM 1993
– **'Maanleys'** SS
Profuse soft yellow flowers over a long period. AGM 1993
– **parvifolia** SS
Small leaves and relatively small rich yellow flowers. We recommend the following:
– – **'Klondike'** DS
Dwarf habit, larger bright, golden-yellow flowers throughout summer. AMT 1965 AGM 1993
– **'Pretty Polly'** DS
A seedling of 'Red Ace' with pale pink flowers, deeper in the centre, with golden stamens.
– **'Primrose Beauty'** SS
Primrose-yellow flowers deeper in centre. Grey-green foliage. Arching branches. AMT 1965 AGM 1993
– **'Princess'** DS
Delicate pale pink with yellow centre, the best colour developed out of hot sun.
– **'Red Ace'** DS
Glowing red flowers over a long period. FCC 1975
– **'Ruth'** SS
Nodding, cup-shaped creamy-yellow flowers turn to white. Upright.
– **'Sunset'** SS
Deep orange to brick-red flowers.

– **'Tangerine'** DS
Wide-spreading, mound-forming. Flowers pale, coppery-yellow. AGM 1993
– **'Tilford Cream'** DS
Large, creamy-white flowers. Dense, spreading habit with rich green foliage. AGM 1993
– **'Vilmoriniana** MS
Erect branched. Silvery leaves and cream flowers. AMT 1965

PRUNUS × amygdalo-persica 'Pollardii'

– **'William Purdom'** SS
Light yellow flowers profusely borne. Upright
habit. FCCT 1966

PROSTANTHERA – Labiatae DS (E) † ○
*Floriferous, aromatic, Australasian shrubs for
mild areas. We recommend the following:*
– **'Chelsea Pink'** SS (E) † ○
Pale pink flowers with purple anthers.
Aromatic grey-green foliage. AM 1986
– **cuneata** DS (E) † ○
Flowers white flushed lilac marked with
purple, May; glossy green leaves. Relatively
hardy. AGM 1993
– **rotundifolia** SS (E) † ○
Dense shrub with tiny leaves and masses of
heliotrope flowers in spring. AM 1924 AGM
1993

PRUNUS – Rosaceae PS-MT
*A large genus containing many beautiful
flowering trees. Peaches and almonds* (Prunus
persica, P. × amygdalo-persica *and* P. dulcis)
*must be sprayed in mid-February and in early
March with Murphy's Traditional Copper
Fungicide, as a control for "Peach Leaf Curl".*
– **'Accolade'** ST ♀
Semi-double, rich pink flowers, 4cm across, in
profusion, early spring. AM 1952 FCC 1954
AGM 1993

– × **amygdalo-persica** ST ♀
A hybrid between the peach and almond of
which we recommend the following:
– – **'Pollardii'** ST ♀
Rich pink, almond-like flowers. FCC 1935
– **amygdalus** see *P. dulcis*
– **avium** MT ♀ "Gean" "Wild Cherry"
Dense clusters of white, cup-shaped flowers,
April-May. Small, glossy, red-purple fruits.
AGM 1993
– – **'Plena'** ('Multiplex') MT ♀ "Double
Gean"
Masses of drooping, double-white flowers.
FCC 1964 AGM 1993
– × **blireana** ST ♀
Metallic, coppery-purple leaves. Double rose-
pink flowers, April. AM 1914 FCC 1923 AGM
1993
– **cerasifera** (*P. myrobalana*) ST ♀ Hdg
(0.5m) "Myrobalan" "Cherry Plum"
Myriads of small white flowers, February-
March. Mature trees bear red or yellow,
edible "cherry-plums". We recommend:
– – **'Nigra'** ST ♀ Hdg (0.5m)
Leaves and stems blackish-purple. Flowers
prolific, single pink fading blush. FCC 1939
AGM 1993
– – **'Pissardii'** ('Atropurpurea') ST ♀ Hdg
(0.5m) "Purple-leaved Plum"
Dark-red young foliage, turning deep purple.
Abundant flowers pink in bud, opening white.
FCC 1884
– – **'Rosea'** LS-ST ♀
Young leaves bronze-purple, turning bronze-
green, then green. Flowers salmon-pink.

PRUNUS × cistena

– **cerasus** ST ♥ "Sour Cherry"
We recommend the following:
– – **'Rhexii'** ST ♥
Very showy, double, white flowers.
– × **cistena** MS Hdg (0.5m) "Purple-leaf Sand Cherry"
Rich red leaves, white flowers in spring. Black-purple fruits. AGM 1993
– **'Collingwood Ingram'** ST ♥
Very deep pink flowers borne in early spring.
– **dulcis** (*P. amygdalus*) T ♥ "Common Almond"
One of the most popular spring-flowering trees. We recommend the following:
– – **'Macrocarpa'** ST ♥
Large, very pale-pink or white flowers. Large fruits. AM 1931
– **glandulosa** SS ○ "Chinese Bush Cherry"
Neat, bushy habit with slender, erect shoots. We recommend the following:

PRUNUS glandulosa 'Alba Plena'

– – **'Alba Plena'** SS ○
Pendant shoots wreathed with double, white flowers, early May. AM 1950 AGM 1993
– – **'Rosea Plena'** ('Sinensis') SS ○
Double, bright-pink flowers. AM 1968 AGM 1993
– **'Hally Jolivette'** LS-ST ♥
Slender, willowy stems, covered in early spring with small, semi-double, blush-white flowers.
– × **hillieri 'Spire'** see *P.* 'Spire'
– **Incisa** LS-ST ♥ "Fuji Cherry"
Abundant, small white flowers, pink-tinged in bud, March. AM 1927
– – **'Praecox'** LS-ST ♥
Flowers during late winter. AM 1957 FCC 1973 AGM 1993

PRUNUS laurocerasus 'Marbled White'

– **'Kursar'** ST ♥
Small, rich deep-pink flowers, March-early April. Young leaves reddish-bronze. AM 1952 AGM 1993
– **laurocerasus** LS (E) "Cherry Laurel"
Vigorous shrub with glossy leaves and white flowers in erect racemes, April. Black, cherry-like fruits. For chalky soils and very cold areas *P. lusitanica* is more suitable. Poisonous foliage and seeds. AGM 1993. We recommend the following forms:
A (f) 5
– – **'Marbled White'** LS (E)
Slow-growing, dense, broadly conical habit Leaves conspicuously marbled with grey-green and white. AM 1986
– – **'Otto Luyken'** SS (E) GC
Outstanding form of dense, dome-shaped habit with narrow, glossy dark-green leaves. AM 1968 AGM 1993
– – **'Rotundifolia'** MS (E) Hdg (0.5m)
Bushy form with short leaves. Recommended for hedging.
– – **'Zabeliana'** SS (E) GC
Horizontally branched, with very narrow leaves. Very free flowering.
– **lusitanica** LS-ST (E) ♥ "Portugal Laurel" Hdg (0.5m)
Glossy, dark-green ovate leaves, with red leaf stalks. White flowers in erect racemes. Dark purple fruits. Good on chalk. AGM 1993. A (f) 5
– – subsp. **azorica** LS (E)
Magnificent densely bushy shrub with larger,

PRUNUS laurocerasus 'Otto Luyken'

PRUNUS lusitanica

bright green leaves, red when young. FCC 1866 AGM 1993
– – **'Myrtifolia'** ('Angustifolia') ('Pyramidalis') LS (E)
Dense, conical habit. Smaller leaves. A good substitute for *Laurus nobilis* ("Bay Tree") in cold areas.
– – **'Variegata'** LS (E)
Leaves conspicuously margined white, sometimes flushed pink in winter.
– **maackii** ST ♥ "Manchurian Cherry"
Shining, golden-brown, flaking bark. Small white flowers, April.
– – **'Amber Beauty'** ST ♥
Selected form with ascending branches and good, amber-coloured bark.
– **mume** ST ♥ "Japanese Apricot"
Pink, almond-scented flowers, late winter-

early spring. We recommend the following forms:
– – **'Alboplena'** ST ♥
Semi-double, white flowers.
– – **'Alphandii'** ST ♥
Semi-double, pink flowers.
– – **'Benichidori'** ST ♥
Strongly fragrant, double, rich madder-pink flowers. AM 1961
– **myrobalana** see *P. cerasifera*
– **'Okame'** ST ♥
Masses of carmine-rose flowers in March. Attractive autumn tints. AM 1947 AGM 1993
– **padus** MT ♥ "Bird Cherry"
Racemes of small, white, almond-scented flowers, May.
– – **'Albertii'** MT ♥
Vigorous, free-flowering form.
– – **'Colorata'** MT ♥
Flowers pale pink, young leaves coppery-purple. AM 1974 AGM 1993
– – **'Watereri'** ('Grandiflora') MT ♥
Flowers in conspicuous racemes up to 20cm long. AM 1969 AGM 1993
– **'Pandora'** ST ♥
Masses of pale, shell-pink flowers, March-early April. AM 1939 AGM 1993
– **persica** LS-ST ♥ "Peach"
We recommend the following ornamental form:
– – **'Klara Meyer'** ('Flore Roseoplena') ST ♥
Double, peach-pink flowers.

PRUNUS padus 'Watereri'

PRUNUS 'Pink Shell'

PRUNUS sargentii

– 'Pink Shell' ST ♥
Elegant tree with drooping branches, abundant, delicate shell-pink flowers. AM 1969 AGM 1993

– × pollardii see *P. × amygdalo-persica* 'Pollardii'

– sargentii MT ♥
One of the loveliest of all cherries. Flowers single, pink, late March-early April. Young leaves bronze-red. Gorgeous autumn colours. AM 1921 FCC 1925 AGM 1993

– – 'Rancho' MT ♦
A form of narrow growth with upswept branches.

– × schmittii MT ♦
Vigorous tree with polished brown bark. Pale-pink flowers, spring.

– serrula ST ♥
Glossy, red-brown, mahogany-like bark. Small, white flowers, late April. AM 1944 AGM 1993

– serrulata 'Autumn Glory' see *P. verecunda* 'Autumn Glory'

– 'Snow Goose' ST ♦
Masses of pure white flowers in spring.

– spinosa LS Hdg (0.5m) "Blackthorn" "Sloe"
Dense, spiny shrub studded with small white flowers March-early April. Black fruits.

– – 'Purpurea' MS
Rich purple leaves. White flowers. Dense habit.

– 'Spire' ST ♦
Narrow habit, soft pink flowers and good autumn colour. Excellent for restricted spaces. AGM 1993

– subhirtella ST ♥ "Spring Cherry"
We recommend the following forms:

– – 'Autumnalis' ST ♥ "Autumn Cherry"
Semi-double, white flowers produced over period November to March. AM 1912 FCC 1966 AGM 1993

– – 'Autumnalis Rosea' ST ♥
Semi-double, blush-pink flowers. AM 1960 AGM 1993

– – 'Fukubana' ST ♥
The most colourful form with masses of semi-double, rose-madder flowers. AGM 1993

– – 'Pendula Plena Rosea' ST ♠
Rose-madder, semi-double, rosette-like flowers on cascading branches. AM 1938

– – 'Pendula Rosea' ST ♠ "Weeping Spring Cherry"
Mushroom habit. Flowers rich pink in bud, fading to blush, late March early April. AGM 1993

– – 'Pendula Rubra' ST ♠
Deep rose flowers, carmine in bud. AM 1938 AGM 1993

– – 'Stellata' ST ♥
Clear pink, star-shaped flowers profusely borne along the branches. AM 1949

– tenella SS "Dwarf Russian Almond"
We recommend the following form:

– – 'Fire Hill' SS ○
Erect stems, wreathed with brilliant rose-red flowers, April. AM 1959 AGM 1993

– triloba 'Multiplex' MS
Large, double, rosette-like clear peach-pink flowers in profusion, late March-early April. FCC 1983 AGM 1993. C (a) 5

– verecunda (*P. serrulata* var. *pubescens*) MT ♥ "Korean Hill Cherry"
White or pink flowers, April-May. Bronze young leaves colouring in autumn. We recommend:

– – 'Autumn Glory' MT ♥
Profuse pale blush flowers, autumn colour rich deep crimson and red. AM 1966

PRUNUS subhirtella 'Pendula Rosea'

PRUNUS tenella 'Fire Hill'

PRUNUS triloba 'Multiplex'

– virginiana 'Shubert' ST ❦
Pale green young leaves quickly change to deep reddish-purple.
– × yedoensis MT ♀ "Yoshino Cherry"
Arching branches. Profusion of almond-

scented blush-white flowers, late March-early April. AM 1927 AGM 1993

JAPANESE CHERRIES of Garden Origin
Mainly small trees of easy cultivation in all well-drained soils. Often with bronze young leaves. Flowers single, semi-double or double, varying from rich pink to white or cream. Flowering times are indicated as follows:
Early – Late March-early April
Mid – Mid-late April
Late – Late April-early May
– 'Amanogawa' ST ❦
Narrow habit. Upright clusters of fragrant, semi-double, shell-pink flowers. Mid to late. AM 1931 AGM 1993

PRUNUS 'Amanogawa'

– 'Asano' ST ♀
Dense clusters of very double, deep pink, flowers. Early.
– 'Cheal's Weeping' ST ▲
Drooping branches, wreathed with very double, clear, deep pink flowers, early. AM 1915 AGM 1993. Usually wrongly grown as 'Kiku-shidare Sakura'
– 'Fudanzakura' ST ♀
Flowers single, white, pink in bud, produced between November and April. AM 1930
– 'Fukubana' see *P. subhirtella* 'Fukubana'

PRUNUS 'Cheal's Weeping'

– 'Hokusai' ST ♀
Vigorous tree. Masses of large, semi-double, pale-pink flowers, in large clusters. Mid.
– 'Ichiyo' ST ♀
Ascending branches. Double, shell-pink flowers, frilled at the edge, in long-stalked clusters. Mid. AM 1959 AGM 1993
– 'Jo-nioi' ST ♀
Single white, deliciously scented flowers. Mid.

PRUNUS 'Shogetsu'

– 'Kanzan' MT ♀
One of the most popular ornamental cherries. Large, showy, double, purplish-pink flowers. Mid. Vigorous. AM 1921 FCC 1937 AGM 1993
– 'Mount Fuji' ST ♀
Slightly drooping branches. Very large, single or semi-double, fragrant, snow-white flowers. Mid. AGM 1993. Usually grown as 'Shirotae'.
– 'Pink Perfection' ST ♀
Flowers double, bright rosy-pink in bud, opening paler, in long, drooping clusters. Mid-late. AM 1945 AGM 1993
– 'Shimidsu Sakura' see 'Shogetsu'
– 'Shirofugen' MT ♀
Flowers large, double, purplish-pink in bud, opening white, fading to purplish-pink, contrasting well with the copper-coloured young leaves, very late. AGM 1993
– 'Shirotae' see under 'Mount Fuji'
– 'Shogetsu' ('Shimidsu Sakura') ST ♀
Most-attractive. Flowers large, fimbriated double, pink tinged in bud, opening pure white, hanging in long-stalked clusters. Mid-late. AM 1930 FCC 1989 AGM 1993
– 'Tai Haku' MT ♀ "Great White Cherry"
Flowers very large, single, dazzling white. Mid. AM 1931 FCC 1944 AGM 1993
– 'Ukon' MT ♀
Flowers semi-double, pale yellowish, tinged green, occasionally pink flushed. Mid. Spreading. AM 1923 AGM 1993
– "Yoshino" see P. × yedoensis

PSEUDOSASA – Gramineae LS (E)
A small genus of bamboos of which we recommend:
– japonica (*Arundinaria japonica*) LS (E)
Most commonly cultivated bamboo, with dense thickets of tall, olive-green canes, arching at the tips with lush masses of dark, glossy green leaves. AGM 1993

PSEUDOWINTERA – Winteraceae MS (E)† ◐
A monotypic genus related to Drimys.
– colorata (*Drimys colorata*) MS (E) † ◐
Remarkable for its unusually coloured oval, leathery leaves – pale yellow-green, flushed pink, edged and blotched deep crimson-purple. AM 1975

PTELEA – Rutaceae LS-ST
We recommend the following:
– trifoliata LS "Hop Tree"
Trifoliolate leaves. Small, very fragrant, yellowish flowers, June. Dense clusters of

persistent, green-winged fruits. AGM 1993
– – **'Aurea'** LS
Leaves soft yellow. FCC 1980 AGM 1993

PTEROCARYA – Juglandaceae LT ♀
*Vigorous trees with handsome, pinnate
leaves. Flowers in catkins. Any fertile soil.*

PTEROCARYA fraxinifolia

– **fraxinifolia** (*P. caucasica*) LT ♀
Wide-spreading tree. Large leaves, with
numerous leaflets. Greenish flowers in
pendulous catkins, the female up to 50cm
long. AGM 1993

PTEROSTYRAX – Styracaceae LS-ST
We recommend the following species:
– **hispida** LS "Epaulette Tree"
Drooping panicles of fragrant white flowers,
June-July. Five-ribbed fruits. AM 1964 AGM
1993

PUNICA – Punicaceae LS † ○
Only one species is in general cultivation.
– **granatum** LS † ○ "Pomegranate"
Glossy-green leaves, coppery when young,
yellow in autumn. Funnel-shaped scarlet or
orange-red flowers with crumpled petals,
late summer-early autumn. Fruits after a
long, hot summer. Best on warm wall. We
recommend:
– – **'Flore Pleno'** LS † ○
Double, orange-red flowers. AGM 1993

PYRACANTHA 'Orange Glow'

PUNICA granatum 'Nana'

– – **'Nana'** DS † ○
Dwarf form with narrow leaves. Orange-scarlet flowers in profusion, September-October. AM 1936

PYRACANTHA – Rosaceae MS-LS (E) Hdg (0.6m) "Firethorn"
Invaluable, thorny evergreens. Masses of small white flowers in summer, spectacular clusters of yellow, orange or red fruits, autumn-winter. A (f) 5
– **'Golden Charmer'** LS (E)
Vigorous, upright habit, orange-yellow fruits.
– **'Golden Dome'** SS (E)
Dense, mound-like habit. Masses of small, deep yellow berries.
– **'Mohave'** LS (E)
Wide spreading habit, masses of large, orange-red fruits. FCC 1984
– **'Orange Charmer'** LS (E)
Upright habit. Large, deep orange fruits, freely borne.

– **'Orange Glow'** LS (E)
Dense habit. Bright orange-red fruits, persisting into winter. Free fruiting. AGM 1993
– **rogersiana** LS (E)
Narrow leaves, reddish-orange fruits. Free fruiting. AM 1953 AGM 1993
– – **'Flava'** LS (E)
Fruits bright yellow. FCC 1919 AGM 1993
– **'Soleil d'Or'** MS (E)
Spreading habit. Orange-yellow fruits. Very useful as ground cover or for mass bedding.
– **'Sparkler'** SS (E) †
Leaves strikingly mottled with white, tinged pink in autumn and winter.
– **'Teton'** LS (E)
Vigorous, upright habit. Profuse, small, orange-yellow berries.
– **'Watereri'** LS (E)
Compact habit. Abundant, bright-red fruits. AM 1955 AGM 1993

PYRUS salicifolia 'Pendula'

PYRACANTHA rogersiana 'Flava'

PYRUS – Rosaceae ST
Ornamental trees often with silvery leaves.
White flowers, April. Tolerant of atmospheric
pollution. All soils.
– betulifolia ST ♥
Slender fast-growing tree. Leaves grey-green at
first, becoming glossy-green. Small, brown
fruits.
– calleryana ST ♥
We recommend the following form:
– – 'Chanticleer' ST ♦
Neat, narrowly conical crown, glossy leaves turn
rich purple and claret in autumn. AGM 1993
– nivalis ST ♥
Abundant, pure white flowers, April, with the
white woolly young leaves. Small, yellowish-
green fruits.
– salicifolia "Willow-leaved Pear" ST ♥
We recommend the following form:
– – 'Pendula' ST ♠
Graceful, small tree. Silvery, willow-like leaves.
Flowers creamy-white. Brown, top-shaped
fruits. AGM 1993

Q

QUERCUS – Fagaceae SS-LT
A large genus of deciduous and evergreen trees. Best on deep, rich soils and mostly lime tolerant, except on shallow chalk soils.
– canariensis (*Q. mirbeckii*) LT ♥ "Algerian Oak"
Fast-growing tree for all soils. Large, shallowly lobed, glossy, green leaves persisting until new year. Young trees have narrow habit. AGM 1993
– castaneifolia MT ♥ "Chestnut-leaved Oak"
Long, narrow, glossy, green leaves with sharp-pointed teeth.
– – 'Green Spire' MT ♥
A vigorous form of compact, broadly columnar habit. AGM 1993
– cerris LT ♥ "Turkey Oak"
Fast-growing tree with shallowly lobed leaves. Excellent on chalk soils and in coastal situations. AGM 1993
– – 'Variegata' MT ♥
Leaves with a very conspicuous creamy white margin. Narrow habit when young.
– coccinea LT ♥ ✗ "Scarlet Oak"
Deeply lobed leaves, glossy green above, with bristle-tipped teeth. Glowing scarlet in autumn. We recommend:

QUERCUS coccinea 'Splendens'

– – 'Splendens' LT ♥ ✗
Rich scarlet autumn colour. FCC 1893 AGM 1993
– conferta see *Q. frainetto*
– ellipsoidalis MT ♥ ✗
Deeply-lobed, slender-stalked leaves turn deep crimson in autumn.
– frainetto (*Q. conferta*) LT ♥ "Hungarian Oak"
Fast-growing tree with fissured bark. Leaves deeply and regularly lobed. Excellent on all soils, including chalk. We recommend:
– – 'Hungarian Crown' LT ♥
A form with upright branches making a compact, broadly oval head. AGM 1993
– henryi see *Lithocarpus henryi*
✗ hispanica LT Semi-(E) ♥
Vigorous hybrids between the "Cork Oak" and the "Turkey Oak". Leaves retained until spring. We recommend the following form:
– – 'Lucombeana' (*Q. lucombeana*) LT Semi-(E) ♥ "Lucombe Oak"
Sharply toothed, glossy, green leaves, grey beneath. AGM 1993
– ilex LT (E) ♥ "Evergreen Oak" "Holm Oak"
Leathery, glossy, dark green, entire or toothed leaves. Branches pendulous at tips on old trees. Good on chalk or in coastal areas. AGM 1993
– ✗ kewensis MT (E) ♥
Vigorous, compact habit with small, dark green, angularly lobed leaves.
– lucombeana see *Q. ✗ hispanica* 'Lucombeana'
– ✗ ludoviciana LT Semi-(E) ♥ ✗
Vigorous tree with deeply and irregularly lobed, glossy, green leaves. Rich autumn colours.
– macranthera MT ♥
Fast-growing tree with stout shoots and large, strongly lobed leaves, softly downy beneath.
– marilandica ST ♥ ✗ "Black Jack Oak"
Slow-growing tree with leaves, three-lobed at the broad apex, glossy green above, tawny-yellow beneath.
– mirbeckii see *Q. canariensis*
– nigra (*Q. aquatica*) MT ♥ ✗ "Water Oak"
Obovate, variously lobed or entire leaves, glossy green on both sides.
– palustris LT ♥ "Pin Oak"
Leaves deeply and sharply lobed, glossy green, often turning rich scarlet in autumn. Branches

droop gracefully at the tips. AGM 1993
– **pedunculata** see *Q. robur*
– **petraea** (*Q. sessiliflora*) LT ⚲ "Sessile Oak" "Durmast Oak"
One of our native oaks, differing from *Q. robur* in its long-stalked leaves and sessile acorns. Good on damp soils. AGM 1993
– – **'Purpurea'** LT ⚲
Young leaves deep, reddish-purple.
– **phellos** LT ⚲ ⟋ "Willow Oak"
Leaves glossy green, narrow, usually entire, willow-like, yellow and orange in autumn. AGM 1993
– × **pseudoturneri** see *Q. × turneri*
– **robur** (*Q. pedunculata*) LT ⚲ "Common Oak" "English Oak"
Our best known native species. Leaves shallowly lobed, nearly sessile; stalked acorns. AGM 1993
– – **'Atropurpurea'** ST ⚲
Slow growing with young leaves and shoots, rich, vinous-purple.
– – **'Concordia'** ST ⚲ "Golden Oak"
Slow growing with golden-yellow foliage.
– – **'Fastigiata'** LT ❘ "Cypress Oak"
A large imposing tree of columnar habit. AGM 1993
– – **'Variegata'** MT ⚲
Leaves with irregular, creamy-white margin.
– **rubra** (*Q. borealis* var. *maxima*) LT ⚲ ⟋ "Red Oak"
Fast-growing tree thriving even in industrial areas. Leaves sharply lobed, matt green; red then red-brown in autumn. AM 1971 AGM 1993
– – **'Aurea'** ('Sunshine') ST ⚲ ⟋ ◑
Young leaves bright yellow. AM 1971
– – **'Limelight'** ST ⟋
Leaves bright yellow-green when young turning to green. Withstands full sun. We propose this name for the plant which is grown on the Continent as *Q. rubra* 'Aurea'.
– **shumardii** ST ⚲
Attractive, deeply-cut leaves, red or golden-brown in autumn.
– **suber** MT (E) ⚲ "Cork Oak"
Thick, rugged, corky bark. Leaves broadly-toothed, leathery, glossy green above, grey-green felted beneath.
– × **turneri** (*Q. × pseudoturneri*) MT Semi-(E) ⚲ "Turner's Oak"
Compact, rounded head. Leaves dark green, toothed.
– **velutina** LT ⚲ ⟋ "Black Oak" "Yellow-bark Oak"
Large, glossy dark-green leaves.
We recommend the following form:

QUERCUS robur 'Fastigiata'

– – **'Rubrifolia'** LT ⚲ ⟋
Enormous leaves up to 40cm long, reddish-brown and yellowish in autumn.

"QUICK" see *Crataegus monogyna*

R

RAPHIOLEPIS see *Rhaphiolepis*

REHDERODENDRON – Styracaceae ST ✓
A small genus of Chinese trees.
– macrocarpum ST ✓
Leaves finely serrate, 7.5 to 10cm long.
Flowers, in pendulous clusters, white, tinged
pink with conspicuous yellow anthers, May.
Oblong, pendulous, bright-red fruits.
Attractive autumn colour. Rare. AM 1947

RHAMNUS – Rhamnaceae MS-LS
*Deciduous or evergreen trees and shrubs with
small but numerous flowers. For all soils in
sun or semi-shade.*
– alaternus LS (E)
Vigorous, bushy habit; glossy, dark green
leaves. Yellowish-green flowers. Fruits red,
then black. Good in coastal and industrial
areas. We recommend:
– – 'Argenteovariegata' MS (E)
Leaves green, marbled grey with irregular
creamy-white margin. AM 1976
– cathartica LS "Common Buckthorn"
Slender, spiny branches with glossy, green,
finely-toothed leaves. Abundant shining, black
fruits. Good on shallow chalk soils.

RHAMNUS alaternus 'Argenteovariegata'

– frangula LS "Alder Buckthorn"
Entire, glossy, green leaves, yellow in autumn.
Fruits red, turning black. Suitable for moist
areas.
– imeretina LS
Very distinct in its stout shoots. Large leaves,
downy beneath usually bronze-purple in
autumn. Large black buds. Good in damp
soils.

RHAPHIOLEPIS – Rosaceae SS (E) ○
*Slow growing shrubs with leathery leaves.
Well drained soil. Good on sunny walls.*
– × delacourii SS (E) † ○
Obovate, glossy, green leaves. Flowers in
erect, terminal panicles in spring or summer.
We recommend the following:
– – 'Coates Crimson' SS (E) † ○
Flowers rose-crimson.
– – 'Spring Song' SS (E) † ○
Apple blossom-pink flowers over a long
period.
– umbellata SS (E) ○
Dense, rounded habit with thick, oval,
inconspicuously toothed leaves. Clusters of
slightly fragrant, white flowers, June. Bronze-
black fruits.

RHODODENDRON (including *Azalea*
– Ericaceae PS-ST ✓ ◑
*Vast group of diverse ornamental plants, both
deciduous and evergreen. Primarily noted for
magnificent inflorescences. Range of
flowering from January-August, although
majority are April-June. Many have handsome
foliage, some of the deciduous kinds being
known for rich autumn leaf colour. They
require moist, well drained, lime-free soil and
relish annual mulching. Large-leaved forms
require shelter from wind damage. Relative
hardiness denoted by use of RHS symbols as
follows:*
   *H4 – hardy anywhere in British Isles,
includes the Hardy Hybrids (HH)*
   *H3– hardy in South and West, and along
seaboard and sheltered inland gardens*
   *H2– requires protection in most sheltered
gardens*
   *H1–should usually only be grown as a
greenhouse plant.*

Grouped RHODODENDRONS

RHODODENDRON SPECIES (including *Azaleas*) PS-ST ✕ ◐
Dwarf species make ideal rock garden subjects. Large-leaved species require wind shelter, ideally thin oak woodland with some evergreen protection.
Awards given to unnamed forms of species are indicated AM (F) or FCC (F)
– **albrechtii** *(Azalea albrechtii)* (Azalea) MS ✕ ◐
Open habit. Leaves clustered at branch tips, turn yellow, autumn. Deep rose flowers, before or with leaves; April-May. AM 1943 AGM 1993 H4
– **arboreum 'Sir Charles Lemon'** see *R.* 'Sir Charles Lemon' under Hybrids.
– **argyrophyllum** LS (E) ✕ ◐
Long leaves silvery or white-felted beneath. Lax trusses of bell-shaped flowers. Slow. AM (F) 1934 H4
We recommend:
– – **'Chinese Silver'** LS (E) ✕ ◐
Leaves silver beneath. Pink flowers, darker on the lobes; May. AM 1957 AGM 1993 H4
– **augustinii** LS (E) ✕ ◐
Small leaves. Delightful blue flowers; April-May. Excellent woodland shrub. AM 1926 H3-4. We recommend:
– – **'Electra'** LS (E) ✕ ◐
Clusters of violet blue flowers marked with greenish-yellow blotches, appearing almost luminous *en masse.* AM 1940 AGM 1993 H3
– **auriculatum** LS (E) ✕ ◐
Richly-scented large, white, funnel-shaped

flowers in huge trusses; July-August. AM 1922 H4
– **bureaui** MS (E) ✕ ◐
Dark shiny leaves, red-woolly beneath. Young growths pale fawn to rust. Compact trusses of bell-shaped rose flowers marked crimson; April-May. AM 1939 (for flowers) AM 1972 (for foliage) AGM 1993 H4
– **calostrotum** DS (E) ✕ ◐
Grey-green foliage. Large saucer-shaped magenta-crimson flowers; May-June. AM (F) 1935 H4
We recommend the form:
– – **'Gigha'** ('Red Form') SS (E) ✕ ◐
Deep claret-red flowers. FCC 1971 AGM 1993

RHODODENDRON calostrotum 'Gigha'

– **campanulatum** LS (E) ✕ ◐
Unfurling leaves coated in suede-like fawn or rust indumentum. Bell-shaped flowers varying pale rose to lavender; April-May. H4
We recommend the forms:
– – subsp. **aeruginosum** *(R. aeruginosum)* MS (E) ✕ ◐
Metallic, green-blue young growths. Slow growth.
– – **'Knap Hill'** MS (E) ✕ ◐
Lavender-blue flowers. AM 1925 AGM 1993
– **ciliatum** SS (E) ✕ ◐
Peeling bark and conspicuously hairy leaves. Fragrant, lilac-rose, bell-shaped, nodding flowers; March-April. AM (F) 1953 AGM 1993 H3-4
– **cinnabarinum** MS-LS (E) ✕ ◐
Scaly leaves. Bright cinnabar red, tubular flowers; May-June. H4. We recommend:
– – **Conroy** group MS (E) ✕ ◐
Narrow, trumpet-shaped, waxy flowers, light orange tinged rose. AM 1950 AGM 1993 H3

– **dauricum** MS Semi-(E) ✎ ◑
1- to 3-flowered trusses of funnel-shaped
rose-purple flowers; January-March. H4.
We recommend the form:
– – **'Midwinter'** MS Semi-(E) ✎ ◑
 Phlox-purple flowers. AM 1963 FCC 1969
AGM 1993
– **davidsonianum** MS-LS (E) ✎ ◑
Lanceolate leaves. Clusters of funnel-shaped
flowers, varying soft pink-purplish-rose. We
recommend a good pale-pink form. AM (F)
1935 FCC (F) 1955 AGM 1993 H3-4
– **decorum** LS-ST (E) ✎ ◑
Glabrous leaves. Lax trusses of large, fragrant,
funnel-shaped flowers, white or shell pink,
sometimes spotted; May-June. H3-4
– **discolor** see *R. fortunei* subsp. *discolor*
– **falconeri** LS-ST (E) ✎ ◑
Large leaves with deeply impressed veins.
Huge trusses of bell-shaped, waxy creamy-
yellow, blotched purple, flowers; April-May.
AM 1922 AGM 1993 H3-4
– **fortunei** LS-ST (E) ✎ ◑
Bell-shaped, lilac-pink, fragrant flowers in
loose trusses; May. H4. We recommend:
– – subsp. **discolor** (*R. discolor*) LS (E) ✎ ◑
Huge trusses of fragrant, funnel-shaped, pink
flowers; June-July. AM 1921 AM (F) 1922 FCC
(F) 1922 AGM 1993 H4
– **fulvum** LS-ST (E) ✎ ◑
Large, polished, dark green leaves, cinnamon
indumentum beneath. Bell-shaped flowers,
blush to deep rose sometimes with crimson

blotch; March-April. AM (F) 1933 FCC (F)
1981 AGM 1993 H4
– **impeditum** DS (E) ✎ ◑
Low mounds of scaly branches. Tiny leaves.
Light purplish-blue, funnel-shaped flowers;
April-May. AM (F) 1944 AGM 1993 H4
– **kaempferi** (Azalea) MS ✎ ◑ Deciduous or
Semi-(E)
Leaves and young shoots hairy. Clusters
of 2 to 4, funnel-shaped flowers, varying
biscuit, salmon, orange, red, rose scarlet;
May-June. AM 1953 AGM 1993 H4. We
recommend:
– – 'Mikado' MS ✎ ◑
Apricot-salmon flowers; late June-July. AM
1988
– **kiusianum** (Azalea) DS (E) ✎ ◑
Funnel-shaped red to lilac-puple flowers.
Dense, spreading habit. AGM 1993
– **lutescens** MS-LS (E) ✎ ◑
Bronze-red young leaves. Primrose-yellow,
funnel-shaped flowers, February to April. H3-
4. We recommend:
 'Bagshot Sands' MS (E) ✎ ◑
Large, primrose-yellow flowers, bronze-red
young foliage. AM 1953 AGM 1993
– **luteum** (*Azalea pontica*) (Azalea) MS-LS ✎ ◑
Common, fragrant yellow azalea. Leaves turn

RHODODENDRON fulvum

RHODODENDRON lutescens

RHODODENDRON SPECIES macabeanum

orange, crimson and purple, autumn. Funnel-shaped, yellow flowers in rounded trusses, May. AM 1979 AGM 1993 H4

– **macabeanum** LS-ST (E) ✕ ◑
Glossy, dark green conspicuously veined leaves, grey-white tomentose beneath, up to 30cm long. Bell-shaped pale yellow, purple spotted flowers in large trusses; March-April. AM 1937 FCC 1938 AGM 1993 H3-4

– **mallotum** LS-ST (E) ✕ ◑
Leaves, rufous woolly beneath. Dark crimson, bell-shaped flowers, March-April. AM 1933 H4

– **moupinense** SS (E) ✕ ◑
Bristly branchlets. Leaves densely scaly beneath. Sweetly scented, funnel-shaped flowers, February-March. We offer a selected form with deep pink flowers spotted and streaked red. AM (F) 1914 AM (F) 1937 AGM 1993 H3-4

– **mucronulatum** MS ✕ ◑
Slender habit. Bright rose-purple, funnel-shaped flowers; January-March. AM (F) 1924 AM (F) 1935 H4. We recommend:

– – '**Winter Brightness**' MS ✕ ◑
A selected form with flowers of a rich purplish-rose. FCC 1957 AGM 1993

– **niveum** LS (E) ✕ ◑
Young leaves covered with dense white hairs.

RHODODENDRON moupinense

Compact, rounded heads of smoky blue to rich purple, bell-shaped flowers; April-May. AM (F) 1951 AGM 1993 H4. We recommend the form:

– – '**Clyne Castle**' LS (E) ✕ ◑
Larger leaves. Rich purple flowers. H4

– **obtusum 'Amoenum'** see R. Obtusum group 'Amoenum' under Evergreen Hybrid Azaleas

– **orbiculare** MS-LS (E) ✕ ◑
Rounded, heart-shaped leaves, glaucous beneath. Bell-shaped, rose-pink flowers, sometimes tinged blue; March-April. AM 1922 H4

– **polycladum** SS (E) ✕ ◑
Upright habit with scaly leaves and blue to purple flowers. H4. We recommend:

– – **Scintillans** group (*R. scintillans*) SS (E) ✕ ◑
Profuse, small, funnel-shaped flowers, April-May, deep violet in the form we offer. AM (F) 1924 FCC 1934 AGM 1993 H4

– **ponticum** LS (E) ✕ ◑
The Common Rhododendron which has become naturalised in the British Isles. Mauve to lilac pink flowers; May-June. Excellent for hedging and as shelter belt. H4

– **quinquefolium** (Azalea) MS-LS ✕ ◑
Leaves in whorls at shoot tips, green, bordered reddish-brown when young, colouring autumn. Clusters of pendulous, saucer-shaped, white flowers with green spots; April-May. AM 1931 AM (F) 1958 AGM 1993 H4

– **racemosum** MS (E) ✕ ◑
Leathery leaves, glaucous beneath. Pale to bright pink, funnel-shaped flowers forming racemes along branchlets; March-April. FCC 1892 H4. We recommend:

– – '**Forrest's Dwarf**' DS (E) ✕ ◑
Red branchlets. Bright pink flowers.

– **roseum** (*Azalea rosea*) (Azalea) MS-LS ✕ ◑
Clusters of clove-scented, funnel-shaped flowers, pale to deep pink, with the leaves; May. AM (F) 1955 AGM 1993 H4

– **roxieanum** SS-MS (E) ✕ ◑
Slow growth. Narrow leaves with fawn or rust indumentum beneath. Tight trusses of bell-shaped creamy-white, rose flushed flowers; April-May – not whilst young. H4. We recommend:

– – **Oreonastes** group SS (E) ✕ ◑
Very narrow, linear leaves. AM 1973 AGM 1993

– **russatum** SS (E) ✕ ◑
Compact habit, leaves 2.5cm long, densely scaly beneath. Flowers funnel-shaped, deep blue-purple to violet, white throat, April-May. AM (F) 1927 FCC (F) 1933 AGM 1993 H4

RHODODENDRON racemosum

RHODODENDRON polycladum Scintillans gp.

– **schlippenbachii** *(Azalea schlippenbachii)* (Azalea) LS ✗ ◑
Rounded habit. Large leaves in whorls at branch tips, suffused purple when young, colouring richly autumn. Saucer-shaped flowers pale to rose-pink or white; April-May. AM (F) 1896 FCC (F) 1944 AGM 1993 H4
– **scintillans** see *R. polycladum* Scintillans group

– **vaseyi** *(Azalea vaseyi)* (Azalea) LS ✗ ◑
Leaves often colouring fiery red, autumn. Widely funnel-shaped flowers, varying pale pink, rose or white with flame spots; April-May. AGM 1993 H4
– **viscosum** *(Azalea viscosa)* (Azalea) MS ✗ ◑
"Swamp Honeysuckle"
Bushy habit. Fragrant spicy, narrow, funnel-shaped flowers. White sometimes pink stained, sticky on outside; June-July. AM (F) 1921 AGM 1993 H4
– **williamsianum** SS (E) ✗ ◑
Spreading habit. Bronze young growths. Small heart-shaped leaves. Bell-shaped shell-pink flowers; April. AM 1938 AGM 1993 H3
– **yakushimanum** SS (E) ✗ ◑
Compact with dark, glossy green leaves, brown tomentose beneath. H4. We recommend:

RHODODENDRON yakushimanum 'Koichiro Wada'

– – **'Koichiro Wada'** SS (E) ✗ ◑
Young growths silvery-white. Compact trusses of bell-shaped flowers rose in bud, opening apple blossom-pink, finally white, May. FCC 1947 AGM 1993 H4
– **yunnanense** LS (E) ✗ ◑
Funnel-shaped generally pink flowers with darker spots; May. AM 1903 AGM 1993 H4

RHODODENDRON HYBRIDS PS-ST (E) ✗ ◑
Original Hardy Hybrids (HH) exhibit ample

RHODODENDRON yunnanense

RHODODENDRON 'Brocade'

foliage, full firm trusses, ability to withstand exposure and complete hardiness. More recent introductions show greater variation in foliage, flower and habit and although generally hardy, will not tolerate such extreme conditions. Average height is 1.8 to 3m. Flowering seasons are:

       Early – April
       Mid – May-mid June
       Late – Late June onwards

A (b) (i) (k) 2 *Old plants of hardy hybrids if straggly may be cut back hard during winter.*
– 'Alice' (HH) LS (E) ✗ ◑
Vigorous upright habit. Tall, conical trusses of funnel-shaped flowers, rose-pink with lighter centre. Mid. AM 1910 AGM 1993 H4

– 'Anna Baldsiefen' DS (E) ✗ ◑
Compact, upright habit. Vivid phlox-pink, funnel-shaped flowers with deeper, wavy margin. Leaves bronzing in winter. Early. AGM 1993 H4

– 'Anna Rose Whitney' MS (E) ✗ ◑
Vigorous, spreading habit. Deep rose-pink, funnel-shaped flowers 10cm across in dense, rounded trusses. Mid. AMT 1987 AGM 1993 H4

– 'Arctic Tern' DS (E) ✗ ◑
Compact with small, glossy green leaves. Small flowers white tinged green in compact, rounded trusses. Mid. AMT 1984 AMT 1989 AGM 1993 H4

– 'Arthur Stevens' MS (E) ✗ ◑
Rounded habit. Bright yellow buds and petioles. Bell-shaped flowers in loose trusses. Pale pink, fading white, with deep rose basal stain. Mid. AM 1976 AGM 1993 H3

– 'Bagshot Ruby' MS (E) ✗ ◑
Vigorous. Widely funnel-shaped, ruby flowers in rounded trusses. Mid. AM 1916 AGM 1993 H4

– 'Bashful' MS (E) ✗ ◑
Spreading habit. Light pink flowers blotched rust-red fade to white. Red-tinged leaves, silvery when young. Mid. AMT 1989 AGM 1993 H4

– 'Beatrice Keir' LS (E) ✗ ◑
Large trusses of funnel-shaped, lemon-yellow flowers. Early. AM 1974 AGM 1993 H3

– 'Beauty of Littleworth' (HH) LS (E) ✗ ◑
Huge conical trusses of white, crimson-spotted flowers. Mid. FCC 1904 FCCT 1953 AGM 1993 H4

RHODODENDRON 'Christmas Cheer'

– **'Betty Wormald'** (HH) MS (E) ✗ ◑
Huge trusses of funnel-shaped, wavy-edged flowers, crimson in bud, opening deep rose, lighter in centre and marked blackish crimson within. Mid. AMT 1935 FCCT 1964 AGM 1993 H4

– **'Bo-peep'** MS (E) ✗ ◑
Slender, loose habit. Primrose-yellow flowers with inner darker ray, in clusters of 1 or 2; March. AM 1937 AGM 1993 H3

– **'Bow Bells'** MS (E) ✗ ◑
Bushy habit. Coppery young growths. Widely bell-shaped, shell-pink flowers, deep cerise in bud. Early-Mid. AM 1935 AGM 1993 H4

– **'Bric-a-brac'** SS (E) ✗ ◑
Neat habit. White, open flowers with chocolate anthers, March. AM 1945 AGM 1993 H3

– **'Britannia'** (HH) MS (E) ✗ ◑
Compact habit. Slow. Glowing crimson scarlet flowers in compact trusses. Mid. AM 1921 FCCT 1937 AGM 1993 H4

– **'Brocade'** MS (E) ✗ ◑
Dome-shaped habit. Loose trusses of frilly, bell-shaped, peach-pink flowers, carmine in bud. Early mid. AGM 1993 H4

– **Carita** LS (E) ✗ ◑
Large, bell-shaped pale lemon flowers with inner cerise basal blotch. Early. AM 1945 H3-4
We recommend:

– – **'Golden Dream'** LS (E) ✗ ◑
Deep cream flushed and shaded pink. AGM 1993

– **'Caroline Allbrook'** SS (E) ✗ ◑
Compact, spreading habit. Widely funnel-shaped flowers with wavy margins, lavender pink with paler centre. Mid. AMT 1977 AGM 1993 H4

– **'Christmas Cheer'** (HH) MS (E) ✗ ◑
Dense, compact habit. Flowers pink in bud, fading white; March or sometimes earlier. Only occasionally in flower at Christmas. AM 1990 H4

– **Cilpinense** SS (E) ✗ ◑
Neat rounded habit to 1m high. Shallowly bell-shaped, white flowers, flushed pink, deeper in bud; March. AM 1927 FCC 1968 AGM 1993 H4

– **'Cinnkeys'** LS (E) ✗ ◑
Dense clusters of tubular, orange-red flowers, shading to yellow in lobes. Mid. AM 1935 H4

– **Conroy** see *R. cinnabarinum* Conroy group under species

– **'Countess of Haddington'** MS (E) † ✗ ◑
Straggling habit. Fragrant, trumpet-shaped, white, flushed pale rose, flowers, in umbels of 2 to 4. Early. FCC 1862 AGM 1993 H2

– **'Crest'** see *Rhododendron* 'Hawk Crest'

– **'Curlew'** DS (E) ✗ ◑
Spreading habit. Widely bell-shaped flowers about 5cm across, pale yellow, marked with greenish-brown. Mid. FCC 1969 AMT 1981 FCCT 1986 AGM 1993 H4

– **'Cynthia'** (HH) LS (E) ✗ ◑
Vigorous. Conical trusses. Widely funnel-shaped rose-crimson flowers, with ray of blackish-crimson markings within. Mid. AGM 1993 H4

– **'Doc'** SS (E) ✗ ◑
Compact habit with rose-pink, funnel-shaped flowers with wavy margins borne in rounded trusses. Mid. AGM 1993 H4

– **'Dopey'** SS (E) ✗ ◑
Bell-shaped, wavy-edged flowers, bright orange-red with paler margins and orange-brown spots, in rounded trusses. Mid. AMT 1977 FCCT 1979 AGM 1993 H4

– **'Dora Amateis'** SS (E) ✗ ◑
Compact with scaly leaves. Flowers funnel-shaped, pink in bud opening white spotted yellow, profuse in open clusters. Early. AMT 1976 FCCT 1981 AGM 1993

– **'Elisabeth Hobbie'** DS (E) ✗ ◑
Translucent, scarlet, bell-shaped flowers in loose umbels. Early. AMT 1986 AGM 1993 H4

– **'Elizabeth'** DS (E) ✗ ◑
Clusters of rich dark red, trumpet-shaped flowers; April. AM 1939 FCC 1943 H4

– **'Emasculum'** MS (E) ✗ ◑
Upright habit with small leaves. Broadly funnel-shaped, lilac-pink flowers 4cm across. Early. AM 1976 AGM 1993 H4

– **'Fabia'** SS (E) ✗ ◑
Dome-shaped bush. Loose flat trusses, scarlet, funnel-shaped flowers, orange inside and speckled pale brown. Mid. AM 1934 FCC 1989 AGM 1993 H4

RHODODENDRON 'Elizabeth'

– **'Fastuosum Flore Pleno'** (HH) LS (E) ✎ ◑
Dome-shaped bush. Lax trusses, rich mauve, double, frilly-edged, funnel-shaped flowers, ray of brown crimson markings within. Mid. AGM 1993 H4

– **'Fragrantissimum'** MS (E) † ✎ ◑
Dark green, corrugated leaves. Flowers widely funnel-shaped, extremely fragrant, white flushed rose, green tinged inside. FCC 1868 AGM 1993 H2-3

– **'Furnivall's Daughter'** MS-LS (E) ✎ ◑
Widely funnel-shaped, light rose-pink flowers with splash of dark markings. Mid-Late. AMT 1958 FCCT 1961 AGM 1993 H4

– **'Fusilier'** LS (E) ✎ ◑
Long narrow leaves. Large trusses of brilliant red bell-shaped flowers. Mid. AM 1938 FCC 1942 AGM 1993 H3

– **'Gartendirektor Glocker'** SS (E) ✎ ◑
Compact, domed habit with rounded, blue-green leaves bronze when young. Deep rose-red, funnel-shaped flowers. Tolerates sun. Mid. H4

– **'Ginny Gee'** DS (E) ✎ ◑
Compact with profusely borne, widely funnel-shaped, pale pink flowers. Early to Mid. AGM 1993 H4

– **'Golden Torch'** SS (E) ✎ ◑
Bell-shaped flowers 5cm across, pale yellow from salmon-pink buds in compact trusses. Mid. AMT 1993 AGM 1993 H4

– **'Gomer Waterer'** (HH) LS (E) ✎ ◑
Large, rounded trusses, funnel-shaped flowers, white tinged mauve, with ochre basal blotch, Mid-Late. AM 1906 AGM 1993 H4

RHODODENDRON 'Gomer Waterer'

– **Hawk** MS (E) ✎ ◑
Yellow-flowered hybrids of which we recommend:

– – **'Crest'** MS (E) ✎ ◑
Bell-shaped primrose-yellow flowers in large trusses. Mid. FCC 1953 AGM 1993

– **'Hotei'** MS (E) ✎ ◑
Compact with narrow, dark green leaves. Widely bell-shaped deep yellow flowers. Mid. AM 1973 AGM 1993 H4

– **'Hydon Dawn'** DS (E) ✎ ◑
Compact rounded trusses of funnel-shaped, light pink flowers with wavy margins and reddish spots. Mid. AMT 1986 FCCT 1987 AGM 1993 H4

– **'Hydon Hunter'** SS (E) ✎ ◑
Compact, upright habit with dark green leaves. Domed trusses of funnel-shaped flowers, white flushed pale pink with yellow spots. Mid. AM 1976 FCCT 1979 AGM 1993 H4

– **'Isabel Pearce'** LS (E) ✎ ◑
Large trusses of conspicuously spotted, rose-red flowers fading to pink with deeper margins. Mid. AGM 1993 H4

– **Jalisco** MS (E) ✎ ◑
Straw-coloured flowers, tinged orange-rose at tips. Late. H3-4. We recommend:

– – **'Elect'** MS (E) ✎ ◑
Primrose-yellow flowers with paler lobes, brownish-red markings within. AM 1948 FCCT 1987 AGM 1993

– **'Jenny'** ('Creeping Jenny') PS (E) ✎ ◑
Large, deep red, bell-shaped flowers. Mid. AGM 1993 H4

– **'Kluis Sensation'** MS (E) ✎ ◑
Bright scarlet flowers, darker spots on upper lobes. Mid. AGM 1993 H4

– **'Lady Clementine Mitford'** (HH) LS (E) ✎ ◑
Large glossy leaves. Widely funnel-shaped peach-pink flowers, shaded white; with pink,

RHODODENDRON Loderi 'Venus'

174

green and brown inner markings. Mid-Late.
AMT 1971 AGM 1993 H4

– **'Lavender Girl'** MS (E) ✓ ◑
Vigorous, compact habit. Dome-shaped
trusses, fragrant funnel-shaped lavender
flowers, lilac-mauve in bud. Mid. AMT 1950
FCCT 1967 AGM 1993 H4

– **'Lem's Cameo'** MS (E) ✓ ◑
Rounded trusses of funnel-shaped flowers to
9cm across, red in bud opening cream and
apricot flushed red and spotted pink. Mid.
AGM 1993 H4

– **'Lem's Monarch'** LS (E) ✓ ◑
Very large trusses of pale pink flowers fading
to white edged pink. Mid. AGM 1993 H4

– **'Lodauric Iceberg'** LS-ST (E) ✓ ◑
Nodding trusses of large, fragrant white
flowers 13cm across, streaked red-brown at
the base. Late. AM 1958 AGM 1993 H4

– **Loderi** LS-ST (E) ✓ ◑
Enormous trusses, fragrant, lily-like trumpet-
shaped flowers, 13-15cm across, varying
white to cream and soft pink. Early-Mid. H4.
We recommend the clones:

– – **'King George'** LS-ST (E) ✓ ◑
Pure white with pale green inner basal
markings, soft pink in bud. AM 1968 FCC
1970 AGM 1993

– – **'Pink Diamond'** LS-ST (E) ✓ ◑
Pale pink, with crimson basal markings,
turning to green, flushed brown. FCC 1914
AGM 1993

– – **'Venus'** LS-ST (E) ✓ ◑
Rhodamine pink paling with age, deep pink in
bud. AGM 1993

– **'Loder's White'** (HH) LS (E) ✓ ◑
Conical trusses. Widely funnel-shaped, pure
white flowers, edged pink and marked with
crimson spots; mauve pink in bud. Mid. AM
1911 AGM 1993 H4

– **'Marinus Koster'** MS (E) ✓ ◑
Large trusses, white flowers, shaded pink with
inner purple blotch, deep pink in bud. Mid.
AMT 1937 FCCT 1948 AGM 1993 H4

– **'May Day'** MS (E) ✓ ◑
Wide spreading. Loose trusses, slightly
pendulous, funnel-shaped, signal-red or
orange-red flowers, with large calyces. Mid.
AGM 1993 H3

– **'Moerheim'** DS (E) ✓ ◑
Compact with glossy leaves, maroon in
winter. Freely borne, aster-violet flowers. Mid.
AGM 1993 H4

– **'Morning Red'** ('Morgenrot') SS (E) ✓ ◑
Compact, rounded habit. Large trusses of
rose-red flowers deep red in bud. Mid. AGM
1993 H4

RHODODENDRON 'Loder's White'

– **'Mrs A. T. de la Mare'** (HH) MS (E) ✓ ◑
Vigorous, upright habit. Dome-shaped
trusses, frilly-edged, funnel-shaped, white
flowers with greenish spots, pink tinted in
bud. Mid. AMT 1958 AGM 1993 H4

– **'Mrs Charles E. Pearson'** (HH) MS (E) ✓ ◑
Stout, erect branches. Conical trusses, widely
funnel-shaped, pale mauve-pink flowers
fading to white, with brown markings,
mauve-pink in bud. Mid. AMT 1933 FCCT
1955 AGM 1993 H4

– **'Mrs P. D. Williams'** MS (E) ✓ ◑
Flattened trusses; ivory flowers with brown
blotch on upper lobes, freely produced. Mid-
Late. AMT 1936 AGM 1993 H4

– **Nobleanum** (HH) LS-ST (E) ✓ ◑
Slow growth. Compact trusses, widely funnel-
shaped, rich rose flowers, flushed white
inside, with crimson spots, rose scarlet in bud;
January-March or earlier. H4

– – **'Venustum'** (HH) MS (E) ✓ ◑
Dome-shaped habit. Pink flowers shading to
white with inner dark crimson basal markings;
late winter. AM 1973

– **'P. J. Mezzit'** SS (E) ✓ ◑
Dark green, scaly leaves tinged purple in
winter. Dense clusters of saucer-shaped lilac
flowers 4cm across. Early. AM 1972 AGM
1993 H4

– **'Patty Bee'** DS (E) ✓ ◑
Compact with dark green leaves bronze in
winter. Dense trusses of pale yellow, funnel-
shaped flowers 4.5cm across with wavy
margins. Early. AMT 1989 AGM 1993 H4

– **'Penheale Blue'** SS (E) ✓ ◑
Compact, rounded habit with small, dark
green leaves. Small clusters of deep violet-
blue, widely funnel-shaped flowers are freely

RHODODENDRON 'Penheale Blue'

RHODODENDRON 'Praecox'

borne. Early. AMT 1974 FCCT 1981 AGM
1993 H4
– **'Percy Wiseman'** SS (E) ✕ ◑
Compact with dark, glossy green leaves.
Globular trusses of funnel-shaped flowers
5cm across, cream flushed pink fading to
creamy-white. Mid. AMT 1982 AGM 1993 H4
– **'Pink Cherub'** SS (E) ✕ ◑
Funnel-shaped, wavy-margined flowers pink
in bud open to nearly white flushed pale pink,
freely borne in large, rounded trusses. Mid.
AMT 1968 FCCT 1988 AGM 1993 H4
– 'Pink Pebble' SS (E) ✕
Compact habit. Rose-pink, widely bell-shaped
flowers from red buds. Mid. AGM 1993
– **'Polar Bear'** LS-ST (E) ✕ ◑
Large leaves. Large trusses, fragrant, trumpet-
shaped, white flowers, green flash inside.
Late. FCC 1946 AGM 1993 H4
– **'Praecox'** SS Semi-(E) ✕ ◑
Leaves aromatic when crushed. Widely
funnel-shaped, rosy-purple flowers; February-
March. FCC 1978 AGM 1993 H4
– **'Princess Anne'** DS (E) ✕ ◑
Dense habit. Small, pale yellow, funnel-
shaped flowers. Mid. AMT 1978 FCCT 1983
AGM 1993 H4
– **'Ptarmigan'** DS (E) ✕ ◑
Spreading. Small neat heads of white flowers;
March-April. FCC 1965 AGM 1993 H4
– **'Purple Splendour'** (HH) LS (E) ✕ ◑
Erect branches. Widely funnel-shaped, rich
purple flowers with black markings. Mid-Late.
AM 1931 AGM 1993 H4
– **'Queen Elizabeth II'** MS (E) ✕ ◑
Fine clear yellow flowers. Mid. Strong-
growing. AM 1967 FCC 1974 AGM 1993
– **'Razorbill'** SS (E) ✕ ◑
Compact with small, scaly leaves. Dense
trusses of rose-pink, tubular flowers 2cm long
open from deep pink buds. Early to Mid. AM

1978 AMT 1981 FCCT 1983 AGM 1993 H4
– **'Red Carpet'** DS (E) ✕ ◑
Compact, spreading habit. Bright red, bell-
shaped flowers 5cm across with wavy
margins. Mid. AMT 1983 AGM 1993 H4
– **'Saint Tudy'** SS (E) ✕ ◑
Dense bushy habit. Dense trusses, shallowly
bell-shaped, lobelia-blue flowers. Early-Mid.
AM 1960 FCCT 1973 AGM 1993 H4
– **'Sapphire'** DS (E) ✕ ◑
Open habit. Small leaves. Pale lavender-blue
flowers. Early. AMT 1967 AGM 1993 H4
– **'Sappho'** (HH) MS ✕ ◑
Dome-shaped habit. Conical trusses. Widely
funnel-shaped, white flowers, blotched purple-
black, mauve in bud. Mid. AMT 1974 AGM
1993 H4
– **'Scarlet Wonder'** DS (E) ✕ ◑
Mound-forming. Loose terminal trusses,
trumpet-shaped, frilly-edged, ruby-red
flowers. Mid. AMT 1989 AGM 1993 H4
– **'Seven Stars'** LS (E) ✕ ◑
Vigorous. Bell-shaped, frilly-edged white
flowers flushed pink, reddish in bud. Mid. AM
1967 FCCT 1974 AGM 1993 H3-4

RHODODENDRON 'Scarlet Wonder'

– **'Silver Cloud'** ('Silberwolke') DS (E) ✗ ◐
Dense, rounded habit. Pale purple flowers darker outside with frilled margins and yellow-green spots. Mid. H4

– **'Silver Sixpence'** SS (E) ✗ ◐
Upright habit. Creamy-white spotted with yellow, from green and mauve-tinged buds. Mid. AMT 1986 AGM 1993 H4

– **'Sir Charles Lemon'** (*R. arboreum* 'Sir Charles Lemon') LS-ST (E) ✗ ◐
Vigorous with handsome leaves, rusty-brown beneath. Dense trusses of white flowers. Early. AGM 1993 H3

– **'Snow Lady'** SS (E) ✗ ◐
Spreading habit with bristly leaves. Lax trusses of fragrant white flowers. Mid. AGM 1993 H3

– **'Snow Queen'** LS (E) ✗ ◐
Compact habit. Dome-shaped trusses, large funnel-shaped, white flowers with inner red basal blotch, dark pink in bud. Mid. AM 1934 AMT 1946 FCCT 1970 AGM 1993 H3-4

– **'Souvenir de Dr S. Endtz'** MS (E) ✗ ◐
Compact habit. Dome-shaped trusses. Widely funnel-shaped, mottled pink flowers marked crimson, rich rose in bud. Mid. AM 1924 FCCT 1970 AGM 1993 H4

– **'Surrey Heath'** SS (E) ✗ ◐
Bushy, spreading habit with leaves covered in white hairs when young. Rounded trusses of funnel-shaped, pale rose-pink flowers with deeper margins. Mid. AMT 1982 AGM 1993 H4

– **'Susan'** LS (E) ✗ ◐
Bushy habit. Large trusses of bluish-mauve flowers, spotted purple. Early-Mid. AM 1930 AMT 1948 FCC 1954 AGM 1993 H4

– **'Temple Belle'** SS (E) ✗ ◐
Neat rounded habit. Loose clusters of bell-shaped, Persian-rose flowers. Early-Mid. AGM 1993 H3

– **'Tessa Roza'** SS (E) ✗ ◐
Loose clusters of deep pink flowers. Early. AM 1953 AGM 1993 H4

– **'The Hon. Jean Marie de Montague'** MS (E) ✗ ◐
Compact, spreading habit. Large, domed trusses of deep crimson-scarlet, wavy-margined flowers with darker spots. Mid. AMT 1989 AGM 1993 H4

– **'Titian Beauty'** SS (E) ✗ ◐
Compact, upright habit. Waxy-red flowers. Mid. AGM 1993 H4

– **'Tortoiseshell Champagne'** MS (E) ✗ ◐
Funnel-shaped flowers, rich yellow, fading to pale yellow tinged pink at the margins. Mid-Late. AMT 1967 AGM 1993 H3-4

– **'Unique'** SS (E) ✗ ◐
Dense leafy habit. Dome-shaped trusses. Funnel-shaped creamy flowers with crimson spots. Early-Mid. AMT 1934 FCCT 1935 AGM 1993 H4

– **Vanessa** MS (E) ✗ ◐
Spreading habit. Loose trusses. Soft pink flowers spotted carmine within. Mid-Late. FCC 1929 H3-4. We recommend:

– – **'Pastel'** MS (E) ✗ ◐
Spreading habit. Cream flowers flushed shell-pink, stained scarlet outside. Mid-Late. AM 1946 FCCT 1971 AGM 1993

RHODODENDRON 'Temple Belle'

RHODODENDRON Vanessa 'Pastel'

– **'Vintage Rosé'** SS (E) ✓ ◑
Large, conical trusses of funnel-shaped, wavy-margined flowers 6cm across, rose-pink with deeper centres. Mid-Late. AGM 1993 H4
– **'Vulcan'** MS (E) ✓ ◑
Compact habit. Bright red, funnel-shaped flowers 6cm across with wavy margins in domed trusses. Mid. AMT 1957 AGM 1993 H4
– **'W.F.H.'** SS (E) ✓ ◑
Spreading habit. Clusters of funnel-shaped, scarlet flowers. Mid. AGM 1993 H3
– **'Windlesham Scarlet'** MS (E) ✓ ◑
Compact habit. Widely bell-shaped, frilly-margined flowers, deep crimson speckled with black. Mid-Late. AMT 1968 FCCT 1971 AGM 1993 H4
– **'Winsome'** MS (E) ✓ ◑
Deep coppery young growths. Loose pendant trusses. Long wavy-edged, deep-pink flowers. Mid. AM 1950 AGM 1993 H3-4
– **'Yellow Hammer'** MS (E) ✓ ◑
Slender habit. Tubular or narrowly bell-shaped, bright yellow flowers in pairs from terminal and axillary buds. Early. AGM 1993 H3-4

RHODODENDRON 'Yellow Hammer'

AZALEODENDRONS SS-MS Semi-(E) ✓ ◑
Hybrids between deciduous azaleas and evergreen species of other series. Very hardy. Flowering May-June. H4
– **'Glory of Littleworth'** SS Semi-(E) ✓
Stiff, erect habit. Fragrant funnel-shaped flowers, cream turning milky white, with conspicuous coppery blotch; May. AM 1911

– **'Hardijzer Beauty'** SS (E) ✓
Compact habit, small, compact trusses of pale pink flowers, May. AMT 1970 AGM 1993

AZALEODENDRON 'Glory of Littleworth'

DECIDUOUS HYBRID AZALEAS SS-MS
Generally trumpet-shaped, single flowers with wide colour range. Many have rich autumn leaf colour. Divided into groups of hybrids with following characteristics:
Ghent Hybrids (Gh) – Usually fragrant, long-tubed, honeysuckle-like flowers, produced end of May onwards. Average height in an open position 1.8 to 2.5m. H4
Knap Hill Hybrids (Kn) – Usually unscented, colourful, trumpet-shaped flowers opening May. Includes Exbury azaleas (Kn-Ex). Average height in an open position 1.8 to 2.5m. H4
Mollis Hybrids (M) – Scentless, vividly coloured flowers in showy trusses before leaves; generally May. Average height in open position 1.2 to 1.8m. H4
Occidentale Hybrids (O) – Fragrant, pastel-coloured flowers opening late May. Average height in open position 1.8 to 2.5m. H4
A (i) (k) all Azaleas
– **'Ballerina'** (Kn-Ex) MS ✓
White with orange flash, suffused flesh-pink in bud. Large, frilly-edged flowers.
– **'Berryrose'** (Kn-Ex) MS ✓
Rose-pink, yellow flash. Coppery young foliage. AM 1934 AGM 1993
– **'Coccineum Speciosum'** (Gh) MS ✓
Brilliant orange-red. AGM 1993
– **'Corneille'** (Gh) MS ✓
Cream, flushed pink; pink in bud. Excellent autumn leaf colour. AMT 1958 AGM 1993
– **'Daviesii'** (Gh) MS ✓
White, yellow flare. Fragrant. AM 1989 AGM 1993

– **'Exquisitum'** (O) MS ✗
Flesh-pink, deep pink outside; orange flare.
Frilly edged. Fragrant. AMT 1950 FCCT 1968
AGM 1993
– **'Gibraltar'** (Kn-Ex) MS ✗
Flame orange, yellow flash, deep orange-
crimson in bud. Large crinkly petals. AGM 1993

AZALEA 'Persil'

AZALEA 'Gibraltar'

– **'Homebush'** (Kn) MS ✗
Rose-madder, paler shading. Semi-double.
AMT 1950 AGM 1993
– **'Irene Koster'** (O) MS ✗
Rose-pink, yellow blotch. Late. AGM 1993
– **'Klondyke'** (Kn-Ex) MS ✗
Glowing orange-gold, tinted red. Large
flowers. Coppery red young foliage. AGM
1993
– **'Nancy Waterer'** (Gh) MS ✗
Golden yellow. Large. AGM 1993

– **'Narcissiflorum'** (Gh) MS ✗
Pale yellow, darker centre and outside.
Fragrant; double. Vigorous, compact habit.
AMT 1954 AGM 1993
– **'Persil'** (Kn) MS ✗
White, orange flare. AGM 1993
– **'Royal Lodge'** (Kn-Ex) MS
Deep vermilion-red turning to crimson-red.
AGM 1993
– **'Satan'** (Kn) MS ✗
Geranium red, darker buds. AGM 1993
– **'Silver Slipper'** (Kn-Ex) MS ✗
White, flushed pink, orange flare. Copper
tinted young foliage. AMT 1962 FCCT 1963
AGM 1993
– **'Spek's Orange'** (M) SS ✗
Orange, deeper in bud. Late. AMT 1948 FCCT
1953 AGM 1993
– **'Strawberry Ice'** (Kn-Ex) MS ✗
Flesh-pink, deeper at margins, gold flare.
Deep pink in bud. AMT 1963 AGM 1993
– **'Whitethroat'** (Kn) MS ✗
Pure white. Double, frilly edged. Compact
habit. AMT 1962 AGM 1993

EVERGREEN HYBRID AZALEAS SS-MS (E)
✗ ◑

*Low spreading shrubs. April, or more generally
May, flowering. Foliage is often completely
obscured by mass of flowers. Some shelter
from cold winds, and partial shade is ideal.
Average height 0.6-1.2m. Main groups are:
Gable Hybrids (G) – flowers medium, 4-6cm
across
Glenn Dale Hybrids (GD) – flowers medium to
very large 5-10cm across
Kaempferi Hybrids (Kf) – flowers medium 4 to
5cm across
Kurume Hybrids (K) – flowers small, 2.5 to
3.5cm across. Includes "Wilson's Fifty"*

AZALEA 'Homebush'

EVERGREEN HYBRID AZALEAS

Vuyk Hybrids (V) – flowers large, 5 to 7.5cm across
– **'Addy Wery'** (K) SS (E) ✓ ◑
Deep vermilion red. AMT 1950 AGM 1993 H4
– **'Aladdin'** (K) SS (E) ✓ ◑
Intense geranium-red fading to salmon. H4
– **'Azuma-kagami'** (K) MS (E) ✓ ◑
Phlox-pink, darker shading. Hose-in-hose.
AMT 1950 AGM 1993 H3
– **'Betty'** (Kf) SS (E) ✓◑
Salmon-pink, deeper centre. AMT 1940 FCCT
1972 AGM 1993 H4
– **'Blaauw's Pink'** (K) SS (E) ✓ ◑
Salmon-pink, shaded paler; early. AGM 1993
H4

– **'Blue Danube'** (V) SS (E) ✓ ◑
Distinctive bluish-violet. AMT 1970 FCCT
1975 AGM 1993
– **'Connie'** (Kf) SS (E) ✓ ◑
Reddish-orange. H4
– **'Fedora'** (Kf) SS (E) ✓ ◑
Pale pink, darker flash. AM 1931 FCCT 1960
AGM 1993 H4
– **'Hardy Gardenia'** DS (E) ✓ ◑
Dwarf, spreading habit. Double white flowers
6cm across.
– **'Hatsugiri'** (K) SS (E) ✓ ◑
Bright crimson-purple. AMT 1956 FCCT 1969
AGM 1993 H4

AZALEA 'Hinode Giri'

AZALEA 'Blue Danube'

AZALEA 'Hinomayo'

– **'Hino Crimson'** (K) SS (E) ✄ ◑
Crimson-scarlet. AGM 1993
– **'Hinode Giri'** (K) SS (E) ✄ ◑
Bright crimson. AMT 1965 AGM 1993 H4
– **'Hinomayo'** (K) SS (E) ✄ ◑
Clear pink. AM 1921 FCCT 1945 AGM 1993 H4
– **'Ima Shojo'** (K) ('Christmas Cheer') SS (E) ✄◑
Bright red, hose-in-hose. AMT 1959 AGM 1993 H4
– 'Isabella' SS (E) ✄ ◑
Translucent pink. H4
– **'John Cairns'** (Kf) SS (E) ✄ ◑
Dark orange-red. AMT 1940 AGM 1993 H4
– **'Kirin'** (K) SS (E) ✄ ◑
Deep rose, silvery rose shading; hose-in-hose. AM 1927 AMT 1952 AGM 1993 H4
– **'Kure-no-yuki'** (K) ('Snowflake') SS (E) ✄ ◑
White, hose-in-hose. AMT 1952 AGM 1993 H4
– **'Madame van Hecke'** SS (E) ✄ ◑
Small, rosy-pink. H4
– **'Mother's Day'** SS (E) ✄ ◑
Rose red. AMT 1959 FCCT 1970 AGM 1993 H4
– **'Niagara'** (GD) SS (E) ✄ ◑
White blotched yellow-green with frilly margin. AGM 1993 H4

AZALEA 'Rosebud'

– **Obtusum** group (*Azalea obtusa*) SS (F) or semi-(E) ✄ ◑ "Kirishima Azalea"
Wide-spreading. Small glossy, oval leaves. Funnel-shaped crimson or scarlet flowers; May. AM 1898 H4. We recommend:
– – **'Amoenum'** (*Azalea amoena*) MS (E) or Semi-(E) ✄ ◑
Taller. Brilliant magenta or rose-purple flowers, hose-in-hose. AM 1907 AMT 1965
– **'Orange Beauty'** (Kf) SS (E) ✄ ◑
Salmon-orange. AMT 1945 FCC 1958 AGM 1993 H4
– **'Palestrina'** (V) SS (E) ✄ ◑
White, faint green ray. AM 1944 FCC 1967 AGM 1993 H4
– **'Purple Splendor'** SS (E) ✄ ◑
Vivid reddish-purple.
– **'Rosebud'** (K) SS (E) ✄ ◑
Rose pink, hose-in-hose. Late. AMT 1972 AGM 1993 H4
– **'Salmon's Leap'** DS (E) ✄ ◑
Leaves with striking silvery-white margin. Clear salmon-pink flowers. H3
– **'Santa Maria'** SS (E) ✄ ◑
Brick-red. H4
– **'Silvester'** (K) SS (E) ✄ ◑
Purple-red with paler margins. H4
– **'Stewartsonianum'** (G) SS (E) ✄ ◑
Vivid red. Foliage reddish in winter. AGM 1993 H4
– **'Terry'** SS (E) ✄ ◑
Deep rose-pink. H4

AZALEA 'Palestrina'

– **'Vuyk's Rosyred'** (V) SS (E) ✗ ◑
Deep rosy red. AMT 1962 AGM 1993 H4
– **'Vuyk's Scarlet'** (V) SS (E) ✗ ◑
Carmine red, fluted petals. AMT 1959 FCCT
1966 AGM 1993 H4

AZALEA 'Vuyk's Scarlet'

RHODOTYPOS – Rosaceae SS ◑
*Monotypic genus. Opposite leaves on erect
branches. Dog-rose-like white flowers. All
fertile soils.*
– **scandens** (*R. kerrioides*) SS ◑
Abundant paper-white flowers, May-July.
Shiny black conspicuous fruits.

RHUS – Anacardiaceae MS-ST "Sumachs"
*Grown primarily for pinnate, finely divided
foliage which colours richly in autumn. Male
and female flowers inconspicuous and
generally on separate plants. Easy cultivation,
any fertile soil – tolerant of atmospheric
pollution.*
– **cotinoides** see *Cotinus obovatus*
– **cotinus** see *Cotinus coggygria*
– **glabra** MS "Smooth Sumach"
Wide-spreading habit. Smooth, bloomy stems
and leaves. Fiery-red or orange-yellow autumn
foliage. Scarlet, erect, fruit clusters. We
recommend:
– – **'Laciniata'** MS
Finely divided fern-like foliage. FCC 1867
AGM 1993
– **trichocarpa** LS-ST ❦
Downy leaves, coppery-pink when young,
deep orange in autumn. Bristly, yellow fruits
in drooping clusters. AM 1979
– **typhina** LS-ST ❦ "Stag's-horn Sumach"
Densely brown-felted stems. Leaves scarlet,
red, orange and yellow in autumn. Dense

RHUS glabra 'Laciniata'

RHUS typhina

cones of dark-crimson bristly fruits, retained
on female plants into winter. AGM 1993
– – **'Dissecta'** ('Laciniata') LS-ST ❦
Female form with deeply cut fern-like foliage
AM 1910 AGM 1993

RIBES – Grossulariaceae DS-MS
*Flowering currants and ornamental
gooseberries. Generally spring flowering,
some evergreen. Easy cultivation – all soils.
Most are extremely hardy.*
(g) 5
– **alpinum** SS-MS
Densely twiggy habit. Small greenish-yellow
flowers. Red berries. Ideal for hedging.
– **aureum** see *R. odoratum*

– laurifolium DS (E)
Large leathery leaves. Dioecious, greenish-white flowers in drooping racemes; February-March. Berries red, turning blackish. AM 1912
– odoratum (*R. aureum* hort.) MS "Buffalo Currant"
Loose, erect habit. Shiny leaves, colouring richly in autumn. Golden-yellow, clove-scented flowers in lax racemes; April. Black berries.
– sanguineum MS "Flowering Currant"
Flowers in drooping racemes, later ascending; April. Black bloomy fruits. Characteristic pungent smell. We recommend the clones:
– – 'Brocklebankii' SS ◑
Golden yellow leaves. Pink flowers AM 1914 AGM 1993
– – 'Pulborough Scarlet' MS
Deep red flowers. AM 1959 AGM 1993

RIBES sanguineum 'Pulborough Scarlet'

RIBES sanguineum 'Brocklebankii'

– – 'Tydemans White' MS
The best white-flowered form and a distinct improvement on 'Album'. AGM 1993
– speciosum MS Semi-(E) "Fuchsia-Flowered Gooseberry"
Glossy leaves. Spiny, bristly, red stems and fruits. Pendulous clusters of rich red flowers; April-May. Best against walls in cold areas. AGM 1993

ROBINIA – Leguminosae LS-LT ❦
Attractive pinnate leaves, often spiny stems, pea-flowers in hanging racemes. Hardy, fast-growing and suitable for all soils, especially useful for dry or sandy soils. Tolerate atmospheric pollution. Poisonous.

– 'Hillieri' see *R.* × *slavinii* 'Hillieri'
– hispida LS "Rose Acacia"
Glandular-bristly branches. Large, deep rose flowers in short racemes. Excellent against sunny wall. AM 1934 AGM 1993
– – 'Macrophylla' LS
Larger leaflets and flowers. Less bristly.

ROBINIA × slavinii 'Hillieri'

– pseudoacacia LT ❦ "Common Acacia" "False Acacia" "Black Locust"
Suckering habit. Grooved and fissured bark. Drooping racemes of white, slightly-scented flowers along branches, June. AGM 1993
– – 'Bessoniana' ST-MT ❦
Compact form, generally spineless.

– – **'Frisia'** ST-MT ❦
Rich golden-yellow foliage throughout spring to autumn. AM 1964 AGM 1993
– – **'Inermis'** see 'Umbraculifera'
– – **'Monophylla'** see 'Unifoliola '
– – **'Umbraculifera'** ('Inermis') ST ❦ "Mop-head Acacia"
Spineless branches. Compact rounded head. Protect from strong winds.
– – **'Unifoliola'** ('Monophylla') Strange form with single large leaflets or accompanied by one or two normal-sized leaflets.
– × **slavinii 'Hillieri'** ST ❦
Slightly fragrant, lilac-pink flowers. June. AM 1962 AGM 1993

ROBINIA pseudoacacia 'Frisia'

"ROCK ROSE" see *Helianthemum* and *Cistus*

ROMNEYA – Papaveraceae SS-MS ○
"Tree Poppy"
Deeply-cut leaves. Large white poppy-like flowers with central mass of golden stamens. Spread quickly by rhizomes once established. A (c) 4
– **coulteri** SS-MS ○
Large, solitary, fragrant flowers 10-15cm across, July-October. Deeply cut blue-green leaves. FCC 1888 AGM 1993
– **'White Cloud'** SS-MS ○
Large flowers. Strong growing.

ROMNEYA coulteri

ROSA – Rosaceae DS-LS The wild rose species.
Variable habit – low suckering shrubs to tall climbers. Normally pinnate leaves, and prickly stems. Flower colour varies from delicate pastel shades to brilliant scarlet and red. Generally colourful hips. Easy cultivation, most soils, except very acid or wet.
Shrub roses – A (g) 2
– × **alba** MS "White Rose of York" "Jacobite Rose"
Strong prickly stems. Greyish-green leaves. Richly-scented generally semi-double, white flowers, 1.5cm across. Oblong red fruits.
– **'Apothecary's Rose'** see *R. gallica* var. *officinalis*
– **'Arthur Hillier'** LS
Vigorous, semi-erect habit. Large rose-crimson flowers, freely borne; June-July. Bright red, flask-shaped fruits. AM 1977
– **banksiae** Semi-(E) ○
Vigorous climber 7.5m plus. Virtually thornless. We recommend:
– – **'Alba Plena'** Semi-(E) ○ "Banksian Rose" "Lady Banks' Rose"
Dense umbels of double, rosette-like, white flowers, 3cm across, violet-scented, May-June.
– – **'Lutea'** Semi-(E) ○ "Yellow Banksian"
Double yellow flowers. AM 1960
– – **'Lutescens'** Semi-(E) ○
Single, yellow, fragrant flowers.
– – **'Normalis'** Semi-(E) ○
Sweetly fragrant, single, creamy-white flowers.

ROSA banksiae 'Lutea'

ROSA 'Canary Bird'

- **"Burnet Rose"** see *R. pimpinellifolia*
- **"Cabbage Rose"** see *R. centifolia*
- **'Canary Bird'** MS
Arching stems. Small, fern like, fresh green leaves. Abundant bright yellow flowers; late May-early June.
- **canina** MS-LS "Dog Rose"
Strong prickly stems. White or pink, scented flowers. Bright red, egg-shaped fruits.
- **'Cantabrigiensis'** MS
Bristly arching stems. Fragrant, fern-like

leaves. Soft yellow flowers, 5cm across, changing to cream AM 1931 AGM 1984
- **centifolia** SS "Cabbage Rose" "Provence Rose" "Rose des Peintres"
Erect prickly stems. Scented leaves. Large, fragrant, double, rose-pink flowers. We recommend:
- - **'Cristata'** SS ('Chapeau de Napoléon') "Crested Cabbage Rose" "Crested Moss" Crested sepals completely enveloping flower buds.
- **chinensis** SS-MS "China Rose"
Stout branches. Crimson, pink or occasionally white flowers June-September. Red obovoid fruits. We recommend:
- - **'Mutabilis'** see *R. × odorata* 'Mutabilis'
- - **'Old Blush'** SS-MS "Monthly Rose"
Compact habit. Sweet-pea scented, pink flowers, darkening with age, produced over long period.
- **'Complicata'** MS
Scrambling habit Very large, fragrant, deep peach-pink flowers with white eye. AM 1951 FCC 1958 AGM 1984
- **damascena** SS "Damask Rose"
Very thorny stems. Greyish-green leaves. Fragrant, large flowers, varying white to red. Red, bristly, obovoid fruits. Petals are used in perfume manufacture. We recommend:
- - **'Versicolor'** SS "York and Lancaster Rose"

ROSA damascena 'Versicolor'

Loosely double, white flowers, blotched rose.
- **"Dog Rose"** see *R. canina*
- **eglanteria** (*R. rubiginosa*) Hdg (0.6m) "Sweet Briar" "Eglantine"
Stout, erect, prickly stems. Arching branches. Aromatic leaves. Fragrant, clear pink flowers.

Oval, bright red, persistent fruits. Good for hedging. AM 1975
– "Eglantine" see *R. eglanteria*
– filipes
Strong rambling or climbing habit. Fragrant white flowers in panicles; late June-July. Red, globose fruits. We recommend the clone:
– – 'Kiftsgate'
Very vigorous. Foliage copper-tinted when young. Massive panicles of scented flowers. AGM 1984

ROSA filipes 'Kiftsgate'

– gallica *(R. rubra)* SS "French Rose"
Erect, slender, prickly stems. Deep pink flowers, 5-7cm across. Rounded or top-shaped, terracotta fruits. We recommend:
– – var. officinalis *(R. officinalis)* SS "Apothecary's Rose" "Red Rose of Lancaster"
Fragrant, semi-double, rose-crimson flowers with prominent yellow anthers. AGM 1984
– – 'Versicolor' SS "Rosa Mundi"
Semi-double, rose-red striped white flowers, with some entirely red. AM 1961 AGM 1984

ROSA glauca

– glauca *(R. rubrifolia)* MS
Reddish-violet, almost thornless stems. Silvery-purple foliage. Clear pink flowers. Red, ovoid fruits. AM 1949 AGM 1984
– hugonis MS
Graceful arching habit. Fern-like leaves, often bronzed in autumn. Abundant soft yellow flowers, 5cm across, May. Small, dark red round fruits. AM 1917
– "Lady Banks' Rose" see *R. banksiae* 'Alba Plena'
– longicuspis Semi-(E)
Vigorous rambler or climber. Glossy dark green leaves. Large terminal panicles of white, banana-scented flowers, 5cm across. Scarlet-orange ovoid fruits. AM 1964 AGM 1984
– lucida see *R. virginiana*
– 'Max Graf' PS GC
Long trailing stems. Fragrant, rose-pink, golden centred flowers, 5cm across, over extended period. AM 1964
– 'Mermaid' (E) ○
Rambling habit. Glossy green foliage. Sulphur yellow flowers with golden stamens, 13 to 15cm across. Best against warm sunny wall. AM 1917 AGM 1984
– "Monthly Rose" see *R. chinensis* 'Old Blush'
– moyesii MS-LS
Loose open habit, erect branches. Rich blood-crimson flowers, 6-7.5cm across; June-July. Large, flagon-shaped, crimson fruits. AM 1908 FCC 1916 AGM 1984. We recommend:

ROSA 'Mermaid'

ROSA moyesii 'Geranium'

– – **'Geranium'** MS
More compact habit. Brilliant geranium-red
flowers. Larger smoother fruits. AM 1950
AGM 1984
– **nitida** DS GC
Suckering habit. Slender, reddish stems with
fine prickles. Rich autumn leaf colour. Rose-
red flowers, 5cm across. Scarlet fruit.
– × **odorata** LS ○ "Tea Rose"
Group of old hybrids. We recommend the
clone:
– – **'Mutabilis'** (R. chinensis 'Mutabilis') ('Tipo
Ideale') SS MS

ROSA × odorata 'Mutabilis'

Vigorous, slender habit. Purplish young shoots
and coppery young leaves. Richly tea-scented,
orange buds opening buff, shaded carmine,
turning rose then crimson. AM 1957
– **omeiensis** f. **pteracantha** see R. sericea f.
pteracantha
– × **paulii** SS GC
Vigorous, mound-forming habit. Thorny
stems. White, clove-scented flowers.
– **pimpinellifolia** (R. spinosissima) SS "Scotch
Rose" "Burnet Rose"
Suckering, thicket-forming habit. Abundant
small white or pale pink flowers; May-June.
Shiny, small, maroon-black or black fruits.
– – **Double White** MS
Form with double white flowers.
– – **'Glory of Edzell'** MS
Slender branches. Abundant, clear pink
flowers, with lemon-yellow centre; May

ROSA pimpinellifolia 'Glory of Edzell'

– – **'William III'** DS
Dense bushy habit. Greyish-green leaves. Semi-
double magenta-crimson flowers turning to
rich plum, paler reverse. Black fruits.
– **"Provence Rose"** see R. centifolia
– **'Red Max Graf'** PS GC
Similar to 'Max Graf' but with scarlet flowers.
– **"Ramanas Rose"** see R. rugosa
– **"Red Rose of Lancaster"** see R. gallica var.
officinalis
– **'Rosa Mundi'** see R. gallica 'Versicolor'
– **'Rose d'Amour'** (R. virginiana 'Plena') MS
"St Mark's Rose"
Almost thornless. Abundant, fragrant, double,
deep pink flowers; over long period mid-late
summer. FCC 1980

– **"Rose des Peintres"** see *R. centifolia*
– **rubiginosa** see *R. eglanteria*
– **rubra** see *R. gallica*
– **rubrifolia** see *R. glauca*
– **rugosa** MS Hdg (0.6m) "Ramanas Rose"
Strong growing. Stout, prickly, bristly stems.
Fragrant, purplish rose flowers, 8-9cm across.
Recurrent. Bright red tomato-shaped fruits.
Excellent for hedging. AM 1896
– – **'Alba'** MS
Very vigorous. White flowers, tinted blush in
bud. AGM 1984
– – **'Blanc Double de Coubert'** see *R.* 'Blanc
Double de Coubert' under Hybrids
– – **'Frau Dagmar Hastrup'** see *R.* 'Fru
Dagmar Hastrup' under Hybrids
– – **'Roseraie de l'Hay'** see *R.* 'Roseraie de
l'Hay' under Hybrids
– – **'Rubra'** MS
Fragrant, wine-crimson flowers. Conspicuous
large fruits. AM 1955

ROSA rugosa 'Rubra'

– – **'Scabrosa'** see R. 'Scabrosa' under Hybrids
– **"Scotch Rose"** see *R. pimpinellifolia*
– **semperflorens** see *R. chinensis* 'Old Blush '
– **sericea** MS
Vigorous, thorny shrub bearing creamy-white,
four-petalled flowers in May followed by
conspicuous, red, pear-shaped hips. We
recommend:
– – f. **pteracantha** (*R. omeiensis* f.
pteracantha) MS
A striking form, the young shoots with
conspicuous, flattened, translucent red
thorns. FCC 1905 AM 1976

– **spinosissima** see *R. pimpinellifolia*
– **"Sweet Briar"** see *R. eglanteria*
– **"Tea Rose"** see *R.* × *odorata*
– **virginiana** *(R. lucida)* SS
Suckering habit. Leaves colour well in
autumn. Bright pink flowers, 5-6cm across;
June-August. Small round red fruits. AM 1953
AGM 1984
– **'Wedding Day'** LS
Vigorous climbing or rambling habit, to 10m.
Deeply-scented, large trusses of flowers,
cream with orange-yellow stamens, fading to
pink; deep yellow in bud. AM 1950
– **'White Max Graf'**
Large, single, pure white flowers. Prostrate or
climbing to 2m.
– **wichuraiana** PS Semi-(E) GC
Vigorous trailing stems, to 6m long. Fragrant
white flowers in clusters, late summer. Tiny,
round, red fruits. Excellent for covering tree-
stumps or eyesores. AM 1985
– **"York and Lancaster Rose"** see *R.
damascena* 'Versicolor'

ROSE HYBRIDS
Other rose hybrids are listed here
alphabetically. The group to which they
belong is indicated as follows:
B: Bourbon – Flowering from early June. A
very hardy class of strong-growing roses. The
vigorous sorts are admirably suited for
pergolas, arches, etc, the others for pillars,
massing in beds, pegging down, etc.
C: China or Monthly – Flowering
continuously from early June to late autumn.
The most abundant of all roses, some being
of unique colours, thriving best in a sunny
position.
E: English – Mainly small shrubs, combining
the scent and flower shape of some of the
best old roses with the colour range and
recurrent flowering of modern Floribundas
and Hybrid Teas.
HM:Hybrid Musk – Flowering June to late
autumn. Perpetual flowering, cluster roses of
bushy habit usually 1.2-2m high, all more or
less musk-scented.
HP: Hybrid Perpetual – An old group of
complex hybrids with large recurrent flowers.
Mainly 1-1.5m.
M: Modern Shrub – Flowering June to late
autumn. Strong bushes averaging 1.2-2.2m in
height. Worthy inhabitants of the rose world.
OF: Old Fashioned – Including Cabbage,
Damask, Gallica, Moss and other roses which
were favourites before the advent of the
Hybrid Perpetuals. Flowering June and July.

SHRUB ROSES as ground cover

These old roses, mostly double flowered, have many charms, not least of which is their unrivalled perfume. All grow best with liberal cultivation, but after the first season only light pruning is necessary.

R: Rambler – Vigorous shrubs with arching branches and usually relatively small flowers. Ideal for training on arches, pergolas or walls. Many suitable for growing as weeping standards.

RG: Rugosa Hybrids – Flowering June to late autumn. Extremely ornamental and the hardiest of all roses, mostly making compact bushes with large flowers. Dark green, glossy foliage and very prickly stems. Height about 1.5m. Most make good hedges.

ROSA 'Ballerina'

– **'Abraham Darby'** (E)
Fragrant, cup-shaped, apricot-yellow. Repeat-flowering. Arching habit to 1.5m.
– **'Armada'** (E)
Large clusters of semi-double, rich, clear, rose-pink flowers, not fading. Handsome hips.1.4m.
– **'Ballerina'** (HM)
Apple-blossom pink, with white eye, small, single, very free flowering in large clusters, fragrant, recurrent flowers. Makes a neat bush. AGM 1984
– **'Blanc Double de Coubert'** (RG)
Semi-double white flowers, tinted blush in bud. AM 1895 AGM 1984
– **'Bonica'** (M) GC
Cupped, loose, rose-pink with deeper centre, recurrent. Arching with light coppery-green foliage. 75cm.

ROSA 'Buff Beauty'

ROSA 'Bonica'

– **'Boule de Neige'** (B)
Creamy-white edged crimson in bud, very fragrant. Foliage smooth, leathery. Vigorous, erect.
– **'Buff Beauty'** (HM)
Apricot-yellow, lighter at the edges, double, prettily shaped, tea-scented, recurrent. Vigorous, spreading. AGM 1984
– **'Cardinal de Richelieu'** (OF – Gallica group)
Deep purple-crimson, turning purplish, opening to a reflexed ball. Height 1.5m.
– **'Cécile Brunner'** (C)
Rose-pink shaded rose, small, in lax sprays; nearly thornless. AGM 1984
– **'Cerise Bouquet'** (M)
Cerise-pink, semi-double, fragrant. Vigorous, arching habit to 3m.
– **'Chapeau de Napoléon'** see *R. centifolia* 'Cristata' under species
– **'Charles Rennie Mackintosh'** (E)
Very fragrant, double flowers of an unusual lilac-pink. 1m.

ROSA 'Cardinal de Richelieu'

– **'City of London'** (M)
Large, double, pale pink, repeat-flowering, very highly fragrant. Vigorous habit with healthy, bright green foliage. 1-1.5m.
– **'Claire Rose'** (M)
Fragrant, cup-shaped flowers opening to rosette-shaped, blush-pink paling to nearly white. Upright to 1.25m.
– **'Comte de Chambord'** (OF – Portland group)
Rich pink fading to lilac, very full, flat, very fragrant, flowering intermittently through the season. Vigorous, upright. Height 1.2m.
– **'Constance Spry'** (M)
Clear rose-pink, large and cupped with myrrh fragrance. Coppery young foliage, later grey-green. AM 1965 AGM 1984
– **'Cornelia'** (HM)
Coppery-pink with yellow base, double. Very

fragrant; foliage dark green, ample; vigorous. A reliable, perpetual cluster rose. AGM 1984
– **'English Garden'** (E)
Old-fashioned rose-shaped, fragrant, soft apricot-yellow centre, paler towards the edge. Upright to 1m.
– **'Fantin Latour'** (OF – Centifolia group)
Blush, double, freely produced, foliage good, bushy. Height 2m. AM 1959
– **'Felicia'** (HM)
Salmon-pink shaded yellow, double, very fragrant in large clusters. Foliage abundant. An ideal, compact, bushy plant. AGM 1984
– **'Ferdinand Pichard'** (HP)
Rich red striped with white and pink; large, rounded fragrant flowers.
– **'Fisherman's Friend'** (E)
Deep red, fully cupped with heavy damask fragrance. Bushy to 1m. Earned over £12,000 for BBC Children in Need Appeal.
– **'Fru Dagmar Hastrup'** (RG)
Dense, compact habit. Pale rose-pink flowers, with cream stamens, vivid pink in bud. Abundant, large, crimson, round fruits. AM 1958 AGM 1984
– **'Gertrude Jekyll'** (E)
Rich pink, old-fashioned rose-shaped, fragrant. 1.25m.
– **'Gipsy Boy'** (B)
Dark crimson-purple, reflexed petals, flattish, robust, arching. A handsome bush.
– **'Golden Wings'** (M)
Yellow, mahogany-amber stamens, very large, single, deliciously scented, continuous flowering. Compact habit. AM 1965 AGM 1984
– **'Graham Thomas'** (E)
Rich apricot-yellow, fully double, old rose style. Continuous flowering. Arching to 1.2m.

ROSA 'Heritage'

– **'Heritage'** (E)
Fragrant, blush-pink, cupped flowers. Strong branching growth to 1.3m.
– **'Jacqueline Du Pré'** (M)
Semi-double, white with golden stamens, musk-scented. Summer and autumn.
– **'Jayne Austin'** (E)
Soft yellow shading to apricot, noisette-shaped, freely produced. 1m.
– **'Königin von Dänemark'** (OF – Alba group)
Intense pink, deepest in the centre, well shaped, quartered and button-eyed. Height 1.5m. Resembles *R. × alba* in foliage and habit but shows "Damask" influence.
– **'L. D. Braithwaite'** (E)
Large, cup-shaped, brilliant crimson, very fragrant flowers over a long period.
– **'La Reine Victoria'** (B)
Rich pink, exquisite cupped shape, fragrant. Foliage light green. Vigorous and erect.

ROSA 'Graham Thomas'

ROSA 'La Reine Victoria'

– **'Little White Pet'** (M) GC
Large trusses of white, fully double, pompon-like flowers throughout summer. Dark green foliage. 60cm.

– **'Madame Hardy'** (OF – Damask group)
Creamy-white passing to pure white, incurved petals, flat, fully double, quartered, with button eye. Green, pointed foliage. Height 2m. Sturdy growth.

– **'Madame Isaac Pereire'** (B)
Rose-carmine, very large, fully double, richly fragrant. Foliage handsome. Very vigorous – a large, free bush. AGM 1984

ROSA 'Madame Isaac Pereire'

ROSA 'Marguerite Hilling'

– **'Maiden's Blush, Great'** (OF – Alba group)
White tinged blush-pink, margined creamy-pink; large, double and fragrant. Vigorous, with arching stems to 2m.

– **'Marguerite Hilling'** (MS)
Deep pink, single. Graceful bush. A sport of 'Nevada' and similar in growth. AM 1960 AGM 1984

– **'Marjorie Fair'** (MS)
Large trusses of single, fragrant, red flowers, each with a conspicuous white eye.

– **'Mary Rose'** (E)
Glowing rose-pink, old-fashioned style and very fragrant. Continuous flowering. 1.2m.

– **'Madame Pierre Oger'** (B)
Cream shades of pink shaded rosy-violet, globular, very fragrant, free intermittent flowering. Growth slender, erect. AM 1951

– **'Nevada'** (M)
Creamy-white, pale in bud, single, up to 10cm across, recurrent. Very attractive bush, 2 to 2.5m high. AM 1949 FCC 1954 AGM 1984

ROSA 'Nevada'

– **'Nozomi'** (M) GC
Low, compact, spreading habit. Pearl-pink, single flowers.

– **'Penelope'** (HM)
Shell-pink shaded saffron with yellow stamens. Semi-double, strong musk fragrance, perpetual. Leaves broad, glossy. Sturdy and stout branching. AGM 1984

– **'Perle d'Or'** (C)
Buff to pale yellow, beautifully formed, small, in large sprays. AGM 1984

– **'Pretty Jessica'** (M)
Rich pink, fragrant, old-fashioned rose-shaped. 0.8m.

ROSA 'Penelope'

– 'Prosperity' (HM)
Large, semi-double, ivory-white flushed yellow in large trusses. Dark green foliage on arching shoots.

– 'Rose de Meaux' (OF – Centifolia group)
Clear pink, flat pompon double. Leaves small. Erect growing. Height 1.2m.

ROSA 'Rose de Meaux'

– 'Roseraie de l'Hay' (RG)
Vigorous growth. Double, crimson-purple flowers with creamy stamens 10-12cm across. AGM 1984

– 'Rosy Cushion' (R) GC
Lilac-pink with ivory heart, semi-double.

– 'Sally Holmes' (M)
Pale pink to white, single, in large trusses. Upright habit to 1.2m.

ROSA 'Sally Holmes'

– 'Scabrosa' (RG)
Vigorous. Huge, violet-crimson flowers to 14cm across. Large, tomato-shaped fruits; persistent sepals. AGM 1984

– 'Shailer's White' (OF – Moss group)
Full white flowers tinged pink, very freely borne with mossy sepals.

– 'St Cecilia' (E)
Medium-sized, deeply cupped, creamy-buff flowers with strong myrrh fragrance, produced continuously. Small leaves. 1.2m.

– 'Sir Walter Raleigh' (E)
Large, double and fragrant, clear warm pink with golden stamens. Bushy, to 1.5m.

– 'Souvenir de la Malmaison' (B)
Soft, creamy-blush, large, flat and well quartered, delicate fragrance. Superb in a hot season. Strong growing.

– 'Souvenir de St Anne's' (B)
Semi-double, fragrant flowers pearly-pink outside nearly white, with yellow stamens.

– 'Stanwell Perpetual' (M)
Blush, fading white, petals quilled and folded, large, double. Long flowering, slightly fragrant. Stems arching, thorny. Foliage greyish. Possibly a Damask hybrid.

– 'Suma' (M)
Miniature climber, to 1.5m or ground cover. Rich, ruby-red with yellow stamens, slightly fragrant; repeat-flowering.

– 'Swany' (M) GC
Pure white, very double, profusely borne. 90cm.

– 'Sweet Juliet' (E)
Soft apricot, deeper in bud, repeating well in autumn.

– 'The Countryman' (E)
Rose-pink, opening to rosette of true old rose type, very strongly fragrant. 0.75m.

– 'The Fairy' (M) GC
Sprays of small, rounded, fragrant, pink flowers, July-late autumn. Compact, dwarf, spreading habit with attractive, glossy foliage.

– 'The Prince' (E)
Rosette-shaped and very fragrant, deep crimson shading to rich purple. 1.25m.

– 'Variegata di Bologna' (B)
White-flecked, deep carmine, globular, double, well filled, fragrant. The most distinct of the striped roses. Best in blackspot-free areas.

– 'Warwick Castle' (E)
Rosette-shaped, pink, fragrant. Arching, to 0.8m.

– 'Wedding Day' (R)
Large trusses of fragrant flowers, cream with orange stamens from yellow buds. Vigorous, with bright green leaves and few thorns.

– 'Westerland' (M)
Golden-orange, large and strongly scented, profuse and recurrent. Large, bright green leaves.

– 'William Lobb' (OF – Moss group)
Crimson, passing to slate-blue, flat, in clusters. Strong growing. Height 2m. Suitable for the back of a border.

– 'Winchester Cathedral' (E)
White or with buff centre, old-fashioned rose-shaped, fragrant. 1.25m. Part of the proceeds from the sale of this plant will be donated to Winchester Cathedral Trust.

– 'Yellow Button' (E)
Rosette-shaped, light yellow, fragrant. Glossy leaves. 1m.

– 'Yesterday' (M)
Lilac-pink with golden stamens, semi-double and very fragrant, flowering throughout the season.

– 'Zéphirine Drouhin' (B)
Bright carmine pink, loosely double, sweetly scented, continuous. Very vigorous, tall, stems thornless. Can be pruned to form a large bush or hedge but best as a climber. AGM 1984

ROSA 'Zéphirine Drouhin'

"ROSE OF SHARON" see *Hypericum calycinum*

"ROSEMARY" see *Rosmarinus*

ROSMARINUS – Labiatae PS-MS (E) ○
"Rosemary"

ROSA 'William Lobb'

Aromatic narrow leaves, used in cooking. Blue flowers. Suits all well-drained soils.
– **lavandulaceus** see *R. officinalis* 'Prostratus'
– **officinalis** MS (E) ○ "Common Rosemary"
Dense habit. Green or grey-green leaves, white beneath. Flowers in axillary clusters. Good informal hedge. We recommend:

ROSMARINUS officinalis

– – **'Fastigiatus'** see 'Miss Jessopp's Upright'
– – **'Miss Jessopp's Upright'** ('Fastigiatus') MS (F) ○
A vigorous form of upright habit. AGM 1993
– – **'Prostratus'** (*R. lavandulaceus* hort.) PS (E)

† ○
Dense, mat-forming habit. Clusters of flowers, May-June. Excellent for tops of sunny walls. AGM 1993
– – **'Severn Sea'** DS (E) ○
Arching branches. Brilliant flowers. AM 1989 AGM 1993
– – **'Sissinghurst Blue'** SS (E)
Upright habit with profuse, rich blue flowers. AM 1983 AGM 1993
– – **'Tuscan Blue'** SS (E) ○
Striking, deep blue flowers in winter and spring.

"ROWAN" see *Sorbus aucuparia*

RUBUS – Rosaceae PS-MS "Ornamental Brambles"
Variable genus exhibiting variously attractive foliage, flowers, or ornamental stems. Generally prickly. Easy cultivation – some excellent for poor soils.
D 1, 2, 3
– **'Benenden'** (*R.* Tridel 'Benenden') LS
Vigorous shrub with tall, arching, spineless stems and 3 to 5-lobed leaves. Scented white flowers up to 5cm across are borne in May. AM 1958 FCC 1963 AGM 1993
– – **'Betty Ashburner'** PS (E) GC
Spreading habit, large, rounded glossy leaves with crinkled edges.
– **cockburnianus** MS
Strong arching habit. Purple stems clothed in white bloom. Fern-like leaves, white or grey

RUBUS 'Benenden'

RUBUS cockburnianus

beneath. Small purple flowers June. Bloomy black fruits. AGM 1993

  microphyllus 'Variegatus' SS
Mound-forming habit. Three-lobed leaves, green mottled pink and cream.

– **odoratus** MS
Vigorous erect habit. Thornless, peeling stems. Large velvety leaves. Clusters of fragrant purplish-rose flowers, June-September. Edible red fruits.

– **thibetanus** MS
Semi-erect, purple-brown stems covered in blue-white bloom. Grey, silky, fern-like leaves, white or grey-felted beneath. Small purple flowers. Black or red fruits. AM 1915. We recommend:

– – **'Silver Fern'** SS
Dainty form with small, silver-grey leaves and very silvery shoots. AGM 1993

– **tricolor** PS (E) GC
Long, trailing, red bristly stems. Glossy green leaves, white-felted beneath. White flowers, July. Sometimes bears large red edible fruits.

– **Tridel 'Benenden'** see *R.* 'Benenden'

– **ulmifolius** LS
Vigorous, scrambling stems. Leaves, white-felted beneath. We recommend:

– – **'Bellidiflorus'** LS
Double pink flowers in large panicles, July-August. Exceedingly vigorous, suitable for a wild garden.

RUSCUS – Ruscaceae DS-SS (E)
Dense clumps of stiff green stems. Leaves reduced to tiny scales. Apparent leaves are flattened stems. Tiny, dioecious flowers. Attractive fruits on female plants. For all soils.

– **aculeatus** SS (E) "Butcher's Broom"
Small, spine-tipped "apparent" leaves, bright red cherry-like fruits where plants of both sexes are present. Fruits poisonous.

RUTA graveolens 'Jackman's Blue'

– **hypoglossum** DS (E) GC
Large "apparent" leaves, with single tiny green flower on upper surface. Similarly large red fruits on female plants.

– **racemosus** see *Danae racemosa*

RUTA – Rutaceae SS ○
Aromatic plants for well-drained situation in any soil. Irritant foliage.

– **graveolens** SS (E) ○ "Rue"
Fern-like, glaucous leaves. Small mustard-yellow flowers, June-August. We recommend the form:

– – **'Jackman's Blue'** SS (E) ○
Compact, bushy habit. Vivid glaucous-blue foliage. AGM 1993

S

"ST JOHN'S WORT" see *Hypericum*

SALIX – Salicaceae PS-LT The "Willows"
*Large diverse genus. Generally vigorous, hardy
and of easy cultivation – some excellent for
damp situations. They are dioecious, many
with attractive catkins, the male forms usually
more showy. Some have colourful stems in
winter; prune hard alternate years in March to
encourage these. B3*
– acutifolia (*S. daphnoides* var. *acutifolia*)
LS
Graceful habit. Long pointed leaves and
slender shoots. Catkins before the leaves. We
recommend:
– – 'Blue Streak' LS
Polished black-purple stems clothed in blue-
white bloom. AGM 1993
– alba LT ♥ "White Willow"
Slender branches drooping at tips. Narrow
silver-backed leaves. Excellent for wet sites,
maritime exposure and as a windbreak.

SALIX alba

– – 'Britzensis' ('Chermesina') LT ♥ "Scarlet
Willow"
Conspicuous brilliant orange-scarlet young
stems in winter. AGM 1993
– – var. caerulea (*S.* 'Caerulea') LT ♥ "Cricket
Bat Willow"
Ascending branches. Sea-green lanceolate
leaves, glaucous beneath. Best willow for

SALIX alba 'Britzensis'

cricket bats. Female.
– var. sericea ('Argentea') MT ♥
Slower growing. Leaves intensely silvery. AGM
1993
– – 'Tristis' see *S.* × *sepulcralis* 'Chrysocoma'
– – var. vitellina (*S. vitellina*) MT ♥ "Golden
Willow"
Young shoots of brilliant egg-yolk yellow.
Male. AMT 1967 AGM 1993
– – 'Vitellina Pendula' see *S.* × *sepulcralis*
'Chrysocoma'
– babylonica MT
Most cultivated plants belong to var.
pekinensis (*S. matsudana*) with slender
stems and narrow green leaves. The follow-
ing are excellent for dry soils and cold,
barren areas:
– – 'Pendula' MT ♠
Graceful, weeping habit.
– – 'Tortuosa' MT ♥
Twisted branches and twigs, especially
noticeable in winter. AGM 1993
– 'Caerulea' see *S. alba* var. *caerulea*
– caprea LS–ST ♥ "Goat Willow" "Great
Sallow"

SALIX caprea 'Kilmarnock'

Male form has large yellow spring catkins known as "Palm". Female, silvery catkins known as "Pussy Willow".

– – **'Kilmarnock'** ST ♠ "Kilmarnock Willow" Stiffly pendulous branches. Male. AM 1977 AGM 1993

– × **chrysocoma** see *S.* × *sepulcralis* 'Chrysocoma'

SALIX daphnoides

– **cinerea** LS-ST ♀ "Grey Sallow" Grey downy stout twigs. Silky catkins, early spring before leaves.

– **daphnoides** ST ♀ "Violet Willow" Vigorous deep purple shoots, clothed in white bloom. Catkins in spring, before leaves. AM 1957

– **elaeagnos** (*S. incana*) (*S. rosmarinifolia* hort.) LS "Hoary Willow" Dense, bushy habit. Slender reddish-brown stems. Linear leaves, greyish hoary, becoming green, white beneath. Catkins, with leaves, spring. AM 1989 AGM 1993

– × **erythroflexuosa** see *S.* × *sepulcralis* 'Erythroflexuosa'

– **exigua** LS-ST "Coyote Willow" Slender greyish-brown branches. Linear, silky, silver leaves, minutely toothed. Slender catkins, with the leaves.

– **fargesii** MS-LS Open habit. Stout shoots becoming polished reddish-brown. Conspicuous reddish winter buds. Slender, ascending catkins with or after leaves.

– **fragilis** LT ♀ "Crack Willow" Rugged grooved bark. Brittle-jointed twigs. Shiny, lanceolate leaves, green or bluish-green below. Slender catkins, with leaves, spring.

– **gracilistyla** MS Vigorous. Grey downy young shoots and leaves. Silky, grey, male catkins, with reddish anthers, ripening to bright yellow; spring before leaves. AM 1925

– – **'Melanostachys'** (*S. melanostachys*) SS-MS Stout twigs. Catkins before the leaves, very

SALIX hastata 'Wehrhahnii'

dark, with blackish scales and brick-red anthers ripening yellow. AGM 1993
– **hastata** SS
Leaves sea-green beneath. Catkins, before or with leaves in spring. We recommend:
– – **'Wehrhahnii'** (*S. wehrhahnii*) SS-MS
Spreading habit. Silver-grey, male catkins, turning yellow, spring. AM 1964 AGM 1993
– **helvetica** SS
Bushy habit. Soft greyish pubescence on young stems, leaves and catkins. Grey-green leaves, white beneath. Catkins, with leaves in spring. AGM 1993
– **incana** see *S. elaeagnos*
– **lanata** SS "Woolly Willow"
Slow spreading habit. Silvery grey downy leaves. Erect, yellowish-grey, woolly catkins, spring. AGM 1993
– **magnifica** LS-ST
Sparse habit. Large magnolia-like leaves. Catkins with leaves, spring, females often 15-25cm long. AM 1913 AGM 1993
– **matsudana** and cultivars see under *S. babylonica*
– **pentandra** MT ♥ "Bay Willow"
Glossy twigs. Lustrous green, bay-like leaves, aromatic when crushed. Catkins, late spring with leaves, males yellow.
– **purpurea** MS-LS "Purple Osier"
Graceful arching shoots, often purplish. Narrow blue-green leaves. Slender catkins, before leaves in spring. Wood of young shoots is bright yellow beneath bark.
– – **'Nana'** ('Gracilis') SS
Compact habit. Good low hedge for damp sites.
– – **'Pendula'** ST ♠
Long hanging branches. Excellent for a small garden. AGM 1993
– **repens** SS "Creeping Willow"
Creeping habit. Greyish-green leaves, silvery beneath. Small catkins, before leaves in spring. We recommend:
– – var. **argentea** SS
Silvery silky leaves. Revels in moist, sandy areas by the sea. AGM 1993
– **rosmarinifolia** see *S. elaeagnos*
– × **rubens** MT ♥
Vigorous tree with long, slender leaves. We recommend:
– – **'Basfordiana'** MT ♥
Young shoots orange-red in winter. Yellow male catkins in spring. AGM 1993
– × **sepulcralis** MT
A group of hybrids of which we recommend:
– – **'Chrysocoma'** (*S. alba* 'Vitellina Pendula') (*S. alba* 'Tristis') (*S. babylonica* 'Ramulis

SALIX lanata

Aureis') (*S.* × *chrysocoma*) MT ♠ "Golden Weeping Willow"
Wide-spreading. Strongly arching branches ending in golden-yellow branchlets eventually to the ground. Slender bright green leaves. AGM 1993
– – **'Erythroflexuosa'** (*S.* × *erythroflexuosa*) ST
Vigorous, contorted, orange-yellow, pendulous shoots. Twisted leaves.
subopposita DS
Slender, erect, spreading stems. Small leaves, generally opposite. Catkins, early spring before leaves, the males with brick-red anthers.
– **viminalis** LS-ST "Common Osier"
Vigorous. Long straight shoots, grey tomentose when young. Long, narrow, dull green leaves, silvery silky beneath. Catkins before leaves. Cultivated for basket making.
– **wehrhahnii** see *S. hastata* 'Wehrhahnii'

"SALLOW" see *Salix caprea* and *S. cinerea*

SALVIA – Labiatae DS-MS ○
Aromatic sub-shrubs. Flowers normally in whorls along stems late summer-early autumn. Require a warm, dry, well-drained site. Tender species are ideal for cool conservatory.
– **elegans** (*S. rutilans*) SS † ○ "Pineapple Sage"
Downy, heart-shaped, pineapple-scented leaves. Magenta-crimson flowers, summer. Needs a sheltered south wall.
– **gesneriiflora** SS † ○
Heart-shaped leaves. Long racemes of showy, intense scarlet flowers. AM 1950
– **guaranitica** (*S. ambigens*) (*S. caerulea*) SS † ○

Erect habit. Downy, heart-shaped leaves. Deep azure-blue flowers in long racemes, late summer-autumn. AM 1926
– involucrata SS † ○
Racemes of rose-magenta flowers, sticky to the touch. We recommend the form:
– – 'Bethellii' (*S. bethellii*) MS ○
Large, heart-shaped leaves. Magenta-crimson flowers in stout racemes, mid-summer onwards. FCC 1880
– microphylla (*S. grahamii*) SS † ○
Bright red flowers fading bluish-red, June-late autumn. We recommend the following:
– – var. neurepia (*S. neurepia*) SS † ○
Larger leaves. Showier, rosy-red flowers, late summer-autumn.
– officinalis DS Semi-(E) ○ "Common Sage"
Strongly aromatic, grey-green, leaves; used in cooking. Bluish-purple flowers, summer.
– – 'Icterina' DS Semi-(E) ○
Variegated leaves, green and gold. AGM 1993
– – 'Purpurascens' DS Semi-(E) ○ "Purple-Leaf Sage"
Stems and young foliage soft purple. AGM 1993
– – 'Tricolor' DS Semi-(E) ○
Grey-green leaves, splashed creamy white, suffused pink and purple.
– rutilans see *S. elegans*

SALVIA officinalis 'Tricolor'

SAMBUCUS – Caprifoliaceae SS-ST
"Elder"
Grown for ornamental foliage and fruit. Pinnate leaves with serrated leaflets. Tolerate most situations and soils.
– nigra LS-ST "Common Elder"
Fissured bark. Fragrant, cream flowers in flattened heads, June. Clusters of shiny black fruits. Good on chalk. All parts poisonous except processed flowers and fruits.

– – 'Aurea' MS "Golden Elder"
Golden yellow leaves. AGM 1993
– – 'Aureomarginata' MS
Irregular bright yellow leaf margins.
– – 'Guincho Purple' LS
Leaves deep blackish-purple, turning red in autumn, flowers tinged with pink. AM 1977 AGM 1993
– – f. laciniata MS "Fern-leaved Elder"
Finely cut, fern-like leaves. AM 1988 AGM 1993
– – 'Pulverulenta' MS
Leaves mottled and striped white. AM 1991
– racemosa MS-LS "Red-berried Elder"
Coarsely serrated leaflets. Conical heads of yellowish white flowers, April. Bright scarlet fruit clusters. AM 1936. We recommend:

SAMBUCUS racemosa 'Plumosa Aurea'

– – 'Plumosa Aurea' ('Serratifolia Aurea') SS
Deeply divided golden leaves. Rich yellow flowers. Slower growing. AM 1895 AM 1956
– – 'Sutherland Gold' SS
Similar to 'Plumosa Aurea' but less liable to scorching in full sun. AGM 1993
– – 'Tenuifolia' SS
Mound-like habit. Arching branches. Fern-like, finely divided leaves. Slow growth. AM 1917 AGM 1993

SANTOLINA – Compositae DS (E) ○
"Cotton Lavender"
Mound-forming. Grey, green or silvery finely divided foliage. Dainty button-like flower heads on tall stalks, July. Needs well drained soil.
– chamaecyparissus (*S. incana*) DS (E) ○
Woolly, silvery filigree foliage. Lemon-yellow flower heads. AGM 1993

SANTOLINA chamaecyparissus

– – var. **corsica** see 'Nana'
– – **'Nana'** (var. *corsica* hort.) DS (E) ○
More compact, dwarf habit. AGM 1993
– **neapolitana 'Edward Bowles'** see *S. pinnata* 'Edward Bowles'
– **pinnata** (*S. neapolitana*) DS (E) ○
Feathery, silver leaves. Lemon-yellow flowers. We recommend:
– – **'Edward Bowles'** (*S. neapolitana* 'Edward Bowles') DS (E) ○
Grey-green foliage. Creamy-white to pale primrose flower heads
– **rosmarinifolia** (*S. virens*) DS (E) ○
Vivid green, filigree leaves. Lemon-yellow flower heads.
– – **'Primrose Gem'** DS (E) ○
Pale, primrose-yellow flower heads. AGM 1993
– **virens** see *S. rosmarinifolia*.

SARCOCOCCA – Buxaceae DS-SS (E) ◑
"Christmas Box"
Glossy foliage. Clusters of small, white, fragrant flowers, late winter. For any fertile soil; good on chalk.
– **confusa** SS (E) ◑
Dense, spreading habit. Long, slender pointed leaves. Very fragrant flowers, with cream anthers. Shiny black fruits. AM 1989 AGM 1993
– **hookeriana** SS (E) ◑
Erect habit. Hairy green stems. Lanceolate leaves. Black berries. AM 1936 AM 1983 AGM 1993. We recommend:
– – var. **digyna** SS (E) ◑
More slender habit. Narrower leaves. AM 1970 AGM 1993
– – var. **humilis** (*S. humilis*) DS (E) ◑ GC
Suckering, densely branched habit. Shiny

SARCOCOCCA hookeriana var. humilis

deep green leaves. Male flowers have pink anthers. Black berries.
– – **'Purple Stem'** SS (E) ◑
Purple flushed young stems, petioles and midribs.
– **humilis** see *S. hookeriana* var. *humilis*
– **orientalis** SS (E) ◑
Dark green leaves on vigrous, upright shoots. Pink-tinged flowers followed by black berries.

SASA – Gramineae DS-MS (E)
Genus of thicket-forming bamboos, of low habit with relatively broad leaves. Usually solitary branches forming each node.

SASA veitchii

– palmata MS (E)
Vigorous and thicket-forming with large leaves and bright green canes. FCC 1896 AGM 1993
– – f. nebulosa MS (E)
The most commonly grown form with purple-blotched stems.
– ramosa (*Arundinaria vagans*) DS (E) GC
Vigorous, carpeting plant with bright green foliage. Canes bright green, becoming deep olive-green.
– tessellata see *Indocalamus tessellatus*
– veitchii (*S. albo-marginata*) (*Arundinaria veitchii*) DS-SS (E)
Thicket-forming. Deep purplish-green canes, later dull purple. Leaves 10-25cm long, pale straw or whitish along margins in autumn, giving variegated effect through winter. AM 1898

SASSAFRAS – Lauraceae MT ✗ ❦
Require loamy, lime-free soil and the shelter of woodland.
– albidum MT ✗ ❦
Distinctive aromatic tree. Flexuous branches, particularly conspicuous in winter. Variously shaped leaves, colouring well in autumn. Inconspicuous racemes of greenish-yellow flowers, May.

"SEA BUCKTHORN" see *Hippophae rhamnoides*

SENECIO – Compositae SS (E) ○
Attractive, often grey, foliage. Daisy-like, white or yellow flowers, summer. Excellent wind resisters and maritime shrubs.
– elaeagnifolius MS (E) ○
Rigid dense habit. Glossy, oval, leathery leaves, buff-felted beneath, as are flower-stalks and young shoots.

SENECIO 'Sunshine'

– greyi see *S.* 'Sunshine'
– monroi SS (E) ○
Dense, dome-like habit. Oval wavy edged leaves, white felted beneath, as are flower-stalks and young shoots. Yellow flower-heads. AGM 1993
– 'Sunshine' (*S. greyi* hort.) SS (F) ○
Dense mound-like habit. Silvery grey leaves becoming green, white felted beneath. Yellow flower-heads. AGM 1993
– viravira (*S. leucostachys* hort.) DS (E) † ○
Striking, silvery white, finely cut leaves. Small white flower-heads in summer. AM 1973

SENNA – Leguminosae MS † ○
A large genus, mainly from the tropics. The following requires a warm, sheltered wall or conservatory.
– × floribunda (*Cassia obtusa* hort.) MS † ○
Vigorous shrub with clusters of large, deep yellow flowers in summer and autumn. AGM 1993

SHIBATAEA – Gramineae DS (E)
Low growing bamboo with creeping rootstock. Branches short, leafy, in clusters of three to five at each node.
– kumasaca (*Phyllostachys ruscifolia*) DS (E)
Compact. Dense leafy clumps. Zig-zag canes, pale green maturing dull brown. Leaves 5 to 10cm long. FCC 1896

SINARUNDINARIA – Gramineae LS (E)
Genus of attractive bamboos previously included in Arundinaria. *We recommend:*
– anceps LS (E)
Vigorous, wide-spreading species good for screens and hedges. Erect, glossy green canes, useful in the garden when mature. AGM 1993
– murielae see *Thamnocalamus spathaceus*
– nitida LS (E)
Purple flushed, arching canes making a dense clump. Delicate, narrow leaves. FCC 1898 AGM 1993

SKIMMIA – Rutaceae DS-SS (E)
Slow growing, aromatic shrubs. Compact habit. Dioecious, apart from S. japonica *subsp.* reevesiana; *both sexes necessary for production of bright, persistent, fruits. Excellent for maritime and industrial sites.*
– × confusa SS (E)
Dense, mound-forming habit with very aromatic leaves and creamy-white flowers in spring. We recommend:
– – 'Kew Green' SS (E)
Large clusters of fragrant flowers freely borne.

Male. The best of the genus in flower and thriving in sun or shade. AM 1991 AGM 1993
– **japonica** DS-SS (E)
Dense, dome-shaped habit. Leathery leaves. White, often fragrant flowers, April-May. Bright red, globular fruits on female plants. FCC 1863. We recommend:
– – **'Foremanii'** see under 'Veitchii'
– – **'Fragrans'** SS (E)
Dense panicles of "Lily-of-the-Valley" scented, white flowers. Male. AGM 1993
– – **'Nymans'** SS (E)
Comparatively large fruits, freely borne. Female. AGM 1993
– – subsp. **reevesiana** (*S. reevesiana*) DS (E) ✗
Hermaphrodite white flowers in terminal panicles. May. We recommend 'Robert Fortune' with crimson fruits persisting through winter. AM 1982 AGM 1993
– – **'Rubella'** SS (E)
Large panicles of red buds, winter; opening to white, yellow anthered flowers, early spring. Male. AM 1962 AGM1993

SKIMMIA japonica 'Rubella'

– – **'Veitchii'** SS (E)
Vigorous. Broad leaves. Large bunches of brilliant fruits. Female. Usually grown as 'Foremanii'. FCC 1888
– **reevesiana** see *S. japonica* subsp. *reevesiana*

"SLOE" see *Prunus spinosa*

"SMOKE TREE" see *Cotinus coggygria*

"SNOWBALL" see *Viburnum opulus* 'Roseum'

"SNOWBALL, JAPANESE" see *Viburnum plicatum* 'Sterile'

"SNOWBERRY" see *Symphoricarpos albus* var. *laevigatus*

"SNOWDROP TREE" see *Halesia carolina*

"SNOWDROP TREE, MOUNTAIN" see *Halesia monticola*

"SNOWY MESIPILUS" see *Amelanchier*

SOLANUM see under CLIMBERS

SOPHORA – Leguminosae LS-LT
Elegant, pinnate leaves. Attractive pea-flowers. Require well drained, fertile soil. Sun-loving.
– **japonica** MT-LT ♀ "Japanese Pagoda Tree"
Leaves up to 30cm long. Creamy-white flowers in large terminal panicles, late summer-autumn on mature trees. AGM 1993. We recommend:
– – **'Pendula'** ST ♠
Stiffly weeping branches, eventually touching the ground.
– – **'Regent'** LT ♀
A vigorous form with glossy leaves which flowers when young.
– **microphylla** LS-ST (E) ♀ † ○
Dense, wiry habit when juvenile. Leaves with small, numerous leaflets. Drooping clusters of yellow flowers May. AM 1951. We recommend:

SOPHORA microphylla 'Sun King'

– – 'Sun King' LS (E) ○
A hardy form of dense, bushy habit producing large, bright yellow flowers over a long period during late winter and spring.
– tetraptera LS-ST (E) ♀ † ○ New Zealand "Kowhai"
Spreading or drooping branches. Yellow, slightly tubular flowers in hanging clusters, May. Beaded, 4-winged seed pods. AM 1943 AGM 1993 We recommend the form:
– – 'Grandiflora' LS-ST (E) ♀ † ○
Large leaflets. Slightly larger flowers. AM 1977

SORBARIA – Rosaceae MS-LS
Vigorous, elegant, pinnate leaves. Large conical panicles of creamy-white or white flowers. Suitable for most soils. Best in full sun. Associate well with water.
– aitchisonii MS
Long, spreading branches, reddish when young. Sharply serrated, tapering leaflets. Flowers, July-August. AM 1905 AGM 1993
– arborea LS
Robust habit. Large leaves, downy beneath. Flowers at ends of current year's growth, July-August. AM 1963

SORBARIA arborea

SORBUS – Rosaceae DS-LT
Ornamental foliage, often colouring richly in autumn. Usually white flowers, May-June. Colourful berry-like fruits; generally the yellow or white forms remaining longer in winter, than orange or red. Raw fruits are poisonous. Mostly hardy and of easy cultivation on any well drained fertile soil.
Majority fall into the first two of three groups:
Aria Section – Simple, toothed or lobed leaves. Good on chalk "The Whitebeams "
Aucuparia Section – Pinnate leaves "The Mountain Ashes "
Micromeles Section – Similar to Aria Section but fruits with deciduous calyces.

– alnifolia (Micromeles Section) ST-MT ♀
Dense purplish-brown branches. Heavily veined, double toothed leaves, colouring orange and scarlet, autumn. Small red fruits. AM 1924
– aria ST-MT ♀ "Whitebeam"
Compact, rounded head. Greyish-white, oval leaves, becoming green, white beneath, then russet and gold in autumn. Bunches of deep crimson fruit. Tolerates industrial pollution and sea winds.
– – 'Chrysophylla' ST ♀
Yellowish leaves, turning rich butter-yellow, autumn.
– – 'Decaisneana' see 'Majestica'
– – 'Lutescens' ST ♀
Emerging leaves covered in dense, creamy-white tomentum on upper surfaces, becoming grey-green in summer. AM 1952 AGM 1993

SORBUS aria 'Lutescens'

– – 'Majestica' ('Decaisneana') ST-MT ♀
Large leaves, 10-15cm long. Large berries. AGM 1993
– aucuparia ST-MT ♀ "Mountain Ash" "Rowan"
Pinnate leaves. Large, dense bunches of bright red fruits, autumn. Tolerant of extreme acidity. Not for shallow chalk. AM 1962
– – 'Aspleniifolia' ('Laciniata') ST ♀
Fern-like leaves, deeply divided.
– – 'Beissneri' ST ♦
Dark coral-red young shoots and leaf petioles. Trunk and stems, coppery russet. Yellowish-green leaves, the leaflets varying deeply incised to pinnately lobed.

– – **'Cardinal Royal'** ST ♦
A form of upright habit with bright red fruits profusely borne.

– – **'Edulis'** MT ♥
Larger leaves. Heavy bunches of large, sweet, edible fruits.

– – **'Sheerwater Seedling'** ST ♦
Vigorous, ascending branches. Orange-red berries in large clusters. Good street tree. AGM 1993

– **cashmiriana** (Aucuparia Section) ST ♥
Open branched habit. Pale pink flowers, May. Gleaming white, marble-like fruits in hanging clusters, persisting after leaf fall. AM 1952 FCC 1971 AGM 1993

– **commixta** (Aucuparia Section) ST ♥
Glossy green leaves, coppery when young, colouring brightly in autumn. Erect bunches of small, round, orange-red fruits. AM 1979. We recommend:

– – **'Embley'** ST-MT ♦
Profuse, orange-red fruits, leaves turn bright red in autumn. AM 1971 AGM 1993

– **domestica** MT ♥ "Service Tree"
Open habit. Scaly bark. Pinnate leaves. Apple- or pear-shaped, edible, green fruits flushed red, 2.5-3cm long.

– **'Eastern Promise'** (Aucuparia Section) ST ♥
Upright habit. Leaves turning purple then flame in autumn. Heavy bunches of rose-pink fruits.

– **'Embley'** see *S. commixta* 'Embley'

– **'Ethel's Gold'** (Aucuparia Section) ST ♥
Bright green leaves. Golden amber fruits, persisting into the New Year. AM 1989

– **folgneri** (Micromeles Section) ST ♥
Usually spreading or arching habit. Variable leaves often colouring well in autumn. Hanging clusters of dark red or purplish-red fruits. AM 1915. We recommend:

– – **'Lemon Drop'** ST ♥
Arching branches bear profuse, bright yellow fruits.

– **hupehensis** (Aucuparia Section) ST ♥
Strong ascending purplish-brown branches. Distinctive, bluish-green leaves. Loose, drooping clusters of white or pink tinged fruits, persisting late into winter. AM 1955 AGM 1993

– – var. **obtusa** ST ♦
A form with pink berries. AGM 1993

– **hybrida** ST ♥
Compact tree with dark green leaves divided into few leaflets at the base. Red fruits in large clusters in autumn. We recommend:

– – **'Fastigiata'** see *S.* × *thuringiaca* 'Fastigiata'

SORBUS hupehensis

– – **'Gibbsii'** ST ♦
A form of dense habit with relatively large fruits. AM 1925 AM 1953 AGM 1993

– **intermedia** (Aria Section) ST-MT ♥
"Swedish Whitebeam"
Dense, rounded head. Leaves, grey felted beneath. Orange-red fruits in bunches. Good for town or city gardens.

– – **'Brouwers'** ST ♥
Ascending branches make an oval crown. Good for street planting. AGM 1993

– **'Joseph Rock'** (Aucuparia Section) ST ♦
Erect, compact head. Leaves colouring fiery red, orange, copper and purple in autumn. Clusters of round, creamy-yellow fruits, maturing to amber. AM 1950 FCC 1962 AGM 1993

SORBUS 'Joseph Rock'

– × **kewensis** (Aucuparia Section)
(*S. pohuashanensis* hort.) ST ♥
Heavy cropper. Dense bunches of orange-red berries weigh down the branches in September. AM 1947 FCC 1973 AGM 1993

– **'Leonard Messel'** ST ♥
Compact, broadly upright habit with large blue-green leaves turning red-purple in autumn. Bright pink fruits in large clusters. AM 1973 FCC 1987

SORBUS × kewensis

–'**Mitchellii**' See *S. thibetica* 'John Mitchell'
– **reducta** (Aucuparia Section) DS
Thicket forming, suckering shrub. Red stalked leaves, bronze and purplish in autumn. Small round fruits, white flushed rose. AM 1974
– **sargentiana** (Aucuparia Section) ST ♀
Rigidly branched habit. Large, sticky, crimson, winter buds. Red-stalked leaves, colouring red in autumn. Large rounded heads of small scarlet fruits. AM 1954 FCC 1956 AGM 1993
– '**Savill Orange**' ST ♀
Dense clusters of large, orange-red berries.
– **scalaris** (Aucuparia Section) ST ♀
Wide-spreading habit. Dark glossy frond-like leaves, grey downy beneath. Colouring purple and red in autumn. Flattened heads of small, red fruits. AM 1934 AGM 1993
– '**Sunshine**' (Aucuparia Section) ST ♀
Erect habit when young. Large, lax, dense bunches of golden yellow fruits.
– **thibetica** (Aria Section) MT-LT ♀
Vigorous, large-leaved tree of which we recommend the following. For the plant previously grown under this name see *S. wardii*.
– – '**John Mitchell**' (*S. mitchellii*) MT-LT ♀
Large, rounded, green leaves, white tomentose beneath, up to 15cm long and across. AGM 1993
– × **thuringiaca** ST ♀
Leaves divided to the midrib at the base, shallowly lobed elsewhere. Bunches of scarlet berries, lightly freckled. AM 1924. We recommend the form:
– – '**Fastigiata**' (*S. hybrida* 'Fastigiata') ST ♀
Closely packed, stiffly ascending branches. A good street tree.
– **torminalis** MT ♀ "Chequer Tree" "Wild Service Tree"
Scaly bark. Twigs, woolly pubescent when young. Dark, glossy, maple-like leaves, bronzy yellow in autumn. Russety brown fruits.

SORBUS 'Sunshine'

SORBUS vilmorinii

– **vilmorinii** (Aucuparia Section) ST ♀
Spreading habit. Leaves, red and purple in autumn. Drooping clusters of rose-red fruits, turning pink to white flushed rose. AM 1916 AGM 1993
– **wardii** (*S. thibetica* hort.) (KW21127) (Aria Section) ST ♀
Stiff, erect branches. Ribbed leaves, sparsely hairy beneath, grey and downy when young. Corymbs of amber fruits, speckled greyish brown.
– '**White Wax**' ST ♀
Fern-like leaves. Drooping clusters of white berries.

– **'Winter Cheer'** (Aucuparia Section) ST ♀
Open branched habit. Large, flat bunches of
chrome yellow fruits, ripening orange-red,
persistent. AM 1971

SPARTIUM – Leguminosae MS ○
*Monotypic genus. Revels in sunny, well
drained position. Good maritime shrub. (b) 3*
– **junceum** MS ○ "Spanish Broom"
Loose habit. Erect, green, rush-like stems.
Loose, terminal racemes of fragrant, yellow
pea-flowers, summer-early autumn. AM 1968
FCC 1977 AGM 1993

SPARTIUM junceum

"SPICE BUSH" see *Lindera benzoin*

"SPINDLE" see *Euonymus*

SPIRAEA – Rosaceae DS-LS
*Variable flowering shrubs, some with attractive
foliage, of easy cultivation in ordinary soil and a
sunny site – a few dislike shallow chalk.*
– **aitchisonii** see *Sorbaria aitchisonii*
– **bullata** see *S. japonica* 'Bullata'
– × **bumalda 'Anthony Waterer'** see *S.
japonica* 'Anthony Waterer'
– – **'Goldflame'** see *S. japonica* 'Goldflame'
– × **cinerea** SS
Arching stems. Narrow leaves, grey downy
when young. Dense clusters of small white
flowers along branches, late April-early May.
We particularly recommend:
– – **'Grefsheim'** MS
Excellent free-flowering clone. AGM 1993
– **crispifolia** see *S. japonica* 'Bullata'
– **discolor** see *Holodiscus discolor*
– **fritschiana** DS
Mound-forming with blue-green leaves and
broad corymbs of white, pink-tinged flowers
in June.
– **japonica** SS
Erect habit. Coarsely serrated, lanceolate to
ovate leaves. Large, flattened heads of pink
flowers, midsummer. Variable species, we
recommend the forms:

SPIRAEA japonica 'Anthony Waterer'

– – **'Alpina'** see 'Nana'
– – **'Anthony Waterer'** (*S.* × *bumalda*
'Anthony Waterer') DS
Bright crimson flowers. Leaves occasionally
variegated cream and pink. FCC 1893 AGM
1993
– – **'Bullata'** (*S. crispifolia*) (*S. bullata*) DS
Compact habit. Small, puckered leaves. Rose-
crimson flowers in flat-topped clusters. Slow
growth. FCC 1884
– – **'Candlelight'** DS
Soft, buttery-yellow young foliage turns to
deep yellow. Pink flowers.
– – **'Firelight'** DS
Orange-red young foliage turns bright
orange-yellow then green, fiery red in
autumn. Deep rose-pink flowers.
– – **'Golden Dome'** DS
Mound-forming habit with bright yellow
foliage.
– – **'Goldflame'** (*S.* × *bumalda* 'Goldflame') DS
Young growths gold and flame coloured in
spring, turning green. Best in moist soil. AGM
1993

SPIRAEA japonica 'Goldflame'

SPIRAEA japonica 'Nana'

– – **'Little Princess'** SS
Mound-forming habit. Rose-crimson flowers.
– – **'Nana'** ('Alpina') DS
Mound-forming habit. Smaller leaves and
flower-heads. Rose-pink flowers in tiny heads.
AGM 1993
– – **'Shirobana'** DS
Mixture of white and deep pink flowers borne
in the same and different heads. AGM 1993
– **nipponica** MS
Dense bushy habit. Long, arching stems.
Clusters of white flowers, along upperside of
branches, June. We recommend the form:
– – **'Snowmound'** (var. *tosaensis* hort.) SS
Dense, mound-like habit. Abundant flowers,
smothering branches, June. AM 1982 AGM
1993. C or D 2 or 7
– – var. **tosaensis** see 'Snowmound'
– **thunbergii** SS-MS
Dense, twiggy, spreading habit. Wiry stems.
Abundant white flowers in clusters on branches, March-April. AGM 1993 C or D 2 or 7
– × **vanhouttei** MS
Vigorous, arching habit. Dense umbels of
white flowers along branches, June. AM 1984
AGM 1993

STACHYURUS – Stachyuraceae MS-LS
*Stiffly pendulous racemes of flowers form in
autumn and open early following spring.
Suitable for all fertile soils.*
– **chinensis** MS-LS
Spreading habit. Purplish branchlets.
Tapering, dull green leaves, shiny pale green
below. Soft yellow, cup-shaped flowers,
February-March. AM 1925. We offer:
– – **'Magpie'** MS
Variegated form, grey green leaves margined
cream and tinged rose.
– **praecox** MS-LS
Reddish brown branchlets. Broad, taper-
pointed leaves. Short racemes of pale yellow,
cup-shaped flowers, March or earlier. AM
1925 FCC 1976 AGM 1993

STACHYURUS praecox

STAPHYLEA – Staphyleaceae LS-ST
"Bladder Nut"
*Hardy flowering shrubs. Curious inflated
bladder-like fruits. For all fertile soils.*
– **colchica** LS
Strong growing, erect habit. Conspicuous
erect panicles of white flowers, May. Capsules
up to 10cm long. FCC 1879 AGM 1993
– **holocarpa** LS-ST ♥
Trifoliolate leaves. White flowers in drooping
panicles, April-May. AM 1924. We
recommend the form:
– – **'Rosea'** LS-ST ♥
Spreading branches. Young leaves bronze.
Drooping clusters of soft pink flowers. AM
1953

STEPHANANDRA – Rosaceae DS-MS
*Graceful habit. Leaves often colouring richly in
autumn. Small greenish-white flowers. Suit
most soils.*
– **incisa** (*S. flexuosa*) MS
Dense habit. Slender, zig-zag stems. Ovate
leaves, deeply toothed and lobed. Crowded
flower panicles, June. We recommend:

STEPHANANDRA incisa 'Crispa'

– – **'Crispa'** DS GC
Mound-forming habit. Small, crinkly leaves.
Tiny creamy flowers, June.
– **tanakae** MS
Arching, brown stems. Broadly ovate or
triangular leaves. Flowers slightly larger than
S. incisa.

STEWARTIA see *Stuartia*

× **STRANVINIA 'Redstart'** see *Photinia*
'Redstart'

"STRAWBERRY TREE" see *Arbutus unedo*

STUARTIA (*Stewartia*) – **Theaceae** LS-MT
⚘ ◖
*Notable for flowers, autumn leaf colour and
ornamental bark. White or cream, generally
solitary, flowers produced in leaf axils. Short-
lived but produced continuously, July-August.
Need moist, loamy, lime-free soil, ideally in
woodland conditions. Resent disturbance.*
– **koreana** see *S. pseudocamellia* var. *koreana*
– **malacodendron** LS-ST ⚘ ◖
White flowers with purple stamens and bluish
anthers. FCC 1934
– **pseudocamellia** (*S. grandiflora*) ST-MT ⚘
⚘ ◖
Open habit. Attractive, flaking bark. Leaves
colouring red and yellow in autumn. White
flowers with yellow anthers. FCC 1888 AGM
1993

STUARTIA pseudocamellia

– var. **koreana** (*S. koreana*) ST-MT ⚘ ⚘ ◖
Larger camellia-like flowers opening more
widely. Striking, patchwork-effect bark.
AGM 1993
– **serrata** ST ⚘ ⚘ ◖
Warm brown stems. Leathery leaves,
colouring richly, autumn. White flowers with
red basal stain outside, yellow anthers; June.
AM 1932

– **sinensis** LS-ST ⚘ ⚘ ◖
Attractive, flaking bark. Leaves, rich crimson in
autumn. Cup-shaped, fragrant flowers. AGM
1993

STYRAX – Styraceae LS-ST ⚘ ⚘ "Snowbell"
*Pure white, pendulous flowers, late spring-
summer. Require moist, loamy, lime-free soil,
sun or semi-shade.*
– **hemsleyana** ST ⚘
Open branched habit. Leaves almost round
oblique at base. Lax, downy racemes of
flowers with central cone of yellow anthers,
June. AM 1930 FCC 1942 AGM 1993. A (e) 3
– **japonica** ST ⚘ ⚘
Wide-spreading, fan-like branches. Bell-
shaped flowers with central cluster of yellow
stamens, hang along branches, June. FCC
1993 AGM 1984. A (e) 3

STYRAX japonica

– – **'Pink Chimes'** ST ⚘
Slightly drooping branches bear pale pink
flowers deeper at base.
– **obassia** LS-ST ⚘ ⚘
Large, almost round leaves, velvety beneath.
Long, lax, terminal racemes of fragrant, bell-
shaped flowers, June. FCC 1888 AGM 1993

"SUMACH" see *Cotinus coggygria* and *Rhus
typhina*

"SUN ROSE" see *Helianthemum* and *Cistus*,
Halimium and × *Halimiocistus*

"SWEET BRIAR" see *Rosa eglanteria*

"SWEET CHESTNUT' see *Castanea sativa*

"SWEET GALE" see *Myrica gale*

"SWEET GUM" see *Liquidambar styraciflua*

"SWEET PEPPER BUSH" see *Clethra
alnifolia*

"SYCAMORE" see *Acer pseudoplatanus*

SYCOPSIS – Hamamelidaceae LS-ST (E) ♥
*One species in general cultivtion with
leathery, pointed, lanceolate leaves and early
spring flowers.*
– sinensis LS-ST (E) ♥
Monoecious flowers without petals, small
clusters of red-anthered, yellow stamens
surrounded by dark brown tomentose scales,
opening February-March.

SYMPHORICARPOS – Caprifoliaceae
DS-MS
*Small flowers. Ornamental pink or white
berries, abundantly produced autumn and
persisting well into winter. Grow in all soils.
Some are excellent for hedging. Poisonous.*
– albus SS
Dense bushy shrub with white berries of
which we recommend:
– – var. laevigatus (*S. rivularis*) MS
"Snowberry"
Dense, thicket-forming habit. Profuse, marble-
like, glistening white berries. Excellent for
poor soils and dense shade. FCC 1913

SYMPHORICARPOS albus var. laevigatus

– × chenaultii SS
Dense habit. Clusters or spikes of purplish-red
berries, pinkish-white where unexposed. We
recommend the form:
– – 'Hancock' DS GC
Dwarf form, excellent as ground cover
beneath trees.
– Doorenbos Hybrids (*S. × doorenbosii*) MS
Strong growth. White fruits flushed rose. We
recommend the following clones:
– – 'Magic Berry' SS
Compact spreading habit. Abundant rose-
pink berries.
– – 'Mother of Pearl' SS
Dense habit. Heavy crops of marble-like white

SYMPHORICARPOS Doorenbos Hybrids 'Mother of Pearl'

berries flushed rose. AM 1971
– – 'White Hedge' SS Hdg (0.5m)
Strong, erect, compact growth. Erect clusters
of abundant small white berries. Excellent
hedger.
– rivularis see *S. albus* var. *laevigatus*

SYRINGA – Oleaceae SS-LS ○ "Lilac"
*Generally strong-growing tree-like shrubs,
flowering May-June. Many delightfully
fragrant. Grow in most soils, especially good
on chalk.* A (j) (k) 2
– × hyacinthiflora LS
Early flowering, variable hybrid. We
recommend the clone:
– – 'Esther Staley' LS
Abundant, single, pink flowers, carmine in
bud, late April-May. AM 1961 AGM 1993
– × josiflexa MS-LS
Deep green leaves. Loose plume like panicles
of fragrant, rose-pink flowers. We particularly
recommend:
– – 'Bellicent' LS
Enormous flower panicles. FCC 1946 AGM
1993

SYRINGA × josiflexa 'Bellicent'

– × **laciniata** (*S.afghanica* hort.) SS
Slender stems and dainty pinnately divided leaves. Slender panicles of lilac flowers, May.
– **meyeri** MS
An elegant, bushy lilac of which we recommend:
– – **'Palibin'** (*S. palibiniana* hort.) (*S. velutina* hort.) SS-MS
Dense, compact habit. Velvety, dark green leaves. Abundant panicles of pale lilac or lilac-pink flowers. AGM 1993
– **microphylla** MS
Small ovate leaves. Small panicles of fragrant, rosy-lilac flowers, June and September. We recommend the form:
– – **'Superba'** MS
Abundant rosy-pink flowers, May and inter-mittently until October. AM 1957 AGM 1993

SYRINGA microphylla 'Superba'

– **palibiniana** see *S. meyeri* 'Palibin'
– **patula** MS "Korean Lilac"
Bushy, small-leaved lilac with small panicles of fragrant flowers May-June. We recommend:
– – **'Miss Kim'** MS
Compact habit, wider than tall, profuse, small panicles of white flowers, purple in bud and when first open. AGM 1993
– × **persica** MS "Persian Lilac"
Rounded, bushy habit. Slender branches. Small panicles of fragrant, lilac flowers, May. AGM 1993
– – **'Alba'** MS
White flowers. AGM 1993
– × **prestoniae** "Canadian Hybrids"
Vigorous, late-flowering hybrids. We recommend the forms:
– – **'Elinor'** LS
Pale lavender flowers, purplish-red in bud, in erect panicles. AM 1951 AGM 1993

– **reflexa** LS
Large, rough, oval leaves, up to 20cm. Long narrow drooping panicles of purplish-pink flowers, whitish within, AM 1914 AGM 1993
– × **swegiflexa** MS
Strong-growing, open habit. Large cylindrical panicles of generally pink flowers. We recommend:
– – **'Fountain'** MS
Compact habit. Long drooping panicles of fragrant, soft pink flowers.
– **sweginzowii** MS
Vigorous. Elegant habit. Long loose panicles of fragrant, flesh-pink flowers. AM 1915. We recommend:
– – **'Superba'** MS
Larger flower panicles. AM 1918
– **velutina** see *S. meyeri* 'Palibin'
– **vulgaris** LS "Common Lilac"
Vigorous suckering habit. Richly scented flowers, May-June. Numerous cultivars have arisen from this. The following are recommended:
– – **'Charles Joly'** LS
Double, dark purplish-red, late. AGM 1993
– – **'Edward J. Gardener'** LS
Double pink flowers. Among the best of its colour.
– – **'Firmament'** LS
Single, lilac-blue, early. AGM 1993
– – **'Katherine Havemeyer'** LS
Double, lavender-purple, fading soft lilac-pink. Broad, compact panicles. AM 1933 AGM 1993
– – **'Madame Antoine Buchner'** LS
Double, pink to rosy-mauve, late. Loose narrow panicles. AM 1982 AGM 1993
– – **'Madame Lemoine'** LS
Double, pure white, creamy-yellow in bud. AM 1891 FCC 1894 AGM 1993

SYRINGA vulgaris 'Madame Lemoine'

SYRINGA vulgaris 'Souvenir de Louis Späth'

– – **'Mrs Edward Harding'** LS
Double, claret-red, shaded pink, late. Free-
flowering. AGM 1993
– – **'Paul Thirion'** LS
Double, claret rose, fading lilac-pink, carmine
in bud. Late.
– – **'Primrose'** LS
Single, pale primrose-yellow. Small, dense
panicles. AM 1950
– – **'Sensation'** LS
Single, purplish-red florets, margined white.
Large panicles.
– – **'Souvenir de Louis Späth'** LS
Single. Wine-red. FCC 1894 AGM 1993

T

TAMARIX – Tamaricaceae LS "Tamarisks"
*Graceful, slender branches. Feathery plume-like
foliage and inflorescences. Tiny pink flowers in
slender racemes. Excellent in windy or coastal
sites. Any soils except shallow chalk.*
– **pentandra** see *T. ramosissima*
– **ramosissima** (*T. pentandra*) LS
Reddish-brown branches. Glaucous foliage.
Rose pink flowers, late summer-early autumn.
AM 1933. We offer:
– – **'Rubra'** LS
Darker coloured flowers. AGM 1993. A (a) 2, 3
– **tetrandra** (*T. caspica* hort.) LS
Loose, open habit. Dark branches. Light pink
flowers, May-early June. AGM 1993. A (f) 7

TAMARIX tetrandra

TELOPEA – Proteaceae LS (E) ∠ ◑
*Require moist, well-drained, fertile, lime-free
soil.*
– **truncata** LS (E) ∠ ◑ "Tasmanian Waratah"
Stout, downy shoots. Thick leathery leaves. Rich
crimson flowers in dense terminal heads, June.
AM 1934 FCC 1938

TETRADIUM – Rutaceae MT ♦
*A small genus of trees with pinnate leaves.
The following is suitable for all types of soil.*
– **danielli** (*Euodia daniellii, E. hupehensis*)
MT ♦
Vigorous, with white, fragrant flowers, late
summer–autumn, and red to purple or black
fruits. AM 1949 FCC 1976

TELOPEA truncata

TEUCRIUM – Labiatae SS (E) ○
*Square stems. Double lipped flowers. Need
well-drained site in full sun.*
– **fruticans** SS (E) † ○ "Shrubby Germander"
Dense, white tomentum on stems and leaf
undersides. Terminal racemes of pale blue
flowers. Needs wall shelter. AM 1982. We
recommend:
– – **'Azureum'** SS (E) † ○
Deep blue flowers contrast well with the
foliage. AGM 1933

TEUCRIUM fruticans

THAMNOCALAMUS – Gramineae LS (E)
*A small genus of elegant bamboos of which we
recommend:*
– **spathaceus** (*Arundinaria murielae*) LS (E)
Canes bright green, becoming yellow-green
and making dense, non-rampant clumps. AGM
1993
– **spathiflorus** (*Arundinaria spathiflora*) LS (E)

THAMNOCALAMUS spathaceus

"THORN, GLASTONBURY" see *Crataegus monogyna* 'Biflora'

TIBOUCHINA – Melastomataceae LS-ST †
Not hardy. Suitable for sheltered warm wall in very mild area, or conservatory.
– **urvilleana** (*T. semidecandra* hort.) LS (E) †
Four-sided stems. Prominently veined, velvety leaves. Large, rich purple flowers, continuous summer-autumn. FCC 1868

TILIA – Tiliaceae ST-LT The "Limes" or "Lindens"
Basically heart-shaped leaves. Clusters of small fragrant, greenish-yellow flowers, July. Suitable for all soils. Tolerant of atmospheric pollution. May be hard pruned.
– **cordata** (*T. parvifolia*) MT-LT ♥ "Small-leaved Lime"
Leathery, dark green leaves, pale green beneath. Sweetly scented, tiny, ivory flowers. AGM 1993
– – **'Greenspire'** MT ♥
Fast-growing selection developing a narrowly oval crown. AGM 1993
– × **euchlora** MT ♥
Elegant, arching, juvenile habit, densely twiggy in maturity. Rounded, glossy green leaves, paler beneath. Free from aphids and associated stickiness. FCC 1890 AGM 1993
– × **europaea** LT ♥ "Common Lime"
Vigorous. Dense suckering habit. Greenish, smooth, zig-zag shoots. Common avenue tree. We recommend the forms:
– – **'Pallida'** MT ♥
Ascending branches forming broadly conical crown. Wind resistant.
– – **'Wratislaviensis'** MT ♥
Golden yellow young leaves, becoming green with maturity. AGM 1993

TILIA × euchlora

– **'Harold Hillier'** MT ♥
Elegant tree of narrow habit with lobed and sharply toothed, often maple-like leaves turning clear butter-yellow in autumn.
– **henryana** MT ♥
Softly downy, bristle-edged leaves, axillary tufts beneath.
– **mongolica** ST ♥ "Mongolian Lime"
Compact, rounded head of branches. Distinctive ivy-like, lobed leaves, glossy green turning bright yellow in autumn. AGM 1993
– **oliveri** MT-LT ♥
Slightly pendulous shoots. Dark green finely serrated leaves, silvery-white tomentose beneath.
– **parvifolia** see *T. cordata*
– **petiolaris 'Chelsea Sentinel'** see *T. tomentosa* 'Chelsea Sentinel'

TILIA × europaea 'Wratislaviensis'

– **platyphyllos** (*T. grandifolia*) LT ♀ "Broad-leaved Lime"
Vigorous, rounded habit. Downy shoots and leaves. Relatively few suckers produced. FCC 1892
– – **'Aurea'** LT ♀
Conspicuous yellow young shoots, maturing olive green.
– – **'Prince's Street'** LT ♦
Vigorous form of upright habit with bright red winter shoots.
– – **'Rubra'** ('Corallina') LT ♀ "Red Twigged Lime"
Semi-erect branched habit. Conspicuous reddish young twigs. Good for industrial areas. AGM 1993
– **tomentosa** (*T. argentea*) (*T. alba*) LT ♀ "Silver Lime"
Strong ascending branches, often pendulous at tips. White-felted shoots. Dark green leaves, white-felted beneath. Sweetly scented flowers are narcotic to bees. We offer:
– – **'Brabant'** LT ♦
Broadly conical form with upright branches. AGM 1993
– – **'Chelsea Sentinel'** (*T. petiolaris* 'Chelsea Sentinel') LT ♀
Long-stalked leaves on attractively drooping shoots show white undersides in the breeze. In effect, a narrower form of *petiolaris*. AGM 1993

TOONA – Meliaceae MT ♀
Mainly tropical genus. We recommend:
– **sinensis** (*Ailanthus flavescens*) (*Cedrela sinensis*) MT ♀
Large, pinnate leaves. Panicles of fragrant white flowers. Yellow autumn tints. Fast growing. We recommend:
– – **'Flamingo'** ST ♦
Slow-growing, brilliant pink young foliage.

TRACHYCARPUS – Palmae ST (E)
Palms with very large, fan-shaped leaves. Male and female flowers usually on separate trees.
– **fortunei** (*T. excelsus*) (*Chamaerops excelsa*) ST (E) ♀ "Chusan Palm"
Tall fibrous-coated trunk. Leaves, 1-1.5m across, borne in a cluster at trunk apex. Terminal panicles of numerous small yellow flowers. Bluish black fruits. AM 1970 AGM 1993

"TREE DAISY" see *Olearia*

"TREE OF HEAVEN" see *Ailanthus altissima*

TRACHYCARPUS fortunei

TROCHODENDRON aralioides

"TREE POPPY" see *Romneya*

TRICUSPIDARIA see *Crinodendron*

**TROCHODENDRON –
Trochodendraceae** LS (E) ✗
Monotypic genus. Suits most fertile soils except shallow chalk.
– **aralioides** LS (E) ✗
Slow, spreading growth. Aromatic bark. Bright apple-green, leathery, scallop-edged leaves. Erect terminal racemes of green flowers, spring-early summer. AM 1976

"TULIP TREE" see *Liriodendron tulipifera*

"TUPELO" see *Nyssa sylvatica*

U

ULEX – Leguminosae SS-MS (E) "Furze"
"Gorse" "Whin"
*Revels in poor, dry, acid soils. Unsuitable for
shallow chalk. Useful for clothing dry banks,
and for gale-swept, coastal sites.*
– **europaeus** MS (E) "Common Gorse"
Green, viciously-spiny, densely branched
shrub. Chrome-yellow pea flowers, March-
May and intermittently at other times.
– – **'Flore Pleno'** ('Plenus') SS (E)
Abundant, semi-double, persistent flowers,
April-May. AM 1967 AGM 1993

ULEX europaeus 'Flore Pleno'

ULMUS – Ulmaceae MS-LT "Elms"
*Hardy and fast growing. Grow in most soils,
and tolerate sea gales and atmospheric
pollution. As a result of "Dutch Elm Disease",
the planting of Elms has virtually ceased. The*

ULMUS minor 'Jacqueline Hillier'

*following so far appear to be resistant to the
disease.*
– × **elegantissima 'Jacqueline Hillier'** see *U.
minor* 'Jacqueline Hillier'
– × **hollandica** ST-LT
Hybrids between the "Wych Elm" and the
"Field Elm" of which we recommend:
– – **'Dampieri Aurea'** ST ❋
Conspicuous, bright golden-yellow foliage.
FCC 1893
– **minor 'Jacqueline Hillier'** (*U.* ×
elegantissima 'Jacqueline Hillier') MS
Dense suckering habit. Slender downy twigs.
Small double-toothed leaves, rough to the
touch. Good low hedge.

V

VACCINIUM – Ericaceae PS-LS ✓
Attractive, usually edible berries. Deciduous species notable for autumn leaf colour. Thrive in extremely acid soils. Generally prefer moisture and some shade.
– **corymbosum** MS ✓ "Swamp Blueberry"
Thicket-forming shrub with erect stems. Bright green leaves turn scarlet and bronze in autumn. Pale pink or white flowers, May. Sweet, edible, usually black berries. AM 1990 AGM 1993. We recommend:

VACCINIUM corymbosum

– – **'Jersey'** MS ✓
A superior selection grown for its edible fruit.
– **cylindraceum** LS ✓ Semi-(E)
Erect habit. Bright green leaves. Short racemes of cylindrical flowers, pale yellowish-green, tinged red, red in bud. Blue-black, bloomy berries. AM 1990 AGM 1993
– **glauco-album** SS (E) ✓
Suckering habit. Grey-green leaves, vivid blue-white beneath. Racemes of pink flowers amid conspicuous rosy, silvery bracts; May-June. Blue-black, bloomy berries. AM 1931 AGM 1993
– **vitis-idaea** DS (E) ✓ ◑ GC "Cowberry"
Creeping habit. Glossy, box-like leaves. Terminal racemes of bell-shaped, white tinged pink flowers; June-August. Edible, acid, red berries. We recommend:
– – **'Koralle'** DS (E) ✓ ◑ GC
Free-fruiting with large, bright red berries. AM 1976 AGM 1993

VIBURNUM – Caprifoliaceae SS-LS
Easily cultivated shrubs. Some evergreen, often ornamental leaves. Deciduous species

VACCINIUM vitis-idaea

usually have rich autumn colour. Flowers usually white, often heavily fragrant. Some have brightly coloured fruits.
– **alnifolium** see *V. lantanoides*
– **'Anne Russell'** see *V. × burkwoodii* 'Anne Russell'
– × **bodnantense** MS-LS
Strong, upright habit. Fragrant, flowers in dense clusters, October onwards. We recommend the clones:
– – **'Charles Lamont'** MS-LS
Fragrant, pure deep pink flowers over a long period. AGM 1993
– – **'Dawn'** MS-LS
Vigorous. Richly scented, rose-tinted flowers, late autumn-winter. AM 1947 AGM 1993
– – **'Deben'** MS-LS
Sweetly fragrant white flowers, pink in bud, in mild weather October-April. AM 1962 FCC 1965 AGM 1993

VIBURNUM × bodnantense 'Dawn'

217

– × **burkwoodii** MS (E)
Dark shiny leaves, brown-grey felted beneath.
Fragrant white flower clusters, pink in bud;
January-May. AM 1929
– – **'Anne Russell'** MS (E)
Clusters of fragrant white flowers, pink in
bud. AM 1957 AGM 1993
– – **'Park Farm Hybrid'** MS (E)
Strong, spreading habit. Fragrant white
flowers, pink in bud; April-May. AM 1949
AGM 1993
– × **carlcephalum** MS
Compact habit. Often rich autumn leaf
colour. Large, rounded flower corymbs, pink
in bud; May. AM 1946 AGM 1993
– **carlesii** MS
Rounded habit. Downy leaves, greyish
beneath, often colouring autumn. Heavily
scented, rounded, white flower clusters, pink
in bud; April-May. AM 1908 FCC 1909. We
recommend:
– – **'Aurora'** MS
Sweetly fragrant pink flowers, red in bud.
AGM 1993
– – **'Diana'** MS
Compact habit. Strongly fragrant flowers,
opening red turning pink.
– **'Chesapeake'** SS Semi-(E)
Mound-forming habit with dark, glossy green
leaves. Heads of fragrant white flowers open
from pink buds in May. Fruits red becoming
black.
– **davidii** SS (E)
Wide-spreading, mound-like habit. Dark,
glossy, leathery leaves, conspicuously three-
veined. Bright turquoise berries when group-
planted to ensure pollination. AM 1912 AM
1971 (to female plant) AGM 1993
– **'Eskimo'** SS Semi-(E)
Snowball-like flower heads, pink in bud
opening white. Dense habit with glossy
leaves.
– **farreri** (*V. fragrans*) MS-LS
Broad, rounded habit. Bronze young foliage.
Sweetly scented white flower clusters, pink in

VIBURNUM carlesii 'Diana'

VIBURNUM davidii

bud; November onwards. Occasional red
fruits. AM 1921 AGM 1993
– – **'Nanum'** DS
Dense, rounded habit. AM 1937
– **fragrans** see *V. farreri*
– **furcatum** LS ✕
Upright habit. Leaves colouring richly in
autumn. Hydrangea-like flowers with
marginal ray florets, May. Red fruits ripening
black. Good woodland shrub. AM 1944 AGM
1993
– × **globosum 'Jermyns Globe'** MS (E)
Dense, rounded habit. Dark green leathery
leaves on reddish petioles. Small, white
flowers May, and intermittently at other
times; blue fruits occasionally produced.
– **henryi** MS (E)
Open erect habit. Glossy, leathery leaves.
White flowers in pyramidal panicles, June.
Bright red fruits ripening black. FCC 1910
– × **hillieri** MS Semi-(E)
Spreading habit. Copper-tinted young foliage,
bronze-red in autumn. Abundant creamy
flowers in panicles, June. Bright red fruits
ripening black. We recommend:
– – **'Winton'** MS Semi-(E)
The only form in general cultivation. AM 1956
AGM 1993
– **'Jermyns Globe'** see *V.* × *globosum*
'Jermyns Globe'
– × **juddii** MS
Bushy habit. Clusters of sweetly fragrant, pink
tinged flowers; April-May. AGM 1993
– **lantana** LS "Wayfaring Tree"
Native shrub common on chalk. Leaves
sometimes dark crimson in autumn. Creamy
flowers, May-June. Red fruits maturing
black.
– **lantanoides** (*V. alnifolium*) MS ✕ ◑
"Hobble Bush"
Large, strongly veined leaves, claret-red in

autumn. Large, hydrangea-like inflorescences, marginal white sterile florets, May-June. Red fruits ripening blackish-purple. Ideal for woodland. AM 1952

– **macrocephalum** MS Semi-(E)
Rounded shrub of which we recommend:

– – **'Sterile'** MS Semi-(E)
Large, rounded heads of sterile white flowers in May. Best against a sunny wall in cold areas. AM 1927

– **opulus** LS "Guelder Rose" "Water Elder"
Maple-like leaves, colouring autumn. Hydrangea-like flowers with marginal ray florets; June-July. Persistent, red, translucent fruit clusters.

– – **'Compactum'** SS
Dense compact habit. AM 1962 AGM 1993

– – **'Notcutt's Variety'** LS
Larger flowers and fruits. AM 1930 AGM 1993

– – **'Roseum'** ('Sterile') LS "Snowball"
Conspicuous, creamy white, round heads of sterile flowers. AGM 1993

VIBURNUM opulus 'Xanthocarpum'

VIBURNUM × burkwoodii 'Park Farm Hybrid'

VIBURNUM opulus 'Roseum'

– – **'Xanthocarpum'** LS
Clear golden fruits, almost translucent when ripe. AM 1932 FCC 1966 AGM 1993

– **'Park Farm Hybrid'** see *V. × burkwoodii* 'Park Farm Hybrid'

– **plicatum** (*V. tomentosum*) (*V. plicatum* f. *tomentosum*) MS-LS
Tiered branches. Pleated leaves, often colouring autumn. Flattened heads of creamy flowers with marginal sterile ray florets, in double rows on branch uppers; May-June. Red fruits ripening black. We recommend:

– – **'Grandiflorum'** MS
Larger heads of flowers, tinged pink at margins. AM 1961 AGM 1993

– – **'Lanarth'** MS
Strong-growing. Characteristic, tiered

VIBURNUM plicatum 'Mariesii'

branching. AM 1930

– – **'Mariesii'** MS
Distinctive horizontally tiered branches. Abundant flowers. AGM 1993

– – **'Nanum Semperflorens'** ('Watanabe') MS
Compact habit. Horizontal branching. Flattened heads of flowers, intermittently summer-late autumn.

– – **'Pink Beauty'** MS
Ray florets turn pink with maturity. AGM 1993

VIBURNUM plicatum 'Pink Beauty'

VIBURNUM 'Pragense'

– – **'Rowallane'** MS
Lacecap heads with large ray florets. Profuse small red fruits. Good autumn colour. AM 1942 FCC 1956 AGM 1993
– – **'Sterile'** MS "Japanese Snowball"
Dense, spreading habit. Globular heads of white, sterile florets in double rows; May-June. FCC 1893
– – f. **tomentosum** see *V. plicatum*
– – **'Watanabe'** see 'Nanum Semper-florens'
– **'Pragense'** MS-LS (E)

VIBURNUM rhytidophyllum

Spreading habit. Elliptic, corrugated leaves to 10cm, glossy, dark green, white-felted below. Creamy white flowers, in terminal cymes, May. AGM 1993
– **rhytidophyllum** LS (E)
Fast-growing. Glossy, corrugated leaves, grey tomentose beneath. Heads of creamy-white flowers, May. Red fruits turning black. Plant two, to ensure fruiting. FCC 1907
– **sargentii** LS
Attractively lobed leaves colouring well in autumn. Lacecap-like heads of white flowers followed by red fruits. AM 1967. We recommend:
– – **'Onondaga'** LS
Upright habit with deep maroon young leaves turning reddish-purple in autumn. Flower heads with white marginal florets surrounding deep red buds. AGM 1993
– **setigerum** (*V. theiferum*) MS
Open, lax habit. Distinctive leaves, altering colour constantly, from metallic-blue-red through greens to orange-yellow. Flowers early summer. Orange-yellow fruit clusters, ripening bright red. AM 1925
– **tinus** LS (E) "Laurustinus" Hdg (0.5m)
Dense bushy habit. Dark glossy leaves. Flattened heads of flowers, late autumn-early spring. Metallic blue fruits ripening black.

VIBURNUM tinus 'Eve Price'

Good for coastal sites. We recommend:
– – **'Eve Price'** MS (E)
Dense, compact habit. Carmine buds, flowers pink-tinged. AM 1961 AGM 1993
– – **'French White'** LS (E)
Vigorous with large heads of white flowers.
– – **'Gwenllian'** MS (E)
Compact with small leaves. White flowers from deep pink buds. AGM 1993
– – **'Lucidum'** LS (E)
Vigorous. Larger leaves. Larger flower heads; March-April. AM 1972
– – **'Pink Prelude'** LS (E)
White flowers turn to pale then deep pink.
– – **'Variegatum'** MS (E) †
Leaves variegated creamy-yellow.

VINCA major 'Variegata'

VITEX agnus-castus

VINCA minor 'Argenteo-variegata'

– wrightii MS
Metallic green leaves, often colouring autumn. Flowers, May. Glistening red fruits. We recommend:
– – 'Hessei' SS
Broad, attractively-veined leaves. Conspicuous sealing wax-red fruits.

VINCA – Apocynaceae PS (E) GC
"Periwinkle"
Vigorous, trailing shrubs. Suitable for all fertile soils. A (f) 3
– major PS (E) GC "Greater Periwinkle"
Rampant trailing habit, rooting at tips. Glossy, hairy leaves. Bright blue flowers in leaf axils, April-June.
– – 'Variegata' ('Elegantissima') PS (E) GC

Leaves margined and mottled creamy-white. AM 1977 AMT 1982 AGM 1993
– minor PS (E) GC "Lesser Periwinkle"
Trailing habit, rooting at intervals. Bright blue flowers single in leaf axils; April-June, and intermittently to autumn.
– – 'Argenteo-variegata' PS (E) GC
Blue flowers. Leaves variegated creamy-white. AGM 1993
– – 'Atropurpurea' PS (E) GC
Plum-purple flowers. AMT 1983 AGM 1993
– – 'Azurea Flore Pleno' PS (E) GC
Sky blue, double flowers. AMT 1983 AGM 1993
– – 'Bowles' Variety' PS (F) GC
Small, pale blue flowers.
– – 'Gertrude Jekyll' PS (E) GC
White flowers. AMT 1983 AGM 1993
– – 'La Grave' PS (E) GC
Large, azure-blue flowers. AMT 1983 AGM 1993

VITEX – Verbenaceae MS ○
Requires good drainage and sun to ripen growth and produce flowers. Excellent for sunny wall
– agnus-castus MS ○ "Chaste Tree"
Spreading habit. Aromatic. Grey downy shoots. Slender racemes of fragrant, violet flowers. September-October. AM 1934

W

"WALNUT" see *Juglans*

"WATTLE" see *Acacia*

"WAYFARING TREE" *see Viburnum lantana*

WEIGELA – Caprifoliaceae SS-MS
Fresh green leaves. Funnel-shaped flowers varying in colour, red-pink-white, produced May-June. Easy cultivation, withstand atmospheric pollution. C7
– **'Abel Carrière'** MS
Large, rosy carmine, yellow-throated flowers AGM 1993
– **'Bristol Ruby'** MS
Vigorous, erect habit. Ruby red flowers. AM 1954

WEIGELA 'Bristol Ruby'

– **'Evita'** DS
Low, spreading habit, bright red flowers over a long period.
– **'Fiesta'** MS
Glossy red flowers profusely borne. AGM 1993
– **florida** MS
Reddish or rose-pink flowers, paler within. We recommend the forms:
– – **'Foliis Purpureis'** SS
Slower growing, compact habit. Purple-flushed leaves. Pink flowers. AGM 1993
– – **'Variegata'** MS
Compact. Leaves margined creamy-white. Pink flowers, AM 1968 AM 1988 AGM 1993
– – **'Versicolor'** SS
Flowers creamy-white changing to red.
– **'Looymansii Aurea'** MS ◑
Light golden foliage. Pink flowers.

WEIGELA florida 'Variegata'

– **'Majestueux'** MS
Erect habit. Large madder-pink, carmine-throated flowers.
– **middendorffiana** SS ◑
Peeling bark. Bell-shaped sulphur-yellow flowers with dark orange markings. April-May. Best given shelter. AM 1931
– **'Mont Blanc'** MS
Vigorous. Large, fragrant white flowers. AGM 1993
– **praecox** MS
Vigorous. Honey-scented, rose-pink flowers with yellow markings, May onwards. We recommend:
– – **'Variegata'** MS
Leaves variegated creamy-white. AGM 1993
– **'Rubidor'** SS
Yellow foliage, carmine-red flowers.
– **'Victoria'** SS
Deep bronze-purple foliage. Purple-pink flowers. Upright habit.

"WHITEBEAM" see *Sorbus aria*

"WHITEBEAM, SWEDISH" see *Sorbus intermedia*

"WILLOW" see *Salix*

"WING NUT" see *Pterocarya*

"WINTER JASMINE" see *Jasminum nudiflorum*

"WITCH HAZEL" see *Hamamelis*

X

XANTHOCERAS – Sapindaceae LS
Monotypic genus. Pinnate leaves and erect, horse chestnut-like flower panicles. For all fertile soils, good on chalk.
– sorbifolium LS
Upright habit. White flowers with carmine eye, May. Top-shaped fruits. FCC 1876 AGM 1993

XANTHORHIZA – Ranunculaceae SS
Monotypic genus. Suckering, thicket-forming shrub. Requires a moist or clay soil – not for shallow chalk.
– simplicissima SS "Yellow-root"
Pinnate leaves, burnished bronze-purple in autumn. Drooping panicles of tiny purple flowers, March-April. Bright yellow roots and inner bark, bitter to the taste. AM 1975

Y

"YELLOW ROOT" see *Xanthorhiza simplicissima*

"YELLOW WOOD" see *Cladrastis lutea*

YUCCA – Agavaceae DS-MS (E) ○
Distinctive architectural plants. Long, sword-like leaves in clumps or rosettes. Spectacular panicles of drooping, lily-like, bell-shaped flowers; July-August. Require hot, dry, well drained site.
– filamentosa DS (E) ○
Stemless. Dense clumps of leaves, margined

YUCCA filamentosa 'Bright Edge'

YUCCA filamentosa

with curly white threads. Creamy-white flowers in conical panicles 1-2m tall. AGM 1993
– – **'Bright Edge'** DS (E) ○
Leaves margined golden-yellow. AGM 1993
– – **'Variegata'** DS (E) ○
Leaves striped and margined yellow. AGM 1993
– **flaccida** DS (E) ○
Stemless. Tufts of leaves with bent tips and curly white threads along margins. Creamy flowers in downy panicles 0.6-1.2m tall. We recommend the clone:
– – **'Golden Sword'** DS (E) ○
Leaves, with broad, central, yellow stripe. AGM 1993
– – **'Ivory'** DS (E) ○
Large panicles of creamy-white, green-stained flowers. AM 1966 FCC 1968 AGM 1993
– **gloriosa** MS (E) ○ "Adam's Needle"
Trunk-like stem. Dense terminal head of vicious spine-tipped leaves. Creamy-white flowers in erect conical panicles, 1-2m high. AGM 1993
– – **'Variegata'** MS (E)
Leaves with creamy-yellow stripes and margins. FCC 1883 AGM 1993

YUCCA flaccida 'Ivory'

– **recurvifolia** SS (E) ○
Short stem. Long tapered leaves, recurved, except for central leaves. Dense panicles of creamy-white flowers, 0.6-1m high; late summer. AGM 1993
– **whipplei** (*Hesperoyucca whipplei*) SS (E) †
○
Stemless. Dense globular clump of leaves. Dense panicles of large, fragrant greenish-white flowers, edged purple – 1.8-3.6m tall; July-August. AM 1945

"YULAN" see *Magnolia denudata*

Z

ZAUSCHNERIA – Onagraceae DS †
Excellent rock garden plants requiring warm, sunny, well drained sites.
– **californica** DS † "Californian Fuchsia"
Bushy habit. Downy, grey-green stems and leaves. Loose spikes of fuchsia-like red flowers with scarlet tubes, late summer-autumn. We recommend:
– – **'Dublin'** DS †
Flowers profusely borne over a long period during late summer and autumn. AM 1893 AGM 1993
– – subsp. **mexicana** DS †
Equally floriferous with broader, green leaves.

ZELKOVA – Ulmaceae MT-LT ❀
Smooth-barked trees. Simple toothed leaves. Small, monoecious, greenish flowers. Thrive in

deep moist loamy soils, tolerate shade.
– **carpinifolia** LT ❀
Slow growth. Smooth grey bark, flaking with age. Hairy shoots. Coarsely toothed leaves.
– **serrata** MT ❀
Smooth, grey bark flaking with age. Coarsely toothed leaves turn bronze or red, autumn. AGM 1993

ZENOBIA – Ericaceae MS Semi-(E) ✗ ◑
Monotypic genus. Requires lime-free soil and preferably semi-shade.
– **pulverulenta** MS Semi-(E) ✗ ◑
Loose habit. Bloomy young shoots and leaves. Pendulous clusters of aniseed-scented, white, bell-shaped flowers; June-July. AM 1932 FCC 1934

CLIMBERS

A

Contains some of the most beautiful of all woody plants. Reference is also made here to plants described in the Tree and Shrub section often treated as wall shrubs, including tender plants best grown against sheltered walls. All climbers, even the self-clingers, require initial support until established. Many are useful ground cover plants.

ABELIA floribunda see Tree and Shrub section

ABUTILON see Tree and Shrub section

ACACIA see Tree and Shrub section

ACTINIDIA – Actinidiaceae
Vigorous climbers, often with edible fruit, suitable for walls, pergolas or tall stumps.
– **chinensis** "Chinese Gooseberry"
Large, heart-shaped leaves. Conspicuous creamy-white flowers in late summer. To secure edible fruits, both male and female plants are required. AM 1907

ACTINIDIA kolomikta

– **kolomikta**
Strikingly variegated leaves, white flushed pink in the terminal half, developing best in sun. Slightly fragrant white flowers, June. AM 1931 AGM 1993

AKEBIA – Lardizabalaceae Semi-(E)
Vigorous, semi-evergreen twiners with attractive foliage. Good for training over hedges, small trees or old stumps. Unusual fruits, only produced after a mild spring and hot summer.
– **quinata** Semi (E)
Leaves with five leaflets. Red-purple, fragrant flowers, April. Sausage-shaped, dark purple fruits. AM 1956

AKEBIA quinata

AMPELOPSIS – Vitaceae
Ornamental vines climbing by tendrils. Good for covering walls, hedges, etc or training into trees. Attractive fruits formed after a long, hot summer and mild autumn. See also Parthenocissus and Vitis. A (f) 12
– **brevipedunculata**
Vigorous climber, with "Hop"-like leaves. We recommend the following form:
– – **'Elegans'**
Leaves densely mottled white and tinged pink. Less vigorous habit.

– **megalophylla** (*Vitis megalophylla*)
Large, bi-pinnate leaves up to 60cm long.
Fruits purple, becoming black. A good
specimen plant for a tall post or tree. AM
1903
– **veitchii** see *Parthenocissus tricuspidata*
'Veitchii '

ARISTOLOCHIA – Aristolochiaceae
*Twining plants with mostly heart-shaped
leaves and unusual flowers. Good for covering
walls, fences or stumps or for training into
trees .*

– **macrophylla** (*A. sipho*) "Dutchman's Pipe"
Vigorous climber. Syphon-like, yellowish-
green flowers, brownish-purple flared mouth,
June.

ASTERANTHERA – Gesneriaceae Cl (E) †
◑
*A monotypic genus climbing by aerial roots.
Best in leafy, acid or neutral soil.*
– **ovata** Cl (E) † ◑
Trailing creeper, climbing walls or tree trunks
in suitable conditions. Tubular, red flowers,
white in throat, June. AM 1939

B

BERBERIDOPSIS corallina

BERBERIDOPSIS – Flacourtiaceae (E) † ●
*A monotypic genus. Best suited to a sheltered
position in a moist, peaty soil.*

– **corallina** (E) † ● "Coral Plant"
Leathery, dark green, spiny leaves, deep
crimson flowers in pendant, terminal racemes,
late summer. AM 1901

BIGNONIA – Bignoniaceae (E) ○
A monotypic genus related to Campsis *but
climbing by tendrils*
– **capreolata** (E) ○
Leaves with two leaflets 5-13 cm long.
Flowers tubular, orange-red in clusters, June.
AM 1958

"BLUEBELL CREEPER" see *Sollya
heterophylla*

C

CALLISTEMON see Tree and Shrub section

CAMELLIA see Tree and Shrub section

CAMPSIS – Bignoniaceae ○
*Two species of scandent shrubs with pinnate
leaves and conspicuous, trumpet-shaped
flowers August-September.*

– **grandiflora** ○
Leaves with seven or nine glabrous leaflets.
Flowers deep orange and red in drooping
terminal panicles. Best on sheltered wall. AM
1949
– **radicans** Cl ○ "Trumpet Vine"
Climbing by aerial roots but best given initial
support. Leaves with nine or eleven leaflets.

CAMPSIS × tagliabuana 'Madame Galen'

Flowers brilliant orange and scarlet in terminal clusters. AM 1990. We recommend:
– – **'Flava'** ('Yellow Trumpet') Cl ○
Flowers rich yellow. AM 1969 AGM 1993
– × **tagliabuana** ○
A hybrid intermediate between the preceding two species. We recommend the following form:
– – **'Madame Galen'** ○
Panicles of salmon-red flowers. Vigorous. Requires some support. AM 1959 AGM 1993

CANTUA buxifolia see Tree and Shrub section

CARPENTERIA californica see Tree and Shrub section

CEANOTHUS see Tree and Shrub section

CELASTRUS – Celastraceae
Vigorous, rampant climbers suitable for growing over hedges, walls, tall shrubs or trees.
– **orbiculatus**
Twining, spiny shoots bear rounded leaves which turn clear yellow in autumn. Scarlet

CELASTRUS orbiculatus

and gold-spangled split seed capsules in autumn. Normally, male and female required for fruits but the form we grow is hermaphrodite. AGM 1993

CESTRUM see Tree and Shrub section

CHAENOMELES see Tree and Shrub section

CHIMONANTHUS see Tree and Shrub section

CLEMATIS – Ranunculaceae
The species of Clematis are in general of easier cultivation than the large-flowered hybrids. They are excellent climbers for wooden supports, fences, or walls while the more vigorous species are suitable for training into large shrubs or trees. The flowers are often followed by attractive, silken seed heads. See also "Large Flowered Garden Clematis". Poisonous and irritant foliage.
– **alpina**
Blue or violet-blue flowers on long, slender stalks, April-May. Good on a low wall or small bush. AM 1894
– – **'Frances Rivis'**
A vigorous, free flowering form with larger flowers. AM 1965 AGM 1993

CLEMATIS alpina 'Frances Rivis'

– – **'Helsingborg'**
Deep blue flowers. AGM 1993
– – **'Ruby'**
Deep rose-red flowers.
– **armandii** (E)
A vigorous and beautiful species. Flowers 5-6.5cm across in clusters, April-May. Best on a sunny wall. We recommend the following forms:

CLEMATIS armandii

– – 'Apple Blossom' (E)
Flowers white tinged pink. Young leaves bronze. AM 1926 FCC 1936
– – 'Snowdrift' (E)
Flowers pure white.
– 'Bill Mackenzie'
A splendid hybrid of *C. tangutica*, the long-stalked, bright yellow flowers opening widely with a centre of purple filaments. AM 1976 AGM 1993
– campaniflora
A vigorous climber. Small, bowl-shaped, blue-tinted flowers, borne profusely, July-September.
– chrysocoma
Soft pink flowers 5 to 6.5cm across, borne profusely; early May-June, and again in late summer. AM 1936
– cirrhosa (E)
We recommend the following forms:
– – var. balearica (E) "Fern-leaved Clematis"
Prettily divided leaves, bronze in winter. Flowers 4 to 5cm across, pale yellow, spotted reddish-purple within, throughout winter. AM 1974 AGM 1993

CLEMATIS 'Bill Mackenzie'

CLEMATIS cirrhosa var. balearica

– – 'Freckles' (E)
Flowers heavily spotted and streaked with red. AM 1989 AGM 1993
– × durandii
Entire leaves up to 15cm long. Flowers dark blue, with central cluster of white stamens, often more than 10cm across. AGM 1993
– × eriostemon
Semi-herbaceous, reaching 2 to 2.5m, each year. We recommend the following form:
– – 'Hendersonii'
Flowers deep bluish-purple, widely bell-shaped and slightly fragrant. 5 to 6.5cm across, July-September. AM 1965
– flammula
Vigorous, slender stems and bright green leaves making a dense tangle. Loose panicles of small, white, fragrant flowers. August to October. Good on tall hedges and walls. AM 1984
– – 'Rubromarginata' see *C. × triternata* 'Rubromarginata'
– florida
We recommend the following forms:
– – 'Alba Plena'
Fully double, greenish-white flowers borne over a long period.
– – 'Sieboldii' ('Bicolor')
Flowers recalling a "Passion Flower", 8cm across, white with conspicuous central boss of violet-purple petaloid stamens, June-July. AM 1914
– × jackmanii
A spectacular climber with violet-purple flowers up to 13cm across. July-October. FCC 1863 AGM 1993
– × jouiniana
Sub-shrubby climber, reaching 3.5m. We grow an attractive form with sweetly scented flowers.

CLEMATIS macropetala 'Markham's Pink'

– – 'Cote d'Azur'
Small, azure-blue flowers, autumn. Excellent
for covering low walls, mounds or tree stumps.
– macropetala
Relatively low growing climber to 2.5m with
prettily divided leaves. Flowers 5.5 to 7.5cm
across, violet-purple with conspicuous petaloid
staminodes. Good on a low wall or fence. AM
1923. We recommend:
– – 'Lagoon' ('Blue Lagoon')
Deep blue flowers. AGM 1993
– – 'Maidwell Hall'
Deep lavender blue flowers.
– – 'Markham's Pink'
Flowers the shade of crushed strawberries.
AM 1935 AGM 1993
– – 'White Moth'
Flowers pure white.
– montana
Very vigorous. Trifoliolate leaves. Flowers 5-
6.5cm across in profusion, May-June. Good
for growing into trees, large shrubs or over
hedges and walls. We recommend:
– – 'Alexander'
Creamy-white, sweetly-scented flowers.
– – 'Elizabeth'
Large, slightly fragrant, soft pink flowers.
AGM 1993
– – f. grandiflora
Vigorous form reaching 12m. Flowers white.
AGM 1993
– – 'Picton's Variety'
Deep rosy-mauve with up to six sepals.
– – 'Pink Perfection'
Fragrant flowers similar to 'Elizabeth' but
deeper in colour.
– – var. rubens
Bronze-purple foliage, rose-pink flowers. AM
1905 AGM 1993
– – 'Tetrarose'
Bronze foliage, lilac-rose flowers up to 7.5cm
across. AGM 1993
– – var. wilsonii
Profuse, chocolate-scented white flowers in
June.

CLEMATIS montana 'Tetrarose'

– nutans see *C. rehderiana*
– rehderiana (*C. nutans*)
Nodding, bell-shaped, soft primrose-yellow
flowers up to 2cm long and cowslip-scented,
in erect panicles, late summer and autumn.
AM 1936
– tangutica
Prettily divided, sea-green leaves and nodding,
rich-yellow, lantern-like flowers on long stalks
in autumn. Silky seed heads. Good on low
walls, fences, trellis and banks.
– tibetana
We recommend:
– – subsp. vernayi "Orange-peel Clematis"
Graceful with finely divided, blue-green
leaves. Nodding yellow flowers with thick
sepals and purple stamens, August-
September. AM 1950 AGM 1993
– × triternata
Vigorous climber of which we recommend:
– – 'Rubromarginata'
Masses of fragrant flowers, white with reddish-
violet margin, late summer. AGM 1993
– viticella
Slender climber to 3.5m. Flowers violet,
reddish-purple or blue, 4cm across, on slender
stalks, summer-early autumn. We recommend:
– – 'Alba Luxurians'
Flowers white, tinted mauve. AGM 1993
– – 'Minuet'
Upright creamy-white flowers with a broad,
purple band at the end of each sepal. AGM
1993
– – 'Purpurea Plena Elegans'
Large, lilac-purple double flowers with
numerous sepals. FCC 1987 AGM 1993
– – 'Royal Velours'
Flowers deep, velvety purple. AM 1948 AGM
1993
– 'White Swan'
A hybrid of *C. macropetala* with pure white,
double flowers up to 12cm across.

LARGE-FLOWERED GARDEN CLEMATIS

Spectacular and colourful flowering climbers. Best planted with the "heads" in sun and the roots in shade in well-drained, good loamy soil, to which has been added some well-rotted manure and lime in some form. Can be trained to wires on a wall or grown over pergolas, trellises, tripods or into shrubs or small trees but should be planted well away from the roots of intended hosts. Respond well to an annual mulch of well-rotted manure or compost plus an ample supply of water. Sometimes subject to "Clematis Wilt" for which there is no known cure. This mainly affects young plants with the sudden collapse of a single shoot or the whole plant. Usually if wilted shoots are pruned out, new young growth will occur from the root or lower stem.

Pruning

a. FLORIDA (F) LANUGINOSA (L) and PATENS (P) groups. These normally flower in May and June on the previous year's wood. Trim back old flowering shoots immediately after flowering. Old, dense habited plants may be hard pruned in February, but the first crop of flowers will be lost.

b. JACKMANII (J), TEXENSIS (T) and VITICELLA (V) groups. These normally flower in late summer and autumn on the current year's shoots. May be hard pruned to within 30cm of the ground in February or March. Old plants tend to become bare at the base.

– 'Asao' (P)
Large flowers have 6-7 broad, rose-carmine sepals.

– 'Barbara Jackman' (P)
Deep violet, striped magenta, up to 15cm across with 5 to 6 overlapping sepals. May-June.

CLEMATIS 'Countess of Lovelace'

– 'Beauty of Worcester' (L)
Blue-violet, creamy-white stamens, occasionally double, May-August.

– 'Bee's Jubilee' (L)
Blush-pink, banded carmine-rose. Overlapping sepals. AGM 1993

– 'Blue Gem' (L)
Sky-blue, large. June-October.

– 'Carnaby' (L)
Deep raspberry pink, compact and free-flowering. Good in shade.

– 'Comtesse de Bouchaud' (J)
Soft rose-pink with yellow stamens, vigorous and free flowering, June-August. AM 1936 AGM 1993

– 'Countess of Lovelace' (P)
Bluish-lilac, 15cm across with cream anthers. Double and single on the same plant. May-July.

– 'Daniel Deronda' (P)
Large, violet-blue, paler at centre with creamy stamens, often double. June-September. AGM 1993

– 'Dr Ruppel' (P)
Deep pink with carmine bar and yellow stamens. Up to 20cm across. AGM 1993

– 'Duchess of Albany' (T)
Nodding, tubular, bright pink flowers. July to September. AM 1897 AGM 1993

– 'Duchess of Edinburgh' (F)
Double and rosette-like, white shaded green, scented. Up to 10cm across. May-June.

– 'Elsa Späth' (P)
Lavender-blue with red stamens. Up to 20cm across. May-June and September. AGM 1993

– 'Ernest Markham' (V)
Glowing petunia-red, with a velvety sheen, sepals rounded, June-September. AGM 1993

– 'Etoile Violette' (T)
Deep purple with 4-6 sepals, up to 10cm across. Vigorous and free-flowering. July-September. AGM 1993

– 'Fujimu-Sumi' (L)
Deep lavender blue, 6 pointed sepals with white bar on reverse and centre of green-white stamens.

– 'General Sikorski' (L)
Mid-blue, with red-based sepals. To 15cm across. June-July. AGM 1993

– 'Gravetye Beauty' (T)
Bell-shaped, cherry-red. July to September. AM 1935

– 'Hagley Hybrid' (J)
Shell-pink with chocolate-brown anthers, free flowering. June-September.

– 'Henryi' (L)
Large, creamy-white with pointed sepals and

dark stamens, vigorous and free flowering;
May-June, and again in August-September
AGM 1993

– **'H. F. Young'** (L)
Large Wedgwood-blue, with broad,
overlapping, acuminate sepals and yellow
stamens. AGM 1993

– **'Huldine'** (V) ○
Pearly white, pointed sepals banded mauve
on the reverse; vigorous and free flowering,
July-October. AM 1934

– **'Jackmanii Alba'** (J)
Very vigorous with white flowers veined blue
to 13cm across, early flowers double, late
single. July-September. FCC 1883

– **'Jackmanii Superba'** (J)
Large, rich, violet-purple with broad sepals;
vigorous and free flowering. July-September.
AGM 1993

– **'Lady Betty Balfour'** (V)
Deep velvety purple with golden stamens;
very vigorous, best in full sun, August-
October. AM 1912

– **'Lasurstern'** (P)
Deep lavender blue, conspicuous white
stamens, broad, tapering, wavy-edged sepals;
May-June and again in early autumn. AGM
1993

– **'Lincoln Star'** (P)
Brilliant raspberry-pink, 15cm across with dark
red stamens. May-June with paler flowers in
September.

– **'Marie Boisselot'** (P)
Large, pure white with cream stamens and
broad, rounded, overlapping sepals; vigorous
and free flowering. May-October. AGM 1993

– **'Miss Bateman'** (P)
White, 15cm across, banded pale green when
first open. May-June. AGM 1993

– **'Mme Julia Correvon'** (V)
Deep wine-red, 7cm across. AGM 1993

– **'Mrs Cholmondely'** (J)
Large, pale blue with long-pointed sepals

CLEMATIS 'Nelly Moser'

vigorous and free flowering, May-August.
FCC 1873 AGM 1993

– **'Mrs N. Thompson'** (P)
Deep violet with a scarlet bar, pointed sepals.
May-June, and September.

– **'Multi-Blue'**
Deep violet-blue, fully double flowers with
centre of blue and white staminodes, May-
June and again in autumn.

– **'Nelly Moser'** (L)
Large pale mauve-pink with carmine bar. Very
free flowering. Best on a north wall, or in
some shade. May-June, and again August-
September. AGM 1993

CLEMATIS 'The President'

CLEMATIS 'Marie Boisselot'

CLEMATIS 'Ville de Lyon'

– **'Niobe'** (J)
Deep red, to 15cm across with yellow anthers. The best red clematis. AGM 1993
– **'Perle d'Azur'** (J)
Light blue with broad sepals. Vigorous and free flowering, June-August. AGM 1993
– **'Rouge Cardinal'** (J)
Crimson velvet to 15cm across with brown anthers. June-August.
– **'The President'** (P)
Deep purple-blue, silvery reverse, free flowering. June-September. FCC 1876 AGM 1993
– **'Venosa Violacea'** (V)
Purple, conspicuously veined with white. AGM 1993
– **'Ville de Lyon'** (V)
Bright carmine-red, deeper at margins, with golden stamens. July-October. AM 1901
– **'Vyvyan Pennell'** (P)
Deep violet blue suffused purple and carmine in the centre, fully double. May-July. Single flowers in autumn. AGM 1993

– **'Wada's Primrose'** (P)
Pale creamy-yellow, best in shade.
– **'William Kennet'** (L)
Lavender-blue with dark stamens, sepals with crimped margins. June-August.

CLIANTHUS puniceus see Tree and Shrub section

"CLIMBING HYDRANGEA" see *Hydrangea petiolaris*

CORONILLA see Tree and Shrub section

COTONEASTER see Tree and Shrub section

CRINODENDRON see Tree and Shrub section

CYTISUS battandieri see Tree and Shrub section
– **'Porlock'** see Tree and Shrub section

D

DAPHNE odora see Tree and Shrub section

DECUMARIA – Hydrangeaceae Cl
Two species, climbing by aerial roots. Succeed in sun or shade, on a wall or tree trunk.
– **barbara** Cl Semi-(E)
Climber to 9m. Leaves ovate, to 13cm long. Small, white flowers in small clusters, June-July.
– **sinensis** Cl (E)
Climber to 5m, narrow leaves to 9cm long. Small, green and white, honey-scented flowers in clusters, May. AM 1974

DENDROMECON see Tree and Shrub section

DREGEA – Asclepiadaceae
We recommend the following species for a warm, sheltered wall or conservatory.
– **sinensis** (*Wattakaka sinensis*) †
Slender-stemmed climber to 3m with ovate leaves, grey felted beneath. Deliciously scented white flowers with central zone of red spots, in long-stalked umbels, summer. AM 1954

DRIMYS see Tree and Shrub section

E

ECCREMOCARPUS – Bignoniaceae
The following species is hardy in a sheltered corner in mild areas.

– **scaber**
Vigorous climber with bipinnate leaves ending in slender tendrils. Scarlet to orange-yellow,

tubular flowers produced throughout summer and autumn. AGM 1993

ERIOBOTRYA see Tree and Shrub section

ESCALLONIA see Tree and Shrub section

F

FALLOPIA – Polygonaceae
Of the climbing species of this genus we

FALLOPIA baldschuanica

recommend the following. Good for covering unsightly objects, hedges, fences or for growing into trees.
– baldschuanica (*Polygonum baldschuanicum*) "Russian Vine"
Very vigorous climber up to 12m.Conspicuous panicles of tiny, pink-tinged flowers, summer and autumn. AM 1899 AGM 1993

FEIJOA see Tree and Shrub section

FORSYTHIA suspensa see Tree and Shrub section

FREMONTODENDRON see Tree and Shrub section

G

GARRYA elliptica see Tree and Shrub section

"GRANADILLA" see *Passiflora quadrangularis*

"GRANADILLA, PURPLE" see *Passiflora edulis*

H

HEDERA – Araliaceae "Ivy" Cl (E)
Evergreen climbers, clinging by aerial roots. They thrive in almost any soil or situation, sun or shade and are tolerant of atmospheric pollution. Foliage can be irritant. A (f) 2 and 5

– algeriensis (*H. canariensis* hort.) Cl (E) GC "Algerian Ivy"
Leaves bright, glossy green, up to 15 or 20cm long, entire or obscurely three-lobed, often bronze in winter.

– – **'Gloire de Marengo'** Cl (E) GC
Leaves deep green in centre merging to
silvery grey and margined creamy-white. FCC
1880 AMT 1979 AGM 1993
– – **'Margino-maculata'** Cl (E) GC
Leaves green strikingly mottled with creamy-
white.
– **canariensis** see *H. algeriensis*
– **colchica** Cl (E) GC "Persian Ivy"
Vigorous species. Dark green, thick, leathery
leaves up to 20cm or more long, usually
entire. AGM 1993
– – **'Dentata'** Cl (E) GC
Leaves very large, softer green more irregular
and occasionally toothed. AMT 1979
– – **'Dentata Variegata'** Cl (E) GC
Leaves conspicuously margined creamy-
yellow, maturing creamy-white. AM 1907
FCCT 1979 AGM 1993

HEDERA colchica 'Dentata Variegata'

– – **'Sulphur Heart'** ('Paddy's Pride') Cl (E)
GC
Large leaves, boldly marked with an irregular
central splash of yellow. AMT 1979 AGM
1993
– **helix** Cl (E) GC "Common Ivy"
A very variable climber useful for growing on
walls or trees or as ground cover, where little
else will grow. We recommend the following
forms:
– – **'Adam'** Cl (E) GC
Leaves small, conspicuously margined with
white.
– – **'Buttercup'** Cl (E) GC
Leaves rich yellow, becoming yellowish-green
or pale green with age. AGM 1993
– – **'Caecelia'** Cl (E) GC
Leaves with crisped margins edged with
creamy-white.
– – **'Caenwoodiana'** Cl (E) GC
Small leaves regularly divided into narrow
lobes. AGM 1993
– – **'Glacier'** Cl (E) GC
Leaves silver-grey with a narrow white
margin. AMT 1979 AGM 1993
– – **'Goldchild'** Cl (E) GC
Leaves conspicuously margined with bright
yellow. AM 1971 AGM 1993
– – **'Goldheart'** Cl (E)
A striking form. Leaves with conspicuous
yellow central splash. AM 1970
– – **'Harald'** ('Chicago Variegata') Cl (E) GC
Shallowly lobed leaves with broad, creamy-
white margin.
– – **'Hibernica'** see *H. hibernica*
– – **'Ivalace'** Cl (E) GC
Glossy, green leaves, crimped at the margin.
FCCT 1979 AGM 1993

HEDERA helix 'Goldheart'

HEDERA helix 'Little Diamond'

– – **'Kolibri'** Cl (E)
Dark green leaves conspicuously blotched with creamy-white. Best as a house plant. AGM 1993
– – **'Little Diamond'** (E) GC
Leaves green, mottled grey, with creamy-white margin, entire or three-lobed. Dwarf, bushy habit. AMT 1979 AGM 1993
– – **'Manda's Crested'** Cl (E) GC
Bright green sharply pointed five-lobed leaves, colouring reddish in winter. Neat, mound-forming habit. Slow. FCCT 1980 AGM 1993
– – **'Marginata Elegantissima'** see 'Tricolor'
– – **'Shamrock'** Cl (E) GC "Clover-Leaf Ivy"
Small, bright green, three-lobed or entire leaves bronzing in winter. AGM 1993
– – **'Tricolor'** ('Marginata Elegantissima') Cl (E) GC
Small, grey-green leaves margined white, edged rose-pink in winter.
– **hibernica** Cl (E) GC "Irish Ivy"
Large, dark green, usually five-lobed leaves up to 15cm across. Vigorous and particularly useful as ground cover. AMT 1979 AGM 1993

HOLBOELLIA – Lardizabalaceae (E) ○
Twiners with compound leaves.
– **coriacea** (E) ○
Vigorous climber to 6m or more. Leaves with three glossy green leaflets. Small flowers April-May; purplish, fleshy pods.

"HONEYSUCKLE" see *Lonicera*

"HONEYSUCKLE, CAPE" see *Tecomaria capensis*

"HOP" see *Humulus*

HUMULUS – Cannabidaceae
The following species is herbaceous but useful for covering hedges, shrubs etc.
– **lupulus** "Hop"
Scrambling climber, three to five lobed, coarsely toothed leaves. Small flowers in late summer followed by"Hops". We offer:
– – **'Aureus'**
Leaves soft yellow. Best in full sun. AGM 1993

HYDRANGEA – Hydrangeaceae Cl
Climbing shrubs with aerial roots. Happy in

HUMULUS lupulus 'Aureus'

HYDRANGEA petiolaris

sun or shade in all soils. Tolerant of atmospheric pollution.
– **petiolaris** Cl "Climbing Hydrangea"
Vigorous climber, excellent on walls or trees. Mound-forming when grown as a shrub. Greenish-white flowers, with several white sterile florets; large clusters, June. AGM 1993
– **serratifolia** Cl (E)
Dark green, entire, leathery leaves. Small, creamy-white flowers in dense panicles, late summer. AM 1952

I

ITEA ilicifolia see Tree and Shrub section

"IVY" see *Hedera*

"IVY, BOSTON" see *Parthenocissus tricuspidata*

J

"JASMINE" see *Jasminum*

"JASMINE, CHILEAN" see *Mandevilla suaveolens*

JASMINUM – Oleaceae "Jasmine"
"Jessamine"
Twining, scandent shrubs. Small, trumpet-shaped, usually fragrant flowers. Best in full sun. Tender species are excellent for conservatory.
– beesianum
Vigorous and hardy. Small, fragrant deep velvety red flowers, May-June. Black berries.
– humile see Tree and Shrub section
– mesnyi (*J. primulinum*) Semi-(E) †
Four-angled shoots. Trifoliolate leaves. Bright yellow, semi-double flowers 4cm long, March-May. FCC 1903 AGM 1993
– nudiflorum see Tree and Shrub section
– officinale "Common White Jasmine"
Vigorous twiner with pinnate leaves. Flowers white, deliciously fragrant, in clusters, June-September. AGM 1993. A (g) 10
– – f. affine ('Grandiflorum')
Flowers slightly larger, pink tinged on the outside.
– – 'Argenteovariegatum'
Leaves grey-green, margined creamy white. AGM 1993
– – 'Aureum'
Leaves blotched and suffused with yellow.

JASMINUM officinale

– polyanthum (E) †
Pinnate leaves with up to seven leaflets. Flowers white, flushed pink, intensely fragrant, throughout summer. AM 1941 FCC 1949 AGM 1993
– sambac "Arabian Jasmine" (E) †
Glossy, undivided leaves to 8cm long. Clusters of very fragrant, white flowers, pink with age, are continuously produced.
– × stephanense
Leaves simple or with up to five leaflets, often variegated on vigorous shoots. Pale pink, fragrant flowers, June-July. AM 1937 AGM 1993
– suavissimum †
Slender, twining stems. Linear leaves up to 6cm long. Sweetly fragrant, white flowers in loose panicles, late summer.

K

KERRIA japonica 'Pleniflora' see Tree and Shrub section

L

LAPAGERIA – Philesiaceae (E) † ✕ ◑
A monotypic genus; for a cool, moist soil, on a sheltered wall. An excellent conservatory plant.
– rosea (E) † ✕ ◑
Strong, wiry stems reaching 4 to 5m leathery leaves. Flowers rose-crimson, fleshy, bell-shaped, 7.5cm long by 5cm across, borne singly or in pendulous clusters, summer and autumn. FCC 1974 AGM 1993

LAPAGERIA rosea

– – var. albiflora (E) † ✕ ◑
Flowers white.
– – 'Flesh Pink' (E) † ✕ ◑
Flowers flesh-pink. AGM 1993
– – 'Nash Court' (E) † ✕ ◑
Flowers soft pink marbled deeper pink. FCC 1884 AGM 1993

LONICERA – Caprifoliaceae "Honeysuckle"
Includes some of the loveliest and most popular of all climbers. Seen at their best when scrambling over bushes or tree stumps, trellises or pergolas.
– ✕ americana
Vigorous, free-flowering. Flowers, 4 to 5cm long, fragrant, white, pale then deep yellow, tinged purple, June-July. AM 1937 AGM 1993
– ✕ brownii "Scarlet Trumpet Honeysuckle"
Deciduous or Semi-(E). With long leaves, glaucous beneath. We recommend the following form:
– – 'Dropmore Scarlet'
Vigorous climber with clusters of bright scarlet, tubular flowers, July-October.
– caprifolium (*L.* 'Early Cream') "Perfoliate Honeysuckle"
Vigorous. Glaucous leaves. Flowers fragrant, 4 to 5cm long creamy-white, often tinged pink, June-July. Berries orange-red. AGM 1993
– 'Dropmore Scarlet' see *L.* ✕ *brownii* 'Dropmore Scarlet'

LONICERA japonica 'Aureoreticulata'

– etrusca
Vigorous, deciduous or semi-(E). Flowers fragrant, cream, becoming yellow, June-July. Best in full sun.

– – 'Donald Waterer'
Red flowers white inside turn to orange-yellow. Young shoots red. AM 1985

– – 'Superba'
Creamy-white flowers in large clusters turn to orange-yellow. Vigorous with red shoots. AM 1953

– flexuosa see *L. japonica* var. *repens*

– × heckrottii
Spreading shrub with scandent branches. Flowers fragrant, 4 to 5cm long, yellow, heavily flushed purple. We recommend:

– – 'Gold Flame'
A form with deep green leaves and more brightly coloured flowers.

– henryi (E) or Semi-(E)
A vigorous climber with long, dark green, leathery leaves. Flowers yellow stained red, June-July. Black berries.

– japonica (E) or Semi-(E) GC
Vigorous. Useful for concealing unsightly objects. Flowers produced continuously from June onwards. We recommend the following forms:
A (g) or (b) 4

– – 'Aureoreticulata' (E) or Semi-(E)
Bright green leaves conspicuously veined with golden yellow.

– – 'Halliana' (E) or Semi-(E)
Flowers white, changing to yellow, very fragrant. AGM 1993

– – var. repens (*L. flexuosa*) (E) or Semi-(E)
Leaves and shoots flushed purple. Flowers very fragrant, flushed purple on the outside.

– periclymenum "Woodbine"
Our common, native honeysuckle. Vigorous. Richly fragrant flowers; red berries. We recommend the following forms:
C or E 8 or 9

– – 'Belgica' "Early Dutch Honeysuckle"
Flowers reddish-purple outside fading yellowish, May-June, and again late summer. AGM 1993

– – 'Graham Thomas'
White flowers turn to yellow. AGM 1993

– – 'Serotina' "Late Dutch Honeysuckle"
Flowers rich reddish-purple outside, July-October. AM 1988 AGM 1993

LONICERA sempervirens

LONICERA tragophylla

– sempervirens (E) or Semi-(E) "Trumpet Honeysuckle"
Rich green leaves. Flowers 4 to 5cm long, rich orange-scarlet outside, yellow within, late summer-early autumn. AM 1964 AGM 1993. A (g) or (b) 4

– × tellmanniana
Flowers 5cm long, rich, coppery-yellow flushed red in bud in large clusters, June-July. Best with the roots in shade. AM 1931 AGM 1993

– tragophylla
The largest flowered and most showy climbing honeysuckle. Flowers 6 to 9cm long, bright yellow in large clusters, June-July. At its best with the roots in shade. AM 1913 AGM 1993

M

MAGNOLIA, in particular *M. delavayi* and *M. grandiflora* see Tree and Shrub section

MANDEVILLA – Apocynaceae
Mainly tropical climbers. The following succeed on a sheltered wall in mild areas. Make excellent conservatory plants.
– × amabilis 'Alice du Pont' † ○
Vigorous climber with deeply veined leaves. Bright pink, trumpet-shaped flowers are produced over a long period in summer. Mild area or conservatory.
– laxa (*M. suaveolens*) † ○ "Chilean Jasmine"
Slender-stemmed climber with pointed, heart-shaped leaves. Fragrant, white, periwinkle-like flowers in clusters, summer. AM 1957

– suaveolens see *M. laxa*

MUTISIA – Compositae (E) ○ "Climbing Gazania"
Climbing or trailing shrubs. Colourful, gazania-like flower-heads produced singly on long stalks. Best in a well drained soil with the roots in shade.
– oligodon (E) ○
Suckering, trailing shrub to 1.5m. Oblong, coarsely toothed leaves forming a low thicket. Flower heads 5 to 7.5cm across, salmon-pink petals, summer and intermittently into autumn. AM 1928

MYRTUS see Tree and Shrub section

O

OXYPETALUM – Asclepiadaceae
Herbs and sub-shrubs, some climbing. The following is suitable for mild areas or conservatory.

– – caeruleum (*Tweedia caerulea*) † ○
Twining sub-shrub with softly hairy, sage-green leaves. Clusters of flowers during summer are powder-blue turning to purple then lilac. AM 1936

P

PARTHENOCISSUS – Vitaceae
High climbing, mainly self-clinging vines, useful for covering large walls or tree trunks. Leaves often richly coloured in autumn. See also Ampelopsis *and* Vitis. A (f) 12
– henryana (*Vitis henryana*) Cl
Leaves with three to five leaflets, dark green or bronze with silvery white veins, red in autumn. AM 1906 AGM 1993

– quinquefolia (*Vitis quinquefolia*) Cl "Virginia Creeper"
Tall growing. Excellent for high walls, trees, etc. Leaves with five leaflets, brilliant orange and scarlet in autumn. AGM 1993
– tricuspidata (*Vitis inconstans*) Cl "Boston Ivy"
Vigorous climber commonly planted on old walls. Leaves very variable, ovate or trifoliolate

PARTHENOCISSUS henryana

on young plants, three lobed on mature plants, rich crimson and scarlet in autumn. Often incorrectly called "Virginia Creeper". FCC 1868 AGM 1993
– – **'Veitchii'** (*Ampelopsis veitchii*) Cl
Smaller leaves, purple tinged when young.

PARTHENOCISSUS tricuspidata 'Veitchii'

PASSIFLORA – Passifloraceae † ○
"Passion Flower"
Climbing by tendrils, best on sunny, sheltered wall. The unusual flowers are borne singly on long stalks. Petals and sepals often similar and known as tepals. Inside these is a conspicuous ring of filaments (corona).
– × **allardii** † ○
Large, three-lobed leaves. Flowers 9 to 11.5cm across, tepals white shaded pink, corona white and deep cobalt-blue, summer-autumn.
– **antioquiensis** (*Tacsonia vanvolxemii*) † ○
Leaves entire or deeply three-lobed. Flowers pendulous 10 to 13cm across, tube rich rose-red, small, violet corona, late summer-autumn. AGM 1993
– **caerulea** † ○ "Blue Passion Flower"
Vigorous, fairly hardy species. Dense habit. Evergreen in mild areas. Leaves five to seven lobed. Flowers slightly fragrant, 7.5 to 10cm

across, tepals white or pink tinged, corona blue at tips, white in centre, purple at base; summer-autumn. AGM 1993

PASSIFLORA caerulea

– – **'Constance Elliott'** † ○
Flowers ivory white. FCC 1884 AGM 1993
– × **caerulea – racemosa** † ○
Vigorous, with three-to five-lobed leaves. Deep pink flowers have a white corona, black-violet at the base. Best in the conservatory.
– **edulis** † ○ "Purple Granadilla"
Vigorous. Deeply three-lobed leaves. Flowers 6cm across, tepals white, green without, curly white filaments banded with purple, throughout summer.
– **'Exoniensis'** † ○
Beautiful hybrid. Deeply three-lobed leaves. Flowers pendulous, 10 to 13cm across, tepals rose-pink. Conservatory only.
– **'Lavender Lady'** † ○
Vigorous with glossy foliage and rich lavender flowers over a long period.
– **mollissima** † ○
Vigorous with deeply three-lobed leaves. Pendulous flowers have a long tube, pink tepals and a small, purple corona.
– **quadrangularis** † ○ "Granadilla"
Very vigorous with stout, four-angled stems and large, unlobed leaves. Fragrant flowers are green outside and white to red or violet within with the corona banded reddish-purple. Large, edible yellow fruits.
– **racemosa** † ○ "Red Passion Flower"
Leaves usually three-lobed. Flowers vivid scarlet with purple, white-tipped, outer filaments, in drooping racemes – summer. Conservatory only. AGM 1993
– **umbilicata** † ○
Vigorous, fairly hardy species. Small violet flowers.

"PASSION FLOWER" see *Passiflora*

PILEOSTEGIA – Hydrangeaceae Cl (E)
Evergreen climbers with aerial roots. The
following is suitable for wall or tree trunk.
– viburnoides Cl (E)
Dark green, leathery leaves, up to 15cm long.
Flowers creamy-white in crowded, terminal
panicles – late summer-autumn. AM 1914
AGM 1993

PLUMBAGO – Plumbaginaceae
The best-known species of this genus related
to Ceratostigma *is a striking conservatory plant*
flowering throughout summer and autumn.
– auriculata (*P. capensis*) (E) † ○
Vigorous, with arching stems and profuse
clusters of pale sky-blue flowers 2.5cm across.
AGM 1993

PILEOSTEGIA viburnoides

POLYGONUM baldschuanicum see *Fallopia*
baldschuanica

PUNICA see Tree and Shrub section

PYRACANTHA see Tree and Shrub section

R

RHAPHIOLEPIS see Tree and Shrub section

RHODOCHITON – Scrophulariaceae
An attractive and unusual climber suitable for
a conservatory or sunny wall.
– atrosanguineum † ○
Slender stems to 3m bear bell-shaped, deep
purple flowers with a tubular purple-red
centre over a long period in summer. AM
1985 AGM 1993

RUBUS – Rosaceae
Of the climbing species of this genus, we
recommend the following:

– henryi (E)
Attractive climber with handsome foliage. We
recommend:
– – var. bambusarum (E)
Long, scandent stems reaching 6m, on
suitable support. Leaves with three narrow
leaflets, glossy dark green above, white-felted
beneath. Pink flowers, summer. Black fruits.
FCC 1907

"RUSSIAN VINE" see *Fallopia*
baldschuanica

S

SCHISANDRA – Schisandraceae
Attractive, flowering climbers for walls, fences
or for growing into shrubs or trees. Female
plants bear attractive berries.

– propinqua
A slender-stemmed twiner of which we
recommend:
– – var. chinensis

Short-stalked, yellowish terracotta flowers –
late summer-autumn. Berries scarlet.
– **rubriflora** (*S. grandiflora* var. *rubriflora*)
Leathery, conspicuously veined leaves, deep
crimson flowers in late spring followed by
scarlet berries. AM 1925

SCHIZOPHRAGMA – Hydrangeaceae Cl
*Ornamental climbers with aerial roots. Small
creamy-white flowers in large heads, each
head margined with several cream-coloured
sterile florets. Suitable for walls, trees or
stumps. Flower best in full sun.*
– **hydrangeoides** Cl
Rounded, coarsely toothed leaves. Flower-
heads up to 25cm across, July. FCC 1885
– – **'Roseum'** Cl
Sterile florets rose-flushed. AM 1939
– **integrifolium** Cl
Slender-pointed, entire or slightly toothed
leaves. Flower-heads to 30cm across with
large sterile florets up to 9cm long, July. AM
1936 FCC 1963 AGM 1993

SENECIO – Compositae
*This large genus contains only a few climbers
of which we recommend:*
– **scandens** Semi-(E) ○
Long scandent stems up to 6m. Coarsely
toothed, often lobed leaves. Small, bright
yellow flower-heads in large panicles,
autumn. Best in a sheltered position and
allowed to scramble over a bush or hedge.

SOLANUM – Solanaceae ○
*The climbing members of this genus make
spectacular wall plants given a sunny,
sheltered position.*

SCHIZOPHRAGMA integrifolium

SOLANUM crispum 'Glasnevin'

– **crispum** Semi-(E) ○
We recommend the following form:
– – **'Glasnevin'** ('Autumnale') Semi-(E) ○
A vigorous scrambling shrub bearing loose
corymbs of rich purple-blue, yellow centred
flowers, summer and autumn. AM 1955 AGM
1993
– **jasminoides** Semi-(E) † ○
Fast-growing, twining shrub. Glossy green
leaves. Flowers pale slate-blue, yellow in the
centre, in loose clusters, summer-autumn.
– – **'Album'** Semi-(E) † ○
Flowers white with a yellow centre. AM 1977
AGM 1993

SOLLYA– Pittosporaceae (E) † ○
*Beautiful twining plants for very mild area or
conservatory. We recommend the following:*
– **heterophylla** (E) † ○ "Bluebell Creeper"
Slender stems to 2m or more. Nodding
clusters of delicate, bell-shaped, sky-blue
flowers, summer-autumn.

SOPHORA see Tree and Shrub section

STAUNTONIA – Lardizabalaceae (E)
Evergreen, twining shrubs. The following

species requires a sheltered wall in sun or semi-shade.
– hexaphylla (E)
Vigorous climber to 10m or more. Leaves with three to seven, leathery leaflets. Flowers 2cm

across, fragrant, white tinged violet, borne in racemes in spring. Edible, purple-tinged fruits produced after a warm, dry summer. AM 1960

T

TECOMARIA – Bignoniaceae
The following species requires a warm, sunny wall in a sheltered position or a conservatory.
– capensis (E) † ○
Vigorous twining shrub with pinnate leaves. Brilliant scarlet, trumpet-shaped flowers, late summer.

TIBOUCHINA see Tree and Shrub section

TRACHELOSPERMUM – Apocynaceae Cl
(E) † ○
Beautiful, self-clinging climbers with attractive sweetly scented, jasmine-like flowers, suitable for a sheltered wall in all but the coldest localities.
– asiaticum Cl (E) † ○
Dark, glossy green leaves, flowers 2cm across, creamy-white, buff yellow in centre, becoming yellow, fragrant. AGM 1993
– jasminoides Cl (E) † ○
Dark, polished green leaves. Flowers 2.5cm across, white becoming cream. Requires a warm wall or conservatory.

TRACHELOSPERMUM asiaticum

AM 1934 AGM 1993
– – 'Japonicum' Cl (E) ○
Vigorous form with large leaves bronzing in winter.
– – 'Variegatum' Cl (E) † ○
Leaves margined and splashed creamy-white.

TWEEDIA caerulea see *Oxypetalum caeruleum*

V

"VINE, TRUMPET" see *Campsis radicans*

"VIRGINIA CREEPER" see *Parthenocissus quinquefolia* and *P. tricuspidata*

VITEX see Tree and Shrub section

VITIS – Vitaceae
Ornamental vines, climbing by tendrils, often giving rich autumn colour. Most effective

when growing into a large tree or covering an old hedge or stump but can be trained to cover walls, bridges or fences. Small greenish flowers are followed by small grapes after a hot, dry season. (f) 12 or 1
– 'Brant' (*V. vinifera* 'Brant')
Popular, hardy, fruiting vine reaching 9m, or more on suitable support. Dark purple-black, bloomy, sweet grapes. AM 1970 AGM 1993

VITIS coignetiae

– coignetiae
Possibly the most spectacular vine. Large leaves up to 30cm across, brilliant crimson and scarlet in autumn. Fruits 12mm across, black, bloomed purple. AGM 1993
– davidii
Vigorous climber with spiny shoots. Leaves heart-shaped, dark glossy green above,

glaucous and bristly beneath, rich crimson in autumn. AM 1903
– henryana see *Parthenocissus henryana*
– himalayana see *Parthenocissus himalayana*
– inconstans see *Parthenocissus tricuspidata*
– pulchra
Reddish shoots and coarsely toothed leaves reddish when young, brilliant scarlet in autumn.
– thomsonii see *Parthenocissus thomsonii*
– vinifera "Grape Vine"
We recommend the following forms which are useful for ornamental foliage as well as fruits.
– – 'Brant' see *V.* 'Brant'
– – 'Incana' "Dusty Miller Grape"
Leaves grey-green, with a white, cobwebby down. Fruits black.
– – 'Purpurea' "Teinturier Grape"
Leaves claret-red when young becoming deep vinous purple. AM 1959 AGM 1993

W

WATTAKAKA sinensis see *Dregea sinensis*

WISTERIA – Leguminosae
Beautiful climbers with pinnate leaves and long racemes of white, pink, blue or mauve pea-flowers, May and June, and often later. Best in full sun on a wall, pergola or into a tree. Poisonous, especially the seeds.
– floribunda "Japanese Wisteria"
Up to 4m or more. Leaves with thirteen to nineteen leaflets. Flowers fragrant, with the leaves. AM 1984. We recommend the following forms:
– – 'Alba'
Flowers white, tinted lilac in racemes 45 to 60cm long. AM 1931 AGM 1993
– – f. macrobotrys
Racemes up to 1m long or more. Flowers fragrant, lilac tinged blue-purple. AGM 1993
– – 'Rosea'
Flowers pale rose, tipped purple, in long racemes. AGM 1993
– – 'Violacea Plena'
Flowers violet blue, double.

WISTERIA floribunda 'Alba'

– sinensis "Chinese Wisteria"
Perhaps the most popular wisteria, reaching 18 to 30m in a suitable tree. Leaves with nine to thirteen leaflets. Flowers fragrant, mauve or deep lilac in racemes up to 30cm long before the leaves. AGM 1993
– – 'Alba'
Flowers white. FCC 1892 AGM 1993
– – 'Plena'
Flowers double, rosette-shaped, lilac.

CONIFERS

A

A CONIFER GARDEN

ABIES balsamea 'Hudsonia'

The wide range of shape and colour shown by conifers makes them valuable garden plants. Mainly evergreen, they range from prostrate dwarf shrubs to large trees. Some are suitable for maritime exposures, hedging or ground cover. The deciduous conifers are no less attractive and contain several beautiful and unusual trees.

Apart from the naturally low growing species, several conifers have given rise to numerous dwarf forms which enables the beauty of these plants to be enjoyed in even the smallest of gardens.

ABIES – Pinaceae ST-LT (E) ♦ "Silver Firs"
Mainly conical trees with narrow flattened leaves often white beneath. Erect cylindrical cones, in some species attractively blue-purple or violet, when young. Require a deep, moist soil for best development. Apart from A. cephalonica and A. pinsapo they are largely intolerant of industrial atmosphere and shallow chalk soils.
– **balsamea** MT (E) ♦ ∠ "Balsam Fir" "Balm of Gilead"

We recommend the following form:
– – **'Hudsonia'** DS (E)
Dense, compact habit with densely arranged, short balsam-scented leaves. Fairly lime tolerant. AGM 1993
– **cephalonica** LT (E) ♦ "Grecian Fir"
A handsome tree with rigid, pointed, glossy, green leaves, white beneath. One of the best for chalk soils.

ABIES concolor 'Candicans'

ABIES koreana

– **concolor** MT-LT (E) ♦ "Colorado White Fir"
Young trees with smooth, grey bark. Leaves 2-3cm, blue-green or grey-green. Cones cylindrical 16-25cm long. AGM 1993. We recommend:
– – **'Candicans'** LT (E) ♦
Leaves vivid grey or silvery white.
– – **'Compacta'** SS
Dense habit with bright silvery blue foliage. AGM 1993
– **grandis** LT (E) ♦ "Giant Fir"
Fast growing tree with dark, glossy green, horizontally arranged leaves with two glaucous-grey bands beneath. Cones bright green 7.5-10cm. Moderately lime tolerant. AGM 1993
– **koreana** ST (E) ♦
Slow growing, neat habit. Dark green leaves, 1-2cm gleaming white beneath. Even young plants usually produce abundant small, violet-purple cylindrical cones, 5-7cm. AGM 1984. Some plants in cultivation are more vigorous and may be hybrids
– – **'Silberlocke'** ('Horstmann's Silberlocke') DS
Leaves twist upwards to reveal their white undersides. AGM 1993
– **lasiocarpa** MT (E) ♦ "Alpine Fir"
We recommend the following form:
– – **'Compacta'** MS (E)

Slow-growing, tree-like shrub of dense conical habit with bright blue-grey foliage. AGM 1993
– **nobilis** see *A. procera*
– **nordmanniana** LT (E) ♦ "Caucasian Fir"
Ornamental tree with tiered, down-sweeping branches. Leaves 2-3cm glossy green above white banded beneath, densely arranged. Cones cylindrical, greenish when young 15-20cm. AGM 1993
– – **'Golden Spreader'** DS (E)
Slow growing, wide spreading form with light yellow leaves. AGM 1993
– **pinsapo** MT-LT (E) ♦ "Spanish Fir"
Short, rigid, radially arranged, dark green leaves to 1.5cm. Cones cylindrical 10-15cm, purplish when young. One of the best for chalk. We offer:
– – **'Glauca'** LT (E) ♦
Leaves a striking blue-grey. AGM 1993
– **procera** (*A. nobilis*) LT (E) ♦ ✗ "Noble Fir"
Bluish-green leaves, glaucous banded beneath, crowded above the shoots. Huge cylindrical cones up to 25cm long, green when young. AM 1973 FCC 1979 AGM 1993
– **spectabilis** LT (E) ♦ "Himalayan Fir"
Densely two-ranked leaves up to 6cm long, glossy dark green above, silvery-white beneath. Cones cylindrical to 18cm, violet-purple when young. AM 1974

ARAUCARIA – Araucariaceae MT-LT (E) ♥
Remarkable trees of symmetrical appearance bearing whorled branches. The following is the only hardy species:

ARAUCARIA araucana

– **araucana** (*A. imbricata*) MT-LT (E) ♥ "Chile Pine" "Monkey Puzzle"
Long, spidery branches densely covered with overlapping, rigid, spine-tipped, dark green leaves. AM 1980

C

CALOCEDRUS – Cupressaceae ST-LT (E) ⚑
A small genus of trees related to Thuja. *We
recommend the following species and forms:*
– decurrens (*Libocedrus decurrens*) LT (E) ⚑
"Incense Cedar"
Characteristic, columnar habit, with dark
green leaves, arranged in dense, fan-like
sprays. A good formal tree. AGM 1993
– – 'Aureovariegata' MT (E) ⚑
A form in which some leaf sprays are golden-
yellow.
– – 'Berrima Gold' ST (E) ⚑
Pale yellow-green foliage tipped with orange
in winter, bark orange. Slow-growing.

CEDRUS – Pinaceae MT-LT (E) ♠ "Cedar"
*A small genus of large trees ideally suited for
specimen planting. Conical when young,
spreading with age. Leaves in rosettes on
short side-shoots, single on young growths.
Cones erect, barrel-shaped*
– atlantica LT (E) ♠ "Atlas Cedar"
Vigorous tree with green or grey-green leaves,
2-3.5cm, thickly covering the branches. Cones
5-7cm. AGM 1993. We recommend:
– – 'Aurea' MT (E) ♠
Foliage golden-yellow.

CALOCEDRUS decurrens 'Berrima Gold'

CEDRUS atlantica 'Glauca Pendula'

– – Glauca group LT (E) ♠ "Blue Cedar"
Spectacular form with silvery-blue leaves. A
very effective specimen tree. FCC 1972 AGM
1993

CEDRUS atlantica Glauca group

– – **'Glauca Pendula'** ST (E) ♠
Most effective when the long, weeping
branches are supported. Leaves glaucous-blue.
– **deodara** LT (E) ♦ "Deodar"
Very distinct tree of somewhat pendant habit
with a drooping leader and shoot tips and
leaves up to 5cm long, glaucous when young,
becoming bright green. Cones 7-10cm. AGM
1993
– – **'Aurea'** MT (E) ♦ "Golden Deodar"
Young leaves golden yellow in spring. AGM
1993
– – **'Golden Horizon'** SS (E)
A form of spreading habit with golden-yellow
foliage.
– **libani** LT (E) ♦
Conical when young gradually developing flat-
topped tiers of branches. Leaves green or
grey-green. AGM 1993
– – **'Comte de Dijon'** MS (E)
Slow growing bush of dense, conical habit.
– – **'Sargentii'** ('Pendula Sargentii') MS (E)
A prostrate form most effective when trained
upwards to make a dense, weeping bush.

CEDRUS libani 'Sargentii'

CEPHALOTAXUS – Cephalotaxaceae SS-
ST (E)
*Rather like large-leaved yews. Suitable for
dense shade even under other conifers, as
well as open sites. Excellent on chalk. Olive-
like fruits on female plants.*
– **fortunei** LS-ST (E) "Chinese Plum Yew"
Bushy spreading habit – usually wider than
high. Dark green, narrow leaves 6-9cm in two
opposite rows. AM 1975. We recommend the
following:
– – **'Prostrate Spreader'** ('Prostrata') DS (E)
GC
Low growing form of wide-spreading habit
with deep green leaves. Superb ground-cover
plant.

– **harringtonia** LS-ST (E)
Leaves 3.5-6.5cm. Paler green than *C.
fortunei*. We recommend the following form:
– – **'Fastigiata'** MS-LS (E)
Erect-branched habit, resembling the "Irish
Yew". Almost black-green, radially arranged
leaves.

CHAMAECYPARIS – Cupressaceae ST-LT
(E) "False Cypress"
*Although containing only a few species this
genus has contributed to gardens a vast
number of forms from dwarfs to large trees.
Differing from* Cupressus *in their frond-like
branchlets and smaller globose cones.*
– **lawsoniana** LT (E) ♦ Hdg (0.6m) "Lawson
Cypress"
Drooping branches. Broad, fan-like sprays of
foliage, arranged in flattened planes. An
excellent hedge even in exposed or shady
positions. We offer:
– – **'Alumigold'** ST (E) ♦
Soft blue-grey foliage edged golden yellow.
Compact, upright habit.
– – **'Backhouse Silver'** see 'Pygmaea
Argentea'
– – **'Bleu Nantais'** SS
Slow-growing. Conical habit with striking
silvery-blue foliage.
– – **'Chilworth Silver'** LS (E)
Broadly columnar habit with densely packed,
silvery-blue, juvenile foliage. AGM 1993
– – **'Elegantissima'** ST (E) ♦
Broad, drooping sprays of silvery grey or grey-
cream foliage.
– – **'Ellwoodii'** LS (E)
Closely columnar habit with short, feathery
sprays of grey-green foliage, steel-blue in
winter. Slow growing. AM 1934 AGM 1993
– – **'Ellwood's Gold'** MS-LS (E)
Similar to 'Ellwoodii' but slower growing and
with the tips of the sprays yellow tinged. AGM
1993
– – **'Ellwood's Pillar'** MS (E)
Compact, narrow habit. Foliage blue-grey and
feathery.
– – **'Erecta Witzeliana'** see 'Witzeliana'
– – **'Fletcheri'** LS (E)
Broad, columnar habit with grey-green semi-
juvenile foliage, bronze in winter. FCC 1913
AGM 1993
– – **'Gimbornii'** SS (E)
Dense, slow growing bush with blue-green
foliage, tipped mauve. AGM 1993
– – **'Green Hedger'** MT-LT (E) ♦ Hdg (0.6m)
Dense habit with branches ascending from the
base, rich green foliage. AGM 1993

CHAMAECYPARIS lawsoniana 'Gimbornii'

CHAMAECYPARIS lawsoniana 'Minima Aurea'

CHAMAECYPARIS lawsoniana 'Kilmacurragh'

– – **'Kilmacurragh'** MT-LT (E) ♥
Very narrow, columnar habit with irregular sprays of dark green foliage on short branches. AGM 1993

– – **'Lane'** MT (E)
Feathery sprays of golden-yellow foliage. One of the best golden Cypresses. AGM 1993

– – **'Minima Aurea'** SS (E)
Conical bush of dense habit. Vertically held sprays of soft, golden-yellow foliage. One of the best golden conifers for the rock garden. AGM 1993

– – **'Minima Glauca'** SS (E)
Slow growing bush of rounded habit with densely packed sprays of sea-green foliage. AGM 1993

– – **'Naberi'** MT (E) ♦
Green foliage, sulphur-yellow at tips; creamy blue in winter.

CHAMAECYPARIS lawsoniana 'Pembury Blue'

– – **'Pembury Blue'** MT (E) ♦
Striking tree. Silvery-blue foliage. Perhaps the best blue "Lawson Cypress". AGM 1993

– – **'Pottenii'** MT (E) ♥
Dense, slow growth. Sea-green foliage in soft, crowded, feathery sprays. AM 1916

– – **'Pygmaea Argentea'** ('Backhouse Silver') SS (E)
Slow growing rounded bush. Dark bluish-green foliage, creamy-white at the tips. Perhaps the best dwarf, white variegated conifer. AM 1900 AGM 1993

CHAMAECYPARIS lawsoniana 'Pygmaea Argentea'

CHAMAECYPARIS lawsoniana 'Stardust'

– – **'Snow White'** SS (E)
Slow growing with white-tipped juvenile foliage.
– – **'Stardust'** MT (E) ♦
Narrow habit. Yellow foliage, bronze at the tips. AGM 1993
– – **'Summer Snow'** SS (E)
Foliage bright creamy-white in summer turning to green.
– – **'Van Pelt'** ST (E) ♦
Narrow habit with deep blue-grey, later blue-green foliage. AGM 1993
– – **'Westermannii'** MT (E) ♦
Dense, broad habit. Spreading branches

bearing large sprays of light yellow foliage when young, becoming yellowish-green.
– – **'White Spot'** MT (E) ♦
Grey-green sprays of foliage, flecked creamy-white at the tips.
– – **'Winston Churchill'** ST-MT (E) ¶
Broadly columnar. Foliage rich, golden-yellow throughout the year. One of the best golden Lawson Cypresses.
– – **'Wisselii'** MT-LT (E) ♦
Distinct tree of slender habit. Ascending branches. Blue-green foliage borne in short, crowded, fern-like sprays. AM 1899 AGM 1993
– – **'Witzeliana'** ('Erecta Witzeliana') ST (E) ¶
Narrow habit with long, ascending branches. Foliage vivid green, crowded sprays.
– – **'Yellow Transparent'** LS (E)
Similar to 'Fletcheri' but slower growing, with yellow young foliage, transparent in sunshine, bronze in winter.
– **nootkatensis** LT (E) ♦ "Nootka Cypress"
Drooping branchlets. Long, flattened sprays of green foliage, rough to the touch. AM 1978. We recommend:
– – **'Pendula'** MT-LT (E) ♦
Spreading and upcurved branches bearing long, pendulous branchlets. AM 1988 AGM 1993

CHAMAECYPARIS nootkatensis 'Pendula'

– **obtusa** LT (E) ♦ "Hinoki Cypress"
Spreading branches with glossy green foliage in thick, flattened sprays. We recommend the following forms:
– – **'Aurora'** SS (E)
Compact bush with shell-like sprays of yellow-green foliage.
– – **'Crippsii'** ST (E) ♦
Frond-like sprays of rich golden-yellow foliage. One of the best small golden conifers. FCC 1899 AGM 1993

CHAMAECYPARIS obtusa 'Crippsii'

– – **'Fernspray Gold'** SS (E)
Fern-like sprays of golden-yellow foliage.
– – **'Nana Aurea'** MS (E)
A slow growing bush, ideal for the rock
garden, golden-yellow foliage. Perhaps the
best dwarf golden conifer. AGM 1993
– – **'Nana Gracilis'** MS (E)
Slow growing bush of compact habit. Dark
green foliage in short, neat, shell-like sprays
AGM 1993

CHAMAECYPARIS obtusa 'Nana Aurea'

– **pisifera** LT (E) ♦ "Sawara Cypress"
Horizontally flattened sprays of dark green
foliage with sharply pointed, scale-like leaves.
FCC 1861. We recommend the following
forms:

CHAMAECYPARIS obtusa 'Nana Gracilis'

– – **'Boulevard'** ('Cyanoviridis') LS (E)
Dense, narrowly columnar habit. Steel-blue
foliage, soft to the touch. One of the most
popular of conifers. AGM 1993
– – **'Gold Spangle'** ST (E) ♦
Narrow habit with thread-like, bright yellow
foliage.
– – **'Golden Mop'** ('Filifera Aurea Nana') SS
(E)
Mounded habit with bright yellow, thread-like
foliage. AGM 1993
– – **'Sungold'** MS-LS (F)
Slender, thread-like shoots of golden-yellow
foliage. Withstands full sun.

CHAMAECYPARIS pisifera 'Boulevard'

– **thyoides** ST-MT (E) ♦ ∠ "White Cypress"
Erect, fan-shaped sprays of aromatic,
glaucous-green foliage. We recommend the
following forms:
– – **'Ericoides'** SS (E) ∠
Compact, conical bush with sea-green
juvenile foliage, soft to the touch, becoming
bronze-purple in winter. AGM 1993
– – **'Purple Heather'** ('Heatherbun') DS (E) ∠
Dense, round-topped bush with juvenile
foliage rich plum-purple in winter.

CRYPTOMERIA – Taxodiaceae
A monotypic genus. Cones solitary, globular.
– **japonica** LT (E) ♥ "Japanese Cedar"
Vigorous tree with reddish, shredding bark
and densely crowded, awl-shaped leaves on
long, slender branchlets. AGM 1993
– – **'Elegans Compacta'** MS (E)
Dense billowy bush with very soft, plumose
foliage rich purple in winter. AGM 1993
– – **'Elegans Nana'** SS (E)
Very dense, rounded habit with juvenile
foliage, bronze in winter. Differs from
'Elegans Compacta' in its straight fairly stiff
leaves.
– – **'Sekkan-sugi'** ST (E) ♦
Young foliage pale creamy-yellow becoming
dark green.
– – **'Vilmoriniana'** DS (E)
Very slow growing bush with short crowded
branchlets, making a dense, rigid globe,
reddish-purple in winter. AGM 1993

CRYPTOMERIA japonica 'Vilmoriniana'

CUNNINGHAMIA – Taxodiaceae ST-MT (E) ♥
Two species of trees recalling Araucaria. *The
following is hardy but best planted in a
sheltered position.*
– **lanceolata** ST-MT (E) ♥ "Chinese Fir"
Lanceolate leaves, 3-7cm, emerald green
above, marked with two white bands

beneath, becoming bronzy in autumn. AM
1977

× **CUPRESSOCYPARIS** (*Cupressus* ×
Chamaecyparis) – **Cupressaceae** MT-LT (E) ♥
Fast growing, popular trees with many uses.
– **leylandii** LT (E) ♥ Hdg (0.6m) "Leyland
Cypress"
Vigorous tree of dense habit. Foliage in
irregular, slightly drooping sprays. Excellent
for tall hedges and screens and tolerant of
coastal conditions and chalk soils. The fastest
growing conifer in this country. AM 1941
– – **'Castlewellan Gold'** MT (E) ♥
A form with yellow foliage.

CUPRESSUS – Cupressaceae ST-LT (E)
Impressive trees differing from Chamaecyparis
*in their usually rounded branchlets and larger
cones.*
– **cashmeriana** ST-MT (E) ♦ † "Kashmir
Cypress"
Ascending branches draped with long
pendulous branchlets with conspicuously
blue-grey foliage in flattened sprays. FCC
1971 AGM 1993
– **glabra** (*C. arizonica* hort.) MT (E) ♦
We recommend the following forms:

CUPRESSUS glabra 'Pyramidalis'

CUPRESSUS sempervirens

CUPRESSUS macrocarpa 'Goldcrest'

– – **'Aurea'** ST (E) ♦
Young foliage, yellow during summer.
– – **'Pyramidalis'** MT (E) ♦
Dense, conical habit with conspicuous, blue-grey foliage. An excellent formal tree. AGM 1993
– **macrocarpa** MT-LT (E) ♥ "Monterey Cypress"
Vigorous tree becoming broad-crowned with age. Bright green foliage, densely packed sprays. Excellent for shelter in coastal areas.

The yellow forms are best in full sun. We offer:
– – **'Goldcrest'** MT (E) ♥
Dense, narrow habit with rich yellow, feathery, juvenile foliage. AGM 1993
– – **'Gold Spread'** SS (E) GC
Dense and wide-spreading with bright golden-yellow foliage, yellow-green in winter. AGM 1993
– **sempervirens** MT (E) ♦ "Italian Cypress" "Mediterranean Cypress"
The familiar narrow cypress of the Mediterranean region. Branches strictly ascending with dark green foliage. AGM 1993
– – **'Green Pencil'** ('Green Spire') MT (E) ♦
Selected clone of closely erect habit.
– – **'Swane's Golden'** ST (E)
Compact, narrow habit with bright golden foliage. AGM 1993

F

"FIR" see *Abies*

G

GINKGO – Ginkgoaceae MT-LT ♦
The only member of this genus is the sole living representative of a large group of plants which occurred throughout the world in prehistoric times.
– **biloba** (*Salisburia adiantifolia*) MT-LT ♦
"Maidenhair Tree"
A remarkable, deciduous tree with bi-lobed fan-like leaves, clear yellow in autumn .
Tolerant of industrial areas. AGM 1993
– – **'Tremonia'** MT ♦
A form of narrowly conical habit

GINKGO biloba

H

"HEMLOCK" see *Tsuga*

J

JUNIPERUS – Cupressaceae PS-LT (E)
"Juniper"
A large group of plants of varying habit. Leaves narrow and pointed on juvenile plants, usually scale-like on adult plants. Excellent on chalk.
– **chinensis** MT-LT (E) ♥

Variable tree, normally of columnar habit. Generally both adult and juvenile foliage. We recommend the following forms:
– – **'Aurea'** ST (E) ♥ "Young's Golden Juniper"
Foliage golden yellow. Inclined to burn in full sun. FCC 1871 AGM 1993

– – **'Blue Alps'** LS
Vigorous habit with striking steel-blue foliage.
– – **'Obelisk'** MS (E)
Erect, columnar habit with densely packed, bluish-green, juvenile foliage. AGM 1993
– – **'Pyramidalis'** MS (E)
Slow growing, conical bush of dense habit, almost all juvenile foliage. FCC 1868 AGM 1993

JUNIPERUS chinensis 'Pyramidalis'

– **communis** MS-LS (E) "Common Juniper"
Narrow, prickly silver-backed leaves. The prostrate forms make excellent ground cover in full sun. AM 1890. We offer:

JUNIPERUS communis 'Compressa'

– – **'Compressa'** DS (E)
Slow growing narrow column. A gem for the rock garden. AGM 1993
– – **'Depressa Aurea'** DS (E) GC
Low, spreading habit with golden-yellow young foliage.
– – **'Gold Cone'** ('Suecica Aurea') SS (E)
Compact, upright habit with bright yellow foliage.
– – **'Golden Rod'** ('Schneverdinger Goldmachangel') SS (E)
Slender, columnar habit with bright yellow young foliage green in winter.
– – **'Green Carpet'** PS (E) GC
Wide spreading with bright green foliage.
– – **'Hibernica'** ('Stricta') (*J. hibernica*) LS (E) "Irish Juniper"
Dense form of slender, columnar habit. An excellent formal specimen. AGM 1993
– – **'Hornibrookii'** PS (E) GC
Prostrate form. Rather small, sharply pointed leaves, silvery beneath. AGM 1993
– – **'Repanda'** PS (E) GC
Densely packed, semi-prostrate stems. Loosely arranged leaves, soft to the touch. AGM 1993

JUNIPERUS communis 'Repanda'

– – **'Sentinel'** LS (E)
Dense, very narrow habit. Blue-green leaves on purple shoots.
– **conferta** PS (E) GC "Shore Juniper"
Apple-green, prickly leaves banded white above. Excellent cover in full sun where it will form large patches. We recommend:
– – **'Blue Pacific'** PS (E) GC
Shorter and broader, less prickly leaves, deeper green.
– **drupacea** ST (E) ⚘ "Syrian Juniper"
Distinctive narrow columnar habit. Short, densely crowded branches. Leaves awl-shaped, sharply pointed, broadly banded white above.
– **'Grey Owl'** (*J. virginiana* 'Grey Owl') MS (E)
Vigorous shrub with wide-spreading branches and soft, silvery-grey foliage. AM 1968 AGM 1993

– **'Holger'** SS (E) GC
Spreading habit with blue-grey foliage, creamy-yellow when young. AGM 1993

– **horizontalis** PS-DS (E) GC "Creeping Juniper"
Long, usually creeping branches, forming large carpets. Excellent, dense ground cover. We recommend the following forms:

– – **'Blue Chip'** PS (E) GC
Foliage bright blue throughout the year.

– – **'Blue Rug'** see 'Wiltonii'

– – **'Hughes'** DS (E) GC
Wide-spreading, slightly ascending branches with grey-green foliage.

– – **'Wiltonii'** ('Blue Rug') PS (E) GC
Long, prostrate branches with glaucous-blue foliage. AGM 1993

– **japonica** hort. see *J. × media* 'Plumosa'

– **× media** SS-LS (E)
A variable hybrid, usually of wide-spreading habit. Several forms make excellent ground cover and are plants of architectural quality. The following are recommended:

– – **'Blaauw'** SS (E)
Strongly ascending branches densely clothed with feathery sprays of mainly scale-like, greyish-blue leaves. AGM 1993

– – **'Carberry Gold'** PS (E) GC
Conspicuous, creamy-yellow foliage throughout the year. Slow growing.

– – **'Gold Coast'** SS (E) GC
Flat-topped, wide-spreading bush with golden-yellow foliage.

– – **'Mint Julep'** MS (E)
Wide spreading habit with arching shoots. Foliage rich green.

– – **'Old Gold'** MS (E) GC
Similar to 'Pfitzeriana' but of more compact habit with bronze-gold foliage throughout the year. AGM 1993

JUNIPERUS × media 'Pfitzeriana Aurea'

– – **'Pfitzeriana'** MS (E) GC (AGM 1993)
This large, wide-spreading shrub has generally been superseded by others such as 'Mint Julep', 'Pfitzeriana Aurea' and 'Pfitzeriana Compacta' qv.

– – **'Pfitzeriana Aurea'** MS (E) GC "Golden Pfitzer"
A low growing, flat-topped form of 'Pfitzeriana' with the young foliage golden yellow.

– – **'Pfitzeriana Compacta'** SS (E) GC
A low growing but wide-spreading form of 'Pfitzeriana' with mainly juvenile, prickly leaves. AGM 1993

– – **'Plumosa Aurea'** MS (E)
Ascending branches arching at the tips with dense, plume-like sprays of yellow foliage, bronze-gold in winter. AGM 1993

– – **'Sulphur Spray'** SS (E)
Foliage pale sulphur-yellow, brighter in summer. Spreading. AGM 1993

– **procumbens** PS (E) GC "Creeping Juniper"
Wide-spreading, mound-forming shrub with long, stiff branches bearing glaucous-green, sharply pointed leaves. We offer:

– – **'Nana'** ('Bonin Isles') PS (E) GC
A more compact form with shorter branches. AGM 1993

JUNIPERUS procumbens 'Nana'

– **sabina** SS (E) GC "Savin"
Variable shrubs of usually wide-spreading habit with green or grey-green, mainly scale-like leaves. We recommend the following form:

– – **'Tam No Blight'** ('New Blue') DS (E) GC
Compact, wide-spreading and flat-topped with blue-green foliage. A disease-resistant form of var. *tamariscifolia*.

– **scopulorum** ST (E) ♠ " Rocky Mountain Juniper"
Cypress-like tree with reddish-brown, shredding bark and slender branchlets. Tightly adpressed, scale-like leaves. We recommend the following:

JUNIPERUS squamata 'Blue Star'

JUNIPERUS scopulorum 'Skyrocket'

– – **'Moonglow'** ST (E) ⦙
Bright blue-grey foliage. Narrow upright habit.
– – **'Skyrocket'** (*J. virginiana* 'Skyrocket') ST
(E) ⦙
Very narrow habit with erect branches and
blue-grey foliage. One of the narrowest of
conifers.
– – **'Springbank'** ST (E) ⦙
Ascending and spreading branches bear
silvery grey-green foliage.
– **squamata** PS-ST (E)
A variable species. Shoots with characteristic,
nodding tips. Leaves short, awl-shaped, white
or pale green above. We recommend:
– – **'Blue Carpet'** PS (E) GC
Bright blue-grey, prickly foliage. AGM 1993
– – **'Blue Star'** DS (E)
Dense bush with silvery-blue, awl-shaped
leaves. AGM 1993
– – **'Chinese Silver'** MS LS (E)
Many-stemmed shrub of dense habit with

awl-shaped leaves, intense silvery blue-green.
– – **'Embley Park'** (*J. recurva* 'Embley Park')
SS (E)
A distinct form with ascending branches and
rich, grass-green, awl-shaped leaves.
– – **'Meyeri'** LS (E)
Vigorous, semi-erect shrub with ascending,
angular branches and densely packed,
glaucous-blue leaves. AM 1931
– **virginiana 'Grey Owl'** see *J.* 'Grey Owl'
– – **'Skyrocket'** see *J. scopulorum* 'Skyrocket'

L

LARIX – Pinaceae LT ♠ "Larch"
*Vigorous, deciduous trees with linear leaves
borne in dense rosettes on short shoots and
singly on young shoots, turning yellow in
autumn. Suitable for most soils except very
wet or dry, shallow chalk.*
– **decidua** (*L. europaea*) LT ♠ "European
Larch" "Common Larch"
Crown slender conical when young. Branches
and branchlets drooping on older specimens.
Shoots yellowish or grey. Leaves light green.
AGM 1993
– **europaea** see *L. decidua*

LARIX kaempferi 'Pendula'

– **kaempferi** (*L. leptolepis*) LT ♦ "Japanese Larch"
Vigorous tree with reddish shoots and sea-green leaves. Commonly used in forestry plantations. Withstands exposure well. AGM 1993
– – **'Pendula'** LT ♦
A form with long, weeping branches.

– **leptolepis** see *L. kaempferi*

"LEYLAND CYPRESS" see × *Cupressocyparis leylandii*

LIBOCEDRUS decurrens see *Calocedrus decurrens*

M

"MAIDENHAIR TREE" see *Ginkgo biloba*

METASEQUOIA – Taxodiaceae MT-LT ♦
A monotypic genus. The first living representative was found in China in 1941, the same year in which the genus was named from fossil specimens. It has quickly become a very popular conifer.
– **glyptostroboides** MT-LT ♦ "Dawn Redwood"
Vigorous, deciduous tree conical when young, developing a rounded head with age. Bright green, linear leaves borne on short, deciduous branchlets resembling a pinnate leaf, pink and old gold in autumn. Best in a moist, well-drained soil. AM 1969 AGM 1993. We recommend the following form:
– – **'Emerald Feathers'** MT-LT ♦
A form, selected for vegetative propagation, of regular habit with dense, lush-green foliage.

MICROBIOTA – Cupressaceae DS (E)
A monotypic genus related to Juniperus.

METASEQUOIA glyptostroboides 'Emerald Feathers'

– **decussata** DS (E) GC
Densely branched, spreading habit. Leaves mostly scale-like, bright green, turning brownish in winter. AM 1973 AGM 1993

P

PICEA – Pinaceae MT-LT (E) ♦ "Spruce"
Ornamental trees usually of conical habit with whorled branches and needle-like, usually sharp pointed leaves. Cones pendulous. Not recommended (apart from the dwarf forms) for poor, shallow, chalky or dry soils or very exposed situations.

– **abies** LT (E) ♦ "Common Spruce" "Norway Spruce" "Christmas Tree"
Orange or reddish-brown shoots and bright green leaves. There are numerous forms.
– – **'Acrocona'** LS-ST (E)
Branches semi-pendulous usually terminating in a large cone even when young.

PICEA abies 'Nidiformis'

– – **'Inversa'** ('Pendula') ST (E) ♠
Branches pendulous. Needs to be trained
when young to reach tree form.
– – **'Nidiformis'** DS (E)
A flat-topped bush of dense spreading habit
with branches in horizontal layers. AGM 1993
– **breweriana** ST-MT (E) ♠ "Brewer's
Weeping Spruce"
Spreading branches bear long, slender,
hanging, tail-like branchlets. Leaves flattened,
shining dark blue-green above, white
beneath. Perhaps the most beautiful of all
spruces. AM 1958 FCC 1974 AGM 1993
   glauca LT (E) ♠ "White Spruce"
Dense habit with decurved branches
ascending at the tips. Leaves four-angled,
glaucous-green and densely arranged. Very
hardy and suitable for exposed positions. We
recommend the following form:
– – var. **albertiana 'Conica'** MS (F)
Slow growing, perfectly cone-shaped bush of
dense habit. A deservedly popular form. AM
1933 AGM 1993
– **likiangensis** MT (F) ♠
Vigorous, ornamental tree with pale brown or

PICEA glauca var. albertiana 'Conica'

reddish young shoots. Leaves flattened, green
or bluish-green above, glaucous beneath.
Young cones and male flowers brilliant red in
April-May. AM 1961 FCC 1974
– **mariana** MT (E) ♠ "Black Spruce"
Narrow habit with densely hairy, brown
shoots. Leaves dark bluish-green. Cones dark
purple when young. We recommend:
– – **'Nana'** DS (E)
Globular bush of dense habit with grey-green
leaves. Suitable for the rock garden. AGM
1993
– **omorika** MT-LT (E) ♠ "Serbian Spruce"
A graceful tree of slender habit with relatively
short, drooping branches curving upwards at
the tips. Leaves flattened, dark green above,
glaucous beneath. AGM 1993

PICEA omorika

– – **'Nana'** SS (E)
Dense conical habit. Leaves bright blue-white
beneath.
– – **'Pendula'** MT (E)
Narrow habit with drooping branches. AGM
1993
– **orientalis** LT (E) ♠ "Oriental Spruce"
Densely branched tree of broad habit,
branched to the ground. Leaves glossy dark
green, short and blunt, very densely arranged.
AGM 1993
– – **'Aurea'** MT (E) ♠
Young shoots creamy yellow becoming
golden yellow and finally green. FCC 1893
AGM 1993

PICEA orientalis 'Aurea'

– **pungens** MT-LT (E) "Colorado Spruce"
Stout, orange-brown young shoots and rigid,
sharply pointed green to grey leaves. FCC
1887
More common in cultivation are members of
the Glauca group ("Blue Spruce") of which a
selection is given below.
– – **'Globosa'** ('Glauca Globosa') SS (E)
Flat-topped, globular bush of dense habit
with glaucous-blue leaves. AGM 1993
– – **'Hoopsii'** ST-MT (E) ♦
Dense habit with vividly glaucous-blue leaves.
AGM 1993
– – **'Koster'** ST-MT (E) ♦
Leaves an intense silvery-blue. AGM 1993

PICEA pungens 'Globosa'

PICEA pungens 'Koster'

– – **'Procumbens'** ('Glauca Procumbens') PS
(E) GC
Low growing, wide spreading shrub with
glaucous-blue foliage. AGM 1993
– **smithiana** (*P. morinda*) LT (E) ♦ "West
Himalayan Spruce"
Branches upcurved at tips bearing long,
pendulous branchlets. Leaves relatively long,
needle-like and dark green. AGM 1993

PINUS – Pinaceae ST-LT (E) "Pine"
*A large genus of evergreen trees. Normally
conical when young, broadening in maturity.
Leaves long and needle-like, borne in bundles
of 2-5. Some survive in the poorest soils, acid
or alkaline, but generally the 5-needled
species are not satisfactory on shallow chalk
soils. Some make excellent windbreaks
especially in coastal districts. All dislike shade
and few will tolerate a smoke-polluted air.
Numerous dwarf forms are cultivated.*
– **aristata** LS-ST (E) "Bristlecone Pine"
Dense habit. Stout, reddish-brown, young
shoots. Leaves in fives, tightly bunched, dark
green, flecked with white resin spots.
Specimens up to 2,000 years old have been
recorded in the wild.

– **armandii** MT (E) ❦ "Armand's Pine"
An ornamental tree with drooping, slender, glaucous leaves borne in fives. Long, decorative, eventually pendulous cones
– **bungeana** ST-MT (E) ♦ "Lace-bark Pine"
Often branched from near the base with characteristic, patchwork bark like a "London Plane". Shoots grey-green, leaves in threes, rigid.
– **cembra** ST-MT (E) ♦ "Arolla Pine"
Characteristic, dense conical or columnar habit. Young shoots densely rusty-hairy. Leaves in fives, densely crowded, dark blue-green, glaucous on the inner surface. Cones deep blue, never opening. A good formal tree. AGM 1993

PINUS cembra

– **contorta** MT-LT (E) ♦ ✗ "Beach Pine"
Young shoots green. Leaves in pairs, yellowish-green and characteristically twisted. We recommend the following form:
– – subsp. **latifolia** MT (E) ♦ ✗ "Lodgepole Pine"
Leaves longer and slightly broader.
– **coulteri** MT-LT (E) ♦ "Big-Cone Pine"
Striking tree with stout, glaucous shoots. Leaves in threes, very long, grey-green, stiff and curved. Huge cones are produced on mature trees. AM 1961 AGM 1993
– **densiflora** MT (E) ❦ ✗ "Japanese Red Pine"
Reddish, flaking bark. Leaves in pairs, slender and dark green. We offer:
– – **'Oculus Draconis'** ST (E) ❦ ✗ "Dragon-eye Pine"

A slow growing form with the terminal leaves banded yellow.
– **jeffreyi** LT (E) ♦ "Jeffrey Pine"
Narrow, spire-like crown. Young shoots stout and glaucous. Leaves to 20cm long, bluish-green, in threes, crowded at the ends of the branchlets. AGM 1993
– **koraiensis** MT (E) ♦ "Korean Pine"
Open-branched tree with densely rusty hairy young shoots. Leaves usually in fives, blue-green, stiff and rough to the touch. We recommend:
– – **'Compacta Glauca'** (P. cembra 'Compacta Glauca' ST (E) ♦
Compact form with short, stout branches and densely packed, conspicuously glaucous foliage.
– **leucodermis** MT (E) ♦ "Bosnian Pine"
Dense, ovoid habit. Young shoots glaucous. Leaves in pairs, very dark green, rigid and erect. Young cones bright blue. Suitable for dry and shallow chalk soils. AGM 1993
– – **'Schmidtii'** DS (E)
Very slow growing, dense bush with bright green leaves. AGM 1993
– **montezumae** MT-LT (E) ❦ † "Montezuma Pine"
Magnificent tree. Large, domed crown. Young shoots stout, orange-brown. Leaves to 25cm long, usually in fives, blue-grey, spreading or drooping.
– **mugo** LS-ST (E) ❦ "Mountain Pine"
Dense, bushy habit. Leaves in pairs, dark green, short, rigid and curved. Succeeds in almost all soils including chalk.
– – **'Gnom'** MS (E)
A compact form making a dark green, globular mound.
– – **'Mops'** MS (E)
Slow growing, dense bush of rounded habit. AGM 1993
– – **'Ophir'** DS (E)
Compact, rounded habit. Foliage golden-yellow in winter.

PINUS montezumae

PINUS mugo var. pumilio

– – var. **pumilio** PS-MS (E)
Branches prostrate or ascending to 2m. AGM 1993
– – **'Winter Gold'** SS (E)
Bright yellow winter foliage.
– **nigra** (*P. nigra* var. *austriaca*) LT (E) ♦ "Austrian Pine"
Commonly planted tree with dark bark and yellowish-brown young shoots. Leaves in pairs, dark green and rigid, densely crowded. Good in exposed positions as a windbreak, on chalky soils and coastal areas. AGM 1993
– – **'Hornibrookiana'** SS (E)
A slow growing form of spreading habit with many stout, ascending branches.
– – subsp. **laricio** (var. *maritima*) LT (E) ♦ "Corsican Pine"
Differs from the "Austrian Pine" in its straighter, more openly branched trunk and more flexible, grey-green leaves. A common forestry tree happy in almost any soil and situation. AGM 1993
– – var. **maritima** see subsp. *laricio*

PINUS parviflora

– **parviflora** ST-MT (E) ♦ "Japanese White Pine"
A slow growing, bushy tree becoming flat-topped with age. Leaves in fives, slightly curved, deep blue-green, blue-white on the inner surface. AM 1977 AGM 1993. We recommend:
– – **'Adcock's Dwarf'** MS (E)
A compact, slow growing bush with very short leaves produced in congested bunches at the shoot tips. AGM 1993
– – **'Tempelhof'** ST (E)
Vigorous form of upright growth with glaucous-blue foliage.
– **patula** ST-MT (E) ♥ ✗ †
A very beautiful tree with reddish bark and spreading branches. Leaves normally in threes, 15-30cm long, slender and pendulous. Requires a sheltered position or mild area. AGM 1993
– **pinaster** MT-LT (E) ♦ "Maritime Pine" "Bournemouth Pine"
Fast-growing, sparsely branched tree. Leaves in pairs to 25cm long, rigid and curved, dull grey. Excellent for sandy soils and coastal areas particularly in the south and west. AGM 1993
– **ponderosa** LT (E) ♦ "Western Yellow Pine"
Stately tree with a tall, straight trunk, and relatively short spreading or drooping branches. Leaves in threes to 25cm long and stiff. AM 1980 AGM 1993

PINUS ponderosa

PINUS strobus 'Nana'

– radiata LT (E) ♠ "Monterey Pine"
Thick, rugged, dark brown bark. Leaves in threes, bright green and densely crowded. Cones often remaining intact for many years. Grows rapidly in coastal areas of the south and west where it is suitable for a windbreak. AGM 1993

– strobus LT (E) ♠ "Weymouth Pine" "White Pine"
Older trees develop a rounded head. Leaves in fives, slender and glaucous-green. A fast growing, ornamental tree.

– – **'Nana'** SS (F)
A dwarf form of dense habit. AGM 1993

– – **'Nivea'** ST (E) ♠
Slow growing tree with glaucous leaves tipped milky-white.

– sylvestris LT (E) ♠ "Scots Pine"
Common tree with characteristic, reddish young bark. Leaves in pairs, twisted, grey-green or blue-green. Suitable for all soils. AGM 1993

– – **'Argentea'** see 'Edwin Hillier' LT (E) ♠

– – **'Aurea'** ST (E) ♠
Slow growing tree with leaves golden-yellow in winter. AM 1964 AGM 1993

– – **'Beuvronensis'** SS (E)
A compact, dome-shaped bush, ideal for the rock garden. AM 1968 AGM 1993

– – **'Edwin Hillier'** ('Argentea') LT (E) ♠
Leaves silvery blue-green.

– – **'Fastigiata'** ST (E) ♦
A remarkable form of very narrow habit with erect branches. A superb tree where space is limited.

– – **'Gold Coin'** DS (E)
Bun-shaped habit, leaves turn pale golden-yellow in winter.

– – **'Moseri'** MS (E)
Slow-growing, dense globular bush or

PINUS sylvestris 'Aurea'

PINUS wallichiana

miniature tree with the foliage turning yellow-green in winter. AGM 1993
– – **'Pumila'** see 'Watereri'
– – **'Watereri'** ('Pumila') LS-ST (E) ✿
A slow growing bush or small tree of dense, rounded habit.
– **wallichiana** LT (E) ✿ "Bhutan Pine"
Vigorous broad-headed tree. Young shoots glaucous. Leaves in fives to 20cm long, slender, blue-green, drooping with age. Long, banana-shaped resin-smeared cones. AM 1979 AGM 1993

PODOCARPUS – Podocarpaceae PS-LT (E)
A large genus of trees and shrubs from the southern hemisphere containing several hardy species. Mainly suitable for most soils, acid or alkaline.
– **nivalis** DS-MS (E) GC "Alpine Totara"
A variable shrub, usually low and spreading but sometimes up to 2m. Leaves narrow and

leathery, olive green, crowded. Very hardy and excellent on chalk.

PSEUDOLARIX – Pinaceae MT ♦ ✗
A monotypic genus related to Larix.
– **amabilis** MT ♦ ✗ "Golden Larch"
A beautiful and very hardy slow-growing deciduous tree. Leaves in clusters on short shoots as the Larch, golden yellow in autumn. Cones like pale green artichokes, reddish-brown when ripe. AM 1976 AGM 1993

PSEUDOTSUGA – Pinaceae ST-LT (E) ♦ ✗
Evergreen trees with whorled branches and spindle-shaped buds. Leaves linear, soft to the touch, with glaucous bands beneath.
– **menziesii** LT (E) ♦ ✗ "Douglas Fir"
A vigorous tree with downswept lower branches and pendulous branchlets. A commonly planted and very important forestry tree. Many trees have exceeded 45m in this country. AGM 1993

R

"REDWOOD" see *Sequoia sempervirens*

S

SCIADOPITYS – Pinaceae MT (E) ♦ ✗
A monotypic genus.
– **verticillata** MT (E) ♦ ✗ "Umbrella Pine"
A very distinct, slow growing tree of dense habit. Leaves long and linear, in dense whorls like the spokes of an umbrella. AM 1979 AGM 1993

SEQUOIA – Taxodiaceae LT (E) ♦
A monotypic genus. The world's tallest tree, reaching more than 100m in the wild.
– **sempervirens** LT (E) ♦ "Californian Redwood"

A very large tree which has reached more than 40m in this country. Bark soft, reddish-brown. Leaves dark green above with two white bands beneath. AGM 1993
– – **'Adpressa'** ('Albospica') ST (E) ♦
A slow growing form with the young shoots tipped creamy white. FCC 1890
– **wellingtonia** see *Sequoiadendron giganteum*

SEQUOIADENDRON – Taxodiaceae LT (E) ♦
A monotypic genus. Not as tall in the wild as

SEQUOIADENDRON giganteum

the "Californian Redwood" but more massive and acknowledged to be the world's largest living thing.
– **giganteum** (*Sequoia gigantea*) (*Sequoia wellingtonia*) LT (E) ♠ "Wellingtonia" "Mammoth Tree" "Big Tree"
Vigorous tree of dense habit with downswept branches. Bark deeply furrowed, reddish-brown. Leaves awl-shaped, bright green, prickly pointed. AGM 1993
– – **'Pendulum'** ST (E) ♥
An unusual tree of unique appearance. Usually forming a narrow column with long

SCIADOPITYS verticillata

branches hanging down along the trunk. FCC 1882

"SPRUCE" see *Picea*

T

TAXODIUM – Taxodiaceae ST-LT ✍
Deciduous. Attractive, frond-like, feathery foliage. Male and female strobili on same tree. Grow on all soils except chalk. Tolerant of waterlogged conditions.
– **ascendens** ST-MT ✍ ♥
Bright green awl-shaped leaves, rich brown in autumn. Round cones, purple and resinous when young. We recommend:
– – **'Nutans'** ST-MT ✍ ♥
Shortly spreading or ascending branches. Branchlets erect at first, later nodding. AGM 1993

– **distichum** LT ✍♠ "Deciduous Cypress" "Swamp Cypress"
Fibrous, reddish-brown bark, buttressed trunk. Bright green feathery foliage, bronze in autumn. Small round cones, purple when young. Best conifer for wet or swampy soils. AM 1973 AGM 1993

TAXUS – Taxaceae MS-ST (E) "Yew"
Dark green leaves with two grey-green or yellow-green bands beneath. Male and female strobili usually on separate plants. Fruits with fleshy cup containing single

poisonous seed. Tolerate most soils and situations. Good for hedging. All parts except fruit flesh are poisonous.

TAXODIUM ascendens 'Nutans'

TAXUS baccata

– baccata ST-MT (E) ♀ Hdg (0.6m) "Common Yew" "English Yew"
Dark green leaves, yellowish-green beneath. Fruits with red cup. Needs good drainage. Will grow on shallow chalk or very acid soil. Good for hedging. AGM 1993
– – 'Adpressa Variegata' LS (E)
Young leaves old gold turning yellow, restricted to margins as they age. Male. FCC 1889 AGM 1993
– – 'Dovastoniana' ST (E) ♀ "Westfelton Yew"
Long, horizontal branches and weeping branchlets. Blackish-green leaves. Generally female. AGM 1993

– – 'Dovastonii Aurea' LS (E)
Leaves margined yellow. Male. AGM 1993
– – 'Elegantissima' LS (E)
Dense habit. Ascending branches. Yellow young leaves turning paler, confined to margins with age. Female. AGM 1993

TAXUS baccata 'Fastigiata'

– – 'Fastigiata' LS (E) "Irish Yew"
Erect, broadly columnar habit. Black-green leaves. Female. FCC 1863 AGM 1993
– – 'Fastigiata Aureomarginata' LS (E)
"Golden Irish Yew"
Similar in habit to the "Irish Yew". Leaves margined yellow. Male. AGM 1993
– – 'Repens Aurea' DS (E)
Low spreading habit. Leaves yellow margined when young, cream later. AGM 1993
– – 'Semperaurea' MS (E)
Slow. Ascending branches. Young leaves old gold, turning rusty yellow. Male. AM 1977 AGM 1993

TAXUS baccata 'Repens Aurea'

– – **'Standishii'** ('Fastigiata Standishii') MS (E)
Slow. Dense columnar habit. Golden leaves.
Female. AGM 1993
– × **media** MS-LS (E)
Vigorous, spreading habit. We recommend:
– – **'Hicksii'** LS (E) Hdg (0.6m)
Broadly columnar habit. Female. Good for
hedging. AGM 1993

THUJA – Cupressaceae DS-LT (E) "Arbor-
vitae"
*Aromatic foliage. Small scale-like leaves often
borne in flattened, fan-like sprays. Male and
female strobili on same tree. Small cones.
Thrive in almost any well-drained soil.
Poisonous.*
– **occidentalis** MT (E) ♥ "American
Arborvitae"
Reddish-brown peeling bark. Branches
upcurved at tips. Flattened sprays of dark
green foliage, paler beneath, usually bronze in
winter. We recommend:
– – **'Aureospicata'** ST (E) ♠
Compact, upright habit, yellow foliage turns
to old gold in winter.
– – **'Holmstrup Yellow'** MS (E)
Dense, conical habit with golden-yellow
foliage.
– – **'Little Gem'** DS (E)
Slightly flat-topped, rounded habit. Crowded,
crimpled sprays of deep green foliage.
– – **'Rheingold'** LS (E)
Slow. Ovoid or conical habit. Rich old gold-
amber foliage. AM 1902 AGM 1993
– – **'Smaragd'** ST (E) ♠
Dense, narrow habit. Bright green foliage
does not bronze in winter. AGM 1993
– – **'Sunkist'** SS (E)
Slow growing, bushy shrub with golden-
yellow foliage.
– – **'Wareana Lutescens'** ('Lutescens') SS (E)
Compact conical habit. Thickened sprays of
pale yellow foliage.
– – **'Woodwardii'** SS (E)
Dense ovoid habit. Green foliage throughout
year.
– **orientalis** LS (E) "Chinese Arbor-vitae"
Dense, conical or columnar habit. Erect
branches and branchlets. Frond-like vertical
sprays of small green leaves. Less aromatic
than other species. We recommend:
– – **'Aurea Nana'** DS (E)
Dense, round habit. Light yellow-green
foliage. AGM 1993
– – **'Conspicua'** MS-LS (E)
Compact, conical habit. Golden yellow
foliage.

THUJA orientalis 'Conspicua'

– – **'Elegantissima'** MS-LS (E)
Dense, columnar habit. Golden yellow foliage,
tinged old gold, turning green in winter. AGM
1993
– – **'Rosedalis'** ('Rosedalis Compacta') SS (E)
Dense ovoid habit. Soft juvenile foliage
changes from canary yellow in spring, to sea-
green then plum-purple in winter.
– **plicata** LT ♥ (E) Hdg (0.6m) "Western Red
Cedar"
Reddish brown shredding bark. Bright, glossy
green leaves in flattened, drooping sprays,
fruity when crushed. Tolerates shallow chalk.
Excellent for hedging. AGM 1993

THUJA plicata 'Fastigiata'

THUJA plicata 'Stoneham Gold'

– – **'Aureovariegata'** see 'Zebrina'
– – **'Aurea'** LT (E) ⚘
Rich old gold foliage. FCC 1897 AGM 1993
– – **'Fastigiata'** ('Stricta') LT (E) ⚘
Slender ascending branches, densely arranged. AGM 1993
– – **'Irish Gold'** MT (E) ♦
A striking form, the foliage conspicuously banded with deep yellow. AGM 1993
– – **'Rogersii"** ('Aurea Rogersii') SS (E)
Slow. Compact conical habit. Golden and bronze densely packed foliage.
– – **'Stoneham Gold'** SS (E)
Slow. Dense conical habit. Bright golden foliage, tipped coppery bronze. AGM 1993
– – **'Zebrina'** ('Aureovariegata') LT (E) ⚘
Sprays of green foliage, banded creamy-yellow. Strong growth. FCC 1869

THUJOPSIS – Cupressaceae ST-MT (E) ♦
Monotypic genus. Related to Thuja *but longer leaves and broader, flatter branchlets. For all well-drained soils.*

– **dolabrata** (*Thuja dolabrata*) ST-MT (E) ♦
Dense habit. Large flattened sprays of dark green, silver-backed leaves. FCC 1864 AGM 1993

TSUGA – Pinaceae DS-LT (E) "Hemlock"
Spreading branches and drooping or arching branchlets. Short, linear leaves. Male and female strobili on same tree. Small, pendulous cones. Thrive in well-drained, moist, loamy soil. Not for shallow chalk. Shade tolerant.
– **albertiana** see *T. heterophylla*
– **canadensis** LT (E) ♦ "Eastern Hemlock"
Trunk often forked near base. Densely hairy, greyish-brown young shoots. Leaves with two whitish bands beneath. We offer:
– – **'Jeddeloh'** DS (E)
Dense habit with short, spreading and arching branches. AGM 1993
– – **'Pendula'** MS (E)
Mound-like habit, overlapping, drooping branches. AGM 1993
– – **'Prostrata'** PS (E)
Slow. Mat-like habit. Prostrate stems.
– **heterophylla** LT (E) ♦ "Western Hemlock"
Fast growing. Spreading branches. Greyish hairy young shoots. Leaves with two white bands beneath. Good specimen tree. AGM 1993
– – **'Greenmantle'** LT (E) ⚘
Graceful pendulous branches. Narrow habit.
– **mertensiana** LT (E) ♦
Spire-like habit. Densely hairy, greyish-brown young shoots. Grey-green or blue-grey leaves. Comparatively large cones. We recommend:
– – **'Glauca'** LT (E) ♦
Delightful form with glaucous leaves.

W

"WELLINGTONIA" see *Sequoiadendron giganteum*

Y

"YEW" see *Taxus*

GLOSSARY OF BOTANICAL TERMS

Throughout this book, certain accepted botanical terms have been used as an aid to precise description, and/or for the sake of brevity.

The following glossary explains those terms, and some others which you may find useful if your interest in trees and shrubs inspires you to further reading.

Acicular – Needle-shaped

Acuminate – Tapering at the end, long pointed

Acute – Sharp pointed

Adpressed – Lying close and flat against

Anther – The pollen-bearing part of the stamen

Aristate – Awned, bristle-tipped

Articulate – Jointed

Ascending – Rising somewhat obliquely and curving upwards

Auricle – An ear-shaped projection or appendage

Awl-shaped – Tapering from the base to a slender and stiff point

Axil – The angle formed by a leaf or lateral branch with the stem, or of a vein with the midrib

Axillary – Produced in the axil

Bearded – Furnished with long or stiff hairs

Berry – Strictly a pulpy, normally several seeded, indehiscent fruit

Bifid – Two-cleft

Bipinnate – Twice pinnate

Bisexual – Both male and female organs in the same flower

Blade – The expanded part of a leaf or petal

Bloomy – With a fine powder-like waxy deposit

Bole – Trunk, of a tree

Bract – A modified, usually reduced leaf at the base of a flower-stalk, flower-cluster, or shoot

Bullate – Blistered or puckered

Calcareous – Containing carbonate of lime or limestone, chalky or limy

Calcifuge – Avoiding calcareous soils

Calyx – The outer part of the flower, the sepals

Campanulate – Bell-shaped

Capitate – Head-like, collected into a dense cluster

Capsule – A dry, several-celled pod

Catkin – A normally dense spike or spike-like raceme of tiny, scaly-bracted flowers or fruits

Ciliate – Fringed with hairs

Cladode – Flattened leaf-like stems

Clone – A new individual plant formed by separation and independent growth of a vegetative part of the parent plant. Its genetic factors are thus exactly the same as those of the parent plant

Columnar – Tall, cylindrical or tapering, column-like

Compound – Composed of two or more similar parts

Compressed – Flattened

Conical – Cone-shaped

Cordate – Shaped like a heart, as base of leaf

Coriaceous – Leathery

Corolla – The inner normally conspicuous part of a flower, the petals

Corymb – A flat-topped or dome-shaped flower head with the outer flowers opening first

Corymbose – Having flowers in corymbs

Crenate – Toothed with shallow, rounded teeth, scalloped

Cultivar – Garden variety, or form found in the wild and maintained as a clone in cultivation

Cuneate – Wedge-shaped

Cuspidate – Abruptly sharp pointed

Cyme – A flat-topped or dome-shaped flower head with the inner flowers opening first

Cymose – Having flowers in cymes

Deciduous – Soon or seasonally falling, not persistent

Decumbent – Reclining, the tips ascending

Decurrent – Extending down the stem

Deltoid – Triangular

Dentate – Toothed with teeth directed outward
Denticulate   Minutely dentate
Depressed – Flattened from above
Diffuse – Loosely or widely spreading
Digitate – With the members arising from one point (as in a digitate leaf)
Dioecious – Male and female flowers on different plants
Dissected – Divided into many narrow segments
Distichous – Arranged in two vertical ranks: two-ranked
Divaricate – Spreading far apart
Divergent – Spreading
Divided – Separated to the base
Double – (flowers) with more than the usual number of petals, often with the style and stamens changed to petals
Doubly Serrate – Large teeth and small teeth alternating
Downy – Softly hairy

Elliptic – Widest at or about the middle, narrowing equally at both ends
Elongate – Lengthened
Emarginate – With a shallow notch at the apex
Entire – Undivided and without teeth
Evergreen – Remaining green during winter
Exfoliating – Peeling off in thin strips
Exserted – Projecting beyond (stamens from corolla)

Falcate – Sickle-shaped
Fascicle – A dense cluster
Fastigiate – With branches erect and close together
Ferruginous – Rust-coloured
Fertile – Stamens producing good pollen or fruit containing good seeds, or of stems with flowering organs
Filament – The stalk of a stamen
Filiform – Thread-like
Fimbriate – Fringed
Flexuous – Wavy or zig-zag
Floccose – Clothed with flocks of soft hair or wool
Florets – Small, individual flowers of a dense inflorescence
Floriferous – Flower-bearing
Form – Although 'forma' is a recognised botanical category below 'variety', the term is used more loosely in this book and may refer to a species, subspecies or cultivar.

Genus – An assemblage of closely related species
Gibbous – Swollen, usually at the base (as in corolla)
Glabrous – Hairless
Glandular – With secreting organs
Glaucous – Covered with a 'bloom', bluish-white or bluish-grey
Glutinous – Sticky

Habit – General form of a plant
Hermaphrodite – Bisexual, both male and female organs in the same flower
Hirsute – With rather coarse or stiff hairs
Hispid – Beset with rigid hairs or bristles
Hoary – Covered with a close whitish or greyish-white pubescence
Hybrid – A plant resulting from a cross between different species

Imbricate – Overlapping, as tiles on a roof
Impressed – Sunken (as in veins)
Incised – Sharply and usually deeply and irregularly cut
Indehiscent – Fruits which do not (burst) open
Indumentum – Dense hairy covering
Inflorescence – The flowering part of the plant
Internode – The portion of stem between two nodes or joints
Involucre – A whorl of bracts surrounding a flower or flower cluster

Keel – A central ridge

Lacerate – Torn, irregularly cut or cleft
Laciniate – Cut into narrow pointed lobes
Lanceolate – Lance-shaped, widening above the base and long tapering to the apex
Lanuginose – Woolly or cottony
Lateral – On or at the side
Lax – Loose
Leaflet – Part of a compound leaf
Linear – Long and narrow with nearly parallel margins
Lip – One of the parts of an unequally divided flower
Lobe – Any protruding part of an organ (as in leaf, corolla or calyx)
Lustrous – Shining

Membranous – Thin and rather soft
Midrib – The central vein or rib of a leaf
Monoecious – Male and female flowers separate, but on the same plant

Monotypic – Of a single species (genus)
Mucronate – Terminated abruptly by a spiny tip

Nectary – A nectar-secreting gland, usually a small pit or protuberance
Node – The place upon the stem where the leaves are attached, the 'joint'
Nut – A non-splitting, one-seeded, hard and bony fruit

Oblanceolate – Inversely lanceolate
Oblique – Unequal-sided
Oblong – Longer than broad, with nearly parallel sides
Obovate – Inversely ovate
Obtuse – Blunt (as in apex of leaf or petal)
Orbicular – Almost circular in outline
Oval – Broadest at the middle
Ovary – The basal 'box' part of the pistil, containing the ovules
Ovate – Broadest below the middle (like a hen's egg)
Ovule – The body which, after fertilisation, becomes the seed

Palmate – Lobed or divided in hand-like fashion usually five or seven lobed
Panicle – A branching raceme
Paniculate – Having flowers in panicles
Parted – Cut or cleft almost to the base
Pea-flower – Shaped like a sweet pea blossom
Pectinate – Comb-like (as in leaf margin)
Pedicel – The stalk of an individual flower in an inflorescence
Peduncle – The stalk of a flower cluster or of a solitary flower
Pellucid – Clear, transparent (as in gland)
Pendulous – Hanging, weeping
Perfoliate – A pair of opposite leaves fused at the base, the stem appearing to pass through them
Perianth – The calyx and corolla together; also commonly used for a flower in which there is no distinction between corolla and calyx
Persistent – Remaining attached
Petal – One of the separate segments of a corolla
Petaloid – Petal-like (as in stamen)
Petiole – The leaf-stalk
Pilose – With long, soft straight hairs
Pinnate – With leaflets arranged on either side of a central stalk
Pinnatifid – Cleft or parted in a pinnate way

Pistil – The female organ of a flower, comprising ovary, style and stigma
Plumose – Feathery, as the down of a thistle
Pollen – Spores or grains contained in the anther, containing the male element
Polygamous – Bearing bisexual and uni-sexual flowers on the same plant
Procumbent – Lying or creeping
Prostrate – Lying flat on the ground
Pruinose – Bloomy
Puberulent – Minutely pubescent
Pubescent – Covered with short, soft hairs, downy
Punctate – With translucent or coloured dots or depressions
Pungent – Ending in a stiff, sharp point; also acid (to the taste) or strong smelling
Pyramidal – Pyramid-shaped (broad at base tapering to a point)

Raceme – A simple elongated inflorescence with stalked flowers
Racemose – Having flowers in racemes
Rachis – An axis bearing flowers or leaflets
Recurved – Curved downward or backward
Reflexed – Abruptly turned downward
Reniform – Kidney-shaped
Reticulate – Like a network (as in veins)
Revolute – Rolled backwards, margin rolled under (as in leaf)
Rib – A prominent vein in a leaf
Rotund – Nearly circular
Rufous – Reddish-brown
Rugose – Wrinkled or rough
Runner – A trailing shoot taking root at the nodes

Sagittate – Shaped like an arrow-head
Scabrous – Rough to the touch
Scale – A minute leaf or bract, or a flat gland-like appendage on the surface of a leaf, flower or shoot
Scandent – With climbing stems
Scarious – Thin and dry, not green
Semi-evergreen – Normally evergreen but losing some or all of its leaves in a cold winter or cold area
Sepal – One of the segments of a calyx
Serrate – Saw-toothed (teeth pointing forward)
Serrulate – Minutely serrate
Sessile – Not stalked
Setose – Clothed with bristles
Sheath – A tubular envelope
Shrub – A woody plant which branches from the base with no obvious trunk

Simple – Said of a leaf that is not compound or an unbranched inflorescence

Sinuate – Strongly waved (as in leaf margin)

Sinus – The recess or space between two lobes or divisions of a leaf, calyx or corolla

Spatulate – Spoon-shaped

Species – A group of plants of similar genetical constitution

Spicate – Flowers in spikes

Spike – A simple, elongated inflorescence with sessile flowers

Spine – A sharp-pointed end of a branch or leaf

Spur – A tubular projection from a flower; or a short stiff branchlet

Stamen – The male organ of a flower comprising filament and anther

Staminode – A sterile stamen, or a structure resembling a stamen, sometimes petal-like

Standard – The upper, normally broad and erect petal in a pea-flower; also used in nurseries to describe a tall single-stemmed young tree

Stellate – Star shaped

Stigma – The summit of the pistil which receives the pollen, often sticky or feathery

Stipule – Appendage (normally two) at base of some petioles

Stolon – A shoot on or below the ground which produces a new plant at its tip

Striate – With fine, longitudinal lines

Strigose – Clothed with flattened fine, bristle-like, hairs

Style – The middle part of the pistil, often elongated between the ovary and stigma

Subulate – Awl-shaped

Succulent – Juicy, fleshy, soft and thickened in texture

Suckering – Producing underground stems; also the shoots from the stock of a grafted plant

Tendril – A twining thread-like appendage

Ternate – In threes

Tessellated – Mosaic-like (as in veins)

Tomentose – With dense, woolly pubescence

Tomentum – Dense covering of matted hairs

Tree – A woody plant that produces normally a single trunk and an elevated head of branches

Trifoliate – Three-leaved

Trifoliolate – A leaf with three separate leaflets

Turbinate – Top-shaped

Type – Strictly the original (type) specimen, but used in a general sense to indicate the typical form in cultivation

Umbel – A normally flat-topped inflorescence in which the pedicels or peduncles all arise from a common point

Umbellate – Flowers in umbels

Undulate – With wavy margins

Unisexual – Of one sex

Urceolate – Urn-shaped

Velutinous – Clothed with a velvety indumentum

Venation – The arrangement of the veins

Verrucose – Having a wart-like or nodular surface

Verticillate – Arranged in a whorl or ring

Villous – Bearing long and soft hairs

Viscid – Sticky

Whorl – Three or more flowers or leaves arranged in a ring

40-463-1